Creating
Effective Teaching and
Learning Environments

FIRST RESULTS FROM TALIS

Teaching And Learning International Survey

OECD

ORGANISATION FOR ECONOMIC CO-OPERATION AND DEVELOPMENT

The OECD is a unique forum where the governments of 30 democracies work together to address the economic, social and environmental challenges of globalisation. The OECD is also at the forefront of efforts to understand and to help governments respond to new developments and concerns, such as corporate governance, the information economy and the challenges of an ageing population. The Organisation provides a setting where governments can compare policy experiences, seek answers to common problems, identify good practice and work to co-ordinate domestic and international policies.

The OECD member countries are: Australia, Austria, Belgium, Canada, the Czech Republic, Denmark, Finland, France, Germany, Greece, Hungary, Iceland, Ireland, Italy, Japan, Korea, Luxembourg, Mexico, the Netherlands, New Zealand, Norway, Poland, Portugal, the Slovak Republic, Spain, Sweden, Switzerland, Turkey, the United Kingdom and the United States. The Commission of the European Communities takes part in the work of the OECD.

OECD Publishing disseminates widely the results of the Organisation's statistics gathering and research on economic, social and environmental issues, as well as the conventions, guidelines and standards agreed by its members.

This work is published on the responsibility of the Secretary-General of the OECD. The opinions expressed and arguments employed herein do not necessarily reflect the official views of the Organisation or of the governments of its member countries.

Foreword

The challenges facing education systems and teachers continue to intensify. In modern knowledge-based economies, where the demand for high-level skills will continue to grow substantially, the task in many countries is to transform traditional models of schooling, which have been effective at distinguishing those who are more academically talented from those who are less so, into customised learning systems that identify and develop the talents of all students. This will require the creation of "knowledge-rich", evidence-based education systems, in which school leaders and teachers act as a professional community with the authority to act, the necessary information to do so wisely, and the access to effective support systems to assist them in implementing change.

The OECD's Teaching and Learning International Survey (TALIS) provides insights into how education systems are responding by providing the first internationally comparative perspective on the conditions of teaching and learning. TALIS draws on the OECD's 2005 review of teacher policy, which identified important gaps in international data, and aims to help countries review and develop policies to make the teaching profession more attractive and more effective. TALIS is conceptualised as a programme of surveys, with successive rounds designed to address policy-relevant issues chosen by countries.

With a focus in this initial round on lower secondary education in both the public and private sectors, TALIS examines important aspects of teachers' professional development; teacher beliefs, attitudes and practices; teacher appraisal and feedback; and school leadership in the 23 participating countries.

The results from TALIS suggest that, in many countries, education is still far from being a knowledge industry in the sense that its own practices are not yet being transformed by knowledge about the efficacy of those practices. The 23 countries that have taken part in TALIS illustrate the growing interest in the lessons that might be learned from teacher policies and practices employed elsewhere. TALIS provides a first, groundbreaking instrument to allow countries to see their own teaching profession in the light of what other countries show can be achieved. Naturally, policy solutions should not simply be copies of other educational systems or experiences, but comparative analysis can provide an understanding of the policy drivers that contribute to successful teacher policies and help to situate and configure these policy drivers in the respective national contexts.

TALIS is a collaborative effort by member countries of the OECD and partner countries within the TALIS organisational framework. In addition, collaboration and support from the European Commission has helped TALIS address important information needs of the Commission in its monitoring of progress towards the Lisbon 2010 goals.

The report was produced by the Indicators and Analysis Division of the OECD Directorate for Education. The project has been led by Michael Davidson, who with Ben Jensen, co-ordinated the drafting and analysis for the report. The principal authors of the analytical chapters were: Michael Davidson (Chapter 3), Ben Jensen (Chapters 2, 5 and 7), Eckhard Klieme and Svenja Vieluf (Chapter 4), and David Baker (Chapter 6). Additional advice as well as analytical and editorial support was provided by Juan Almonte, Etienne Albiser, Tracey Burns, Ralph Carstens, Eric Charbonnier, Corinne Heckmann, Donald Hirsch, Maciej Jakubowski, David Kaplan, Miyako Ikeda, Pedro Garcia de Leon, Plamen Mirazchiyski, Soojin Park, Leslie Rutkowski, Andreas Schleicher, Diana Toledo Figueroa, Fons van de Vijver, Elisabeth Villoutreix and Jean Yip. Administrative support was provided by Isabelle Moulherat.

The TALIS questionnaires were developed by an Instrument Development Expert Group (IDEG), led by the OECD Secretariat and comprising David Baker, Aletta Grisay, Eckhard Klieme and Jaap Scheerens. The administration of the survey and the preparation of the data underlying the report were managed by the Data Processing and Research Centre of the International Association for the Evaluation of Educational Achievement (IEA), the appointed international contractor, together with its consortium members Statistics Canada and the IEA Secretariat. Dirk Hastedt and Steffen Knoll acted as co-directors of the consortium.

The development of the report was steered by the TALIS Board of Participating Countries, which is chaired by Anne-Berit Kavli (Norway). Annex A3 of the report lists the members of the various TALIS bodies as well as the individual experts and consultants who have contributed to this report and to TALIS in general.

Barbara Ischinger
Director for Education, OECD

Table of Contents

Reader's Guide

STATISTICS AND ANALYSIS

This report presents statistics and analysis derived from the survey responses of teachers of lower secondary education (level 2 of the International Standard Classification of Education (ISCED-97)) and the principals of their schools.

CLASSIFICATION OF LEVELS OF EDUCATION

The classification of the levels of education is based on the revised International Standard Classification of Education (ISCED-97). ISCED is an instrument for compiling statistics on education internationally and distinguishes among six levels of education:

- Pre-primary education (ISCED level 0).
- Primary education (ISCED level 1).
- Lower secondary education (ISCED level 2).
- Upper secondary education (ISCED level 3).
- Post-secondary non-tertiary level of education (ISCED level 4).
- Tertiary-type A education (ISCED level 5A).
- Tertiary-type B education (ISCED level 5B).
- Advanced Research Qualifications (ISCED level 6).

CALCULATION OF INTERNATIONAL AVERAGE

A TALIS average was calculated for most indicators presented in this report. The TALIS average is calculated as the unweighted mean of the data values of the TALIS countries included in the table. The TALIS average therefore refers to an average of data values at the level of the national systems.

SYMBOLS FOR MISSING DATA

The following symbols are employed in the tables and charts to denote missing data:

a   The category does not apply in the country concerned. Data are therefore missing.

m   Data are not available as the underlying data were either not collected or withdrawn.

ABBREVIATIONS USED IN THIS REPORT

The following abbreviations are used in this report:

CFI   Comparative Fit Index

ISCED   International Standard Classification of Education

RMSEA   Root Mean Square Error of Approximation

r_{xy} Correlation coefficient

(S.E.)   Standard error

SRMR   Root Mean Square Residual

ROUNDING OF FIGURES

Because of rounding, some figures in tables may not exactly add up to the totals. Totals, differences and averages are always calculated on the basis of exact numbers and are rounded only after calculation.

All standard errors in this publication have been rounded to two decimal places. Where the value 0.00 is shown, this does not imply that the standard error is zero, but that it is smaller than 0.005.

TERRITORIAL ENTITIES

In the whole document the Flemish Community of Belgium is referred to as "Belgium (Fl.)".

FURTHER DOCUMENTATION

For further information on TALIS documentation, the instruments and methods, see the *TALIS Technical Report* (forthcoming) and the TALIS website (*www.oecd.org/edu/TALIS*).

This report uses the OECD's StatLinks service. Below each table and chart is a url leading to a corresponding Excel workbook containing the underlying data. These urls are stable and will remain unchanged over time.

Chapter 1

Introduction

OVERVIEW OF TALIS

The OECD's Teaching and Learning International Survey is the first international survey to focus on the working conditions of teachers and the learning environment in schools. Its aim is to help countries to review and develop policies that foster the conditions for effective schooling.

TALIS focuses on lower secondary education teachers and the principals of their schools and seeks to provide policy-relevant data and analysis on the following key aspects of schooling:

- the role and functioning of school leadership;
- how teachers' work is appraised and the feedback they receive;
- teachers' professional development; and
- teachers' beliefs and attitudes about teaching and their pedagogical practices.

In view of the important role that school leadership can play in creating effective schools, TALIS describes the role of school leaders and examines the support they give to their teachers. Because retaining and developing effective teachers is a priority in all school systems, TALIS looks at how teachers' work is recognised, appraised and rewarded and how well their professional development needs are being addressed. Finally, TALIS provides insights into the beliefs and attitudes about teaching that teachers bring to the classroom and the pedagogical practices that they adopt.

TALIS is a collaborative effort by member countries of the OECD and partner countries which has been conceptualised as a programme of surveys. This report presents the initial results from the first round of TALIS, which was implemented in 2007-08.

Figure 1.1
Countries participating in TALIS

OECD countries	Partner countries
Australia	Brazil
Austria	Bulgaria
Belgium (Flemish Community)	Estonia
Denmark	Lithuania
Hungary	Malaysia
Iceland	Malta
Ireland	Slovenia
Italy	
Korea	
Mexico	
Norway	
Poland	
Portugal	
Slovak Republic	
Spain	
Turkey	

Note: TALIS was also conducted in the Netherlands but as the required sampling standards were not achieved, their data are not included in the international comparisons.
Source: OECD, *TALIS Database.*

In all, 24 countries participated in this first round of TALIS (see Figure 1.1). However, as the Netherlands did not meet the sampling standards, their data are not included in the international tables and analyses. A summary of the results for the Netherlands can be found in Annex A2 of this report.

ORIGINS AND AIMS OF TALIS

TALIS has been developed as part of the OECD Indicators of Education Systems (INES) project. Over the past 20 years or so, INES has sought to create a coherent set of indicators that provide a reliable basis for the quantitative comparisons of the functioning and performance of education systems in OECD and partner countries. The main product from the INES project is the annual *Education at a Glance* (OECD, 2008a).

Although the INES programme has made considerable progress over the years in developing indicators on the learning environment and organisation of schools, as well as learning outcomes, significant gaps in the knowledge base on teachers and teaching remained. As a result, the INES General Assembly in 2000 in Tokyo called for increased attention to teachers and teaching in future work. At the meeting of deputy Ministers of Education in Dublin in 2003, the need for better information on the quality of learning and how teaching influences learning was further affirmed.

To address these deficiencies, a strategy was developed to improve the indicators on teachers, teaching and learning. One aspect was an international survey of teachers, which evolved into the TALIS programme. Another important impetus for TALIS came from the OECD review of teacher policy, which concluded with the report *Teachers Matter: Attracting, Developing and Retaining Effective Teachers* (OECD, 2005) and emphasised the need for better national and international information on teachers. The framework used in that policy review and the specific gaps in the data and priorities it highlighted were instrumental in the design of TALIS.

The overall objective of the TALIS surveys is therefore to provide, in a timely and cost-effective manner, robust international indicators and policy-relevant analysis on teachers and teaching in order to help countries to review and develop policies that create the conditions for effective schooling. Cross-country analyses provide the opportunity to compare countries facing similar challenges and to learn about different policy approaches and their impact on the learning environment in schools.

The guiding principles underlying the survey strategy are:

- *Policy relevance*. Clarity about the policy issues and a focus on the questions that are most relevant for participating countries are both essential.
- *Value added*. International comparisons should be a significant source of the study's benefits.
- *Indicator-oriented*. The results should yield information that can be used to develop indicators.
- *Validity, reliability, comparability and rigour*. Based on a rigorous review of the knowledge base, the survey should yield information that is valid, reliable and comparable across participating countries.
- *Interpretability*. Participating countries should be able to interpret the results in a meaningful way.
- *Efficiency and cost-effectiveness*. The work should be carried out in a timely and cost-effective way.

DESIGN OF THE TALIS SURVEY

TALIS is conceived as a sequence of surveys which over time, will survey school teachers from all phases of schooling. Within this broad survey design, specific plans for further rounds of TALIS will be reviewed after the first round is completed.

POPULATION SURVEYED AND SAMPLING OPTIONS

The international sampling and operational parameters applied in TALIS are shown in Box 1.1 and further details, including teacher and school participation rates by country are given in Annex A1.2.

Box 1.1 The TALIS design

- **International target population**: lower secondary education teachers and the principals of their schools.

- **Sample size**: 200 schools per country, 20 teachers in each school.

- **Within school samples**: representative samples of schools and teachers within schools.

- **Target response rates**: 75% of the sampled schools (school considered responding if 50% of sampled teachers respond), aiming for a 75% response from all sampled teachers in the country.

- **Questionnaires**: separate questionnaires for teachers and principals, each requiring around 45 minutes to complete.

- **Mode of data capture**: questionnaires filled in on paper or on line.

- **Survey windows**: October-December 2007 for Southern Hemisphere countries and March-May 2008 for Northern Hemisphere countries.

The participating countries decided that the main focus of the first round of TALIS should be teachers of lower secondary education (level 2 of the 1997 revision of the International Standard Classification of Education, ISCED 97) and their school principals. The design of the first round also proposed international options which allowed countries to survey as well a representative sample of teachers of primary and/or upper secondary education and the principals of their schools. Another option was to survey a representative sample of teachers of 15-year-olds in schools that took part in PISA 2006 and principals of these schools. As too few countries expressed an interest in these options, they were not covered at the international level; however, Iceland and Mexico adopted some national sampling options.

TALIS defines teachers of ISCED level 2 as those who, as part of their regular duties, provide instruction in programmes at ISCED level 2. Teachers in the schools sampled who teach a mixture of programmes at different levels, including ISCED 2 programmes, were included in the target population. There was no minimum cut-off for the amount of their ISCED level 2 teaching. The following were excluded from the teacher target population: teachers only teaching special need students; substitute, emergency or occasional teachers; teachers teaching adults exclusively; teachers on long-term leave; and teachers who were also the principals of their schools.

CHOOSING THE POLICY FOCUS OF THE FIRST ROUND OF TALIS

The original conceptual framework for the TALIS programme was developed by a joint taskforce comprising experts from the INES Network A (learning outcomes) and Network C (learning environment and school organisation). The taskforce was asked to develop a data strategy on teachers, teaching and learning in order to identify gaps in data at the international level and help make the coverage of the INES indicators more complete. A major part of that strategy was a survey programme which developed into TALIS.

The original conceptual framework was adapted to the policy issues that had been studied in the OECD teacher policy review (OECD, 2005): attracting, developing and retaining effective teachers; school policies; and effectiveness and quality teachers and teaching (see the forthcoming *TALIS Technical Report* for details of the framework). On the basis of the indicators included in the framework, the participating countries chose the following themes as the policy focus of the first round of TALIS:

- school leadership;
- appraisal of and feedback to teachers; and
- teaching practices, beliefs and attitudes.

TALIS also chose the professional development of teachers as an important theme. In part this was because of synergies with the three main themes and in part because it allowed TALIS to serve as a way for countries of the European Union to collect information on teachers which the Education Council had identified as important to monitor progress towards the Lisbon 2010 goals. In particular, the data on professional development of teachers are relevant for monitoring the common objective of improving the education and training of teachers and trainers (Council (Education) of the EU (2002; 2005; 2007)).

Aspects of other themes were also included in the survey when they were seen to provide important complementary analytical value to the main themes. In particular, aspects of "School climate" and "Division of working time" and a single item on "Job satisfaction" were also included.

Separate questionnaires for teachers and the principals of their schools were prepared to explore the policy and analytical questions agreed by the participating countries under these policy themes. Considerable effort was devoted to achieving cultural and linguistic validity of the survey instruments, and stringent quality assurance mechanisms were applied both for their translation and for the sampling and data collection (see Annex 1.3).

DEVELOPING TALIS

The development of TALIS has been the result of productive co-operation between the member countries of the OECD and the partner countries participating in the first round. Engagement with bodies representing teachers and regular briefings and exchanges with the Trades Union Advisory Council at the OECD (TUAC) have been very important in the development and implementation of TALIS. In particular, the co-operation of the teachers and principals in the participating schools has been crucial in ensuring the success of TALIS.

A Board of Participating Countries, representing all of the countries taking part in the first round of TALIS, set out the policy objectives for the survey and established the standards for data collection and reporting. An Instrument Development Expert Group (IDEG) was established to translate the policy priorities into questionnaires in order to address the policy and analytical questions that had been agreed by the participating countries.

Participating countries implemented TALIS at the national level through National Project Managers (NPMs) and National Data Managers (NDMs), who were subject to rigorous technical and operational procedures. The NPMs played a crucial role in helping to secure the co-operation of schools, to validate the questionnaires, to manage the national data collection and processing and to verify the results from TALIS. The NDMs co-ordinated the data processing at the national level and liaised in the cleaning of the data.

The co-ordination and management of implementation at the international level was the responsibility of the appointed contractor, the Data Processing Centre of the International Association for the Evaluation of Educational Achievement (IEA). The IEA Secretariat was responsible for overseeing the verification of the translation and for quality control in general. Statistics Canada, as a sub-contractor of the IEA, developed the sampling plan, advised countries on its application, calculated the sampling weights and advised on the calculation of sampling errors.

The OECD Secretariat had overall responsibility for managing the programme, monitoring its implementation on a day-to-day basis and serving as the secretariat of the Board of Participating Countries.

Annex A3 provides the list of contributors to TALIS.

INTERPRETATION OF THE RESULTS

It should be carefully borne in mind that the results derived are based on self-reports from teachers and principals and therefore represent their opinions, perceptions, beliefs and their accounts of their activities. This is powerful information, as it gives insight into how teachers perceive the learning environments in which they work, what motivates them, and how policies and practices that are put in place are carried out in practice. But, like any self-reported data, this information is subjective and therefore differs from objectively measured data. The same is true of school principals' reports about school characteristics, which may differ from descriptions provided by administrative data.

In addition, as a cross-sectional survey, TALIS cannot measure causality. For instance, in examining the relationship between school climate and teacher co-operation, it is not possible to establish whether a positive school climate depends on good teacher co-operation or whether good teacher co-operation depends on a positive school climate. The perspective taken in the analysis, *i.e.* the choice of predicted and predictor variables, is purely based upon theoretical considerations, as laid out in the analytical framework. When a reference is made to "effects", it is to be understood in a statistical sense – *i.e.* an "effect" is a statistical parameter that describes the linear relationship between a "predicted" variable (*e.g.* job satisfaction) and a "predictor" variable (*e.g.* participation in professional development activities) – taking effects of individual and school background as well as other "independent" variables into account. Thus, the "effects" reported are statistical net effects even if they do not imply causality.

Finally, the cross-cultural validity of the results is an important feature of the analysis, particularly with regard to the international scales and indices, developed mainly in Chapters 4 and 6 (see Annex A1.1). The analysis indicates the extent to which the indices can be directly compared among countries; where there appear to be limitations on the comparability of the indices, this is noted in the text. Full details of the cross-cultural validity analysis are provided in the *TALIS Technical Report* (forthcoming).

ORGANISATION OF THE REPORT

The following chapters of this report present the results and the analyses from the first round of TALIS.

- **Chapter 2** presents a description of the characteristics of the lower secondary teacher populations and the schools in which they work. In doing so, it provides an important context for the later analytical chapters.

- **Chapter 3** presents and analyses the TALIS data relating to teachers' in-service professional development. It examines the extent to which teachers' professional development needs are provided for and their patterns of participation, as well as the support they receive and the barriers they perceive regarding their participation. It finishes by considering the types of development teachers find most effective.

- **Chapter 4** turns to an examination of teaching practices and teachers' beliefs and attitudes. Based on the conceptual model presented in the chapter, it analyses teachers' beliefs about the nature of teaching and learning, classroom teaching practices, teachers' professional activities, the classroom and school environments, and teachers' perceptions of their self-efficacy and job satisfaction.

- **Chapter 5** is concerned with teacher appraisal and feedback. It begins with an analysis of the nature and impact of school evaluations and then considers key aspects of teacher appraisal and feedback: its frequency and focus, its outcomes, and its impacts on and for teachers. The link between school evaluations, teacher appraisal and feedback and how this impacts on teachers and their teaching is then examined.

- **Chapter 6** turns to school leadership to present and compare management styles across countries. These are analysed in terms of the characteristics of the school principals and the schools in which they work. It then associates management styles to teachers' professional development, their practices, beliefs and attitudes, and the appraisal and feedback they receive.

- **Chapter 7** draws on the findings from Chapters 2 to 6 to build statistical models to examine the determinants of two important characteristics of a positive learning environment: classroom disciplinary climate and teachers' self-efficacy.

Chapters 2 to 7 all begin with a summary of the chapter's key findings and conclude with a discussion of the implications of these findings for policy and practice.

CHAPTER 2
A Profile of the Teacher Population and the Schools in Which They Work

INTRODUCTION

TALIS examines key policy issues such as teachers' professional development; teachers' teaching practices, beliefs and attitudes; teacher appraisal and feedback; and school leadership. Data have been collected on a number of characteristics of schools and teachers which provide not only essential background information for analysis of these issues but also school- and system-level factors that are important for teachers and teaching. This chapter presents analyses of these characteristics, and helps set the scene for the following analytical chapters.

The chapter is divided into two sections. The first section presents a profile of lower secondary teachers and concentrates on their formal education and demographic and employment profile. The demographic profile focuses on the age and gender of teachers and school principals. Discussion of teachers' employment profile includes data on teachers' contractual status and job experience, including the contrast between permanent and short-term or temporary contract employment.

The second section provides a profile of the schools in which teachers work. It gives information on their personnel, resources, admission policies, autonomy and climate. TALIS includes this background information because of the influence of such factors on student learning and attainment, as a number of studies have demonstrated (OECD, 2007). TALIS does not collect data on student outcomes, but it has included variables which previous research has found to affect student learning, many of which are policy-relevant aspects of education systems.

In reading this chapter, it should be borne in mind that TALIS focuses on teachers. Therefore, most of the tables and charts refer to teachers and their distribution among various types of schools. For example, Table 2.4 presents data of, among other things, the sector to which the school belongs and presents the *percentages of teachers* working in public schools across education systems rather than the *percentage of public schools*. Therefore, TALIS figures may not correspond to other, perhaps official statistics which are expressed in terms of the percentage of public schools or the percentage of students in public schools. They are intended to complement rather than contradict the official statistics.

A PROFILE OF LOWER SECONDARY EDUCATION TEACHERS

The demographic profile of teachers provides information on basic characteristics which are of interest in their own right and as a context for later analysis. For example, the amount of appraisal and feedback a teacher receives may be associated with such characteristics as age or length of employment as a teacher (see Chapter 5). In addition, a teacher's formal education can influence their professional development (Chapter 3) and their response to leadership opportunities in their schools (Chapter 6).

Demographic profile of teachers

Table 2.1 shows gender differences across countries. On average across TALIS countries, almost 70% of teachers were female, and in every TALIS country the majority were female. Females dominated particularly in Bulgaria, Estonia, Lithuania, the Slovak Republic and Slovenia, with between 80 - 85% of the teacher workforce. In these countries, concerns about the effects of the feminisation of teaching on education are potentially greater (OECD, 2005). In addition, when males only represent 15 to 20% of the teacher workforce, the potential supply of teachers could be broadened with greater gender equality.

Given the substantial gender gap in the distribution of teachers across TALIS countries, it is interesting to compare this with the gender distribution among school principals, as this provides insight into issues of gender equality in senior management and promotion opportunities. On average across TALIS countries, 45% of school principals were female compared to just fewer than 70% of teachers (Table 2.1). While TALIS data does not allow for identifying the source of this discrepancy, it seems clear that males far more readily move up the career ladder to become school principals. In this sense, a "glass ceiling" may exist in most TALIS countries, and particularly in Austria, Belgium (Fl.), Ireland, Italy, Korea, Lithuania, Portugal, and Turkey where the percentage of female school principals is over 30 percentage-points below the percentage of female teachers.

Figure 2.1

Gender and age of teachers (2007-08)

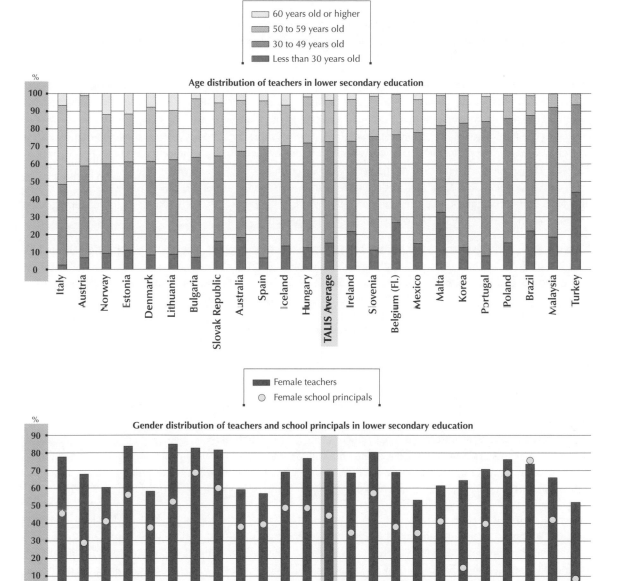

Countries are ranked in descending order, based on the percentage aged 50 or higher.
Source: OECD, Table 2.1.

StatLink ⟐ http://dx.doi.org/10.1787/607784618372

As Figure 2.1 and Table 2.1 show, more than half of teachers across TALIS countries are aged from 30 to 50 years old. Given concerns about an ageing teacher population it is significant that, on average, only 15% of teachers are less than 30 years of age and few teachers were under 25 years of age, perhaps owing to the education and qualification requirements that apply in most countries. That over one-quarter of teachers are over 50 years old is evidence of an ageing teacher population. Indeed in Austria, Italy and Norway at least 40% of teachers are over 50 years old, and in Estonia, Lithuania and Norway, around 10% of teachers are aged 60 or more (Figure 2.1).

An important aspect of an ageing teacher population is the budgetary impact. Staff remuneration is the largest component of education expenditure. In 2005 (the latest year for which data are available), on average across OECD countries, compensation paid to teachers represented 63% of current expenditure on secondary education institutions (OECD, 2008a). In most education systems, teachers with more experience receive a higher salary. In 2006 (the latest year for which data are available), the statutory salaries of teachers with 15 years of experience were, on average across OECD countries, 35% higher than starting salaries for lower secondary teachers (OECD, 2008a). For countries with a substantial proportion of teachers close to retirement age, total staff remuneration may, depending on the nature of the pension system, reduce over the coming years as these teachers are replaced by younger less expensive teachers.

Nevertheless, not all school systems have an ageing teacher population. The teacher population is slightly younger in Belgium (Fl.), Brazil, Ireland, Malaysia, Malta, Poland and Turkey with 50% or more of teachers below the age of 40 (compared to the TALIS average of 43%). Both Malta and Turkey have greater percentages of young teachers, with almost 33 and 44%, respectively, of teachers less than 30 years of age. In these countries, opportunities clearly exist to structure policies for a young teacher workforce (Boyd *et al.,* 2008). Indeed, in Turkey, almost 80% of teachers were under the age of 40 years (Table 2.1).

Teachers' educational attainment

The level of teachers' educational attainment is a combination of their pre-service training and additional qualifications they may have acquired in-service. The quantity and quality of teachers' initial education is clearly important in shaping their work once they begin teaching in schools and should influence their further education and training requirements (see Chapter 3) and other aspects of their development. For example, a low level of formal education or one of poor quality may increase teachers' need for professional development once they enter the profession. On the other hand, extensive formal education may spur greater interest in further education and training to further develop skills obtained during extensive formal education.

Table 2.2 summarises the highest level of formal education successfully completed by teachers and thus provides a context for interpreting teachers' professional development and on-the-job training. Table 2.2 gives the percentages of teachers with various levels of formal education, defined according to the International Standard Classification of Education (ISCED) which identifies comparable levels of education across countries. ISCED level 5 represents the first stages of tertiary education and is split between ISCED levels 5A and 5B. ISCED level 5B programmes are generally more practically oriented and shorter than programmes at ISCED level 5A. ISCED level 5A can be further divided into first and second programmes, typically a Bachelor's degree and a Master's degree from a university or equivalent institution. ISCED level 6 represents further education at the tertiary level which leads to an advanced research qualification such as a PhD.

Very few teachers have not had at least some tertiary education. On average across TALIS countries, the highest level of education completed was below the tertiary level for only 3% of teachers. However, qualifications below ISCED level 5 were more common in Brazil (9% of teachers), Iceland (12%) and Mexico (10%). Differences among countries in the proportion of teachers with different levels of formal education can reflect both the current and past structure of a country's formal education system as well as the requirements for entering the teaching profession. The highest level of tertiary education completed was ISCED level 5B for over half of teachers in Austria (59%) and Belgium (Fl.) (84%) and reflects these countries' qualification requirements. In Belgium (Fl.) an ISCED level 5B qualification is required to be fully certified to teach at ISCED level 2. On average across TALIS countries, just under one-third of teachers had completed a Master's degree and just 1% had completed formal education above this level (Table 2.2).

Large majorities of teachers in Bulgaria (64%), Italy (77%), Poland (94%), the Slovak Republic (96%), and Spain (79%) have completed a Master's degree (Table 2.2); this may reflect these countries' qualification requirements for becoming a teacher or for progressing through the teaching career structure (*e.g.* a requirement for a specific promotion). Teachers' levels of education may also reflect broader education trends within countries and the extent to which formal education is encouraged in schools and in the teaching profession. Chapter 3 also shows the extent to which teachers engage in qualification programmes as part of their ongoing professional development.

Teachers' job experience and contractual status

In general, teaching can be viewed as a relatively stable career with strong job security (OECD, 2005). This can be attractive for those in the profession and those wishing to join it, but it can also create a risk of inertia and lack of flexibility if the teacher workforce becomes comprised largely of older and more risk-averse workers (Atkinson, 2005; Dixit, 2002; Ballou & Podgursky 1997; McKewen, 1995). At the same time, a number of countries are concerned about the decline in teachers' job security and the increase in contract-based employment, particularly of a short-term nature (OECD, 2005), and the impact of teacher turnover (Boyd *et al.,* 2008; Podgursky *et al.,* 2004; Rockoff, 2004).

Table 2.3 shows that on average across TALIS countries, 85% of teachers were employed on a permanent basis. Portugal was the only country in which less than 70% of teachers were permanently employed, followed by Ireland, Brazil and Iceland, with less than 75%. Virtually all teachers were permanently employed in Denmark, Korea, Malaysia and Malta. Permanent employment can be viewed as a benefit of choosing a teaching career and could be linked to the issues discussed in chapter 5 such as the recognition they receive for their efforts and their motivation to improve their effectiveness as teachers.

On average across TALIS countries, only 16% of teachers were employed on fixed-term contracts, and over two-thirds of these teachers were on contracts of less than one year (Table 2.3). This contractual status may affect teachers' job security and how they carry out their work as teachers. Among teachers on fixed-term contracts, all countries except Italy, Korea, Lithuania and Malaysia have more teachers on contracts of less than one year than on longer contracts. Contractual employment of teachers for less than one year was more common in Brazil, Iceland, Ireland, Italy, Poland, Portugal and Spain. A possible explanation for this short-term contractual employment is an effort to increase flexibility in the teacher labour market and to assign teachers to fulfil specific short-term needs. It may also be an aspect of a system which monitors the performance of younger teachers before granting permanent employment. In fact, among the teachers on fixed-term contracts of less than one year, over one-quarter were in their first two years of teaching and three-quarters were in their first ten years of teaching (OECD, *TALIS Database.*). This is consistent with the approach adopted by systems which do not grant permanent employment until at least some fixed-term contract employment has been undertaken (OECD, 2005).

Given the ageing teacher population in some countries and the predominance of permanent employment, it is not surprising to find lengthy experience in the teaching profession. Just under two-thirds of teachers had at least 10 years experience (Table 2.3). On average across TALIS countries, 29% of teachers had worked as teachers for 3 to 10 years, while 27% had taught for 11 to 20 years (Figure 2.2 and Table 2.3). Over one-third (36%) had taught for more than 20 years. This represents a substantial proportion of teachers with considerable experience. While experience can bring important benefits to the job of teaching, owing to greater maturity in the job and increased levels of on-the-job learning, it can also create problems of inertia, lack of innovation and resistance to change which may not occur with a younger teacher population (OECD, 2005; Dixit, 2002; Mante & O'Brien, 2002). This may be particularly apparent in countries whose teachers have been in their positions for a particularly long period of time. For example, in Austria and Italy more than half of teachers have taught for more than 20 years (57 and 53%, respectively), while in Austria, Lithuania and Portugal, fewer than 5% of teachers were in their first two years of teaching.

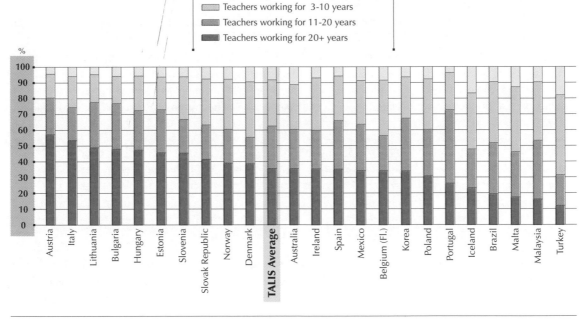

Figure 2.2

Job experience of teachers (2007-08)

- Teachers in their first 2 years of teaching
- Teachers working for 3-10 years
- Teachers working for 11-20 years
- Teachers working for 20+ years

Countries are ranked in descending order of the percentage of teachers who have worked for 20 years or longer.
Source: OECD, Table 2.3.

StatLink ⟐ http://dx.doi.org/10.1787/607784618372

A lack of experience was more common in some countries than in others. In Turkey (18%) and Iceland (17%), over 15% of teachers were in their first two years of teaching (Table 2.3 and Figure 2.2). These countries also have relatively large percentages of teachers below the age of 30. Large proportions of teachers with relatively little experience may point to a need for more training and professional development (Rockoff, 2008). Problems may exist if such teachers are concentrated in particular schools or groups of schools (Boyd *et al.*, 2008). However, this situation also provides opportunities to reinvigorate the teaching profession and school education.

A PROFILE OF THE SCHOOLS IN WHICH TEACHERS WORK

This section looks at the aspects of schools in which teachers work including the sector and size of schools and the composition of school personnel, as well as data collected from school principals concerning schools' admission policies, resources, climate and autonomy.

School sector

Some TALIS countries have sizeable private sectors, with schools that are either privately owned, operated and funded (independent private) or are privately run but receive most of their funds from public sources (government-dependent private) as in Belgium (Fl.). Sectoral differences can affect various aspects of teachers' careers and working lives. There may be differences in salaries and working conditions and differences in the operation and management of schools may lead to differences in teaching practices. Systems in which teachers are appraised and receive feedback on their work may also differ between sectors as teachers in private schools may not be subject to the same regulations and career structure as teachers in public schools.

Table 2.4 shows that, on average across TALIS countries, 83% of teachers worked in public schools yet substantial differences exist across countries. In Ireland and Belgium (Fl.), for example, fewer than 50% of teachers work in public schools. In Belgium (Fl.), private schools are government-dependent. In Ireland private schools are normally not fee-paying and are privately managed. In contrast, over 95% of teachers in Bulgaria, Estonia, Iceland, Italy, Lithuania, Malaysia, Norway and Slovenia work in public schools.

School size

Data collected on teachers' working conditions include the size of schools in which they work and the number and type of colleagues employed to facilitate various management and administrative functions within schools or to support teaching more directly. Table 2.4 presents the average school size in TALIS countries expressed by the average number of students. Information on the type and number of personnel is presented as the ratio of teachers to pedagogical support personnel (such as teacher's aides or other non-professional personnel who either provide or support instruction, professional curricular/instructional specialists, and educational media specialists) and of the ratio of teachers to school administrative or management personnel. These data cover personnel employed by the school and do not include personnel employed outside the school who may offer support in these areas. In Table 2.4, the data correspond to the whole school in which lower secondary teachers work and thus may cover education in addition to the lower-secondary level if schools offer other levels (*e.g.* upper secondary). However, the fourth column of Table 2.4 is an exception as it presents lower secondary teachers' average class size. Teachers provided information about a class they currently teach which was randomly chosen from their weekly timetable.

Teachers worked in schools with an average of 489 students, but there was considerable variation among countries. For example, Malaysia, with a mean of 1 046 students per school, has an average school size just over double the TALIS average. Teachers in Australia, Portugal, and Turkey also worked in relatively large schools with an average number of students ranging from 754 to 800 students. In contrast, smaller schools were more common in Iceland, Norway and Poland, where the average number of students was less than 300. There was thus a difference of over 800 students between the country with the largest average number of students (Malaysia) and the country with the smallest (Poland). In general, the ratio of teachers to pedagogical support personnel (TALIS country average of 13) was higher than the ratio of teachers to administrative support personnel (TALIS country average of 8) showing a greater emphasis on providing administrative rather than pedagogical support. There is less variation among countries in terms of the ratio of teachers to administrative support personnel (Table 2.4).

School resources

The physical, human and financial resources invested in schools influence not only the education provided to students but also aspects of teachers and their teaching that are the focus of this report. The OECD's Programme for International Student Assessment (PISA) shows that the more resource shortages are perceived to hinder instruction, the lower student performance (OECD 2007, p. 263). In addition, inequalities in student's educational performance often reflect disparities in their individual resources and socio-economic status and in the resources invested in schools (OECD, 2008b). In some education systems, there are concerns that schools not only lack the resources to meet the educational requirements of their students, particularly those from disadvantaged backgrounds and those with special learning needs, but that schools with more students from disadvantaged backgrounds may have fewer resources with which to educate their students than those with students from more privileged backgrounds (OECD, 2008b).

Data were collected from school principals concerning the extent to which a lack of resources hindered instruction for students. These data are presented in Table 2.5. School principals were asked to consider eight categories: (availability of) qualified teachers; laboratory technicians; instructional support personnel; other support personnel; instructional materials; computers for instruction; other equipment; and library materials. On average across TALIS countries, between one-third and one-half of teachers taught in schools whose school principal felt that shortages in one or more of these areas hindered their school's capacity to provide instruction "to some extent" or "a lot". This ranged from 33% of teachers whose school principal reported that instruction was hindered to this extent by a lack of laboratory technicians to 50% of teachers whose school principal reported that instruction was hindered to this extent by a shortage of other equipment.

In regard to teachers and support personnel, on average across TALIS countries, 38% of teachers were in schools whose capacity to provide instruction was hindered "to some extent" or "a lot" by a shortage of qualified teachers. This concerned only 12% of teachers in Poland but almost two-thirds of teachers in Estonia and over three-quarters in Turkey (Table 2.5). It is important to recognise that it is not only because of widespread teacher shortages that school principals may report a lack of qualified teachers. The labour market for teachers is complex and multidimensional and shortages can arise in specific subject areas, for particular types of teachers, for teaching of a specific duration, or in certain localities (OECD, 2005). Matters internal to the school such as sudden resignations, unforeseen increases in student numbers, or administrative requirements for the teaching of specific subjects can also lead to a lack of qualified teachers that may affect instruction. Teacher shortages should therefore not be considered homogenous, as the labour market for teachers is affected by the subject area and the year or grade in which they teach. The structure of the labour market and the degree of flexibility in hiring and firing teachers can also create situations that affect instruction within schools. For example, a lack of labour market flexibility may restrict schools' ability to employ teachers to fill short-term vacancies or vacancies that arise at short notice. In addition, a lack of flexibility in teachers' career structure may restrict school principals' ability to differentiate salaries or payments offered to teachers (see Table 2.7) to fill difficult positions or positions that are less attractive to teachers and therefore receive fewer applicants.

On average across TALIS countries, 48% of teachers are in schools whose school principal reported that instruction was hindered "to some extent" or "a lot" due to a lack of instructional support personnel, and 46% taught in schools whose school principal reported that instruction was hindered by a lack of other support personnel. School principals' reports for both of these personnel categories reveal differences among countries. One-third or fewer of teachers worked in schools whose school principal reported that instruction was hindered "to some extent" or "a lot" by lack of instructional support personnel in Bulgaria (15%), Denmark (25%), Malaysia (31%), Poland (21%), and the Slovak Republic (33%). In contrast, a lack of instructional support personnel was reported to hinder instruction in schools in which two-thirds or more of teachers worked in Austria (69%), Portugal (79%), Spain (81%) and Turkey (70%). Over two-thirds of teachers in these countries worked in schools whose school principal also reported that the school's capacity to provide instruction was affected by a lack of other support personnel (Table 2.5).

Analysis of the interaction of these characteristics can indicate the extent to which schools' capacity to provide instruction is hindered by a lack of personnel in a single area (e.g. qualified teachers) or in other categories of school personnel. There is a significant and quantitatively important relationship across TALIS countries between school principals' reports that instruction was hindered by a lack of qualified teachers and by a lack of instructional support and other support personnel. For example, just under half of teachers whose school principal reported that instruction was hindered "a lot" by a lack of qualified teachers also reported this for a lack of instructional support personnel. The relationship was slightly weaker between a lack of qualified teachers and a lack of other support personnel. But was stronger between a lack of instructional support personnel and a lack of other support personnel, with 70% of teachers working in schools whose school principal reported that instruction in their school was hindered "a lot" by a lack of instructional support personnel also reporting that instruction in their school was hindered "a lot" by a lack of other support personnel. The strength of this relationship implies that a distinction between these types of personnel may not be particularly pertinent to decisions made at the school level (OECD, *TALIS Database.*). A situation may exist whereby most resources are devoted to teaching staff and that there are minimal additional resources to allocate for school staff other than qualified teachers. Such an assertion could be reflected in OECD national statistics which showed that in 2005, 63% of current expenditure on educational institutions in secondary education was allocated to the compensation of teachers and 16% was allocated to other staff (OECD, 2008a). Given this figure and the basic requirements or positions that must be filled within schools, perhaps there are few decisions that can be made to, for example, increase the number of instructional support personnel at the expense of teaching personnel. It should also be noted that such decisions can be made at different levels of the education system and are therefore not necessarily school-level decisions.

More than half of teachers in Brazil, Bulgaria, Ireland, Lithuania, Mexico and Turkey worked in schools whose school principal reported that a lack or inadequacy of materials in at least three of four kinds of resources (instructional materials, computers for instruction, library materials and other equipment) hindered instruction. More than half worked in schools where the school principal reported that instruction was hindered "to some extent" or "a lot" by a shortage or inadequacy of instructional materials in Lithuania (62%), Mexico (61%), Poland (52%), and Turkey (61%). More than half worked in schools where the school principal reported that a shortage or inadequacy of library materials hindered instruction in Brazil (58%), Bulgaria (56%), Ireland (66%), Mexico (69%), the Slovak Republic (54%) and Turkey (62%). More than half also worked in schools where the school principal reported that a shortage of computers hindered instruction in Brazil (59%), Bulgaria (51%), Ireland (63%), Lithuania (66%), Mexico (68%), Portugal (67%), the Slovak Republic (57%) and Turkey (57%) (Table 2.5).

Given issues of school resources and tradeoffs in decision making, it is worth noting that countries with higher ratios of teachers to pedagogical or administrative personnel are not necessarily those in which school principals consider that this hinders instruction. Among countries with a relatively high average class size (Table 2.4), an above-average percentage of school principals considered a lack of qualified teachers as a factor hindering instruction in Malaysia (46%) Mexico (64%) and Turkey (78%). In Korea, another country with a high average class size (35 students), only about 19% of teachers worked in schools whose school principal reported that a lack of qualified teachers hindered instruction, one of the lowest percentages among TALIS countries. However, in certain countries with smaller than average class sizes, a large percentage of teachers worked in schools whose school principal reported a lack of qualified teachers which hindered instruction. In Austria, Estonia, Italy, and Lithuania, with average class sizes of less than 22 students, around one-half to two-thirds of teachers' school principals considered that a lack of qualified teachers hindered instruction in their school to at least some extent (Tables 2.4 and 2.5).

Schools in Austria, Ireland, Italy, Spain and Turkey have ratios ranging from 16 to 24 teachers to one person providing pedagogical support (Table 2.4) and a percentage of teachers above the TALIS average who worked in schools whose school principal reported that a lack of instructional support personnel hindered instruction to at least some extent. Conversely, Mexico had a comparatively low average ratio of almost eight teachers to one pedagogical support person, but the school principals of 65% of teachers report that a lack of pedagogical support hindered instruction at least to some extent. Mexico also has one of the lowest ratios of teachers per administrative or management staff but also one of the highest percentages of teachers (almost 70%) whose school principals reported that a lack of support personnel hindered at least to some extent the school's capacity to provide instruction. The pattern is similar, but less striking, for Brazil and Italy. In addition, except for Belgium (Fl.) and Poland, all countries with an above-average ratio of teachers to school administrative or management personnel also had above-average percentages of teachers in schools whose school principals reported that a lack of support personnel hindered the school's capacity to provide instruction.

School admission policies

Admission policies may constitute an important element of the functioning of a school. Such policies can influence the profile of the school's students as well as the type of school or its focus. This can affect teachers in terms not only of their students and their teaching practices, but also their working conditions and the school's requirements and expectations with regard to the teaching staff. School admission policies indicate the extent to which a school selects its students and the extent to which parents and families can choose among schools. Schools with selective admission policies may only allow better-performing students to enter their school and this can help to ensure the school's high performance. Teachers may therefore be required to place a greater emphasis on maintaining or increasing such high performance. They may also face challenges that are different from those in schools with students who perform less well or come from disadvantaged backgrounds. School admission policies that focus on the decisions and needs of students and parents may operate in a system or area that has a greater amount of school choice. Such schools, and teachers working within them, may have to fashion the education they offer to better attract families and meet the specific requirements of students.

Data were collected from school principals on six elements of their school's admission policies: residence in a particular area; students' academic record; recommendation of feeder schools; attendance of other family members at the school; parents' endorsement of the educational or religious philosophy of the school; and students' need or desire for a specific programme. The use of admissions policies varies within and between countries, and in some instances these policies may not apply to all students. For example, in Italy, families are free to choose where they want to send their children, and schools generally have to accede to their request. Specific admission criteria can only be applied when there are specific limitations (e.g. buildings, staff) because enrolments exceed the school's capacity.

As Table 2.6 and Figure 2.3 show, on average across TALIS countries, students' residence was the main deciding factor in admission to a school. Fewer than half of teachers worked in schools whose school principal reported that this was either a pre-requisite or a high priority for admittance; slightly more than 70% of teachers in Portugal and Turkey worked in such schools but less than 25% in Mexico and the Slovak Republic, and less than 1% in Belgium (Fl.).

Belgium (Fl.) is the only country whose school principals did not generally consider students' place of residence a pre-requisite or a high priority (Table 2.6). Following place of residence, an average of 20% of teachers worked in schools where the school principal reported students' desire or need of a special programme as a pre-requisite or a high priority in their school admission policy. This criterion was most prominent in Austria (40% of teachers worked in schools where this was a pre-requisite or a high priority), Belgium (Fl.) (57%),

Bulgaria (43%), and Hungary (58%). Next in order of importance was the attendance of other family members at the school (18% of teachers worked in schools whose school principal reported this as a pre-requisite or a high priority), students' academic record (14%), and the recommendation of feeder schools (10%). In Australia (30%), Belgium (Fl.) (61%), Bulgaria (41%), Denmark (35%) and Hungary (35%), parents' endorsement of the school's instruction or religious philosophy has considerably greater importance than in other TALIS countries (Table 2.6).

Figure 2.3

Percentage of teachers in schools where the principal reported the following as pre-requisites or high priorities for admittance to school (2007-08)

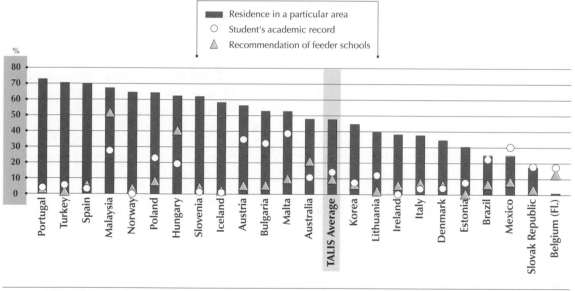

Countries are ranked in descending order of importance attributed by school principals to residence in a particular area.
Source: OECD, Table 2.6.

StatLink ⌐ http://dx.doi.org/10.1787/607784618372

School admission criteria that are selective consider students' academic record and the recommendations of feeder schools important. Attendance of other family members at the school might be included in the admission policies of a selective school and can increase the homogeneity of the student population. However, this criterion does not apply exclusively to selective schools. Non-selective schools may also use it to assist families in the education their children receive. For example, it may be complementary to a policy of giving preference to students who reside in a specific local area. As Table 2.6 shows, 14% of teachers worked in schools which used students' academic records as either a pre-requisite or with a high priority in admission decisions. Such schools are clearly selective and may be more likely to have a higher-performing student population. A greater proportion of teachers worked in these schools in Austria (35% of teachers), Bulgaria (32%), Malta (39%) and Mexico (30%). In addition, the recommendation of feeder schools was considered important in Australia (21% of teachers worked in schools which considered this a pre-requisite or a high priority) but especially in Hungary (41%) and in Malaysia (52%).

School autonomy

A growing belief that schools need to be empowered to better meet the needs of students and families has led to increasing attention on the issue of school autonomy (OECD, 2006a). In a number of education systems, schools have been granted greater autonomy in recent years as decision-making power has been decentralised (OECD 2008a). A key aspect of the underlying rationale for greater school autonomy is the information asymmetries in the education system (Hoxby, 2003). In centralised systems, decisions concerning the provision of specific education programmes are the domain of a central authority rather than individual schools. Similarly, the philosophy underlying the provision of instruction, the allocation of personnel, and a variety of education policies may be mandated centrally. However, information about students' needs and educational demands from parents and local communities are best obtained at the school-level. School principals, teachers and other school staff have the most interaction with these stakeholders and are therefore likely to have the most information on their needs and demands. Furthermore, decisions on appointing teachers and assigning them teaching tasks in a school can be better informed if made at the school level where there is more information on how teachers' skills and abilities match the educational requirements of the school's students.

Data were gathered from school principals on 13 decision-making areas: selecting teachers to hire; firing teachers; establishing teachers' starting salaries; formulating the school budget; deciding on budget allocations within the school; establishing student disciplinary policies; establishing student assessment policies; approving students for admission to the school; deciding which courses are offered; determining course content; choosing appropriate textbooks; and allocating funds for teachers' professional development. The percentage of teachers working in schools whose school principal reported considerable responsibility at the school level for these areas are presented in Table 2.7 and Figure 2.4. It should be noted that considerable responsibility at the school level does not preclude considerable responsibility elsewhere. Considerable responsibility can exist both at the school level and also, for example, with a regional or national education authority. Of most importance to TALIS is decision making that directly affects teachers and their careers. A number of these areas have a direct impact upon teachers' work and their teaching and, as discussed in Chapter 6, the degree of school autonomy will affect school principals' responsibilities within their schools.

Of the 13 areas, the least responsibility at the school level concerned teachers' remuneration. Only around one-quarter of teachers worked in schools whose school principal reported considerable school-level responsibility for establishing teachers' salaries and determining teachers' salary increases. There was considerably more school-level decision-making responsibility in Bulgaria, Estonia, Hungary, Norway, Poland and the Slovak Republic, where over 40% of teachers worked in schools with considerable decision-making power in these areas. In Denmark and Slovenia, over 40% of teachers worked in schools with considerable decision-making power for teachers' salary increases but less responsibility for establishing teachers' starting salaries. Very few teachers (5% or fewer) in Austria, Belgium (Fl.), Ireland, Italy and Spain worked in schools with considerable responsibility for teacher remuneration (Table 2.7). This may have a direct impact upon the form and nature of appraisal and feedback that teachers receive in schools in these countries.

A greater proportion of teachers worked in schools with considerable responsibility for hiring and firing teachers than for decisions concerning teachers' salaries. On average across TALIS countries, 68% of teachers worked in schools whose school principal reported that the school had considerable responsibility for hiring teachers and 61% worked in schools with considerable responsibility for firing teachers. Over 90% of teachers worked in schools with considerable responsibility for hiring and firing teachers in Belgium (Fl.), Bulgaria, Estonia, Hungary, Iceland, Lithuania, Norway, Poland, the Slovak Republic and Slovenia (Table 2.7). In light of this, such schools may also have considerable responsibility for factors affecting teachers' careers, such as teacher appraisal and feedback.

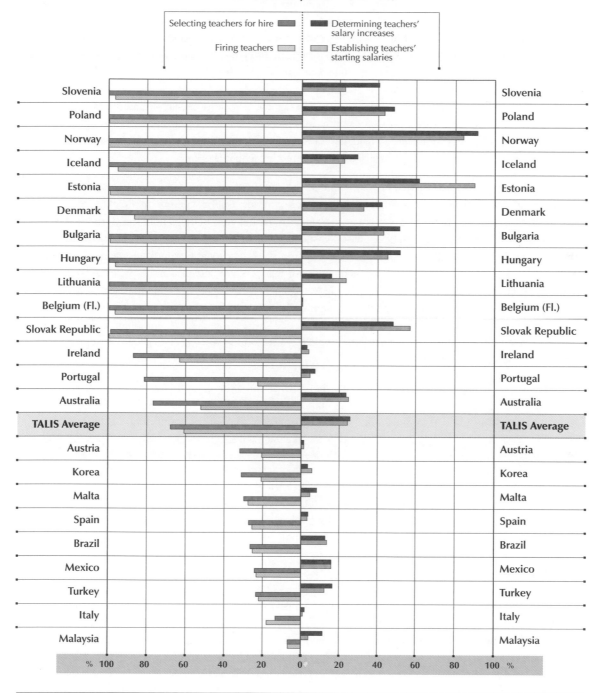

Figure 2.4

School autonomy factors (2007-08)

Countries are ranked in descending order of the percentage of teachers whose principal reported considerable responsibility held at the school for selecting teachers for hire.
Source: OECD, Table 2.7.

StatLink http://dx.doi.org/10.1787/607784618372

On average across TALIS countries, the percentage of teachers working in schools with considerable responsibility for hiring and firing teachers was over twice the percentage of teachers in schools with considerable responsibility for establishing and determining teachers' salaries (Table 2.7). Given this difference, it is apparent that there is a split in decision-making responsibilities concerning the teacher labour market and the career structure for teachers. School-level responsibilities are restricted when it comes to teacher salaries but there is more wide-spread school autonomy in hiring and firing teachers. This split may indicate a centrally determined career structure with a relatively tight control over teacher salaries but greater school autonomy for hiring and firing decisions which are at the interface with the teacher labour market. The split is particularly pronounced in Belgium (Fl.), Iceland and Lithuania where there is widespread school autonomy in hiring and firing teachers but considerably less responsibility for teachers' salaries. For example, 100% of teachers in Belgium (Fl.) worked in schools with considerable responsibility for hiring; virtually none worked in schools with considerable responsibility for establishing or determining teachers' salaries.

With regard to teachers' professional development, school autonomy can be defined in terms of the degree to which decisions concerning the funding of different types of professional development are made at the school-level or centrally. As teachers' development is a focus of TALIS, it is important to note the substantial variation in this area. On average across TALIS countries, just over 60% of teachers worked in schools whose school principal reported considerable responsibility at the school level for allocating funds for teachers' professional development. Countries in which a large percentage of teachers worked in schools with responsibility for allocating professional development funds include Australia (98% of teachers), Denmark (90%), Estonia (87%), Iceland (94%), Ireland (86%), Norway (98%), Poland (97%), the Slovak Republic (86%) and Slovenia (96%). There was less school autonomy in Austria (18%), Mexico (21%), Portugal (23%), and Spain (17%) (Table 2.7). These issues are discussed further in Chapter 3, which focuses on teachers' professional development, and in Chapter 6, which covers school leadership.

For budgetary decisions, there was considerably more decision-making authority within schools across TALIS countries. The majority of teachers in all TALIS countries worked in schools with considerable responsibility for formulating the school budget and deciding on the allocation of the budget within schools. In fact, except in Brazil, Malaysia, Mexico and Spain, more than 85% of teachers worked in schools with considerable decision-making power in this area, an indication a of high degree of school autonomy (Table 2.7).

Information was collected from school principals on the level of school autonomy in six areas covering school policies on student discipline, student assessment, and courses offered, including the types of courses and their content. The great majority of teachers worked in schools where the school principal reported that the school has considerable responsibility for establishing school policies on student discipline and student assessment. As Table 2.7 shows, in all TALIS countries but Malaysia, Portugal and Turkey, over nine out of ten teachers worked in schools with considerable responsibility for student disciplinary policies. However, the same is true in regard to student assessment policies for only 15 TALIS countries, even though on average 89% of teachers worked in schools with considerable responsibility for establishing these policies. On average across TALIS countries, teachers are less likely to work in schools with considerable responsibility for deciding the courses offered. Fewer than three-quarters of teachers worked in schools with considerable responsibility for deciding which courses their school offers. However, while less than half of teachers work in such schools in Brazil (49%), Malaysia (35%), Malta (43%), Mexico (35%), Spain (37%), and Turkey (41%), over 90% worked in schools with considerable responsibility for deciding the courses offered in Australia (100%), Austria (94%), Denmark (91%), Estonia (100%), Hungary (91%), Iceland (98%), Ireland (98%), Italy (100%), and Portugal (94%) (Table 2.7). It should be noted that these decisions may take place within a framework in which some compulsory subjects are determined centrally.

In addition to deciding which courses are offered within schools, decisions on course content and textbooks used by students shed further light on the degree of school autonomy. In all but four TALIS countries (Malaysia, Malta, Mexico and Turkey) over 90% of teachers worked in schools with considerable responsibility for choosing the textbooks used in the courses they teach, and of these four countries, only in Malaysia and Turkey did fewer than 60% of teachers work in such schools. Fewer teachers in TALIS countries worked in schools whose school principal reported considerable school-level responsibility for determining course content. On average across TALIS countries, 66% of teachers worked in schools which had this responsibility. This was more common in Denmark, Hungary and Italy where over 95% of teachers worked in schools with considerable responsibility in determining the content of courses they teach but is found less frequently in Bulgaria (28%), Malaysia (33%), Mexico (33%) and Turkey (27%).

School climate

An important aspect of both the working lives of school principals and teachers and of the education provided to students is school climate, as indicated by the actions of the students and professionals in schools. As previous research has shown, school climate can influence student attainment and learning. For example, analysis of PISA data showed that a positive school climate was associated with higher levels of student achievement (OECD, 2004). A positive school climate can also have a positive impact on teachers and their working lives just as a positive organisational climate can benefit employees, increase their job satisfaction and affect their productivity (Lazear, 2000).

Figure 2.5

Percentage of teachers whose school principal reported that the following teacher behaviours hindered the provision of instruction in their school a lot or to some extent (2007-08)

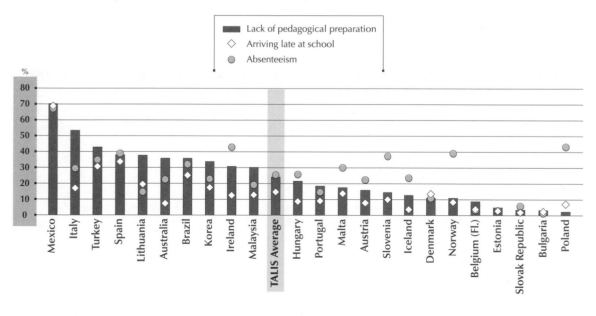

Countries are ranked in descending order of the percentage of teachers whose school principal reported a lack of pedagogical preparation as a factor hindering instruction.
Source: OECD, Table 2.8.

StatLink ⎯⎯⎯ http://dx.doi.org/10.1787/607784618372

School climate is the result of a variety of factors and actions that affect both students and teachers. School principals reported on the extent to which 14 aspects of teacher and student behaviour hindered instruction in their school. Information was collected on three types of teacher behaviour which can hinder instruction: teachers arriving late at school, teacher absenteeism, and teachers' lack of preparation. Information from school principals on the extent to which such behaviour hindered instruction in their school is presented in Table 2.8 and Figure 2.5. Information on student behaviour, which was more generally considered as hindering student learning, is presented in Table 2.8a and includes: students arriving late at school; absenteeism; classroom disturbances; cheating; profanity/swearing; vandalism; theft; intimidation or verbal abuse of other students; physical injury to other students; intimidation or verbal abuse of teachers or staff; and use or possession of drugs and/or alcohol.

Countries varied markedly in the extent to which school principals reported that teachers' actions hindered instruction. While on average across TALIS countries around one-quarter of teachers work in schools whose school principal reported that teacher absenteeism and lack of preparation hindered instruction "to some extent" or "a lot", the problem was greater in certain countries. Over half of teachers worked in schools whose school principal reported a lack of preparation by teachers in Italy (53% of teachers) and Mexico (70%) (Table 2.8). In Mexico, the problem appears to be compounded by a similar proportion of teachers in schools whose school principal reported that instruction was hindered "to some extent" or "a lot" by teacher absenteeism and by teachers arriving late at school. On average across TALIS countries, only 15% of teachers worked in schools whose school principal reported that teachers arriving late at school hindered instruction.

Students' actions were reported to hinder instruction to a greater degree than teachers' actions. The most important were classroom disturbances (60% of teachers worked in schools whose school principal reported that instruction was hindered "to some extent" or "a lot" by classroom disturbances), student absenteeism (46%), students arriving late at school (39%), profanity and swearing (37%), and intimidation or verbal abuse of other students (35%). School principals reported that intimidation or verbal abuse of teachers and other staff (17%), physical injury to other students (16%), theft (15%), and use or possession of drugs and alcohol (11%) were not considered problems to the same extent (Table 2.8a).

Given the cultural context of school principals' reports, it is important to look at differences both within and between countries. Of the student actions reported by school principals as being most important in terms of their impact upon instruction in their school, classroom disturbances, student absenteeism and arriving late at school were the three most frequently reported student-related factors that hinder instruction in Australia, Bulgaria, Estonia, Iceland, Ireland, Lithuania, Malaysia, Mexico, Spain and Turkey (Table 2.8a).

Table 2.1

Gender and age distribution of teachers (2007-08)

Percentage of teachers of lower secondary education with the following characteristics

	Female teachers		Female school principals[1]		Percentage of teachers in each age group											
					Teachers aged under 25 years		Teachers aged 25-29 years		Teachers aged 30-39 years		Teachers aged 40-49 years		Teachers aged 50-59 years		Teachers aged 60 years or more	
	%	(S.E.)	%	(S.E.)	%	(S.E.)	%	(S.E.)	%	(S.E.)	%	(S.E.)	%	(S.E.)	%	(S.E.)
Australia	59.2	(1.14)	38.2	(4.80)	4.5	(0.53)	13.7	(0.74)	22.6	(1.09)	26.5	(0.99)	28.9	(1.16)	3.8	(0.43)
Austria	67.9	(0.74)	29.2	(3.54)	0.7	(0.12)	6.0	(0.48)	15.4	(0.71)	36.9	(0.96)	39.9	(1.12)	1.2	(0.17)
Belgium (Fl.)	68.9	(1.45)	38.2	(4.29)	8.3	(0.67)	18.4	(0.78)	26.3	(0.85)	23.6	(1.18)	22.9	(0.86)	0.5	(0.20)
Brazil	73.6	(1.00)	76.0	(2.76)	6.1	(0.80)	15.9	(0.92)	34.1	(1.10)	31.5	(1.00)	11.2	(0.62)	1.2	(0.19)
Bulgaria	82.7	(1.02)	69.0	(5.98)	1.7	(0.57)	5.2	(0.94)	23.9	(1.17)	32.9	(1.99)	33.2	(1.37)	3.1	(0.44)
Denmark	58.1	(1.22)	37.8	(5.33)	0.9	(0.25)	7.3	(0.64)	30.0	(1.29)	23.3	(1.53)	30.8	(1.31)	7.8	(0.80)
Estonia	83.7	(0.55)	56.4	(3.25)	2.5	(0.34)	8.4	(0.49)	18.2	(0.78)	32.0	(0.87)	27.1	(1.00)	11.7	(0.64)
Hungary	76.9	(1.30)	49.0	(5.40)	1.4	(0.36)	11.0	(1.08)	24.5	(1.07)	35.0	(1.18)	26.2	(1.17)	1.9	(0.35)
Iceland	69.1	(1.46)	49.1	(5.15)	2.6	(0.44)	10.9	(0.88)	26.0	(1.17)	31.0	(1.21)	23.0	(1.13)	6.6	(0.68)
Ireland	68.6	(1.24)	34.9	(4.40)	4.4	(0.48)	17.3	(0.98)	29.2	(1.17)	22.0	(1.06)	23.8	(1.19)	3.3	(0.37)
Italy	77.7	(0.68)	45.8	(4.93)	0.1	(0.08)	2.4	(0.26)	17.2	(0.83)	28.7	(0.77)	44.8	(1.06)	6.7	(0.44)
Korea	64.4	(1.33)	15.0	(4.16)	0.6	(0.14)	11.9	(0.85)	25.4	(0.97)	45.4	(1.23)	15.7	(0.89)	1.1	(0.22)
Lithuania	84.9	(0.60)	52.5	(4.30)	2.3	(0.32)	6.4	(0.50)	21.3	(0.79)	32.4	(0.92)	27.9	(0.88)	9.7	(0.70)
Malaysia	66.0	(0.97)	42.3	(3.68)	1.6	(0.33)	16.9	(0.74)	42.2	(0.92)	31.5	(0.80)	7.6	(0.51)	0.1	(0.13)
Malta	61.4	(1.74)	41.4	(6.45)	10.6	(1.07)	22.1	(1.33)	35.9	(1.78)	13.2	(1.13)	17.1	(1.30)	1.1	(0.28)
Mexico	53.2	(1.26)	34.7	(5.11)	3.0	(0.47)	11.7	(1.01)	25.8	(1.01)	37.3	(1.14)	18.7	(0.94)	3.5	(0.49)
Norway	60.4	(1.07)	41.4	(4.14)	0.8	(0.21)	8.4	(0.66)	31.1	(1.12)	19.8	(0.90)	27.9	(1.10)	12.0	(0.71)
Poland	76.3	(0.68)	68.7	(3.69)	1.7	(0.29)	13.5	(0.72)	36.0	(0.91)	34.5	(1.05)	13.4	(0.66)	0.9	(0.25)
Portugal	70.7	(0.92)	40.0	(4.11)	0.5	(0.14)	7.4	(0.55)	40.0	(1.22)	36.3	(1.15)	14.2	(0.98)	1.7	(0.31)
Slovak Republic	81.7	(0.80)	60.3	(4.86)	3.4	(0.49)	12.7	(0.82)	25.6	(1.16)	22.8	(0.94)	30.1	(1.11)	5.3	(0.66)
Slovenia	80.4	(0.68)	57.4	(3.95)	0.5	(0.13)	10.6	(0.65)	28.1	(0.93)	36.5	(0.91)	22.8	(0.83)	1.5	(0.20)
Spain	56.9	(0.97)	39.6	(5.25)	0.4	(0.17)	6.2	(0.46)	29.7	(1.06)	33.8	(0.95)	25.8	(1.06)	4.1	(0.45)
Turkey	52.0	(2.27)	8.8	(6.30)	10.1	(1.47)	33.8	(2.25)	35.0	(1.33)	14.7	(1.35)	6.2	(0.72)	0.1	(0.08)
TALIS average	69.3	(0.24)	44.6	(0.98)	3.0	(0.11)	12.1	(0.19)	28.0	(0.23)	29.6	(0.23)	23.5	(0.21)	3.9	(0.09)

1. Percentage of principals of schools providing lower secondary education.
Source: OECD, *TALIS Database*.
StatLink ☞ http://dx.doi.org/10.1787/607784618372

Table 2.2

Teachers' educational attainment (2007-08)

Percentage of teachers of lower secondary education by highest level of education completed

	Below ISCED level 5		ISCED level 5B[1]		ISCED level 5A (Bachelor degree)		ISCED level 5A (Master degree)		ISCED level 6	
	%	(S.E.)	%	(S.E.)	%	(S.E.)	%	(S.E.)	%	(S.E.)
Australia	0.3	(0.10)	1.0	(0.25)	82.8	(0.96)	13.7	(0.83)	2.2	(0.33)
Austria	3.1	(0.30)	59.3	(0.78)	1.3	(0.25)	33.6	(0.74)	2.6	(0.29)
Belgium (Fl.)	3.4	(0.38)	84.2	(0.96)	4.2	(0.42)	8.1	(0.73)	0.1	(0.07)
Brazil	8.6	(1.00)	0.2	(0.08)	89.3	(1.02)	1.8	(0.25)	0.1	(0.05)
Bulgaria	3.7	(1.06)	15.7	(1.69)	16.4	(1.21)	64.0	(2.64)	0.2	(0.06)
Denmark	1.9	(0.37)	0.2	(0.10)	90.3	(1.00)	7.5	(0.89)	0.0	(0.03)
Estonia	7.0	(0.51)	6.5	(0.46)	40.3	(1.15)	46.0	(1.21)	0.3	(0.11)
Hungary	0.2	(0.10)	0.1	(0.08)	71.5	(2.13)	27.8	(2.09)	0.4	(0.08)
Iceland	12.1	(0.79)	20.8	(1.15)	60.6	(1.22)	6.3	(0.70)	0.2	(0.12)
Ireland	0.6	(0.20)	3.4	(0.33)	79.4	(0.70)	15.9	(0.78)	0.8	(0.19)
Italy	5.3	(0.30)	9.4	(0.42)	6.9	(0.37)	77.4	(0.58)	0.9	(0.19)
Korea	0.3	(0.11)	0.2	(0.14)	64.7	(1.39)	33.9	(1.35)	0.7	(0.16)
Lithuania	4.1	(0.38)	13.0	(0.77)	47.0	(1.46)	35.7	(1.39)	0.1	(0.07)
Malaysia	1.0	(0.12)	12.1	(0.60)	79.4	(0.79)	7.5	(0.55)	0.0	(0.00)
Malta	3.7	(0.50)	13.3	(1.11)	71.9	(1.50)	10.7	(1.11)	0.4	(0.22)
Mexico	10.4	(0.94)	3.0	(0.43)	75.6	(1.05)	10.7	(0.72)	0.3	(0.11)
Norway	0.9	(0.19)	0.0	(0.00)	76.5	(0.92)	22.5	(0.92)	0.0	(0.04)
Poland	0.3	(0.11)	1.2	(0.27)	4.1	(0.42)	94.0	(0.46)	0.5	(0.18)
Portugal	0.4	(0.11)	4.3	(0.43)	84.4	(0.76)	10.7	(0.71)	0.2	(0.09)
Slovak Republic	2.5	(0.36)	0.0	(0.00)	0.5	(0.15)	96.2	(0.43)	0.8	(0.20)
Slovenia	3.7	(0.34)	41.9	(1.04)	52.9	(1.05)	1.4	(0.20)	0.1	(0.04)
Spain	3.5	(0.35)	1.6	(0.22)	11.4	(0.85)	78.8	(0.89)	4.7	(0.41)
Turkey	0.0	(0.00)	6.0	(0.57)	88.2	(0.96)	5.6	(0.90)	0.2	(0.11)
TALIS average	3.4	(0.10)	12.9	(0.14)	52.1	(0.22)	30.9	(0.22)	0.7	(0.04)

Note: Education categories are based on the International Standard Classification of Education (ISCED).
– ISCED level 5A programmes are generally longer and more theoretically based, while 5B programmes are typically shorter and more practical and skills oriented. A distinction was made between ISCED level 5A (Bachelor) and ISCED level 5A (Master).
– ISCED level 6 is the second stage of tertiary education and leads to an advanced research qualification (*e.g.* PhD).
1. Includes Bachelor degrees for some countries.
Source: OECD, *TALIS Database*.
StatLink ☞ http://dx.doi.org/10.1787/607784618372

Table 2.3

Employment status and job experience of teachers (2007-08)

Percentage of teachers of lower secondary education with the following characteristics

	Employment status						Job experience							
	Permanently employed		Fixed-term contract: More than 1 school year		Fixed-term contract: 1 school year or less		Teachers in their first 2 years of teaching		Teachers working for 3-10 years		Teachers working for 11-20 years		Teachers working for 20+ years	
	%	(S.E.)	%	(S.E.)	%	(S.E.)	%	(S.E.)	%	(S.E.)	%	(S.E.)	%	(S.E.)
Australia	86.8	(1.00)	4.3	(0.73)	8.9	(0.71)	11.3	(0.85)	28.4	(1.22)	24.9	(0.98)	35.4	(1.33)
Austria	89.3	(0.64)	2.0	(0.28)	8.7	(0.55)	4.4	(0.40)	15.1	(0.78)	23.3	(0.81)	57.2	(1.17)
Belgium (Fl.)	80.7	(0.90)	4.8	(0.41)	14.6	(0.83)	8.5	(0.76)	35.1	(1.38)	22.4	(0.94)	34.0	(1.09)
Brazil	74.2	(1.46)	7.1	(0.79)	18.7	(1.41)	9.6	(0.77)	38.6	(1.24)	32.4	(1.09)	19.3	(1.00)
Bulgaria	84.6	(1.25)	4.4	(0.67)	11.0	(1.10)	5.9	(0.69)	17.2	(0.69)	28.9	(1.27)	48.0	(1.53)
Denmark	96.6	(0.63)	0.3	(0.15)	3.1	(0.62)	9.5	(0.84)	35.1	(1.46)	16.9	(1.16)	38.5	(1.38)
Estonia	84.2	(1.12)	5.0	(0.46)	10.8	(0.91)	6.4	(0.51)	20.7	(0.83)	27.3	(1.06)	45.6	(1.09)
Hungary	86.1	(1.75)	2.9	(0.49)	11.0	(1.52)	5.7	(1.76)	21.9	(1.12)	25.0	(0.82)	47.4	(1.41)
Iceland	74.6	(1.12)	6.2	(0.67)	19.2	(0.98)	16.7	(0.99)	35.5	(1.19)	24.6	(1.21)	23.2	(1.06)
Ireland	73.4	(1.10)	7.8	(0.67)	18.8	(1.00)	7.1	(0.60)	33.1	(1.10)	24.6	(1.04)	35.3	(1.35)
Italy	80.6	(0.85)	a	a	19.4	(0.85)	5.9	(0.51)	19.8	(0.87)	20.9	(0.76)	53.4	(1.10)
Korea	95.6	(0.41)	4.2	(0.42)	0.2	(0.08)	6.5	(0.70)	26.2	(1.09)	33.4	(1.01)	33.9	(1.12)
Lithuania	92.4	(0.56)	4.2	(0.40)	3.4	(0.38)	4.8	(0.48)	17.6	(0.76)	28.8	(0.94)	48.8	(1.22)
Malaysia	97.8	(0.29)	1.9	(0.33)	0.4	(0.20)	9.7	(0.63)	37.0	(0.97)	37.2	(0.95)	16.1	(0.68)
Malta	96.3	(0.55)	1.2	(0.34)	2.5	(0.46)	12.8	(1.00)	41.2	(1.42)	28.6	(1.41)	17.4	(1.29)
Mexico	86.8	(1.88)	5.0	(0.56)	8.2	(1.74)	8.7	(1.05)	27.7	(1.15)	29.4	(1.27)	34.2	(1.63)
Norway	89.9	(0.88)	1.8	(0.35)	8.3	(0.80)	7.8	(0.80)	31.7	(1.10)	21.4	(0.98)	39.1	(1.49)
Poland	77.1	(1.11)	5.1	(0.67)	17.8	(0.93)	7.8	(0.64)	31.9	(0.95)	29.6	(0.78)	30.7	(0.97)
Portugal	67.6	(1.39)	15.0	(0.88)	17.4	(0.99)	3.7	(0.34)	23.6	(1.13)	46.5	(1.21)	26.1	(1.60)
Slovak Republic	82.1	(1.09)	3.8	(0.48)	14.1	(1.02)	7.7	(0.82)	29.1	(1.25)	21.7	(0.92)	41.5	(1.41)
Slovenia	82.8	(0.79)	2.2	(0.34)	15.0	(0.78)	6.2	(0.45)	27.0	(1.04)	21.3	(0.94)	45.4	(1.13)
Spain	75.6	(1.06)	6.5	(0.41)	17.9	(1.01)	5.8	(0.49)	28.4	(1.02)	30.6	(0.91)	35.2	(1.36)
Turkey	88.3	(1.32)	4.6	(0.79)	7.0	(0.95)	18.0	(1.85)	50.7	(2.11)	19.4	(1.37)	12.0	(1.26)
TALIS average	**84.5**	**(0.23)**	**4.6**	**(0.11)**	**11.1**	**(0.20)**	**8.3**	**(0.18)**	**29.2**	**(0.24)**	**26.9**	**(0.22)**	**35.5**	**(0.26)**

Source: OECD, *TALIS Database*.
StatLink ᴪ http://dx.doi.org/10.1787/607784618372

Table 2.4

School personnel characteristics and the percentage of teachers in public schools (2007-08)

Average numbers of students and average staff ratios in schools in which teachers of lower secondary education work (includes both public and private schools), and percentage of lower secondary teachers in public schools

	Number of students in schools[1]		Ratio of teachers to number of personnel for pedagogical support		Ratio of teachers to number of school administrative or management personnel		Average class size (Lower secondary education only)		Public schools	
	Mean	(S.E.)	Mean	(S.E.)	Mean	(S.E.)	Mean	(S.E.)	%	(S.E.)
Australia	754.0	(49.85)	8.3	(0.61)	5.5	(0.30)	24.6	0.20	56.1	(1.80)
Austria	300.6	(9.84)	24.1	(1.08)	22.6	(0.82)	21.1	0.14	89.1	(1.91)
Belgium (Fl.)	491.2	(20.15)	20.5	(1.63)	11.7	(0.73)	17.5	0.27	27.6	(1.39)
Brazil	601.2	(16.90)	11.9	(0.72)	6.9	(0.30)	32.2	0.35	84.9	(0.81)
Bulgaria	314.7	(16.22)	12.3	(1.31)	4.8	(0.42)	20.7	0.35	99.1	(0.54)
Denmark	340.4	(20.69)	9.1	(0.97)	7.5	(0.38)	20.0	0.22	71.5	(1.65)
Estonia	361.3	(8.35)	10.4	(0.69)	7.6	(0.21)	20.5	0.32	97.2	(1.49)
Hungary	394.3	(23.16)	7.3	(0.69)	8.3	(0.48)	20.2	0.57	81.3	(4.03)
Iceland	266.5	(12.57)	5.7	(0.60)	6.3	(0.22)	18.6	0.02	98.3	(0.06)
Ireland	454.5	(11.51)	15.8	(1.06)	11.1	(0.41)	21.9	0.18	45.2	(2.54)
Italy	617.9	(30.35)	20.4	(3.22)	7.5	(0.32)	21.3	0.16	96.1	(1.14)
Korea	646.6	(41.75)	14.0	(1.12)	4.9	(0.32)	34.6	0.43	82.1	(2.91)
Lithuania	381.9	(10.11)	16.7	(1.10)	8.3	(0.23)	19.3	0.24	98.5	(0.93)
Malaysia	1046.0	(25.94)	12.4	(1.01)	7.5	(0.45)	34.9	0.28	98.8	(0.57)
Malta	495.8	(20.83)	7.9	(0.74)	8.7	(0.57)	19.6	0.01	67.5	(0.16)
Mexico	436.0	(19.09)	7.9	(0.68)	5.0	(0.34)	37.8	0.55	83.0	(1.20)
Norway	243.0	(10.11)	7.0	(0.41)	8.3	(0.31)	21.4	0.29	96.3	(1.90)
Poland	242.2	(13.35)	9.4	(0.56)	9.0	(0.48)	20.8	0.27	94.4	(1.48)
Portugal	800.8	(33.65)	10.8	(1.64)	10.5	(0.59)	21.3	0.21	89.3	(0.73)
Slovak Republic	351.8	(14.52)	14.3	(1.15)	4.7	(0.17)	21.1	0.26	87.8	(3.03)
Slovenia	377.1	(6.56)	18.3	(1.16)	7.8	(0.34)	18.8	0.18	100.0	(0.00)
Spain	536.7	(25.78)	19.0	(0.91)	8.8	(0.68)	21.7	0.26	75.6	(2.34)
Turkey	795.5	(53.98)	22.2	(2.53)	10.4	(0.49)	31.3	0.75	92.5	(1.16)
TALIS average	**489.1**	**(5.21)**	**13.3**	**(0.27)**	**8.4**	**(0.09)**	**23.5**	**(0.07)**	**83.1**	**(0.37)**

1. These data are means and percentages of characteristics of the schools where lower secondary teachers worked. The education provision in these schools may extend across ISCED levels (*e.g.* in schools that offer both lower and upper secondary education) and therefore may not apply only to teachers or students of lower-secondary education.
Source: OECD, *TALIS Database*.
StatLink ᴪ http://dx.doi.org/10.1787/607784618372

Table 2.5

School resources (2007-08)

Percentage of teachers of lower secondary education whose school principal reported that the following resource issues hinder instruction "a lot" or "to some extent" in their school

	A lack of qualified teachers		A lack of laboratory technicians		A lack of instructional support personnel		A lack of other support personnel		Shortage or inadequacy of instructional materials		Shortage or inadequacy of computers for instruction		Shortage or inadequacy of library materials		Shortage or inadequacy of other equipment	
	%	(S.E.)	%	(S.E.)	%	(S.E.)	%	(S.E.)	%	(S.E.)	%	(S.E.)	%	(S.E.)	%	(S.E.)
Australia	40.5	(4.73)	14.0	(3.25)	38.1	(4.17)	40.4	(4.24)	15.5	(3.13)	32.2	(4.56)	20.9	(3.67)	31.7	(4.36)
Austria	48.8	(3.12)	21.3	(2.66)	68.7	(3.08)	77.5	(2.82)	12.2	(2.30)	25.5	(2.90)	16.8	(2.55)	35.0	(3.44)
Belgium (Fl.)	31.5	(3.76)	7.3	(2.14)	36.7	(3.89)	35.5	(4.11)	13.7	(2.74)	33.2	(3.78)	23.9	(3.43)	29.7	(3.78)
Brazil	31.1	(3.08)	65.1	(3.03)	61.1	(2.98)	63.1	(3.19)	28.6	(2.73)	59.2	(3.18)	57.9	(2.61)	64.1	(2.75)
Bulgaria	25.2	(4.18)	17.8	(2.99)	15.2	(2.92)	13.3	(2.46)	44.7	(3.99)	51.0	(5.60)	55.6	(5.62)	67.0	(5.18)
Denmark	28.2	(4.44)	3.3	(1.84)	25.4	(4.13)	17.5	(3.77)	23.1	(4.10)	22.6	(4.13)	25.5	(4.55)	27.5	(5.01)
Estonia	65.6	(3.58)	17.1	(2.96)	51.6	(3.85)	41.0	(4.12)	36.4	(4.03)	27.1	(3.66)	44.2	(4.36)	45.3	(4.50)
Hungary	22.1	(5.03)	29.6	(6.57)	48.5	(6.36)	36.2	(3.77)	39.4	(4.09)	47.0	(6.26)	37.8	(6.64)	62.9	(5.83)
Iceland	39.0	(0.18)	30.8	(0.18)	36.8	(0.19)	34.1	(0.17)	15.8	(0.13)	27.6	(0.15)	24.6	(0.15)	20.4	(0.15)
Ireland	38.4	(4.63)	82.6	(3.64)	63.6	(5.00)	62.7	(4.69)	34.2	(4.44)	62.5	(4.42)	66.3	(4.78)	62.6	(4.63)
Italy	51.9	(3.45)	53.6	(3.09)	56.6	(3.34)	54.8	(3.41)	42.9	(3.39)	41.6	(3.03)	45.9	(3.13)	46.4	(3.37)
Korea	18.6	(3.36)	39.6	(4.28)	45.2	(4.59)	43.9	(4.28)	27.8	(3.90)	28.4	(3.97)	39.5	(4.30)	41.9	(4.11)
Lithuania	60.6	(3.77)	40.2	(3.91)	47.3	(3.91)	38.9	(4.34)	61.6	(3.72)	66.0	(3.46)	49.3	(3.86)	71.3	(3.79)
Malaysia	45.9	(4.05)	23.8	(2.80)	31.0	(3.46)	32.0	(3.63)	26.2	(3.53)	36.6	(3.83)	36.9	(2.98)	30.3	(3.19)
Malta	26.2	(0.22)	32.8	(0.23)	34.4	(0.18)	51.0	(0.20)	30.1	(0.23)	41.9	(0.20)	28.4	(0.21)	43.8	(0.19)
Mexico	63.8	(4.00)	64.9	(3.39)	64.9	(3.32)	69.2	(3.37)	60.6	(3.37)	68.0	(3.33)	69.3	(3.58)	70.5	(3.35)
Norway	29.7	(3.71)	29.6	(4.14)	51.1	(4.97)	43.7	(5.08)	43.1	(4.50)	41.1	(4.59)	37.3	(4.03)	53.1	(4.85)
Poland	11.8	(2.85)	21.0	(3.26)	21.3	(3.16)	19.0	(2.71)	51.7	(4.38)	35.8	(4.18)	46.5	(4.57)	54.4	(4.56)
Portugal	15.9	(3.23)	47.6	(3.73)	78.5	(3.08)	80.0	(3.18)	36.6	(4.30)	67.3	(3.57)	39.1	(4.33)	70.3	(3.60)
Slovak Republic	30.5	(3.87)	24.9	(4.10)	33.1	(4.57)	23.8	(3.54)	38.7	(4.69)	57.1	(4.27)	53.5	(4.51)	64.1	(4.06)
Slovenia	24.6	(3.34)	17.9	(3.09)	33.9	(3.85)	29.8	(3.41)	18.5	(2.95)	25.0	(3.15)	20.4	(3.07)	33.7	(3.35)
Spain	34.0	(3.40)	13.6	(2.76)	80.5	(3.00)	75.7	(2.61)	24.4	(3.62)	41.0	(3.41)	37.3	(3.62)	50.1	(3.55)
Turkey	78.1	(4.98)	58.7	(4.80)	69.5	(4.55)	72.0	(4.32)	61.3	(4.98)	56.6	(5.88)	61.9	(5.30)	67.0	(5.67)
TALIS average	**37.5**	**(0.77)**	**32.9**	**(0.72)**	**47.5**	**(0.80)**	**45.9**	**(0.74)**	**34.2**	**(0.76)**	**43.2**	**(0.83)**	**40.8**	**(0.83)**	**49.7**	**(0.84)**

Source: OECD, *TALIS Database.*
StatLink ⧉ http://dx.doi.org/10.1787/607784618372

Table 2.6

School admission policies (2007-08)

Percentage of teachers of lower secondary education whose school principal reported the following as pre-requisites or high priority for student admittance to the school

	Residence in a particular area		Student's academic record		Recommendation of feeder schools		Parents' endorsement of the instructional or religious philosophy of the school		Students' need or desire for a special programme		Attendance of other family members at the school	
	%	(S.E.)	%	(S.E.)	%	(S.E.)	%	(S.E.)	%	(S.E.)	%	(S.E.)
Australia	47.8	(3.80)	10.6	(2.57)	21.0	(3.59)	29.5	(3.33)	23.3	(3.26)	42.4	(3.47)
Austria	56.3	(2.92)	34.7	(2.30)	5.4	(1.74)	15.9	(2.53)	40.4	(3.44)	26.9	(2.91)
Belgium (Fl.)	0.8	(0.75)	17.3	(2.80)	12.9	(2.29)	60.6	(4.04)	57.4	(4.05)	12.6	(4.27)
Brazil	25.2	(3.00)	22.3	(3.03)	6.6	(1.68)	7.2	(1.49)	8.0	(1.85)	8.7	(1.90)
Bulgaria	52.7	(3.89)	32.2	(2.77)	5.6	(1.75)	41.0	(5.33)	43.4	(4.72)	50.2	(4.96)
Denmark	34.4	(3.98)	3.9	(1.51)	6.0	(2.56)	34.5	(3.76)	13.0	(2.63)	13.7	(3.17)
Estonia	30.3	(3.48)	7.4	(2.26)	0.4	(0.45)	5.6	(2.11)	15.0	(3.22)	0.4	(0.40)
Hungary	62.3	(5.04)	19.1	(3.38)	40.5	(6.80)	35.0	(4.97)	58.4	(6.63)	33.9	(4.02)
Iceland	58.2	(0.17)	0.9	(0.00)	2.2	(0.06)	3.3	(0.09)	11.5	(0.12)	1.2	(0.06)
Ireland	38.1	(3.75)	0.0	(0.00)	5.8	(2.29)	21.4	(3.17)	9.9	(2.39)	41.5	(4.50)
Italy	37.5	(3.18)	3.6	(1.24)	7.3	(1.54)	6.5	(1.63)	9.8	(1.84)	11.8	(2.02)
Korea	44.5	(4.31)	7.3	(2.36)	6.2	(2.08)	1.2	(0.82)	4.8	(1.79)	0.0	(0.00)
Lithuania	39.5	(3.82)	12.0	(2.84)	2.1	(0.85)	13.8	(2.98)	5.4	(1.85)	19.9	(3.33)
Malaysia	67.2	(3.81)	27.4	(3.41)	51.8	(3.30)	16.2	(2.61)	22.4	(3.32)	12.2	(2.38)
Malta	52.6	(0.23)	38.5	(0.20)	9.8	(0.10)	8.5	(0.06)	16.1	(0.08)	9.8	(0.09)
Mexico	24.7	(3.25)	30.1	(3.70)	8.3	(2.00)	14.0	(3.15)	12.1	(2.33)	16.7	(3.46)
Norway	64.5	(4.27)	0.0	(0.00)	3.4	(1.67)	2.4	(1.79)	7.7	(2.50)	2.8	(1.34)
Poland	64.3	(3.78)	22.8	(3.66)	8.1	(2.31)	11.9	(3.45)	20.9	(3.92)	6.4	(2.01)
Portugal	72.8	(3.70)	3.9	(1.64)	3.2	(1.56)	9.0	(2.36)	29.1	(3.56)	40.5	(3.71)
Slovak Republic	17.2	(3.19)	17.6	(2.69)	3.2	(1.34)	12.0	(3.42)	16.3	(3.48)	7.6	(1.93)
Slovenia	62.0	(3.59)	1.4	(0.98)	4.3	(1.56)	0.4	(0.44)	16.6	(2.71)	8.6	(2.24)
Spain	69.9	(3.52)	3.2	(1.29)	5.6	(1.78)	8.7	(1.97)	8.1	(2.19)	41.4	(3.83)
Turkey	70.4	(6.04)	5.4	(1.26)	1.5	(0.60)	16.9	(4.09)	20.1	(5.03)	11.9	(3.64)
TALIS average	**47.5**	**(0.76)**	**14.0**	**(0.48)**	**9.6**	**(0.49)**	**16.3**	**(0.61)**	**20.4**	**(0.68)**	**18.3**	**(0.62)**

Source: OECD, *TALIS Database.*
StatLink ⧉ http://dx.doi.org/10.1787/607784618372

Table 2.7

School autonomy (2007-08)

Percentage of teachers of lower secondary education whose school principal reported that considerable responsibility for the following tasks is held at the school level[1]

	Selecting teachers for hire		Firing teachers		Establishing teachers' starting salaries		Determining teachers' salary increases		Allocating funds for teachers' professional development		Formulating the school budget		Deciding on budget allocations within the school	
	%	(S.E.)	%	(S.E.)	%	(S.E.)	%	(S.E.)	%	(S.E.)	%	(S.E.)	%	(S.E.)
Australia	76.8	(3.10)	52.2	(3.57)	24.8	(3.50)	23.5	(3.35)	98.2	(1.11)	93.1	(2.56)	100.0	(0.00)
Austria	32.1	(2.95)	20.5	(2.52)	1.4	(0.50)	1.4	(0.51)	17.7	(2.59)	34.9	(2.85)	94.2	(1.65)
Belgium (Fl.)	99.5	(0.39)	96.5	(1.15)	0.3	(0.27)	0.3	(0.27)	73.9	(3.78)	79.6	(3.41)	94.3	(1.80)
Brazil	26.6	(2.32)	25.4	(2.08)	13.7	(0.99)	12.8	(1.04)	28.8	(2.38)	57.2	(3.40)	60.4	(3.09)
Bulgaria	100.0	(0.00)	99.2	(0.59)	42.8	(4.35)	51.3	(4.82)	43.2	(4.88)	86.8	(3.04)	93.4	(2.40)
Denmark	100.0	(0.00)	86.6	(2.67)	32.6	(3.86)	42.0	(4.04)	90.4	(2.74)	76.1	(4.07)	98.0	(1.99)
Estonia	100.0	(0.00)	99.2	(0.51)	89.9	(2.08)	61.5	(3.71)	87.0	(3.00)	88.6	(2.48)	96.5	(1.78)
Hungary	99.8	(0.24)	96.4	(1.77)	45.0	(4.29)	51.6	(4.31)	68.9	(3.79)	89.6	(3.02)	93.4	(2.92)
Iceland	100.0	(0.00)	95.2	(0.17)	22.3	(0.16)	29.3	(0.27)	93.9	(0.18)	71.9	(0.14)	87.3	(0.12)
Ireland	87.0	(2.77)	63.1	(3.63)	3.9	(2.20)	3.0	(2.11)	85.6	(3.19)	69.2	(3.74)	93.3	(1.94)
Italy	13.2	(2.02)	17.9	(2.75)	1.0	(0.59)	2.0	(1.06)	53.5	(2.79)	97.0	(1.06)	99.1	(0.64)
Korea	31.2	(3.67)	20.8	(3.15)	5.7	(2.00)	3.5	(1.55)	63.2	(4.09)	77.3	(3.44)	94.9	(1.86)
Lithuania	99.5	(0.34)	100.0	(0.00)	23.4	(3.39)	15.8	(2.99)	38.5	(3.96)	50.6	(4.28)	90.0	(2.44)
Malaysia	6.9	(1.56)	6.8	(1.66)	4.0	(1.29)	11.4	(2.38)	33.8	(3.28)	68.8	(3.16)	62.5	(3.56)
Malta	30.0	(0.15)	27.7	(0.15)	4.7	(0.09)	8.2	(0.13)	43.0	(0.21)	53.7	(0.21)	86.3	(0.11)
Mexico	24.3	(2.43)	23.3	(2.30)	15.9	(1.65)	16.0	(1.62)	21.1	(2.29)	51.4	(4.01)	45.0	(3.70)
Norway	100.0	(0.00)	100.0	(0.00)	84.0	(3.12)	91.3	(2.23)	98.0	(1.51)	100.0	(0.00)	100.0	(0.00)
Poland	100.0	(0.00)	99.6	(0.36)	43.2	(4.71)	48.2	(4.16)	97.3	(1.40)	99.4	(0.63)	100.0	(0.00)
Portugal	81.3	(3.48)	22.8	(3.03)	4.6	(1.03)	7.2	(1.59)	22.7	(3.01)	92.7	(2.14)	93.1	(2.10)
Slovak Republic	98.8	(0.76)	99.7	(0.33)	57.1	(4.54)	47.9	(4.20)	85.6	(3.15)	80.6	(3.11)	97.3	(1.09)
Slovenia	100.0	(0.00)	96.6	(1.41)	22.7	(3.27)	40.5	(3.86)	95.9	(1.31)	58.2	(3.48)	98.0	(0.99)
Spain	27.4	(2.49)	25.7	(2.30)	3.3	(1.37)	3.7	(1.43)	17.4	(2.66)	76.5	(3.53)	63.8	(3.81)
Turkey	23.5	(4.28)	22.0	(5.36)	12.4	(2.78)	16.6	(3.19)	28.0	(5.33)	79.7	(5.28)	87.9	(4.30)
TALIS average	**67.7**	(0.42)	**60.7**	(0.48)	**24.3**	(0.57)	**25.6**	(0.58)	**60.3**	(0.63)	**75.3**	(0.64)	**88.2**	(0.47)

	Establishing student disciplinary policies		Establishing student assessment policies		Approving students for admission to the school		Deciding which courses are offered		Determining course content		Choosing which textbooks are used	
	%	(S.E.)	%	(S.E.)	%	(S.E.)	%	(S.E.)	%	(S.E.)	%	(S.E.)
Australia	99.5	(0.37)	95.6	(1.99)	96.6	(1.53)	100.0	(0.00)	81.0	(3.25)	99.1	(0.87)
Austria	99.1	(0.62)	91.6	(1.89)	88.0	(1.90)	94.2	(1.46)	80.3	(2.67)	100.0	(0.00)
Belgium (Fl.)	100.0	(0.00)	100.0	(0.00)	89.3	(2.53)	75.9	(4.38)	59.9	(4.12)	100.0	(0.00)
Brazil	93.1	(1.56)	84.0	(2.08)	71.6	(3.11)	48.9	(3.02)	74.7	(2.88)	97.3	(0.91)
Bulgaria	98.4	(0.95)	73.2	(5.97)	91.3	(1.86)	56.3	(4.60)	28.1	(4.72)	98.9	(0.83)
Denmark	96.1	(2.02)	97.1	(1.68)	87.9	(3.18)	91.2	(2.99)	98.2	(1.31)	100.0	(0.00)
Estonia	100.0	(0.00)	100.0	(0.00)	100.0	(0.00)	100.0	(0.00)	89.6	(2.54)	97.2	(1.54)
Hungary	100.0	(0.00)	99.7	(0.27)	98.0	(1.20)	91.3	(2.22)	95.9	(1.91)	100.0	(0.00)
Iceland	100.0	(0.00)	98.7	(0.06)	96.1	(0.09)	98.1	(0.17)	87.9	(0.11)	98.8	(0.00)
Ireland	100.0	(0.00)	100.0	(0.00)	99.4	(0.58)	98.8	(1.15)	68.7	(4.44)	100.0	(0.00)
Italy	100.0	(0.00)	99.5	(0.41)	96.9	(1.00)	100.0	(0.00)	99.0	(0.59)	100.0	(0.00)
Korea	99.6	(0.37)	91.1	(2.40)	85.8	(2.86)	88.7	(2.73)	85.4	(2.87)	96.7	(1.61)
Lithuania	99.4	(0.64)	97.8	(1.18)	85.3	(2.68)	74.0	(3.88)	69.1	(3.88)	98.2	(1.11)
Malaysia	56.7	(3.61)	57.1	(3.43)	21.6	(2.80)	35.4	(3.46)	33.3	(3.12)	19.0	(2.90)
Malta	97.3	(0.01)	85.3	(0.19)	39.7	(0.19)	43.1	(0.02)	48.0	(0.21)	61.2	(0.23)
Mexico	95.8	(1.79)	74.7	(3.42)	74.4	(2.93)	35.3	(3.79)	33.0	(3.92)	68.5	(3.73)
Norway	97.0	(1.48)	79.6	(3.26)	97.2	(1.67)	60.9	(4.39)	78.5	(3.94)	100.0	(0.00)
Poland	100.0	(0.00)	97.3	(1.91)	98.0	(1.26)	59.7	(4.52)	63.9	(4.68)	99.5	(0.53)
Portugal	86.5	(2.85)	98.1	(0.82)	98.0	(1.15)	94.0	(1.77)	43.2	(4.19)	99.6	(0.44)
Slovak Republic	100.0	(0.00)	95.2	(1.97)	99.0	(0.78)	81.7	(2.86)	67.2	(3.67)	91.9	(2.28)
Slovenia	98.9	(0.77)	96.3	(1.51)	92.2	(2.20)	54.0	(3.87)	54.1	(3.70)	100.0	(0.00)
Spain	95.7	(1.62)	65.6	(3.87)	58.5	(3.77)	37.3	(3.47)	44.9	(3.86)	100.0	(0.00)
Turkey	71.5	(5.79)	65.9	(5.37)	91.0	(3.97)	41.2	(6.76)	27.2	(4.14)	43.9	(5.85)
TALIS average	**95.0**	(0.37)	**88.9**	(0.53)	**85.0**	(0.46)	**72.2**	(0.67)	**65.7**	(0.70)	**90.0**	(0.37)

1. School level includes either the school principal, teachers, or the school governing board.
Source: OECD, *TALIS Database*.
StatLink ᗧᗝᗞᗟ http://dx.doi.org/10.1787/607784618372

Table 2.8

School climate – teacher-related factors (2007-08)

Percentage of teachers of lower secondary education whose school principal considered the following teacher behaviours to hinder instruction "a lot" or "to some extent" in their school

	Arriving late at school		Absenteeism		Lack of pedagogical preparation	
	%	(S.E.)	%	(S.E.)	%	(S.E.)
Australia	7.8	(2.08)	22.8	(3.63)	35.8	(4.48)
Austria	8.2	(1.49)	22.7	(2.54)	15.9	(2.39)
Belgium (Fl.)	4.2	(1.53)	3.7	(1.33)	8.8	(2.10)
Brazil	25.5	(2.90)	32.3	(2.99)	35.8	(3.02)
Bulgaria	2.7	(1.19)	1.8	(1.05)	3.3	(1.07)
Denmark	13.8	(3.76)	11.1	(3.52)	11.0	(3.30)
Estonia	3.2	(1.50)	3.4	(1.64)	5.0	(1.76)
Hungary	9.1	(6.00)	26.1	(4.74)	21.5	(4.90)
Iceland	4.1	(0.09)	24.0	(0.12)	12.7	(0.14)
Ireland	12.9	(3.41)	43.3	(4.87)	30.8	(4.86)
Italy	17.4	(2.31)	29.8	(2.69)	53.4	(3.14)
Korea	17.8	(3.02)	23.2	(3.12)	33.8	(3.95)
Lithuania	19.8	(3.19)	15.0	(2.66)	37.7	(3.95)
Malaysia	13.2	(2.69)	19.5	(2.91)	30.2	(3.38)
Malta	14.1	(0.16)	30.4	(0.21)	17.6	(0.19)
Mexico	69.2	(3.93)	67.5	(4.08)	70.2	(3.97)
Norway	8.7	(2.63)	39.5	(4.59)	10.9	(3.09)
Poland	7.4	(2.75)	43.7	(4.14)	2.4	(1.10)
Portugal	9.4	(2.71)	14.9	(3.10)	18.5	(3.34)
Slovak Republic	2.3	(1.44)	6.2	(1.64)	3.5	(1.56)
Slovenia	10.3	(2.35)	37.7	(3.55)	14.5	(2.92)
Spain	34.1	(3.83)	39.2	(3.76)	38.0	(3.84)
Turkey	31.0	(4.45)	35.1	(4.96)	42.9	(5.83)
TALIS average	**15.1**	**(0.61)**	**25.8**	**(0.68)**	**24.1**	**(0.69)**

Source: OECD, *TALIS Database*.
StatLink ᵃᵖˢᵖ http://dx.doi.org/10.1787/607784618372

Table 2.8a (1/2)

School climate – student-related factors (2007-08)

Percentage of teachers of lower secondary education whose school principal considered the following student behaviours to hinder instruction "a lot" or "to some extent" in their school

	Arriving late at school		Absenteeism		Classroom disturbances		Cheating		Profanity/Swearing		Vandalism	
	%	(S.E.)	%	(S.E.)	%	(S.E.)	%	(S.E.)	%	(S.E.)	%	(S.E.)
Australia	43.4	(4.15)	48.2	(4.54)	43.9	(4.48)	6.5	(2.40)	17.0	(3.51)	10.5	(2.67)
Austria	19.1	(2.55)	25.2	(2.95)	61.4	(3.24)	11.1	(2.11)	44.6	(3.03)	30.8	(2.96)
Belgium (Fl.)	28.1	(3.80)	19.7	(2.57)	50.8	(5.01)	5.6	(1.75)	4.8	(1.68)	13.0	(2.81)
Brazil	35.1	(3.36)	50.6	(3.05)	60.2	(3.01)	31.2	(3.22)	40.8	(3.08)	29.3	(2.77)
Bulgaria	33.9	(3.42)	36.1	(4.33)	32.2	(3.89)	16.5	(2.93)	25.2	(3.37)	28.5	(3.74)
Denmark	37.0	(5.23)	26.8	(4.45)	57.3	(3.93)	6.8	(2.06)	42.1	(4.44)	13.8	(3.83)
Estonia	53.0	(3.71)	68.7	(3.71)	70.8	(3.52)	38.8	(3.95)	52.6	(3.59)	15.2	(2.81)
Hungary	36.4	(5.05)	42.7	(4.92)	67.8	(4.28)	26.8	(5.64)	77.2	(3.21)	54.0	(4.03)
Iceland	22.0	(0.17)	17.8	(0.15)	57.8	(0.18)	3.0	(0.04)	17.1	(0.11)	12.3	(0.12)
Ireland	57.7	(4.81)	70.9	(4.35)	53.6	(4.47)	2.9	(1.29)	21.6	(3.83)	10.6	(3.08)
Italy	25.5	(2.67)	37.1	(3.12)	71.6	(2.96)	24.3	(2.57)	22.8	(2.63)	16.2	(2.16)
Korea	35.2	(4.13)	39.7	(4.06)	43.1	(4.19)	25.3	(3.59)	34.3	(3.84)	32.5	(4.00)
Lithuania	65.2	(3.99)	88.5	(2.13)	66.9	(3.84)	38.8	(3.85)	48.5	(4.34)	28.9	(3.61)
Malaysia	34.8	(3.35)	40.7	(3.38)	39.4	(3.29)	14.4	(2.61)	13.5	(2.22)	28.0	(3.13)
Malta	24.7	(0.21)	44.5	(0.20)	57.8	(0.21)	22.9	(0.15)	21.0	(0.15)	24.7	(0.13)
Mexico	78.0	(3.59)	79.0	(3.49)	71.9	(3.60)	54.1	(4.10)	55.5	(4.27)	63.3	(3.93)
Norway	44.5	(4.33)	24.7	(3.91)	65.3	(4.41)	2.2	(1.31)	33.9	(4.47)	22.3	(3.79)
Poland	44.1	(4.12)	62.8	(3.93)	69.0	(3.72)	42.3	(4.48)	60.3	(4.11)	37.4	(4.18)
Portugal	40.8	(4.22)	50.8	(4.14)	69.1	(3.56)	11.2	(2.89)	42.8	(4.37)	20.5	(3.53)
Slovak Republic	13.0	(3.01)	39.8	(4.25)	71.6	(3.62)	38.5	(4.63)	40.1	(4.66)	32.3	(4.52)
Slovenia	23.9	(2.91)	20.7	(2.95)	67.3	(3.44)	13.2	(2.68)	37.5	(4.02)	29.8	(3.84)
Spain	53.3	(3.95)	52.9	(3.52)	70.5	(3.59)	21.6	(3.11)	43.5	(3.55)	28.0	(3.43)
Turkey	57.9	(6.12)	66.7	(5.66)	66.3	(5.99)	21.9	(4.34)	43.2	(3.96)	41.1	(5.62)
TALIS average	**39.4**	**(0.80)**	**45.8**	**(0.77)**	**60.2**	**(0.79)**	**20.9**	**(0.66)**	**36.5**	**(0.74)**	**27.1**	**(0.72)**

Source: OECD, *TALIS Database*.
StatLink ᵃᵖˢᵖ http://dx.doi.org/10.1787/607784618372

Table 2.8a (2/2)

School climate – student-related factors (2007-08)

Percentage of teachers of lower secondary education whose school principal considered the following student behaviours to hinder instruction "a lot" or "to some extent" in their school

	Theft		Intimidation or verbal abuse of other students		Intimidation or verbal abuse of teachers or staff		Physical injury to other students		Use/possession of drugs and/or alcohol	
	%	(S.E.)	%	(S.E.)	%	(S.E.)	%	(S.E.)	%	(S.E.)
Australia	6.9	(2.02)	31.7	(4.19)	13.7	(3.04)	6.2	(1.87)	2.7	(1.45)
Austria	11.5	(2.11)	36.3	(3.22)	8.8	(1.67)	9.0	(1.87)	2.3	(0.99)
Belgium (Fl.)	7.7	(1.98)	39.3	(4.72)	12.2	(2.03)	3.1	(1.17)	7.5	(1.93)
Brazil	13.2	(1.91)	29.3	(2.91)	14.1	(2.17)	10.2	(1.71)	10.7	(2.06)
Bulgaria	4.4	(1.83)	24.2	(4.01)	5.6	(1.43)	7.7	(1.80)	1.6	(0.83)
Denmark	9.4	(3.27)	28.8	(4.66)	13.7	(3.31)	11.7	(3.57)	8.8	(3.06)
Estonia	4.3	(1.66)	47.2	(3.87)	25.6	(3.20)	2.3	(1.08)	10.7	(2.69)
Hungary	23.9	(4.45)	48.2	(4.70)	22.0	(3.99)	37.4	(4.51)	7.9	(6.00)
Iceland	6.9	(0.07)	11.1	(0.09)	8.0	(0.07)	6.9	(0.05)	4.8	(0.04)
Ireland	4.7	(1.85)	36.6	(4.71)	17.9	(3.62)	4.3	(2.08)	15.0	(3.95)
Italy	9.1	(1.74)	30.0	(2.74)	10.4	(1.89)	12.7	(2.19)	4.5	(1.20)
Korea	25.0	(3.54)	36.6	(3.86)	25.3	(3.21)	25.7	(3.20)	16.3	(2.87)
Lithuania	23.4	(3.68)	45.5	(4.24)	28.8	(3.57)	25.9	(3.42)	19.3	(3.02)
Malaysia	13.9	(2.14)	13.5	(2.32)	8.1	(2.09)	10.8	(2.30)	9.2	(2.17)
Malta	11.7	(0.05)	48.8	(0.20)	20.3	(0.14)	7.6	(0.08)	5.4	(0.02)
Mexico	56.0	(4.06)	61.2	(3.36)	47.2	(3.92)	57.1	(3.57)	51.0	(4.08)
Norway	9.5	(2.58)	23.3	(4.03)	10.2	(2.68)	2.7	(1.56)	1.8	(1.30)
Poland	12.1	(2.70)	29.4	(4.26)	5.9	(1.98)	25.3	(3.53)	5.1	(1.91)
Portugal	23.3	(3.30)	28.4	(4.00)	16.9	(2.98)	19.2	(3.18)	8.8	(2.48)
Slovak Republic	9.5	(3.28)	21.6	(3.85)	6.4	(2.81)	5.4	(2.70)	2.2	(2.01)
Slovenia	11.4	(2.47)	46.3	(4.06)	12.8	(2.57)	9.3	(2.37)	4.9	(1.73)
Spain	22.2	(2.91)	40.6	(3.83)	27.4	(3.53)	23.1	(3.11)	20.3	(3.00)
Turkey	32.8	(5.28)	37.0	(4.37)	25.5	(5.74)	42.6	(5.83)	25.9	(3.49)
TALIS average	**15.3**	**(0.59)**	**34.6**	**(0.79)**	**16.8**	**(0.61)**	**15.9**	**(0.58)**	**10.7**	**(0.55)**

Source: OECD, *TALIS Database*.
StatLink ⫘⫘ http://dx.doi.org/10.1787/607784618372

CHAPTER 3

The Professional Development of Teachers

Highlights

- In the participating countries, an average of 89% of teachers in lower secondary education engaged in professional development. The 11% who did not are a source of concern. Around one in four teachers did not participate in professional development in Denmark, the Slovak Republic and Turkey.

- On average in TALIS countries, teachers participated in professional development for just under one day per month.

- A significant proportion of teachers think that professional development does not meet their needs: over half reported wanting more than they received during the previous 18 months.

- The aspect of their work for which teachers most frequently say they require professional development is "Teaching special learning needs students", followed by "ICT teaching skills" and "Student discipline and behaviour".

- Teachers who paid the full cost of professional development took part in more than those who received it free or at partial cost. This is partly because the more time-intensive development activities were more likely to be paid for by teachers themselves.

- Even when development is paid for by teachers, their demand is not satisfied: those who paid towards the cost were more likely to say they wanted more.

- The main reason for unfulfilled demand (according to teachers) is the conflict with their work schedule, but lack of suitable development opportunities is also a significant factor.

- The types of development that teachers regard as the most effective have, on average, lower rates of participation. However, those who do participate in these activities also devote more time to them than those participating in other activities, even though they are more likely to have to pay for them.

- This suggests a need not just for better support for teachers to participate in professional development, but for policy makers and school leaders to ensure that the development opportunities available are effective and meet teachers' needs.

INTRODUCTION

In many countries, the role and functioning of schools are changing and so is what is expected of teachers. Teachers are asked to teach in increasingly multicultural classrooms; to place greater emphasis on integrating students with special learning needs in their classrooms; to make more effective use of information and communication technologies for teaching; to engage more in planning within evaluative and accountability frameworks; and to do more to involve parents in schools.

No matter how good pre-service training for teachers is, it cannot be expected to prepare teachers for all the challenges they will face throughout their careers. Education systems therefore seek to provide teachers with opportunities for in-service professional development in order to maintain a high standard of teaching and to retain a high-quality teacher workforce. As OECD's comparative review on teachers noted (OECD, 2005):

> *Effective professional development is on-going, includes training, practice and feedback, and provides adequate time and follow-up support. Successful programmes involve teachers in learning activities that are similar to ones they will use with their students, and encourage the development of teachers' learning communities. There is growing interest in developing schools as learning organisations, and in ways for teachers to share their expertise and experience more systematically.*

The development of teachers beyond their initial training can serve a number of objectives (OECD, 1998), including:

- to update individuals' knowledge of a subject in light of recent advances in the area;
- to update individuals' skills, attitudes and approaches in light of the development of new teaching techniques and objectives, new circumstances and new educational research;
- to enable individuals to apply changes made to curricula or other aspects of teaching practice;
- to enable schools to develop and apply new strategies concerning the curriculum and other aspects of teaching practice;
- to exchange information and expertise among teachers and others, *e.g.* academics, industrialists; and
- to help weaker teachers become more effective.

To examine these issues, TALIS adopts a broad definition of professional development among teachers:

> *"Professional development is defined as activities that develop an individual's skills, knowledge, expertise and other characteristics as a teacher."*

The definition recognises that development can be provided in many ways, ranging from the formal to the informal. It can be made available through external expertise in the form of courses, workshops or formal qualification programmes, through collaboration between schools or teachers across schools (*e.g.* observational visits to other schools or teacher networks) or within the schools in which teachers work. In this last case, development can be provided through coaching/mentoring, collaborative planning and teaching, and the sharing of good practices.

TALIS asked teachers about their professional development activities during the 18 months prior to the survey (Box 3.1). This period of time was chosen in order to cover activities over almost two school years in order to give a more representative picture and lessen possible distortions due to unusually busy or lean periods of development and to ensure a manageable period for teachers' recall.

Box 3.1 Types of professional development

TALIS asked lower secondary teachers about the professional development they had participated in during the 18 months prior to the survey. Teachers were first asked to indicate whether or not they had participated in each of the following activities:

- **courses/workshops** (*e.g.* on subject matter or methods and/or other education-related topics);
- **education conferences or seminars** (at which teachers and/or researchers present their research results and discuss education problems);
- **qualification programme** (*e.g.* a degree programme);
- **observation visits to other schools**;
- **participation in a network of teachers** formed specifically for the professional development of teachers;
- **individual or collaborative research** on a topic of professional interest; and
- **mentoring and/or peer observation and coaching**, as part of a formal school arrangement.

Teachers were able to indicate participation in multiple activities.

TALIS then asked teachers how many days of professional development they had attended in the 18 months prior to the survey and how many of these days were compulsory. Table 3.1 gives this information.

As TALIS was interested in professional development activities beyond the more structured types listed above, teachers were also asked whether or not they had participated in the following less formal professional development activities:

- **reading professional literature** (*e.g.* journals, evidence-based papers, thesis papers); and
- **engaging in informal dialogue with peers** on how to improve teaching.

Analysis of participation in these activities and their impact is included in Tables 3.2 and 3.8.

TALIS asked teachers about their professional development activities, their impact, the support they received for undertaking them, the extent to which they wanted more than they had engaged in and the barriers they felt had prevented them from doing so, and the areas of their work they found most in need of further development. Therefore, almost all of the results in this chapter are based on teachers' reports. The exception is the discussion of induction and mentoring policies in schools, which reports school principals' responses regarding the existence of such policies in their schools.

In interpreting the results, it is important to bear in mind the self-reporting nature of the survey responses. For example, teachers' reports about the impact of their development activities represent their perceptions; they are not part of an independent evaluation of the effectiveness of these activities. Nevertheless, teachers' perceptions are important and can be expected to influence their behaviour. Also teachers' views about their development needs are to be distinguished from an external assessment of these needs. Chapter 5 will examine the relation between teachers' reports of their development needs and the policies and practices that are in place to assess and appraise teachers' work.

Chapter outline

This chapter seeks to answer the following three questions:

- How much does the amount and profile of teachers' professional development vary within and among countries?
- How well are teachers' professional development needs being met?
- How can unsatisfied demand for professional development be best addressed?

The chapter first examines teachers' participation in professional development and compares the intensity of that participation in terms of number of days. The focus in this section is on more structured activities, such as attendance at courses and workshops, conferences and seminars, etc. More informal activities, such as engagement in informal discussions to improve teaching and reading professional literature, which are not readily measurable in terms of numbers of days, are excluded from these measures (See Box 3.1). The section then looks at the extent to which intensity of participation in professional development differs with the characteristics of the teacher or the schools in which they work and so provides some insight into the distribution of development opportunities. It does not seek to be exhaustive; it focuses on the characteristics that are most often of interest to policy makers. This section thus sheds light on how the policy choices countries make in terms of providing professional development opportunities are reflected in a comparison of participation rates and intensity rates.

The volume (or intensity) of professional development can be influenced by the types of development activities that teachers engage in. The chapter therefore goes on to profile all types of activities listed in Box 3.1, contrasting formal and less formal development activities, and shows how teachers combine different forms of professional development.

In the light of these participation patterns, the chapter then investigates how well teachers' professional development needs are being met. It compares the extent of unsatisfied demand within and between countries and identifies the areas of teachers' work which teachers regard as those in which they have the greatest development need. It concludes by considering how levels of unsatisfied demand relate to the professional development which teachers have received.

Teachers' views of what has helped or hindered their participation in professional development is then examined, in the light of their reports of unsatisfied demand and areas of greatest need. It reveals cross-country variations in the level and types of support received by teachers to participate in professional development and examines the relation between the support received and the level of participation reported in the survey. School-level policies and practices for induction and mentoring of new teachers are revealing of the extent to which they differ among countries; this section looks at how these practices co-exist with other professional development activities in schools.

Finally the chapter considers how unsatisfied demand and development needs might best be addressed. This first involves an analysis of teachers' reports of the factors that prevented them from engaging in more professional development than they did and then proceeds to examine the types of professional development teachers find most effective in meeting their needs. The final section discusses the policy implications arising from the analyses.

Note that further analysis of the professional development data from TALIS is the subject of a separate thematic report being published jointly with the European Commission.

LEVEL AND INTENSITY OF PARTICIPATION IN PROFESSIONAL DEVELOPMENT

This section analyses the level and intensity of participation in professional development across the lower secondary teacher population. Overall levels of participation are measured in terms of teacher participation rates and intensity of participation in terms of the average number of teachers' days of development during the 18-month period prior to the survey.

As noted above, levels of participation and intensity of participation reported in this section do not include the less structured development activities (informal dialogue to improve teaching and reading professional literature), as these are not readily measurable in terms of number of days of activity.

Participation rates

The first column of Table 3.1 shows country-level participation rates in professional development. On average across the 23 participating countries, almost 89% of teachers reported engaging in some professional development (defined as having taken part in at least one day of development in the previous 18 months) over the survey period. This suggests that engagement in professional development is a feature of the lives of the vast majority of teachers in the participating countries. Nevertheless, it is not trivial that some 11% of lower secondary teachers did not take part in any structured development activities.

When participation rates are compared across countries, there are some notable differences. In Australia, Austria, Lithuania and Slovenia, participation is virtually universal, with less than 5% of lower secondary teachers having participated in no development activities. In Spain all teachers reported some participation. This contrasts with the situation in Denmark, Iceland, the Slovak Republic and Turkey, where around one-quarter reported no participation during the period. For these four countries, such relatively high rates of non-participation must be a source of concern (Figure 3.1).

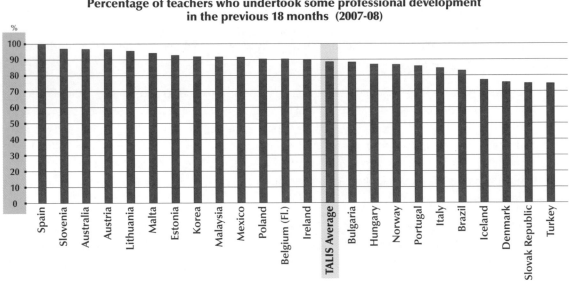

Figure 3.1

**Percentage of teachers who undertook some professional development
in the previous 18 months (2007-08)**

Countries are ranked in descending order of percentage of teachers having had some professional development in the 18 months prior to the survey.
Source: OECD, Table 3.1.

StatLink ⟨⟩ http://dx.doi.org/10.1787/607807256201

Intensity of participation

While participation rates are generally high, intensity of participation may differ among teachers and across countries. TALIS measures the intensity of participation in terms of the number of days of professional development teachers reported having taken during the survey period.

On average among all lower secondary teachers in the participating countries, teachers had 15.3 days of professional development in the 18 months prior to the survey – in other words, an average of just less than one day per month. But countries differ significantly. The highest average numbers were reported by Mexico (34.0 days), followed by Korea (30.0) and Bulgaria (27.2), and the lowest by Ireland (5.6 days), the Slovak Republic (7.2), Malta (7.3), Belgium (Fl.) (8.0) and Slovenia (8.3). Internationally, therefore, there is a six-fold difference between the highest and lowest intensity of participation (Table 3.1).

Are there trade-offs between participation and intensity?

A comparison of the level and intensity of participation can serve to indicate different policy choices that school systems may make, *e.g.* to spread opportunities across all teachers or to concentrate them on a smaller proportion of the teacher population.

As well as showing the average number of days of professional development for all lower secondary teachers, Table 3.1 (third set of columns) shows the average number of days for teachers who had some professional development during the survey period. Figure 3.2 compares the second measure with the proportion of teachers who received some professional development in the previous 18 months, thus providing a contrast between the level and the intensity of participation. From this, some interesting contrasts become apparent.

Figure 3.2

Comparison of the level and intensity of participation in professional development (2007-08)

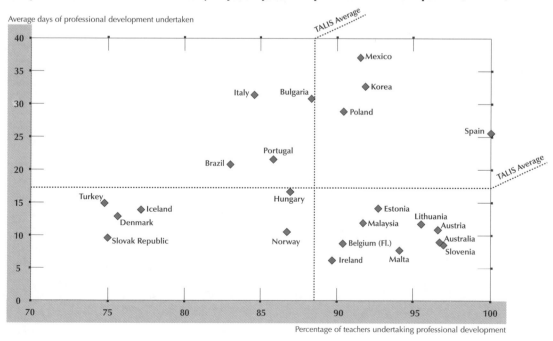

Source: OECD, Table 3.1.

StatLink http://dx.doi.org/10.1787/607807256201

Nine out of 23 countries are in the lower right-hand quadrant, which represents a combination of high levels of participation and low intensity (*i.e.* above average participation and below average number of days of professional development). This may indicate a choice to spread development opportunities across a very large proportion of teachers. The clearest examples are Australia, Austria and Slovenia, where virtually all lower secondary teachers received some professional development but an average of only around 10 days.

In contrast, teachers in Italy reported participation rates somewhat below average at 85%, yet among those who participated, the number of days was a relatively high average of 31. This may indicate a situation in which universal participation is forgone in favour of generous provision for those who have the opportunity to participate.

There are exceptions, however. The four countries with the highest percentages of teachers who received no professional development – Denmark, Iceland, the Slovak Republic and Turkey – are also those with below average number of days of professional development. In these countries participation in professional development is far from universal but also is of low intensity for those who participate.

At the opposite end of the spectrum, Mexico, Korea, Poland and Spain not only have high participation but also high intensity of participation in professional development.

How much variation is there in the intensity of participation?

Examining the variation in the number of days of teachers' professional development can provide an indication of how professional development is distributed across teachers in each country.

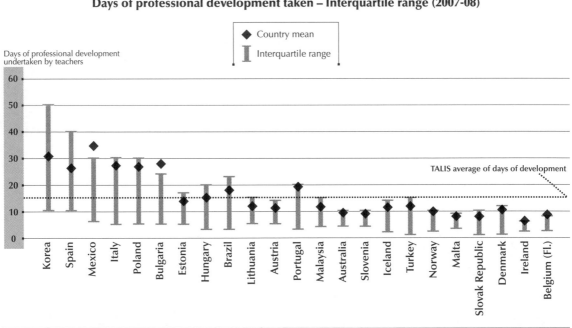

Figure 3.3

Days of professional development taken – Interquartile range (2007-08)

Countries are ranked in descending order of the median number of days of professional development taken.
The interquartile range is the range of days within which the middle 50% of teachers fall.
Source: OECD, Table 3.1d.

StatLink ⬛🗐🗗 http://dx.doi.org/10.1787/607807256201

To assess the overall degree of variation within a country, the percentile distribution of the number of days of teachers' development is analysed. Figure 3.3 illustrates the interquartile range – the range within which the middle 50% of professional development days taken by teachers lies, again measured across all teachers (including those who did not take professional development in the previous 18 months). The longer the bar for a country in Figure 3.3, the more variation there is in the number of days of development taken by teachers, around the mid-point of the distribution. A shorter bar indicates the opposite. The chart ranks countries in descending order of the median value for the number of days of professional development followed; the country mean is included for comparison.

Korea is the country with by far the widest range, followed by Spain, and then Italy, Mexico and Poland. In contrast, the range is much narrower (six days or less) in Australia, Belgium (Fl.), Ireland, Malta and Slovenia. The extent of variation measured in this way is associated with the average number of days of development taken by teachers in each country. Nevertheless, it is evident that, particularly in countries where teachers reported relatively large amounts of professional development on average, participation among teachers is very unequal.

How does participation vary by teacher and school characteristics?

The analysis of the disparity in the take-up of professional development within countries can be more closely focused by examining participation with respect to the characteristics of teachers and the schools in which they work. The comparisons shown in Table 3.1a and 3.1b and discussed here are based on the average days of professional development among teachers with some professional development in the survey period and so are net of teachers who had no professional development during this period.

The teacher and school characteristics chosen for the comparisons are those which are generally of the most policy interest to participating countries.

Gender differences

On average across participating countries, there is no statistically significant difference between male and female teachers – 17.5 days of professional development on average for female teachers compared with 16.9 days for male teachers. The largest differences in favour of female teachers were in Mexico (around six days more on average), followed by Poland and Korea (around four days more), though none of these differences is statistically significant. However, male teachers led in a number of countries, the largest differences being reported in Portugal and Italy (more than four days) and Turkey (less than three days). Again these differences are not statistically significant (Table 3.1a).

Age differences

On average, the amount of professional development that teachers received decreased with the age of the teacher. Averaged across all countries, teachers under 30 years of age received around 21 days of professional development; the number declined steadily to an average of around 14 days for teachers aged 50 years or more; these differences between age groups are all statistically significant. This indicates that on average less experienced teachers receive more days of professional development than more experienced teachers (Table 3.1a).

At the country level such significant differences are most pronounced in Italy, Poland and Portugal, where teachers less than 30 years of age participated in twice as many days of development as teachers aged 50 years and over. Again, country patterns vary. In some countries, lower secondary teachers remain active in professional development throughout their career. In Bulgaria, for example, teachers in each age group took part in well over 20 days of professional development during the previous 18 months. In fact, among those aged 50 years and over, the number was 27 days, the same number as for the youngest age group.

Qualification level differences

On average across participating countries, teachers with a Master's degree or higher qualification received more days of professional development (some 20 days) than those with a Bachelor's degree or less (17-18 days). This pattern is apparent in almost all participating countries, the exceptions being Austria, Belgium (Fl.), Hungary and the Slovak Republic, where teachers with a Master's degree or higher received on average the least number of days (though in the Slovak Republic virtually all teachers are qualified to Master's degree level) (Table 3.1a).

In a number of countries, the least qualified (*i.e.* those with qualifications below the level of a Bachelor's degree) received the least professional development. This would appear to be a worrying finding, as those who arguably might benefit most from further professional development are getting the least. This may raise questions of equity, particularly if such teachers are disproportionately employed in more challenging schools, as previous research has shown (OECD, 2005).

This pattern is most pronounced in Mexico, where those with at least a Master's degree received almost twice the number of days of development as those with less than a Bachelor's degree. Even so, the amount of professional development received by the latter group, at 27 days, is still higher than the amount teachers received on average in most other countries surveyed.

These findings present a notable parallel to results concerning the participation of adults in non-formal, continuing education and training, which indicate that more highly educated adults in the general population are more likely to participate in such training (OECD, 2005). This can be a consequence of issues concerning demand for training as well as its supply on an equitable basis.

Differences between public and private schools

As defined here, private schools comprise both independent private and government-dependent private schools, the latter being privately run but receiving most of their funding from public sources. On average in participating countries, teachers in public schools had one day more professional development than their private school counterparts, a difference that is not statistically significant. Except in Bulgaria, where the proportion of teachers in the private sector is very small (Table 2.4), the largest difference in favour of public school teachers was in Korea (nine days more). Though there were also sizeable differences in favour of private school teachers, none of these is statistically significant (Table 3.1b).

Interestingly, in Italy, this pattern is affected by the fact that teachers in private schools may undertake professional development in order to increase the possibility of obtaining a permanent position in public schools. This is because such activities improve the score and ranking of teachers in the list of qualified staff on which the appointment to public schools is based.

School location differences

On average, the amount of lower secondary teachers' professional development is much the same, regardless of whether the schools in which they teach are located in a village, town or city. Although countries vary in this respect, there is no prevailing trend, and differences are generally not statistically significant. In no country, for instance, does the amount of professional development consistently increase or decrease with the size of the population in the school's locality (Table 3.1b).

For example, in Brazil, teachers in village schools (fewer than 3 000 population) took part in slightly more professional development activities than their counterparts in other types of communities (23 days compared with 21 for all teachers who took professional development in Brazil), while the reverse was true in Bulgaria,

Mexico and Poland. On the basis of this mixed evidence, the geographic locality of the school does not appear to affect participation in professional development.

TYPES OF PROFESSIONAL DEVELOPMENT

Analysis of the types of development activities engaged in can be informative and may go some way towards explaining differences in teachers' average numbers of days of professional development participation. TALIS asked teachers about various activities ranging from more organised and structured to more informal and self-directed learning, all of which are listed in Table 3.2. Therefore, informal dialogue to improve teaching and reading professional literature, which were excluded from the analysis in the previous section are included here.

The type of professional development most often mentioned was "Informal dialogue to improve teaching", with 93% of teachers on average reporting this activity during the survey period. Indeed, in all countries but Hungary and Mexico, it was the development activity most frequently reported, with a participation rate of more than 90% in most countries. For Hungary, "Reading professional literature" (88%) came first, and for Mexico, attendance at "Courses and workshops" (94%) (Table 3.2 and Figure 3.4).

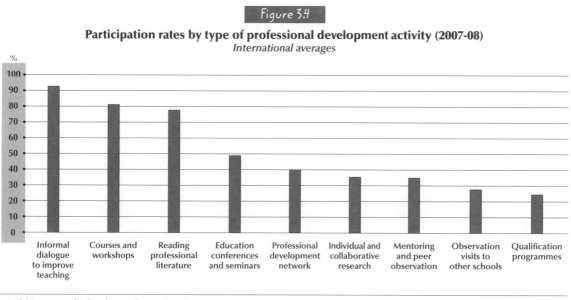

Figure 3.4

Participation rates by type of professional development activity (2007-08)
International averages

Activities are ranked in descending order of participation rates.
Source: OECD, Table 3.2.

StatLink http://dx.doi.org/10.1787/607807256201

After "Informal dialogue to improve teaching", the most frequently reported activities were attending "Courses and workshops" (81%) and "Reading professional literature" (78%). The least common types of professional development were "Qualification programmes" (25%) and "Observation visits to other schools" (28%) (Table 3.2). However, patterns vary widely, particularly for the more structured types of activities. For instance:

- **Courses and workshops:** Participation among teachers was most common in Austria (92%), Estonia (93%), Lithuania (96%) and Mexico (94%) and much less common in Italy (66%), Turkey (62%) and particularly the Slovak Republic (50%).

- **Education conferences and seminars:** Over two-thirds of teachers participated in this activity in Lithuania (68%), Slovenia (75%) and Turkey (68%), but participation was less than half these rates in Belgium (Fl.) (33%), Malaysia (32%) and Mexico (33%).

- **Qualification programmes:** Participation in these programmes was most common in Brazil (41%), Bulgaria (50%) and Lithuania (44%) and least common in Australia (12%), Ireland (11%), Italy (11%) and Slovenia (10%).

- **Observation visits to other schools:** Around two-thirds of teachers in Estonia (63%), Iceland (60%) and Korea (67%) took part in such visits, whereas very few did so in Austria (10%), Denmark (10%), Ireland (8%) and Slovenia (8%).

- **Professional development network:** Participation in development networks was most common in Australia (60%) and Poland (61%) and particularly in Iceland (83%) and Slovenia (72%). In contrast, this was much less a feature of teachers' professional development in Bulgaria (20%), Italy (20%) and especially Portugal (15%).

- **Individual and collaborative research:** While more than half of teachers engaged in this activity in Brazil (55%), Denmark (52%), Italy (57%) and Mexico (63%), it was much less common in Norway (12%) and the Slovak Republic (12%).

- **Mentoring and peer observation:** Around two-thirds of teachers took part in such activities in Korea (69%), Poland (67%) and the Slovak Republic (65%), but it was much less common in Austria (18%), Denmark (18%), Ireland (18%), Malta (17%) and Portugal (15%).

In terms of the overall levels of participation in these activities, it is evident that in some countries participation rates are consistently fairly high across most types of activities. For instance, in Lithuania and Poland participation rates are higher than average for eight out of the nine development activities. These high rates result partly from the fact that individual teachers in these countries took part in a broader combination of development activities than in other countries; analysis of the database shows that in both countries, teachers undertook on average between five and six different types of activities, more than in any other countries. This relatively high level of participation across a broad range of activities may be the sign of a well-developed and active professional development culture. The fact that the percentage of teachers wanting more development than they received is below average in both of these countries (see next section) lends some support to this hypothesis.

On the other hand, participation was below average in Norway on eight out of the nine types of activities, the exception being participation in "Informal dialogue to improve teaching", for which the rate was above the TALIS average. Again, this was partly influenced by the number of types of development activities typically followed by Norwegian teachers. On average, teachers in Norway had only three or four different types of activities during the survey period, the lowest number among countries in the survey, followed by Italy and Ireland.

Clearly the range and type of teachers' professional development activities will influence the number of days reported. Analysis of the TALIS database indicates that enrolment in "Qualification programmes" is likely to be the most time-intensive activity, though "Individual and collaborative research" is also likely to require more time than other activities. It is no surprise therefore that Bulgaria, the country with the highest proportion of teachers engaged in qualification programmes (50%), is also one of the countries with the highest average number of days of professional development reported (31 days). Conversely, in Australia, despite above-average participation in most types of activities, the low rate of participation in qualification programmes is likely to be part of the explanation for the low average number of days reported.

Mexico offers a clear illustration of the association between the types of development activities undertaken by teachers and the resulting number of days of development. It has the highest average number of days of professional development reported by teachers (37 days), and above-average participation in qualification programmes (34%) is combined with the highest participation of all countries in "Individual and collaborative research" (63%). Both are relatively time-intensive activities.

In Italy, high levels and intensity of participation in "Individual and collaborative research" appear to drive the high average number of days of development reported by teachers.

In other countries the picture is less clear. In Lithuania, for example, teachers report a below-average number of days of professional development overall and yet, as noted above, they also reported not only higher than average participation in almost all types of activities, but they also more frequently combined a larger number of activities. In this case, a high percentage of teachers engage in a wide range of activities, but the intensity of participation is not high.

UNSATISFIED DEMAND AND DEVELOPMENT NEEDS

The question of how well teachers' development needs are being met is considered by means of two indicators: the percentage of all teachers who reported that they wanted more professional development than they had received during the survey period and the extent to which they reported development needs in specified areas of their work.

Teachers were asked whether, during the survey period, they had wanted to participate in more professional development than they did. Table 3.3 summarises responses to this question. On average across countries, more than half of the teachers surveyed reported having wanted more professional development than they had received. The extent of unsatisfied demand is sizeable in every country, ranging from 31% in Belgium (Fl.) to over 80% in Brazil, Malaysia and Mexico (Figure 3.5).

Figure 3.5

Percentage of teachers who wanted more development than they received in the previous 18 months (2007-08)

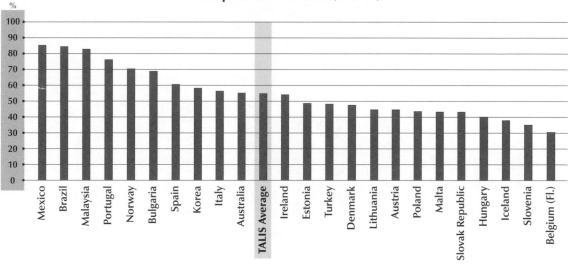

Countries are ranked in descending order of percentage of teachers wanting more development than they received.
Source: OECD, Table 3.3.

StatLink http://dx.doi.org/10.1787/607807256201

Table 3.3 also shows the extent of unsatisfied demand according to a range of teacher and school characteristics. In almost all countries female teachers were more likely than male teachers to report wanting more development than they received, though in most cases the differences are not large. There is a similarly consistent pattern for teachers less than 40 years of age; in most countries they were more likely than older teachers to report a desire for more participation.

There is no consistent cross-country pattern in terms of teachers' qualifications. Although in several countries (and particularly in Australia, Austria, Denmark, Malaysia, Spain and Turkey, where significant differences are evident), more highly qualified teachers are more likely to have reported unsatisfied demand, most countries show no definite pattern.

Similarly, a comparison of teachers in public and private schools does not reveal a consistent pattern. Considering significant differences only, teachers in public schools in Korea, Lithuania and Portugal and Turkey are more likely than their counterparts in private schools to report unsatisfied demand, whereas the reverse is true in Austria and Malta.

What are the areas of greatest development need?

Teachers were asked to rate on a four-point scale, ranging from "Low level of need" to "High level of need", their development needs for various aspects of their work. Table 3.4 presents the percentage of teachers reporting a high level of need in various aspects of their work.

Across the 23 participating countries, the aspect of teachers' work most frequently rated by teachers as an area of high development need was "Teaching special learning needs students". Almost one-third of teachers rated their development need in this area as high (Figure 3.6).

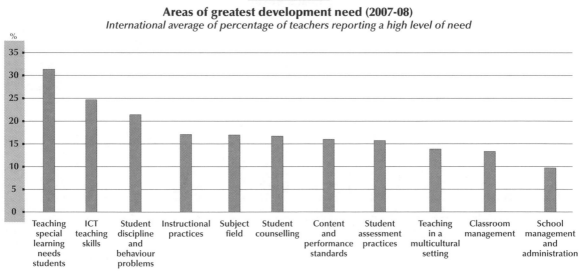

Figure 3.6

Areas of greatest development need (2007-08)
International average of percentage of teachers reporting a high level of need

Areas are ranked in descending order of the international average where teachers report a high level of need for development.
Source: OECD, Table 3.4.

StatLink http://dx.doi.org/10.1787/607807256201

Given that the TALIS target population *excludes* teachers who only teach special learning needs students, this is a noteworthy result. It indicates that classroom teachers in general recognise the importance of developing their competence in this area, and this may be a reflection of two trends: first, the growing calls in some school systems for greater integration of special learning needs students in mainstream schools and classrooms (OECD, 2008) and second, the growing emphasis in education policy on equity as well as quality to ensure that the learning needs of all students are provided for equally. An important message from the TALIS data is that teachers do not feel fully prepared to cope with these challenges.

Sizeable proportions of teachers also reported having a high level of need for "Information and communication technology (ICT) teaching skills" (25%) and "Student discipline and behaviour" (21%). The 2001 OECD survey of upper secondary schools (rather than the lower secondary focus of TALIS) highlighted the lack of use of ICT in classroom instruction but noted the substantial amount of professional development that had taken place in this area (OECD, 2004). That school teachers identify such a high level of need in the use of ICT for instruction almost 10 years later may be a reflection of the speed of technological change which teachers must keep pace with. This may signal a continuing challenge for schools and teachers to keep up to speed in a fast-moving area and to fully exploit technology for the benefit of teaching and learning. But it may also confirm studies which indicate a lack of capacity building in terms of how best to use ICT in the classroom. The IEA SITES study (IEA, 2008), for instance, showed that attendance at ICT-related professional development was significantly and positively correlated with the use of ICT.

In contrast, the aspect of teachers' work which was, on average, the least frequently reported as a high development need was "School management and administration" (10% of teachers) (Table 3.4). The interpretation of this finding is not straightforward. It may indicate that teachers are already well prepared for their role in school management and administration, or it may indicate the relatively low importance of this area for teachers' work.

However, patterns differ sharply across countries. It is striking, for instance, that in Malaysia the extent to which teachers report high levels of development needs (Table 3.4) is, in a number of areas, much higher than the average across countries. This is most evident in the case of "Content and performance standards" (34 percentage points higher than the international average), "Subject field" (40 percentage points higher) and "Instructional practices" (38 percentage points higher).

In Malaysia, not only did the vast majority of teachers want more professional development than they received (83%, much higher than almost all other countries; see Table 3.3), but the strength of that need across almost all areas of their work is much greater than in the other countries surveyed. Interestingly, the only area for which teachers in Malaysia report a high level of need that is lower than the international average is "Teaching special learning needs students", the area which is rated most frequently by teachers overall as a high level need across countries.

A similar though much less marked finding is evident for Lithuania and Italy. In Lithuania a higher than average level of high need is reported by teachers for most aspects of their work, the exceptions being "Teaching special learning needs students" and "Teaching in a multicultural setting". However, the percentage of teachers who wanted more professional development than they received (45%) was slightly below the average across all countries. In Italy the extent of high need is greater than average in all areas of teachers' work except "School management and administration". Among European countries, teachers in Italy report the highest level of need for "Teaching in a multicultural setting".

In Australia, the extent of high development need is below the international average in all eleven areas, most notably in "Teaching special learning needs students" (16 percentage points below the international average), "Student discipline and behaviour" (15 percentage points below) and "Instructional practices"

(13 percentage points below). No other country is below the international average on all eleven areas, though four countries are below on all but one: Denmark (the exception being "Content and performance standards"), Iceland ("Teaching in a multicultural setting"), the Slovak Republic ("Subject Field") and Turkey ("Teaching in a multicultural setting").

Overall index of professional development need

An index of overall need was compiled by assigning a score to each teacher according to the level of need reported for each of the aspects of his/her work: three points for a high level of need; two points for a moderate level of need, one point for a low level of need and no points for cases where teachers noted no development need at all. These were then aggregated and divided by the maximum possible score of 33 (3 times 11) and multiplied by 100 to give an overall percentage of the maximum "need" for each teacher. The index shown in the first column of Table 3.4 is the average of this score across all of a given country's teachers. Thus, an index score of 100 would indicate that teachers reported a high level of need in each of the eleven areas of their work. The results shown in Figure 3.7 indicate that the greatest degree of need for development when aggregated across these areas was reported by teachers in Malaysia, followed by Korea, Italy and Lithuania. The lowest level of need measured by this index was reported by teachers in Hungary, Australia, Denmark and Turkey.

This index should, however, be interpreted with some caution given the consistently high and low reporting of the strength of development need in some countries (discussed in the previous section). These trends may genuinely reflect the level of unsatisfied demand in these countries, but it may also indicate some cultural bias. In other words, teachers in certain countries may systematically tend to report more or less positively than those in other countries. For this reason, a closer focus on differences *within countries* than between countries may be more appropriate, and patterns of high levels of need between topic areas within a country can be compared to identify the relative priorities for each country.

Figure 3.7

Index of professional development need (2007-08)
Scored across 11 aspects of teachers' work

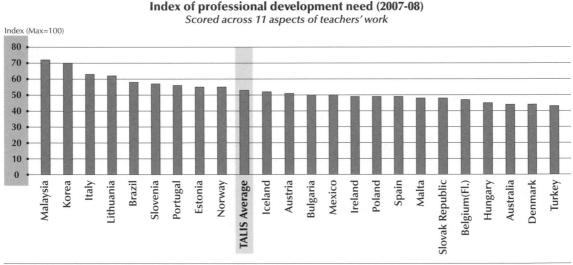

Countries are ranked in descending order of index of professional development need.
Source: OECD, Table 3.4.

StatLink http://dx.doi.org/10.1787/607807256201

As noted, there is a high level of need for "Teaching special learning needs students" compared to other aspects of teachers' work in all countries except Korea, Lithuania and Malaysia. It is particularly pronounced in Brazil and Portugal and is also relatively high in Hungary, Ireland, Malta, Mexico and Spain. The need to develop ICT teaching skills is relatively high in all countries except Korea and is particularly pronounced in Ireland, Norway and Spain.

For other aspects of teachers' work, the following development needs also are relatively high within the countries specified (Table 3.4):

- **Content and performance standards**: Bulgaria, Denmark, Malaysia and Lithuania.
- **Student assessment practices**: Belgium (Fl.), Lithuania and Norway.
- **Subject field**: Belgium (Fl.), Italy, Korea, Lithuania and Malaysia.
- **Instructional practices**: Italy, Korea, Lithuania and Malaysia.
- **Student discipline and behaviour problems**: Austria, Hungary, Iceland, the Slovak Republic and Slovenia;
- **Teaching in a multicultural setting**: Ireland, Italy, Spain and Turkey.
- **Student counselling**: Ireland, Korea, Mexico and Poland.

On average at the country level, there is a weak positive relation between the average number of professional development days engaged in and the percentage of teachers reporting that they wanted more than they had received (Figure 3.8).

Figure 3.8

Comparison of unsatisfied demand for professional development and amount undertaken (2007-08)

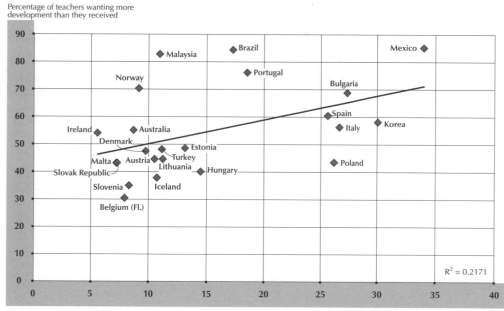

Source: OECD, Tables 3.1 and 3.3.

StatLink http://dx.doi.org/10.1787/607807256201

Although the relation is not very strong, it is interesting that such a pattern exists, though it is important to examine this relation at the country level, and here some divergent trends can be found.

Some countries follow this pattern fairly closely. For instance, in Mexico lower secondary teachers had the highest average number of days of professional development of all participating countries and also the highest percentage of teachers reporting that this did not satisfy their demand. Furthermore, some of the countries with the lowest average number of professional development days – most notably Belgium (Fl.) and Slovenia – also have percentages of teachers wanting more than they had received that is well below average (Table 3.3, column 1). This may indicate that the development received matched teachers' needs and satisfied their demand fairly well or they may be less motivated, for whatever reason, to engage in further professional development. Analysis in the remainder of the chapter will throw further light on this issue.

However, other countries do not show this pattern. In Australia and the Slovak Republic, for example, the teachers who were most likely to want more development were those who had received none during the survey period.

SUPPORT RECEIVED BY TEACHERS FOR PROFESSIONAL DEVELOPMENT

The level and intensity of participation in professional development activities are in part a function of the types of support that teachers receive to undertake them. Support can take many forms, and TALIS asked about possibilities ranging from compulsory development opportunities to formal induction and mentoring support for new teachers.

The following sections examine the different types of support and the relations between the support received and the level and intensity of participation reported.

Compulsory professional development

Teachers' professional development may be, or may not be, compulsory. Some professional development may be deemed compulsory because the skills and knowledge the development activities aim to enhance are considered important for teacher quality. In some cases participation in such activities may even be required for teacher certification. It can also be important for teachers to exercise their own professional judgement by identifying and taking part in development activities which they feel are most beneficial to them. A high degree of compulsory professional development may be indicative of a more highly managed professional development system with less discretion for teachers to choose the development they feel they need.

On average among the participating countries, some 51% of teachers' professional development was compulsory (Table 3.1). The proportion ranged from about one-third or less in Austria, Belgium (Fl.), Denmark and Portugal to 78% in Malta and as high as 88% in Malaysia. The countries with the highest *number* of compulsory days on average were Mexico, Bulgaria, Spain, Italy and Korea and those with the lowest were Austria, Belgium (Fl.) and Ireland.

The question arises as to whether the amount of teachers' professional development depends on the proportion that is compulsory. At the country level, there does not appear to be a clear relation between the average number of days of professional development and the percentage which was compulsory. For instance, Mexico had the highest average number of days of professional development, a figure undoubtedly influenced by the fact that two-thirds of these days were compulsory. In contrast, in Bulgaria, Italy, Korea and Poland, with the next highest average numbers of days of professional development, less than half were compulsory. And in Malaysia, the country with the highest percentage of compulsory days, the average number of days of professional development (among teachers who took personal development) was below average at around 12 days.

Financial support

In addition to formal entitlement to professional development or provision of mandatory programmes, support for professional development can take a variety of forms. TALIS distinguished between financial support – direct payment of the costs of the development activities or salary supplements for undertaking development – and support in the form of time scheduled to allow for development activities.

On average in participating countries, around one-quarter of teachers who engaged in some professional development had to pay some of the cost themselves, and a further 8% had to pay all of the cost. There are certain differences among countries (Table 3.5).

The TALIS survey responses indicate that in no country is all professional development completely free for all teachers. The countries with the highest percentage of teachers who paid nothing for their participation are Belgium (Fl.), Malta, Slovenia and Turkey, where more than 80% of teachers reported having paid nothing towards the cost of their professional development activities. In contrast, less than half of the teachers in Austria, Malaysia, Mexico and Poland received free professional development, and only around one-quarter in Korea, the lowest proportion of all participating countries. The percentage paying the full cost was highest in Portugal (25%), followed by Mexico (19%), Brazil (18%) and Italy (18%).

Figure 3.9

Types of support received for professional development (2007-08)
Percentage of teachers who received support

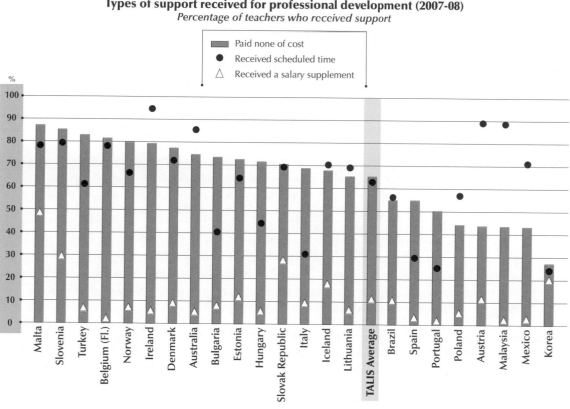

Countries are ranked in descending order of percentage of teachers having paid none of the cost of professional development.
Source: OECD, Table 3.5.

StatLink ⌨🖳 http://dx.doi.org/10.1787/607807256201

Salary supplements

Salary supplements are a less common means of support for professional development, with only 11% of teachers on average receiving them for activities they had taken part in during the survey period. This was a relatively common means of support in Malta, where almost half of teachers received such supplements. It was also a significant means of support in Slovenia (30%) and the Slovak Republic (28%). It is notable that in addition to salary supplements, both Malta and Slovenia have the highest percentage of teachers who paid nothing towards the cost of their professional development, a sign of relatively generous financial support for professional development (Table 3.5).

Scheduled time

Almost two-thirds of teachers received scheduled time to take part in development activities, but the percentage varied substantially between less than 30% in Korea (24%), Portugal (25%) and Spain (30%) to well over 80% in Australia, Austria and Malaysia and over 90% in Ireland (Table 3.5).

Figure 3.9 combines the three forms of support. Relatively high levels of support for all three are reported in Malta, followed by Slovenia, an indication of these countries' extensive and varied support for professional development. In contrast, the levels of support in Poland, Portugal and Spain are below average on all three measures.

What is the relation between support received and levels of participation?

Financial support

The relation between financial support for participation in professional development and levels of participation is not a straightforward one. On the one hand, one might expect higher participation in countries with a high level of financial support for participation. On the other hand, the extent to which financial support is provided for undertaking professional development can be a function of the volume of professional development in the system. On the premise that budgets are limited, it will be easier to pay the full cost of professional development if uptake is low than if it is high. Another model of provision might require teachers to contribute to the cost of the activity but then reward the higher qualifications acquired in their remuneration.

Analysis of the TALIS data reveals a negative relation between the amount of professional development and the extent to which teachers had to pay towards the cost. In other words, the countries in which teachers reported that they had to pay some or all of the costs of their professional development are also typically those in which teachers reported participating in the highest average number of days of development.

To understand the relation better, the average number of days of teachers' professional development can be broken down according to those who paid all, some or none of the costs of the development. On average, teachers who paid nothing towards the cost of their professional development had 13 days of professional development, while those who paid some of the cost had 23 days and those who paid all of the cost had 32 days. This general pattern fits almost every country (Figure 3.10).

Although at first glance counter-intuitive, this result fits the hypothesis that a limited budget will only fully cover the cost of professional development when the volume of professional development is relatively low. In other words, when the average number of days is small, it is more likely that the school or the education authorities will meet the full cost. The negative relation between the volume of professional development and the extent to which teachers have to pay also suggests that, in most countries, the provision of free professional development does not satisfy demand and teachers choose to supplement it by paying for additional development. Thus, the general trend is that higher intensity of participation in professional development goes hand in hand with a higher proportion of teachers having to pay something towards the cost.

Figure 3.10

Average days of development taken by teachers according to personal payment level (2007-08)

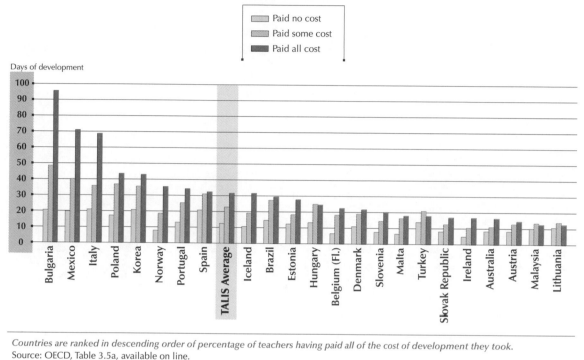

Legend:
- Paid no cost
- Paid some cost
- Paid all cost

Countries are ranked in descending order of percentage of teachers having paid all of the cost of development they took.
Source: OECD, Table 3.5a, available on line.

StatLink ⊟⊞⊒ http://dx.doi.org/10.1787/607807256201

Some countries deviate from this picture. Bulgaria and Italy have relatively high percentages of teachers receiving free professional development (73% and 69%, respectively), with an average number of days in both countries that is well above average (31 days among teachers with some development). In these countries, teachers appear to have high levels of participation in professional development at relatively little cost to themselves. Conversely, in Austria and Malaysia, fewer than 50% of teachers received free professional development, and the average number of days was also low. This would suggest that, in these countries, factors other than budget influence the relatively low intensity of participation in professional development.

Part of the explanation for the relation between the extent of personal payment and the intensity of participation is the fact that development activities that are more time-intensive (qualification programmes and research activities) are also those for which, according to the TALIS survey responses, teachers are more likely to have to pay some or all of the costs (Figure 3.11). Among teachers enrolled in a qualification programme (as a single activity or in combination with other activities), more than half paid some or all of the costs, significantly more than for any of the other activities.

Thus, the strength of the relation between the average days of development received and the degree of personal payment is greatest in Bulgaria (Figure 3.10) where participation in qualification programmes is greatest (Table 3.2).

Figure 3.11

Level of personal payment by type of development activity[1] (2007-08)
International averages

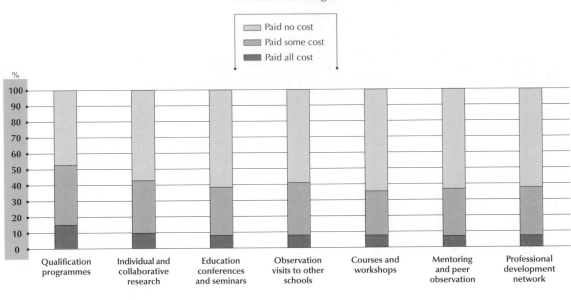

1. Taken alone or in combination with other activities.
Activities are ranked in descending order of the percentage of teachers who paid all of the cost of the development they undertook.
Source: OECD, *TALIS Database.*

StatLink ⬛📊 http://dx.doi.org/10.1787/607807256201

The extent to which teachers who paid for their development did so entirely by choice is not clear from the TALIS data. It may be, for instance, that the cost and time commitment typically required for these activities will provide more of a barrier for some teachers than others, and this may raise some equity concerns. On the other hand, if participation in such programmes can lead to rewards for teachers, perhaps through career advancement or future pay enhancement, this may be less of a concern.

What is the relation between paying for professional development and the extent of unsatisfied demand for development? It might be supposed that if teachers pay for their development, this may help satisfy their demand for development. Analysis of the TALIS database indicates that teachers who paid some or all of the cost of the development they received are more likely to report unfulfilled demand: some 60% of those who paid the full cost said that they had wanted more. The equivalent figure for those who had paid nothing for the development they received was 53% (Table 3.5a available on line). At the country level, only in Norway are teachers who paid nothing towards the development they received more likely to have wanted more than those who had to pay something.

In summary then, those who paid the full cost of their professional development devoted more days to those activities than teachers who either paid some or none of the cost. This is partly indicative of the fact that, according to teachers, more time-intensive professional development activities were less likely to have been provided at no cost. But it also seems to indicate a significant desire among some teachers to take on development activities which are costly financially and in terms of time. In some cases, this can be seen as an investment towards future career progression. Moreover, paying something towards the cost of the development they had received did not satisfy their demand, and these teachers – more than those who received free professional development – had a greater desire for more.

Scheduled time

In terms of the relation between the uptake of professional development and the provision of scheduled time for teachers to undertake development activities, a similar picture emerges. Again, there is no discernable relation at the country level between participation rates and the provision of scheduled time for development but, as Figure 3.12 shows, there is a negative correlation between the extent to which teachers received scheduled time for professional development and the amount of development they undertook during the survey period.

As in the case of personal payment for professional development, the negative relation between support and participation is, at first glance, counter-intuitive, but again the explanation may be resource-related, *i.e.* a high percentage of teachers receiving scheduled time for professional development is only manageable if the number of days is relatively small. Mexico is an exception, with an above-average percentage of teachers receiving time for development and a high level of professional development. The explanation probably lies in part in the fact that a relatively high percentage of this professional development was compulsory (66% of the days taken).

Figure 3.12

Percentage of teachers receiving scheduled time compared to average days of development undertaken (2007-08)
Among those teachers who undertook some development

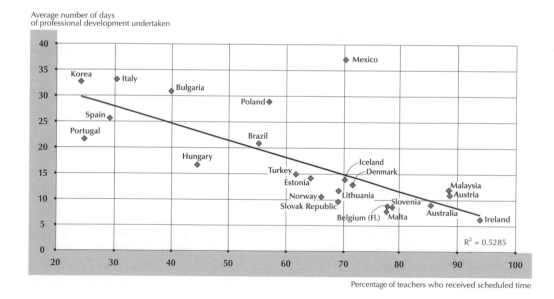

Source: OECD, Tables 3.1 and 3.5.

StatLink ⌐⌐ http://dx.doi.org/10.1787/607807256201

And, as for the relation between personal payment and average days of development, part of the reason that teachers who did not receive scheduled time participated in more days of development on average is that the types of activity more likely to be taken in these situations are relatively time-intensive, namely enrolment in qualification programmes and engaging in research activities. The planned thematic report on teachers' professional development will explore these issues in more detail by attempting to model the determinants of participation in professional development.

Induction and mentoring

Another important type of support for teachers' development takes the form of schools' policies and practices to support teachers who are either new to the profession or new to the school. As noted in the OECD's review of teacher policy (OECD, 2005), the main challenges facing beginning teachers are remarkably similar across countries, such as motivating students to learn, classroom management, and assessing student work. Induction and mentoring programmes may help new teachers cope with these challenges and combat early dropout from the profession.

TALIS sought to learn the extent to which formal policies and practices for induction and for mentoring of new teachers exist in the lower secondary schools in which teachers work. This information was gathered from school principals rather than teachers and permits an examination of the broader development activities in schools where such polices do or do not exist.

On average across the participating countries, some 29% of teachers are in schools where school principals report no formal induction process for teachers new to the school (Table 3.6). A further 27% of lower secondary teachers are in schools where formal induction exists but only for teachers who are new to the profession. Thus, fewer than half of the teachers are in schools with a formal induction process for all teachers new to the school. However, there is enormous variation among countries.

For teachers in Australia and Belgium (Fl.), formal induction is virtually universal for all new teachers to the school. In the Slovak Republic very few teachers are in schools without an induction policy, although it may only be for teachers new to the profession. Also, in Ireland, Poland and Slovenia only a small minority of teachers (less than 10%) are in schools which lack any formal induction process, though in Slovenia and Poland it is predominantly for teachers new to the profession. Formal induction for new teachers is also relatively common in Bulgaria, Estonia, Hungary, Korea and Malaysia (Table 3.6 and Figure 3.13).

The situation in these countries contrasts sharply to that in Brazil, where almost three-quarters of teachers are in schools with no induction process, and in Lithuania, Malta, Mexico and Spain, where the figure exceeds 60%.

A similar picture emerges for mentoring practices. On average across countries, one-quarter of teachers are in schools whose principals report that there is no formal mentoring programme or policy. A further 38% are in schools where mentoring is provided only for teachers new to the profession and some 37% are in schools where all teachers new to the school – whether new to teaching or not – receive organised mentoring.

As for induction, policies for mentoring new teachers vary significantly across countries. The pattern is similar for the two policies. Thus, mentoring practices are extremely common in Australia, Belgium (Fl.), Poland and the Slovak Republic, although in Poland and the Slovak Republic mentoring is more for teachers new to the profession than for all teachers new to the school (Table 3.6). Moreover, as for induction, mentoring is relatively rare in Brazil, Malta, Mexico and Spain, where fewer than 40% of teachers are in schools with formal mentoring practices.

However, mentoring and induction practices do not always go hand in hand. For example, in Lithuania, formal induction of new teachers is relatively rare, but only 20% of teachers are in schools which do not provide mentoring.

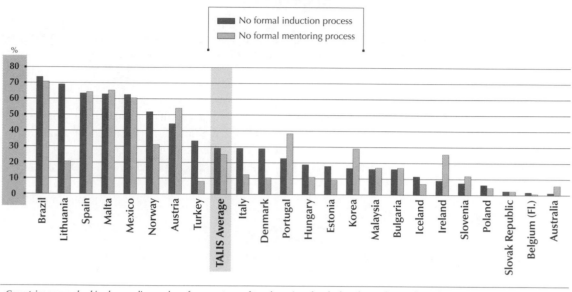

Figure 3.13

Percentage of teachers in schools with no formal induction or mentoring programmes (2007-08)
Based on principals' reports

■ No formal induction process
▨ No formal mentoring process

Countries are ranked in descending order of percentage of teachers in schools that do not have a formal induction programme.
Source: OECD, Table 3.6.

StatLink ⬛ http://dx.doi.org/10.1787/607807256201

Across the participating countries, there is not a strong relation between induction and mentoring policies in schools and the amount of teachers' professional development. In around half of the countries, teachers were likely to have had more professional development if there was a formal induction process in place, and the same is true for mentoring. This positive relation is most prominent in Korea and Mexico, where teachers in schools which had a formal induction process received on average four more days of professional development during the survey period than teachers in schools without such formal programmes. The opposite was true in Bulgaria and Italy, where teachers in schools without formal induction programmes received two or three days more professional development than their counterparts in schools with such programmes (Table 3.6a available on line). It may be that when formal induction policies do not exist in schools, the corresponding support and development may be replaced by other means of development.

These analyses raise questions about how school leadership can support teacher development activities in schools. Chapter 5 will consider this issue in the context of practices to appraise the work of teachers, and Chapter 6 will examine the association between school leadership styles and the professional development activities of teachers.

The relation between unsatisfied demand for professional development and the presence or absence of formal induction or mentoring programmes in schools is similarly mixed (Table 3.6b available on line). On average across the participating countries, the percentage of teachers reporting unsatisfied demand is higher in schools that have formal induction programmes than in those that do not, but in countries such as Slovenia the opposite is true. For schools with and without mentoring programmes, there is on average across the countries surveyed very little difference in the extent of unsatisfied demand. Again there is no consistent pattern among countries.

Part of the reason may be that TALIS only captures whether mentoring programmes exist or not and therefore cannot distinguish between different levels of intensity in the participation in mentoring programmes.

BARRIERS THAT PREVENT MEETING DEMAND

To understand better the take-up of professional development and provide insight into potential policy levers, TALIS asked teachers who had wanted to do more professional development to indicate the reasons that best explain what had prevented them from participating in more professional development. They were entitled to select as many of the options as were appropriate (Figure 3.14).

Across the participating countries, the most commonly cited reasons were "Conflict with work schedule" (47% of teachers) and "No suitable professional development" (42%). In fact, in all but four countries, one or the other of these two factors was the most frequently cited barrier to take-up of additional professional development. The exceptions were Hungary, Mexico and Poland, where the cost of professional development was the reason most often cited (47, 49 and 51%, respectively) and Malta, where "Family responsibilities" was the most cited reason (45%) (Table 3.7).

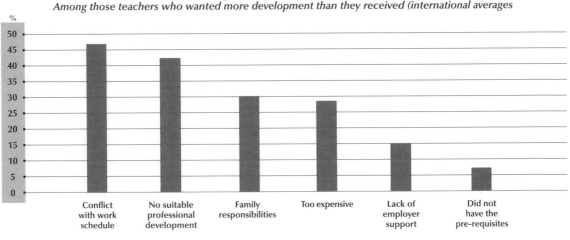

Figure 3.14

Reasons for not taking more professional development (2007-08)
Among those teachers who wanted more development than they received (international averages

Reasons are ranked in descending order of frequency with which the barrier was reported by teachers.
Source: OECD, Table 3.7.

StatLink ⟪⟫ http://dx.doi.org/10.1787/607807256201

No suitable development

Not surprisingly, there is a significant negative correlation between the extent to which teachers reported a lack of suitable professional development and the amount of professional development they actually had. In every country, teachers who reported a lack of suitable development on offer as the reason for not engaging in more development actually participated on average in a smaller number of days of development during the survey period than teachers who did not report this as a barrier. This is good evidence of the association between the perceived lack of suitable development on offer and the amount of development teachers embark on.

The lack of suitable professional development seems to be most acute in Austria. Here almost two-thirds of teachers reported this as a reason for not participating in more professional development than they did, as did more than 50% of teachers in Estonia, Lithuania and the Slovak Republic. In these four countries, the amount of teachers' professional development is below the international average.

Conflict with work schedule

It is notable that the countries where "Conflict with work schedule" was most frequently reported as a barrier – Korea (73% of teachers) and Portugal (65%) – are also those in which teachers were least likely to have received scheduled time for professional development. However, across all countries there is no distinct relation between these two variables. For instance, some 62% of teachers in Australia reported "Conflict with work schedule" as a barrier to participating in more development, the third highest after Korea and Portugal, yet 86% reported that they received scheduled time for professional development (Tables 3.5 and 3.7). This would tend to indicate that the scheduled time was either insufficient or not well aligned with the types of professional development that teachers wanted or perhaps that it was provided for mandatory professional development only. The conflict with the teacher's work schedule was seen as less of a problem in Bulgaria and Denmark, although around one-quarter of teachers still reported this as a barrier.

In virtually all countries, teachers who reported "Conflict with work schedule" as a reason for not engaging in more professional development actually took more days on average than those who did not cite this as a barrier. As noted earlier, this is in part a consequence of the types of development activities undertaken by these teachers. Analysis of the TALIS database shows that those reporting schedule conflict as a barrier are more likely to have engaged in qualification programmes and research activities than those who did not.

Too expensive

Compared with the allocation of scheduled time, there is a slightly stronger relation between the extent to which teachers reported cost as a barrier to taking more professional development and the financial support that they received. In other words countries in which a relatively high percentage of teachers had to pay the full cost of their professional development were more likely to report cost as a barrier to taking more. This is most notable in Brazil and Mexico, as some 50% of teachers reported cost as a reason for not taking part in more development than they did; both countries also reported relatively high percentages (18% and 19% respectively) of teachers having to pay the full cost of these activities. Poland has one of the highest proportions of teachers who had to pay something towards the cost of development, and around 50% reported cost as a barrier to taking part in more (Tables 3.5 and 3.7).

In contrast, cost was less frequently reported as a barrier in Belgium (Fl.) (12%), Ireland (12%) and Turkey (12%), three countries in which relatively few teachers had to pay the cost of their professional development.

It is interesting that teachers who reported expense as a barrier actually had more days of professional development on average than those who did not report this as a barrier. The reason, as noted earlier, is probably that the activities that teachers were more likely to have paid for are also likely to be more time-intensive, particularly enrolment in qualification programmes.

So, in addition to the finding that teachers who had to pay for their development had more unsatisfied demand than those who did not, the preceding analysis shows that for these teachers more than others, cost is a barrier to satisfaction of that demand.

Other barriers

On average across participating countries, "Lack of employer support" was relatively rarely cited as a barrier. However, in Denmark more than one-third of teachers reported this as a factor preventing further professional development. In contrast, only a small minority of teachers in Bulgaria (3%), Italy (6%) and Spain (6%) see this as a barrier (Table 3.7).

The lack of prerequisites to undertake the desired development was reported as a significant problem only in Malaysia (over one-quarter of teachers), followed by more than 15% in Mexico and Turkey (Table 3.7).

IMPACT OF PROFESSIONAL DEVELOPMENT

Having assessed the level of unsatisfied demand for professional development among lower secondary teachers and the areas of their work for which they have greatest development need, the level and intensity of participation in professional development activities and the support on offer to teachers and the perceived barriers against taking more development, this chapter now turns to the question of the types of professional development activities that are most effective in providing the professional development teachers need.

TALIS asked teachers to report the impact of their development activities on their development as a teacher. Since TALIS reports teachers' perceptions, these reports of perceived impact should be treated with some caution as indicators of the effectiveness of these activities. Nevertheless, if teachers feel that a development activity has had limited impact, this is likely to colour their decisions, and perhaps those of their colleagues, regarding future participation in that activity.

Table 3.8 shows the percentage of teachers who reported a moderate or high impact for the types of development they had undertaken during the survey period. It is striking how positively teachers view the impact of these development activities and how consistent this is across all types of development activities. On average across participating countries, teachers reported that the most effective forms of development were "Individual and collaborative research", "Informal dialogue to improve teaching" and "Qualification programmes", all with close to 90% of teachers reporting a moderate or large impact on their development as a teacher. The development activities that were reported to be relatively less effective were attendance at "Education conferences and seminars" and taking part in "Observation visits to other schools", though even for these activities around 75% of teachers reported a moderate or high impact.

In general, there is little variation in this pattern across countries with the exception of teachers in Belgium (Fl.), who take a far less positive view of the impact of their development activities. On average, the percentage of teachers who reported a moderate or large impact was around 20-30 percentage points lower than the international average for most activities. This is in the context of teacher reports indicating relatively low participation in professional development activities, relatively low demand for more professional development, and relatively low financial or work-related barriers to further participation (Tables 3.1 and 3.3). A possible interpretation of the combination of low participation and low demand may be a perceived lack of impact of professional development activities. This need not necessarily raise a concern about the quality of the development on offer but could indicate a teacher workforce whose preparation for teaching is well served through initial teacher training.

Teachers in Australia, Austria and Brazil also view the impact of most types of development less positively than in other countries. In Australia this is most notably the case for "Reading professional literature" (where high or moderate impact was reported by 66% of teachers, 16 percentage points below the international average). For Austria, the reported impact of attendance at "Educational conferences and seminars" was relatively low (18 percentage points below the international average) and in Brazil the impact of "Mentoring and peer observation" activities was 12 percentage points below the international average (Table 3.8).

In contrast, teachers in Denmark, Hungary, Lithuania and Poland rank the impact of the development they had undertaken across all types of development above the international average. Malaysia is more positive than the international average on all aspects except "Individual and collaborative research", where the percentage of teachers reporting moderate or high impact was around the international average.

Education conferences and seminars, although seen as one of the less effective types of activities on average across countries, are considered particularly effective by teachers in Malaysia. Teachers in Lithuania found observational visits to other schools particularly effective, and teachers in Hungary reported a particularly strong impact of mentoring and peer observation (Table 3.8).

How does perceived impact relate to participation?

Given these varying patterns of impact, it is informative to compare impact and participation across the different types of activities. On average across the participating countries, the most obvious contrast between participation and impact is for "Qualification programmes", which ranked second highest in the percentage (87%) of teachers who reported moderate or high impact resulting from their participation, yet the participation rate (25%) was the lowest of all development activities (Figure 3.15).

There is also a notable contrast between participation and impact for "Individual and collaborative research", where impact ranked highest of the nine activities but only sixth in terms of participation.

It is not possible to learn from the TALIS data why these differences occur. However, it can be noted that both qualification programmes and research are relatively time-intensive and, as noted earlier, they are also activities which teachers were more likely to have had to pay for. It may not be possible for education systems to allow very high proportions of its teachers to spend a large part of their time on these activities and to finance them as well. The cost and time commitments are likely to present barriers for some teachers as well.

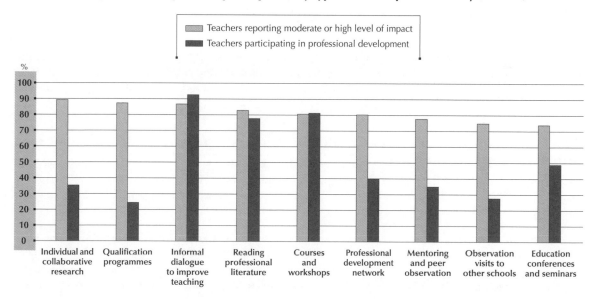

Figure 3.15

Comparison of impact and participation by types of development activity (2007-08)

- Teachers reporting moderate or high level of impact
- Teachers participating in professional development

Activities are ranked in descending order of the percentage of teachers reporting a moderate or high impact of the professional development they took.

Source: OECD, Tables 3.2 and 3.8.

StatLink http://dx.doi.org/10.1787/607807256201

Yet it is striking that the two types of activities that teachers report as having the highest impact on their development are those that they are most likely to have to pay for and commit significant time to. In other words, it is through teachers' own investment that, on average, they engage in the activities they have found to be among the most effective for their development. Even allowing for the fact that teachers are likely to choose to participate in and pay for activities which they expect to be effective, this is an important finding.

In contrast, courses and workshops and, to a lesser degree, education conferences and seminars have relatively high rates of participation when compared with their reported impact on teachers' development. In these cases, while these activities may not generally require a large time commitment, the justification for high levels of participation might be questioned in view of the relatively lower impact that teachers report.

The pattern of participation in different development activities seems to be more closely aligned with the impact reported by teachers in some countries than in others. A broad indication of this alignment can be obtained by calculating the correlation between rankings of participation by activity and rankings of impact by activity. The correlation is strongest in Lithuania (0.57 Spearman Rank correlation coefficient), followed by Mexico and the Slovak Republic (both 0.43). Arguably in these cases, participation is fairly well aligned with the benefits to be obtained from various categories of professional development. In contrast, there is a fairly strong negative correlation between participation and impact in Estonia (-0.37) and weak negative correlations in Hungary, Iceland, Ireland and Korea (around -0.1). In Estonia, a major contributor to this result is that the activities for which teachers were most positive about the impact – "Qualification programmes" and "Individual and collaborative research" – were the two activities with the lowest participation for teachers.

CONCLUSIONS AND IMPLICATIONS FOR POLICY AND PRACTICE

This chapter has reviewed current patterns of participation in professional development activities by lower secondary education teachers. It has examined the extent to which teachers' demand for professional development is being met and how this varies according to the various types of support teachers have received and what they have perceived as hindrances to engaging in more than they did. Finally, it has analysed the types of activities that teachers reported as having had the greatest impact on their development as teachers.

The chapter set out to answer three questions about the amount of teachers' of professional development, the extent to which it meets their needs, and how it could be improved. This now provides the framework for a reiteration of key results and a discussion of what can be learned. Some of these issues will be examined in greater depth in the separate thematic report on teachers' professional development.

How much does the amount and profile of teachers' professional development vary within and among countries?

This chapter first examined the patterns of participation in professional development reported by teachers.

Key results

- The *level and intensity* of participation in professional development varies considerably among countries. Nearly nine in ten teachers take part in some sort of activity, but since the definition of professional development is broadly drawn, the fact that in some countries up to one in four teachers receive none is a source of concern. Moreover, intensity varies across countries more than participation, with Korea and Mexico seeing teachers participating on average for over 30 days in 18 months, twice the average rate (Table 3.1).

- *Within-country* variation in the intensity of professional development can be high and is greatest in Italy, Korea, Mexico, Poland and Spain. Older teachers tend to receive less than the average, though the pattern by gender is more mixed (Tables 3.1d and 3.1a).

- The *types of development* undertaken by teachers explain some of these variations. Countries in which a high percentage of teachers take part in "Qualification programmes" or "Individual and collaborative research" tend to have a higher average number of days of development. However, only a small minority of teachers participate in these activities. On the other hand, virtually all teachers engage in "Informal dialogue to improve teaching" (not counted in the main measure of professional development), and the great majority attend some form of "Course and workshops" (Tables 3.1 and 3.2).

Discussion

The high average participation in development activities among lower secondary teachers is unquestionably a positive message from the TALIS results. Nevertheless, the fact that, among participating countries, an average of some 11% of teachers did not take part in any of the more structured forms of professional development in the 18 months prior to the survey may be a concern (Table 3.1).

On the other hand, even if not all teachers engage in more organised types of activities, it is reassuring that virtually all engage in informal dialogue with others to improve their teaching and that the vast majority read professional literature. However, some of the more collaborative forms of development are more evident in some countries than in others.

How well are teachers' professional development needs being met?

Analysis of the TALIS data reveals that despite high levels of participation in development activities, the professional development needs of a significant proportion of teachers are not being met.

Key results

- More than half of the teachers surveyed reported that they *wanted more* professional development than they received during the 18-month survey period. The extent of unsatisfied demand is sizeable in every country, ranging from 31% in Belgium (Fl.) to over 80% in Brazil, Malaysia and Mexico (Table 3.3).

- Across countries, teachers who were *more likely to report unsatisfied demand* were in public schools, females and under 40 years of age (Table 3.3).

- Across countries, the aspects of teachers' work with *greatest development need* are: "Teaching special learning needs students", followed by "ICT teaching skills" and "Student discipline and behaviour" (Table 3.4).

Discussion

A certain level of unsatisfied demand might be expected; it is natural that a certain proportion of teachers will at some time not feel fully equipped to carry out their work effectively. Nonetheless, the extent of unsatisfied demand appears large, and in some countries the great majority of teachers state that they need more professional development than they receive.

The extent to which this undermines the effectiveness of the teacher workforce in the participating countries cannot be measured by TALIS, but it is difficult to imagine that such deficits are not to some extent detrimental to effective teaching and learning.

The information from TALIS gives policy makers clear pointers to the main deficits in each country. In terms of the topics for which development needs are greatest, it is striking how consistently countries reported a high level of need for development in the area of teaching students with special learning needs. This indicates a clear recognition on the part of teachers that they do not feel properly equipped to deal with increasingly heterogenous groups and to address the learning needs of the weaker as well as the stronger students.

An individual teacher's amount of development is predictably correlated with the type of activity they have taken part in: teachers engaged in qualification programmes and research activities have to devote more time to these activities than those who attend conferences or workshops. An important discovery from TALIS is that unsatisfied demand exists no matter what activities teachers have engaged in.

How best should unsatisfied demand for professional development be addressed?

The chapter examined the support mechanisms that are in place for teachers and also the barriers which teachers reported as preventing them from engaging in more professional development than they did. The analysis also reveals how these relate to teachers' participation and their desire for more professional development.

Key results

- The more teachers *paid* for development, the more they took part in. That is, teachers who paid nothing received 13 days on average, those who paid some of the cost received 23 days, and those who paid all of the cost received 32 days. This seems partly associated with the nature of programmes: those leading to a qualification were both more time-consuming and more likely to be paid for by teachers (Table 3.5a, available on line).

- *Payment and satisfaction* did not go hand in hand: on the contrary, those who paid for professional development were more likely to want more (Table 3.5a, available on line).

- The principal *cause of unfulfilled demand*, according to teachers, is the conflict with their work schedule, but they also often cite lack of suitable development opportunities. Those who participated in the least development were most likely to cite the latter cause (Table 3.7).

- The *most effective types of development*, according to teachers, are those in which they participate least – especially programmes leading to qualifications, and to a lesser degree, research activities. The most effective types of development are also those for which teachers are more likely to have had to pay the full or partial cost and devote most time to (Table 3.8).

Discussion

In seeking to meet teachers' professional development requirements, policy makers and practitioners need to consider both how to support and encourage participation and how to ensure that opportunities match teachers' perceived needs. This must be balanced with the cost in terms both of finance and teachers' time. Teachers' perceived needs should also match the wider goals of school development and how well teachers' professional development is coordinated with appraisal and feedback practices in schools and school evaluations more generally (see Chapter 5).

Even if there is no country in which the professional development of teachers is completely free, TALIS data indicate that teachers feel that the level of support they receive in most countries is significant in terms of finance and separately scheduled time in which to undertake development activities. In the participating countries, an average of around two-thirds of teachers pay nothing, and a similar proportion receive allocated time; schools and public authorities clearly make a significant investment in teachers' professional development.

Yet, the degree of unsatisfied demand reported by teachers remains troubling and may suggest a misalignment between the support provided and teachers' development needs in terms of content and modes of delivery.

For modes of delivery, the evidence from TALIS is very revealing. It is striking that the activities that teachers report as the most effective for their development are also those for which they are more likely to have had to pay full or partial cost and to devote the most time to. This need not mean that the cost of all teachers' participation in qualification programmes and research should be fully paid for, but a better balance should perhaps be sought between who pays and who benefits.

The 42% of teachers who report a lack of suitable professional development activities to satisfy their needs is an equally worrying finding (Table 3.7). It indicates that carefully comparing provision and support with development needs should be a priority in many participating countries.

Further analysis of teachers' professional development

Further to the discussion of teachers' professional development in this chapter, Chapters 4-6 show how teachers' professional development inter-relates with the other key policy themes of TALIS. Chapter 4 shows how teachers' teaching beliefs, their teaching practices and their professional co-operation are related to their participation in different forms of professional development. Chapter 5 examines how teachers' professional development activities are connected to school and teacher evaluation practices and allows an assessment of the extent to which these practices are related to providing the development that teachers need. Chapter 6 examines how different school leadership styles are associated with teachers' professional development activities and sheds light on the degree to which school leaders can shape schools as professional learning communities. Finally, Chapter 7 examines the significance of professional development among the determinants of classroom disciplinary climate and teachers' self-efficacy.

In addition, these findings prompt further policy questions and thus the need for further analysis of the TALIS data. The thematic report on teachers' professional development, which is being produced jointly with the European Commission, will seek to do this. In particular, it will seek to examine more thoroughly the factors that determine participation in professional development as well as the factors that determine the differing impacts that teachers report for alternative types of development activities.

ADDITIONAL MATERIAL

The following additional material relevant to this chapter is available on line at:
StatLink http://dx.doi.org/10.1787/607807256201

Table 3.1c   Percentage distribution of days of professional development undertaken by teachers in the previous 18 months (2007-08)

Table 3.1d   Percentile distribution of days of professional development undertaken by teachers in the previous 18 months (2007-08)

Table 3.5a   Average days of development taken by teachers and desire for more development according to the level of costs teachers paid (2007-08)

Table 3.6a   Average days of development taken by teachers according to whether a formal induction or mentoring programme was in place (2007-08)

Table 3.6b   Teachers who wanted to participate in more development than they did in the previous 18 months according to whether a formal induction or mentoring programme was in place (2007-08)

Table 3.1

Participation of teachers in professional development in the previous 18 months (2007-08)

Participation rates, average number of days and average of compulsory days of professional development undertaken by teachers of lower secondary education in the 18 months prior to the survey

	Percentage of teachers who undertook some professional development in the previous 18 months		Average days of professional development across all teachers		Average days of professional development among those who participated		Average percentage of professional development days taken that were compulsory	
	%	(S.E.)	Mean	(S.E.)	Mean	(S.E.)	%	(S.E.)
Australia	96.7	(0.43)	8.7	(0.19)	9.0	(0.20)	47.3	(1.17)
Austria	96.6	(0.37)	10.5	(0.17)	10.9	(0.16)	31.4	(0.66)
Belgium (Fl.)	90.3	(0.73)	8.0	(0.38)	8.8	(0.42)	33.6	(0.95)
Brazil	83.0	(1.21)	17.3	(0.70)	20.8	(0.79)	40.2	(1.17)
Bulgaria	88.3	(1.17)	27.2	(1.65)	30.8	(2.04)	46.9	(2.11)
Denmark	75.6	(1.26)	9.8	(0.34)	12.9	(0.40)	34.6	(1.43)
Estonia	92.7	(0.50)	13.1	(0.29)	14.2	(0.31)	49.2	(1.20)
Hungary	86.9	(1.77)	14.5	(0.50)	16.7	(0.41)	46.1	(1.58)
Iceland	77.1	(1.10)	10.7	(0.44)	13.9	(0.56)	49.9	(1.30)
Ireland	89.7	(0.78)	5.6	(0.21)	6.2	(0.21)	41.4	(0.99)
Italy	84.6	(0.76)	26.6	(0.98)	31.4	(1.17)	40.0	(1.08)
Korea	91.9	(0.59)	30.0	(0.57)	32.7	(0.55)	46.9	(0.85)
Lithuania	95.5	(0.40)	11.2	(0.21)	11.8	(0.21)	56.6	(0.98)
Malaysia	91.7	(0.67)	11.0	(0.32)	11.9	(0.33)	88.1	(0.64)
Malta	94.1	(0.75)	7.3	(0.25)	7.8	(0.26)	78.4	(1.07)
Mexico	91.5	(0.60)	34.0	(1.60)	37.1	(1.78)	66.4	(1.22)
Norway	86.7	(0.87)	9.2	(0.30)	10.6	(0.34)	55.5	(1.25)
Poland	90.4	(0.67)	26.1	(1.10)	28.9	(1.20)	41.0	(1.14)
Portugal	85.8	(0.87)	18.5	(0.89)	21.6	(1.01)	35.1	(0.99)
Slovak Republic	75.0	(1.13)	7.2	(0.30)	9.6	(0.38)	44.1	(1.19)
Slovenia	96.9	(0.35)	8.3	(0.20)	8.6	(0.20)	60.5	(0.93)
Spain	100.0	(0.03)	25.6	(0.51)	25.6	(0.51)	66.8	(0.99)
Turkey	74.8	(2.09)	11.2	(0.52)	14.9	(0.65)	72.8	(1.65)
TALIS average	**88.5**	**(0.20)**	**15.3**	**(0.14)**	**17.3**	**(0.16)**	**51.0**	**(0.25)**

Source: OECD, *TALIS Database*.

StatLink ⟨≡⟩ http://dx.doi.org/10.1787/607807256201

Table 3.1a

Amount of professional development undertaken by teachers in the previous 18 months (2007-08) – teacher characteristics

Average number of days of professional development undertaken by teachers of different characteristics
[among those teachers of lower secondary education who took some professional development]

	Female teachers		Male teachers		Teachers aged under 30 years		Teachers aged 30-39 years		Teachers aged 40-49 years		Teachers aged 50+ years	
	Mean	(S.E.)	Mean	(S.E.)	Mean	(S.E.)	Mean	(S.E.)	Mean	(S.E.)	Mean	(S.E.)
Australia	9.0	(0.24)	9.0	(0.28)	9.0	(0.52)	8.9	(0.41)	9.1	(0.34)	9.1	(0.31)
Austria	11.2	(0.20)	10.3	(0.23)	12.4	(0.72)	10.5	(0.47)	11.3	(0.25)	10.5	(0.25)
Belgium (Fl.)	8.5	(0.55)	9.5	(0.48)	8.7	(0.62)	8.8	(0.79)	8.6	(0.61)	9.2	(0.88)
Brazil	20.7	(0.88)	21.2	(1.02)	22.2	(1.51)	22.3	(1.15)	19.7	(0.85)	17.0	(1.40)
Bulgaria	30.7	(2.00)	31.5	(3.79)	27.3	(5.36)	34.2	(4.29)	33.6	(4.21)	26.8	(1.67)
Denmark	13.4	(0.53)	12.3	(0.68)	17.3	(3.02)	13.4	(0.70)	15.8	(1.07)	10.3	(0.50)
Estonia	14.6	(0.36)	11.6	(0.51)	15.3	(1.19)	16.8	(0.80)	15.2	(0.55)	11.8	(0.36)
Hungary	16.6	(0.52)	16.9	(1.28)	15.4	(1.05)	16.3	(0.95)	18.3	(0.80)	15.4	(1.29)
Iceland	14.4	(0.68)	12.7	(0.83)	11.5	(1.41)	12.9	(0.84)	15.2	(0.96)	14.2	(0.99)
Ireland	6.0	(0.23)	6.7	(0.45)	5.8	(0.49)	6.6	(0.49)	6.8	(0.45)	5.7	(0.30)
Italy	30.5	(1.12)	34.8	(2.52)	64.1	(12.08)	50.1	(3.36)	30.4	(1.54)	24.1	(1.04)
Korea	34.2	(0.69)	30.0	(0.91)	43.3	(1.61)	36.7	(1.01)	30.3	(0.82)	24.3	(1.51)
Lithuania	12.1	(0.24)	10.1	(0.46)	11.2	(0.75)	11.5	(0.41)	12.5	(0.34)	11.4	(0.31)
Malaysia	11.8	(0.39)	12.3	(0.44)	12.0	(0.56)	11.7	(0.43)	12.2	(0.37)	11.9	(0.65)
Malta	7.9	(0.39)	7.6	(0.32)	7.7	(0.51)	7.5	(0.42)	8.6	(0.86)	7.9	(0.50)
Mexico	39.9	(2.17)	33.9	(2.72)	48.5	(5.64)	41.8	(3.88)	34.5	(2.27)	28.1	(2.26)
Norway	10.9	(0.49)	10.1	(0.47)	10.2	(0.95)	10.4	(0.58)	12.6	(0.86)	9.7	(0.55)
Poland	29.9	(1.40)	25.6	(1.60)	35.2	(3.22)	33.2	(2.08)	25.5	(1.45)	17.9	(1.64)
Portugal	20.3	(1.06)	24.8	(1.95)	38.5	(5.51)	21.3	(1.29)	20.2	(1.12)	17.7	(2.21)
Slovak Republic	9.9	(0.43)	8.3	(0.61)	9.8	(1.05)	9.7	(0.52)	10.9	(0.53)	8.5	(0.45)
Slovenia	8.7	(0.23)	8.3	(0.34)	9.4	(0.54)	9.7	(0.49)	8.4	(0.25)	7.2	(0.26)
Spain	26.7	(0.64)	24.2	(0.60)	29.4	(1.51)	25.7	(0.91)	26.8	(0.73)	23.0	(0.69)
Turkey	13.6	(0.82)	16.2	(1.29)	16.9	(1.13)	13.6	(0.74)	14.4	(1.91)	10.6	(1.18)
TALIS average	**17.5**	**(0.18)**	**16.9**	**(0.29)**	**20.9**	**(0.72)**	**18.9**	**(0.34)**	**17.4**	**(0.28)**	**14.4**	**(0.23)**

	Teachers with qualification at ISCED level 5B or below		Teachers with an ISCED level 5A Bachelor degree		Teachers with an ISCED level 5A Master degree or a higher level of qualification	
	Mean	(S.E.)	Mean	(S.E.)	Mean	(S.E.)
Australia	9.8	(1.24)	8.7	(0.20)	10.6	(0.51)
Austria	11.3	(0.22)	14.1	(2.72)	10.2	(0.25)
Belgium (Fl.)	8.6	(0.44)	15.5	(4.03)	8.0	(0.72)
Brazil	18.9	(2.00)	20.8	(0.87)	24.8	(2.87)
Bulgaria	28.0	(4.37)	28.4	(3.40)	32.3	(2.93)
Denmark	12.8	(4.47)	12.4	(0.39)	18.7	(1.83)
Estonia	14.7	(1.02)	13.3	(0.43)	14.9	(0.43)
Hungary	23.2	(6.28)	17.1	(0.53)	15.7	(0.59)
Iceland	10.4	(0.79)	15.1	(0.74)	17.8	(2.41)
Ireland	5.9	(0.66)	5.9	(0.25)	7.9	(0.65)
Italy	28.4	(1.53)	26.3	(3.81)	32.0	(1.25)
Korea	55.5	(11.32)	31.5	(0.65)	34.4	(0.82)
Lithuania	11.1	(0.54)	11.5	(0.32)	12.5	(0.34)
Malaysia	10.5	(0.65)	12.0	(0.34)	13.6	(0.76)
Malta	7.6	(0.57)	7.8	(0.30)	8.0	(0.67)
Mexico	27.4	(2.62)	36.4	(2.26)	53.1	(5.31)
Norway	16.0	(3.02)	9.9	(0.39)	12.7	(0.81)
Poland	28.7	(8.87)	27.5	(4.46)	29.0	(1.21)
Portugal	21.1	(3.54)	19.8	(1.07)	35.3	(3.34)
Slovak Republic	12.4	(2.90)	9.9	(2.81)	9.6	(0.37)
Slovenia	7.7	(0.22)	9.3	(0.31)	14.0	(2.98)
Spain	23.8	(2.20)	22.1	(1.22)	26.2	(0.49)
Turkey	10.6	(1.07)	15.0	(0.76)	19.3	(2.95)
TALIS average	**17.6**	**(0.80)**	**17.0**	**(0.41)**	**20.0**	**(0.41)**

▨ Denotes categories that include less than 5% of teachers.
Source: OECD, *TALIS Database*.
StatLink ▨▨▨ http://dx.doi.org/10.1787/607807256201

Table 3.1b

Amount of professional development undertaken by teachers in the previous 18 months (2007-08) – school characteristics

Average number of days of professional development undertaken by teachers in schools of different characteristics
[among those teachers of lower secondary education who took some professional development]

	Teachers in public schools		Teachers in private schools		Teachers in schools in a village		Teachers in schools in a small town		Teachers in schools in a town		Teachers in schools in a city		Teachers in schools in a large city	
	Mean	(S.E.)	Mean	(S.E.)	Mean	(S.E.)	Mean	(S.E.)	Mean	(S.E.)	Mean	(S.E.)	Mean	(S.E.)
Australia	8.9	(0.24)	9.2	(0.32)	10.1	(0.57)	9.4	(0.74)	9.0	(0.35)	8.8	(0.40)	9.0	(0.32)
Austria	11.0	(0.19)	10.2	(0.55)	11.3	(0.44)	10.2	(0.24)	12.1	(0.58)	11.2	(0.45)	11.3	(0.40)
Belgium (Fl.)	12.2	(1.31)	7.6	(0.34)	15.6	(4.07)	7.7	(0.46)	9.1	(0.86)	10.3	(0.88)	a	a
Brazil	21.1	(0.91)	19.0	(1.36)	22.8	(3.01)	19.5	(1.18)	20.2	(1.42)	21.3	(1.23)	20.2	(1.19)
Bulgaria	30.9	(2.08)	20.5	(9.36)	27.5	(3.54)	32.9	(6.88)	32.1	(2.56)	30.6	(3.18)	30.2	(2.55)
Denmark	13.4	(0.49)	12.4	(0.99)	11.7	(0.98)	14.0	(1.45)	12.1	(0.77)	15.0	(1.37)	15.4	(1.74)
Estonia	14.2	(0.31)	14.9	(3.11)	13.9	(0.45)	14.1	(0.76)	14.8	(0.85)	14.3	(0.64)	a	a
Hungary	16.6	(0.50)	17.0	(0.81)	16.7	(1.17)	17.6	(1.06)	16.2	(1.04)	17.0	(0.91)	16.0	(0.81)
Iceland	14.3	(0.65)	6.9	(2.27)	13.3	(0.71)	14.9	(1.21)	15.4	(1.37)	13.3	(1.09)	a	a
Ireland	6.4	(0.33)	5.7	(0.35)	5.9	(0.45)	5.9	(0.40)	6.2	(0.57)	6.7	(0.97)	5.9	(0.51)
Italy	30.8	(1.20)	44.5	(7.40)	30.4	(2.91)	33.0	(2.38)	29.5	(1.48)	29.2	(2.43)	35.3	(3.84)
Korea	34.3	(0.76)	25.1	(1.29)	32.9	(2.74)	33.0	(2.12)	32.2	(1.58)	32.2	(1.43)	33.1	(0.94)
Lithuania	11.8	(0.22)	11.4	(1.58)	10.9	(0.32)	11.7	(0.54)	12.3	(0.53)	12.2	(0.38)	a	a
Malaysia	12.0	(0.33)	10.0	(1.45)	12.1	(0.60)	11.6	(0.47)	12.3	(0.96)	11.9	(1.04)	13.4	(0.41)
Malta	7.5	(0.34)	8.2	(0.36)	8.6	(0.78)	7.9	(0.33)	7.6	(0.54)	a	a	a	a
Mexico	35.3	(1.57)	44.0	(6.21)	30.6	(7.64)	38.6	(4.31)	35.6	(3.13)	32.2	(2.47)	38.4	(2.43)
Norway	10.7	(0.36)	7.1	(1.14)	11.8	(0.78)	10.4	(0.64)	10.6	(0.59)	8.7	(0.57)	a	a
Poland	29.0	(1.26)	27.9	(3.86)	26.5	(1.32)	31.7	(3.33)	28.1	(1.92)	29.7	(3.70)	45.1	(7.16)
Portugal	21.9	(1.22)	17.9	(1.49)	23.8	(2.18)	20.2	(2.00)	22.9	(1.74)	19.9	(3.23)	18.0	(3.57)
Slovak Republic	9.7	(0.39)	10.0	(1.19)	10.6	(1.07)	9.4	(0.66)	8.9	(0.46)	10.3	(1.19)	a	a
Slovenia	8.6	(0.21)	a	a	8.9	(0.42)	8.4	(0.29)	9.0	(0.63)	8.6	(0.73)	a	a
Spain	27.1	(0.62)	21.1	(0.79)	25.4	(1.50)	27.0	(0.88)	25.3	(0.86)	25.5	(1.28)	24.6	(1.18)
Turkey	15.0	(0.72)	14.9	(1.13)	15.1	(2.42)	17.4	(3.05)	14.9	(1.48)	14.4	(0.83)	15.8	(1.32)
TALIS average	**17.5**	**(0.18)**	**16.6**	**(0.66)**	**17.2**	**(0.50)**	**17.7**	**(0.46)**	**17.2**	**(0.28)**	**17.4**	**(0.34)**	**22.1**	**(0.44)**

░ Denotes categories that include less than 5% of teachers.

Source: OECD, *TALIS Database.*

StatLink ⌐╗ http://dx.doi.org/10.1787/607807256201

Table 3.2

Types of professional development undertaken by teachers (2007-08)

Percentage of teachers of lower secondary education undertaking specified professional development activities in the previous 18 months

	Courses and workshops		Education conferences and seminars		Qualification programmes		Observation visits to other schools		Professional development network		Individual and collaborative research		Mentoring and peer observation		Reading professional literature		Informal dialogue to improve teaching	
	%	(S.E.)	%	(S.E.)	%	(S.E.)	%	(S.E.)	%	(S.E.)	%	(S.E.)	%	(S.E.)	%	(S.E.)	%	(S.E.)
Australia	90.6	(0.81)	64.0	(1.34)	11.7	(0.80)	22.2	(1.42)	60.1	(1.38)	36.6	(1.21)	48.6	(1.30)	82.4	(1.09)	93.7	(0.70)
Austria	91.9	(0.56)	49.2	(0.97)	19.9	(0.68)	10.3	(0.55)	37.6	(0.98)	25.9	(0.82)	18.4	(0.84)	89.4	(0.57)	91.9	(0.60)
Belgium (Fl.)	85.2	(0.89)	32.6	(1.33)	17.8	(0.83)	15.1	(1.06)	25.7	(1.05)	31.8	(0.87)	22.1	(0.92)	79.6	(0.98)	91.3	(0.71)
Brazil	80.3	(1.31)	61.0	(1.52)	40.8	(1.27)	32.5	(1.03)	21.9	(0.95)	54.7	(1.17)	47.5	(1.37)	82.5	(0.78)	94.2	(0.58)
Bulgaria	73.7	(2.07)	42.2	(3.44)	50.2	(2.56)	22.5	(2.03)	19.8	(2.22)	24.5	(1.73)	35.4	(3.01)	93.5	(0.96)	94.7	(0.70)
Denmark	81.2	(1.33)	41.6	(1.56)	15.4	(1.47)	10.4	(0.92)	43.5	(1.65)	52.3	(1.51)	17.5	(1.66)	77.3	(1.50)	90.4	(0.89)
Estonia	92.5	(0.66)	50.6	(1.29)	27.7	(0.96)	62.8	(1.37)	42.8	(1.16)	26.6	(1.00)	31.5	(1.35)	87.7	(0.85)	93.8	(0.58)
Hungary	68.7	(1.66)	39.9	(1.64)	26.1	(1.13)	34.6	(2.15)	43.7	(1.83)	17.0	(0.84)	46.7	(1.93)	88.4	(1.11)	79.1	(1.39)
Iceland	72.1	(1.30)	52.1	(1.25)	18.8	(1.02)	60.0	(1.27)	82.6	(1.11)	18.2	(1.08)	33.4	(1.16)	82.8	(1.05)	94.9	(0.65)
Ireland	85.7	(0.88)	42.0	(1.41)	11.4	(0.67)	7.6	(0.75)	51.1	(1.20)	26.3	(1.17)	18.2	(1.12)	60.3	(0.96)	87.4	(0.81)
Italy	66.3	(1.10)	43.5	(1.03)	10.8	(0.50)	16.0	(0.89)	20.0	(0.75)	56.5	(0.92)	27.4	(0.93)	66.2	(0.81)	93.1	(0.46)
Korea	85.0	(0.86)	46.9	(1.24)	27.5	(0.88)	66.8	(1.26)	39.6	(1.00)	50.1	(1.03)	69.4	(1.15)	52.5	(1.06)	90.0	(0.63)
Lithuania	95.7	(0.43)	67.6	(1.10)	43.9	(1.16)	57.1	(1.21)	37.6	(1.05)	48.1	(1.00)	39.7	(1.16)	93.5	(0.50)	96.7	(0.38)
Malaysia	88.6	(0.71)	32.4	(0.93)	22.0	(1.01)	30.0	(1.40)	27.8	(1.25)	21.7	(1.08)	41.8	(1.26)	61.5	(1.63)	95.7	(0.36)
Malta	90.2	(0.96)	51.8	(1.88)	18.1	(1.36)	14.8	(1.23)	39.0	(1.70)	37.4	(1.85)	16.5	(1.19)	61.1	(1.90)	92.3	(1.05)
Mexico	94.3	(0.57)	33.1	(1.23)	33.5	(1.21)	30.5	(1.30)	27.5	(1.13)	62.9	(1.05)	38.1	(1.37)	67.4	(1.05)	88.9	(0.86)
Norway	72.5	(1.40)	40.4	(1.61)	17.6	(0.71)	19.1	(1.49)	35.3	(1.55)	12.3	(0.72)	22.0	(1.50)	64.1	(1.12)	94.0	(0.57)
Poland	90.8	(0.77)	64.3	(1.18)	35.0	(0.95)	19.7	(0.84)	60.7	(1.43)	40.0	(1.08)	66.7	(1.40)	95.2	(0.46)	95.8	(0.36)
Portugal	77.0	(0.91)	51.6	(1.31)	29.5	(0.87)	26.4	(1.03)	15.0	(0.82)	47.1	(1.15)	14.6	(0.84)	73.3	(0.97)	94.2	(0.49)
Slovak Republic	50.1	(1.45)	38.2	(1.38)	38.1	(1.28)	33.1	(1.41)	34.6	(1.46)	11.8	(0.83)	64.8	(1.27)	93.2	(0.64)	95.9	(0.48)
Slovenia	88.1	(0.70)	74.7	(1.05)	10.2	(0.65)	7.7	(0.58)	71.9	(1.38)	22.5	(0.97)	29.1	(0.87)	86.4	(0.73)	97.0	(0.35)
Spain	83.9	(0.86)	36.2	(1.10)	17.2	(0.62)	14.7	(0.75)	22.6	(0.84)	49.2	(0.96)	21.4	(1.00)	68.1	(0.93)	92.6	(0.49)
Turkey	62.3	(1.51)	67.8	(1.99)	19.2	(1.09)	21.1	(1.66)	39.4	(1.67)	40.1	(1.35)	32.2	(2.15)	80.6	(2.14)	92.8	(0.82)
TALIS average	**81.2**	**(0.23)**	**48.9**	**(0.32)**	**24.5**	**(0.23)**	**27.6**	**(0.26)**	**40.0**	**(0.28)**	**35.4**	**(0.24)**	**34.9**	**(0.30)**	**77.7**	**(0.23)**	**92.6**	**(0.14)**

Source: OECD, *TALIS Database.*

StatLink ⌐╗ http://dx.doi.org/10.1787/607807256201

Table 3.3

Teachers who wanted to participate in more development than they did in the previous 18 months (2007-08)

Percentage of teachers of lower secondary education who wanted to take more professional development than they did in the previous 18 months, by certain teacher and school characteristics

	All teachers		Female teachers		Male teachers		Teachers aged under 40 years		Teachers aged 40+ years		Teachers with qualification below ISCED level 5A		Teachers with qualification at ISCED level 5A Bachelor degree		Teachers with qualification at ISCED level 5A Masters degree or higher		Teachers in public schools		Teachers in private schools	
	%	(S.E.)	%	(S.E.)	%	(S.E.)	%	(S.E.)	%	(S.E.)	%	(S.E.)	%	(S.E.)	%	(S.E.)	%	(S.E.)	%	(S.E.)
Australia	55.2	(1.37)	57.9	(1.67)	51.3	(1.89)	59.0	(1.70)	52.5	(1.70)	24.6	(11.05)	55.0	(1.37)	58.9	(2.83)	55.5	(1.49)	54.8	(2.49)
Austria	44.7	(0.93)	46.0	(1.17)	41.9	(1.36)	48.8	(1.83)	43.5	(1.00)	40.3	(1.18)	41.8	(8.01)	51.9	(1.43)	43.9	(1.01)	53.4	(2.05)
Belgium (Fl.)	30.5	(0.98)	32.3	(1.40)	26.5	(2.50)	34.9	(1.22)	25.6	(1.34)	30.4	(1.02)	23.0	(3.04)	36.0	(3.42)	32.7	(1.17)	29.7	(1.36)
Brazil	84.4	(0.77)	85.9	(0.88)	80.5	(1.30)	85.8	(1.05)	82.6	(1.21)	86.4	(2.41)	83.9	(0.85)	83.3	(3.56)	84.8	(0.89)	83.6	(1.52)
Bulgaria	68.9	(1.77)	69.5	(1.62)	65.8	(4.77)	70.9	(2.83)	68.0	(1.87)	67.6	(4.25)	71.6	(3.98)	68.5	(2.33)	68.9	(1.78)	64.5	(12.29)
Denmark	47.6	(1.39)	49.6	(1.93)	44.8	(2.50)	47.3	(2.41)	47.8	(1.90)	18.0	(6.30)	47.8	(1.37)	52.9	(5.58)	48.0	(1.80)	45.8	(3.01)
Estonia	48.7	(1.07)	48.6	(1.16)	49.2	(2.38)	48.3	(1.90)	48.8	(1.26)	48.7	(2.89)	49.8	(1.74)	47.8	(1.49)	48.6	(1.10)	50.4	(9.40)
Hungary	40.2	(2.00)	39.9	(2.45)	41.0	(2.10)	41.1	(3.19)	39.6	(1.81)	39.3	(18.39)	38.6	(2.07)	44.6	(2.22)	40.1	(1.63)	40.3	(5.22)
Iceland	37.9	(1.47)	40.6	(1.93)	32.0	(2.36)	36.3	(2.23)	39.0	(1.84)	36.5	(2.33)	39.4	(1.80)	32.9	(5.74)	37.5	(1.61)	35.0	(12.03)
Ireland	54.1	(1.37)	55.7	(1.54)	50.7	(2.56)	54.8	(1.87)	53.5	(1.61)	46.5	(5.83)	54.6	(1.45)	53.6	(2.85)	53.6	(2.28)	53.8	(1.81)
Italy	56.4	(0.98)	58.4	(1.08)	49.2	(1.78)	57.0	(1.85)	56.2	(1.07)	54.0	(2.38)	62.9	(3.09)	56.1	(1.07)	56.5	(1.03)	48.5	(5.20)
Korea	58.2	(1.16)	60.5	(1.28)	54.1	(1.92)	67.6	(1.57)	52.5	(1.53)	68.1	(13.27)	58.5	(1.42)	57.6	(1.72)	59.6	(1.41)	50.8	(3.98)
Lithuania	44.7	(1.10)	45.4	(1.12)	40.9	(2.80)	47.9	(1.79)	43.3	(1.28)	44.0	(2.18)	45.2	(1.40)	44.2	(1.84)	45.0	(1.10)	31.6	(6.43)
Malaysia	82.9	(0.95)	83.8	(1.10)	81.1	(1.30)	86.5	(1.12)	77.3	(1.28)	75.0	(2.21)	83.9	(1.05)	85.8	(2.12)	83.0	(0.97)	66.9	(11.42)
Malta	43.3	(1.79)	44.4	(2.33)	41.4	(3.10)	42.5	(2.22)	44.6	(3.04)	40.5	(4.26)	43.3	(1.99)	48.0	(5.52)	41.1	(2.44)	47.7	(2.04)
Mexico	85.3	(0.85)	86.3	(1.04)	84.1	(1.15)	88.0	(1.04)	83.3	(1.15)	80.8	(3.10)	86.1	(0.88)	86.6	(2.15)	85.7	(0.80)	84.8	(3.28)
Norway	70.3	(1.13)	72.5	(1.43)	67.1	(1.76)	70.3	(1.72)	70.4	(1.45)	52.6	(12.23)	71.1	(1.36)	68.6	(2.11)	70.6	(1.16)	72.9	(8.17)
Poland	43.6	(1.04)	45.1	(1.28)	38.9	(2.07)	49.5	(1.54)	37.3	(1.26)	40.7	(8.80)	47.5	(4.38)	43.3	(1.07)	43.5	(1.01)	45.2	(7.26)
Portugal	76.2	(0.91)	77.5	(1.04)	73.1	(1.56)	77.3	(1.22)	75.1	(1.43)	70.7	(4.35)	76.0	(0.99)	79.8	(2.52)	77.0	(0.98)	66.0	(3.51)
Slovak Republic	43.2	(1.34)	44.3	(1.37)	38.6	(2.98)	48.4	(1.90)	39.6	(1.78)	38.4	(7.68)	47.3	(15.00)	43.6	(1.40)	42.6	(1.35)	46.3	(3.89)
Slovenia	35.1	(1.18)	34.9	(1.23)	36.0	(2.38)	39.5	(1.82)	32.2	(1.36)	28.8	(1.48)	40.7	(1.50)	36.0	(7.85)	34.9	(1.14)	a	a
Spain	60.6	(1.02)	63.8	(1.28)	56.4	(1.43)	68.6	(1.59)	56.0	(1.29)	47.6	(3.83)	56.5	(2.53)	62.0	(1.16)	60.6	(1.23)	59.5	(2.31)
Turkey	48.2	(2.21)	51.3	(2.13)	44.8	(3.22)	51.2	(2.40)	37.2	(3.56)	26.2	(5.62)	48.8	(2.23)	58.8	(6.69)	48.4	(2.51)	41.6	(3.71)
TALIS average	**54.8**	**(0.27)**	**56.3**	**(0.32)**	**51.7**	**(0.49)**	**57.5**	**(0.40)**	**52.4**	**(0.36)**	**48.1**	**(1.47)**	**55.4**	**(0.85)**	**56.6**	**(0.74)**	**54.9**	**(0.31)**	**53.3**	**(1.26)**

░░░ Denotes categories that include less than 5% of teachers.

Source: OECD, *TALIS Database.*

StatLink ▓▓▒▓ http://dx.doi.org/10.1787/607807256201

Table 3.4

Teachers' high professional development needs (2007-08)

Percentage of teachers of lower secondary education indicating they have a "High level of need"
for professional development in the following areas and overall index of need

	Overall index of development need (Maximum=100)[1]		Content and performance standards		Student assessment practices		Classroom management		Subject field		Instructional practices	
	Index	(S.E.)	%	(S.E.)	%	(S.E.)	%	(S.E.)	%	(S.E.)	%	(S.E.)
Australia	44	(0.35)	8.3	(0.64)	7.5	(0.60)	5.2	(0.52)	5.0	(0.53)	3.6	(0.40)
Austria	51	(0.31)	13.9	(0.69)	12.2	(0.53)	13.6	(0.64)	14.8	(0.59)	18.6	(0.75)
Belgium (Fl.)	47	(0.39)	12.0	(0.65)	15.6	(0.74)	12.1	(0.59)	17.5	(0.74)	14.1	(0.77)
Brazil	58	(0.55)	23.1	(1.31)	21.1	(1.15)	13.7	(0.98)	14.9	(1.06)	14.8	(1.06)
Bulgaria	50	(0.59)	25.7	(2.33)	16.1	(1.45)	12.7	(1.46)	21.2	(1.53)	18.3	(1.67)
Denmark	44	(0.59)	17.1	(1.25)	13.6	(0.97)	2.3	(0.55)	4.6	(0.54)	4.7	(0.57)
Estonia	55	(0.49)	17.7	(0.95)	10.4	(0.65)	13.4	(0.76)	22.6	(1.01)	18.2	(0.78)
Hungary	45	(0.51)	9.2	(0.55)	5.9	(0.51)	3.3	(0.36)	7.4	(0.64)	14.7	(0.81)
Iceland	52	(0.48)	7.3	(0.74)	14.3	(1.00)	11.6	(0.90)	10.3	(0.91)	8.2	(0.76)
Ireland	49	(0.48)	6.7	(0.52)	8.2	(0.77)	6.4	(0.59)	4.1	(0.49)	5.4	(0.60)
Italy	63	(0.30)	17.6	(0.69)	24.0	(0.83)	18.9	(0.84)	34.0	(0.75)	34.9	(0.89)
Korea	70	(0.30)	26.8	(0.92)	21.5	(0.79)	30.3	(0.91)	38.3	(0.96)	39.9	(0.91)
Lithuania	62	(0.41)	39.2	(1.01)	37.3	(1.03)	27.9	(0.96)	43.4	(0.89)	44.5	(0.90)
Malaysia	72	(0.64)	49.8	(1.59)	43.8	(1.43)	41.6	(1.41)	56.8	(1.53)	55.2	(1.47)
Malta	48	(0.57)	8.1	(1.00)	7.2	(0.82)	5.3	(0.78)	6.7	(0.86)	3.9	(0.60)
Mexico	50	(0.59)	13.7	(0.77)	15.0	(0.83)	8.8	(0.66)	11.0	(0.88)	12.3	(0.92)
Norway	55	(0.51)	12.9	(0.85)	21.9	(1.29)	7.7	(0.66)	8.6	(0.70)	8.2	(0.61)
Poland	49	(0.50)	11.9	(0.74)	12.8	(0.77)	17.6	(0.95)	17.0	(0.87)	17.5	(0.75)
Portugal	56	(0.31)	9.8	(0.62)	6.9	(0.51)	5.8	(0.47)	4.8	(0.43)	7.7	(0.54)
Slovak Republic	48	(0.56)	8.2	(0.66)	9.0	(0.57)	9.8	(0.81)	17.2	(0.96)	13.4	(0.89)
Slovenia	57	(0.35)	13.4	(0.67)	22.3	(0.89)	24.0	(0.79)	15.9	(0.78)	19.9	(0.80)
Spain	49	(0.44)	6.0	(0.38)	5.8	(0.42)	8.1	(0.57)	5.0	(0.47)	5.5	(0.39)
Turkey	43	(0.72)	9.8	(0.81)	9.2	(0.90)	6.7	(1.29)	8.9	(0.93)	9.0	(0.92)
TALIS average	**53**	**(0.10)**	**16.0**	**(0.20)**	**15.7**	**(0.19)**	**13.3**	**(0.18)**	**17.0**	**(0.18)**	**17.1**	**(0.18)**

	ICT teaching skills		Teaching special learning needs students		Student discipline and behaviour problems		School management and administration		Teaching in a multicultural setting		Student counselling	
	%	(S.E.)	%	(S.E.)	%	(S.E.)	%	(S.E.)	%	(S.E.)	%	(S.E.)
Australia	17.8	(0.94)	15.1	(0.98)	6.6	(0.71)	5.9	(0.53)	4.0	(0.43)	7.3	(0.61)
Austria	23.8	(0.64)	30.3	(0.94)	32.6	(1.03)	3.9	(0.37)	10.0	(0.68)	13.1	(0.65)
Belgium (Fl.)	14.8	(0.72)	12.8	(0.76)	11.8	(0.71)	2.4	(0.31)	3.7	(0.46)	11.0	(0.68)
Brazil	35.6	(1.33)	63.2	(1.21)	26.5	(1.12)	20.0	(0.78)	33.2	(1.22)	20.7	(1.14)
Bulgaria	26.9	(1.58)	24.4	(1.47)	14.9	(1.82)	8.5	(0.95)	15.5	(2.35)	10.4	(1.30)
Denmark	20.1	(1.67)	24.6	(1.44)	9.8	(1.21)	3.9	(0.49)	7.1	(0.98)	5.5	(0.66)
Estonia	27.9	(0.91)	28.1	(0.95)	23.6	(1.02)	4.6	(0.37)	9.7	(0.77)	21.5	(0.95)
Hungary	23.0	(1.15)	42.0	(1.57)	31.2	(1.50)	3.4	(0.96)	10.7	(0.68)	8.4	(0.83)
Iceland	17.3	(1.08)	23.2	(1.16)	20.0	(0.97)	7.9	(0.84)	14.0	(0.92)	12.9	(0.86)
Ireland	34.2	(1.30)	38.3	(1.32)	13.9	(0.98)	11.8	(0.94)	24.3	(1.31)	24.9	(1.33)
Italy	25.8	(0.81)	35.3	(1.05)	28.3	(1.04)	8.6	(0.49)	25.3	(0.85)	19.7	(0.87)
Korea	17.7	(0.67)	25.6	(0.88)	34.6	(0.92)	10.8	(0.62)	10.4	(0.61)	41.5	(1.04)
Lithuania	36.1	(0.93)	25.4	(0.95)	24.3	(0.89)	9.8	(0.68)	9.8	(0.79)	18.6	(1.09)
Malaysia	43.8	(1.18)	25.9	(1.08)	41.6	(1.41)	29.9	(1.14)	30.3	(1.35)	35.1	(1.21)
Malta	22.8	(1.51)	34.4	(1.56)	10.5	(1.18)	12.9	(1.31)	14.0	(1.36)	15.8	(1.29)
Mexico	24.9	(1.09)	38.8	(1.27)	21.4	(1.04)	11.9	(0.71)	18.2	(0.93)	25.9	(1.12)
Norway	28.1	(1.19)	29.2	(1.04)	16.5	(0.93)	5.8	(0.57)	8.3	(0.75)	7.8	(0.63)
Poland	22.2	(0.90)	29.4	(1.28)	23.5	(0.94)	7.8	(0.57)	6.6	(0.58)	25.4	(1.01)
Portugal	24.2	(0.89)	50.0	(1.06)	17.4	(0.88)	18.2	(0.90)	17.0	(0.73)	8.5	(0.61)
Slovak Republic	14.8	(0.97)	20.1	(0.97)	19.2	(1.26)	4.8	(0.46)	4.6	(0.52)	7.9	(0.58)
Slovenia	25.1	(0.81)	40.4	(1.09)	32.0	(1.04)	7.0	(0.59)	9.9	(0.68)	21.1	(0.83)
Spain	26.2	(1.08)	35.8	(1.04)	18.3	(0.76)	14.2	(0.64)	17.5	(0.73)	12.0	(0.62)
Turkey	14.2	(0.85)	27.8	(1.70)	13.4	(1.44)	9.3	(0.78)	14.5	(1.10)	9.5	(1.16)
TALIS average	**24.7**	**(0.23)**	**31.3**	**(0.25)**	**21.4**	**(0.23)**	**9.7**	**(0.15)**	**13.9**	**(0.21)**	**16.7**	**(0.20)**

1. Index derived from aggregating the development need for each teacher over all of the aspects of their work: 3 points for a high level of need; 2 points for a moderate level of need, 1 point for a low level of need and no points for cases where teachers noted no development need at all. These were then aggregated and divided by the maximum possible score of 33 and multiplied by 100.

Source: OECD, *TALIS Database*.

StatLink ᴍᴸ﹖ http://dx.doi.org/10.1787/607807256201

Table 3.5

Support for professional development undertaken by teachers (2007-08)

Percentage of those teachers of lower secondary education who undertook professional development and received the following types of support

| | Teacher contribution to the cost of professional development undertaken | | | | | | Teacher received scheduled time | | Teacher received salary supplement | |
| | Paid none of the costs | | Paid some of the costs | | Paid all of the costs | | | | | |
	%	(S.E.)	%	(S.E.)	%	(S.E.)	%	(S.E.)	%	(S.E.)
Australia	74.5	(1.24)	24.3	(1.24)	1.2	(0.26)	85.5	(0.86)	5.5	(0.57)
Austria	43.7	(1.00)	49.7	(1.01)	6.6	(0.45)	89.0	(0.72)	11.7	(0.68)
Belgium (Fl.)	81.4	(1.32)	15.3	(1.10)	3.2	(0.46)	78.1	(1.63)	2.2	(0.49)
Brazil	54.8	(1.59)	26.9	(1.36)	18.3	(1.22)	56.2	(1.67)	10.9	(0.88)
Bulgaria	73.4	(2.06)	20.5	(2.16)	6.1	(0.68)	40.4	(1.88)	8.1	(0.91)
Denmark	77.3	(1.45)	16.3	(1.13)	6.4	(0.93)	71.8	(2.34)	9.2	(1.64)
Estonia	72.5	(0.98)	25.6	(0.93)	2.0	(0.28)	64.2	(1.37)	12.0	(0.88)
Hungary	71.5	(1.99)	20.5	(1.76)	8.0	(0.76)	44.4	(2.95)	5.9	(0.85)
Iceland	67.8	(1.34)	27.8	(1.42)	4.5	(0.61)	70.3	(1.39)	17.9	(1.24)
Ireland	79.3	(1.03)	17.5	(0.99)	3.2	(0.46)	94.7	(0.53)	5.8	(0.67)
Italy	68.7	(1.04)	13.7	(0.65)	17.6	(0.78)	30.9	(1.38)	9.6	(0.74)
Korea	27.1	(1.07)	58.5	(1.06)	14.4	(0.79)	24.3	(0.94)	19.8	(1.02)
Lithuania	65.2	(1.75)	30.0	(1.48)	4.8	(0.57)	69.1	(1.26)	6.5	(0.58)
Malaysia	43.5	(1.52)	52.7	(1.54)	3.9	(0.38)	88.6	(0.80)	2.5	(0.31)
Malta	87.1	(1.29)	10.6	(1.18)	2.2	(0.51)	78.2	(1.62)	48.7	(1.94)
Mexico	43.2	(1.31)	38.0	(1.12)	18.8	(1.14)	71.1	(1.52)	2.9	(0.45)
Norway	79.8	(1.14)	17.0	(1.05)	3.3	(0.44)	66.3	(1.56)	7.2	(0.74)
Poland	44.2	(1.30)	45.1	(1.12)	10.7	(0.85)	57.0	(1.68)	5.4	(0.61)
Portugal	50.3	(1.43)	25.2	(1.14)	24.5	(1.24)	25.1	(1.68)	2.0	(0.33)
Slovak Republic	70.4	(1.37)	24.1	(1.21)	5.5	(0.57)	69.2	(1.47)	28.3	(1.72)
Slovenia	85.3	(0.91)	13.7	(0.87)	1.0	(0.22)	79.3	(1.28)	29.7	(1.18)
Spain	54.8	(1.33)	29.6	(1.00)	15.6	(0.87)	29.5	(1.48)	3.3	(0.41)
Turkey	82.9	(1.87)	12.1	(1.90)	5.0	(0.95)	61.2	(2.96)	6.9	(1.19)
TALIS average	**65.2**	**(0.29)**	**26.7**	**(0.27)**	**8.1**	**(0.15)**	**62.8**	**(0.34)**	**11.4**	**(0.20)**

Source: OECD, *TALIS Database.*
StatLink 📊 http://dx.doi.org/10.1787/607807256201

Table 3.6

Frequency of mentoring and induction programmes (2007-08)

Percentage of teachers of lower secondary education whose school principal reported the existence of induction processes and mentoring programmes for teachers new to the school

| | Existence of formal induction process in school | | | | | | Existence of a mentoring programme or policy in school | | | | | |
| | Yes, for all teachers new to the school | | Yes but only for those in their first teaching job | | No formal induction process | | Yes, for all teachers new to the school | | Yes but only for those in their first teaching job | | No formal mentoring process | |
	%	(S.E.)	%	(S.E.)	%	(S.E.)	%	(S.E.)	%	(S.E.)	%	(S.E.)
Australia	93.1	(2.41)	5.6	(2.21)	1.3	(0.96)	70.4	(4.59)	23.8	(4.27)	5.8	(1.84)
Austria	32.1	(3.15)	23.6	(2.61)	44.3	(2.99)	23.0	(2.73)	23.0	(2.64)	54.1	(3.24)
Belgium (Fl.)	94.4	(1.69)	3.9	(1.21)	1.7	(1.08)	90.5	(2.08)	8.8	(2.02)	0.7	(0.49)
Brazil	19.8	(2.38)	6.5	(1.42)	73.7	(2.46)	17.7	(2.11)	11.7	(2.03)	70.7	(2.91)
Bulgaria	53.2	(4.94)	30.7	(6.13)	16.2	(3.85)	29.6	(3.95)	53.5	(4.87)	16.9	(3.51)
Denmark	47.7	(5.22)	23.5	(4.51)	28.8	(3.81)	62.6	(4.52)	27.0	(3.77)	10.4	(2.65)
Estonia	23.1	(3.68)	59.1	(4.19)	17.8	(3.14)	25.8	(3.49)	64.9	(3.81)	9.2	(1.98)
Hungary	34.8	(5.06)	46.4	(5.26)	18.8	(3.46)	44.8	(4.50)	44.2	(4.68)	11.0	(2.40)
Iceland	72.8	(0.17)	15.7	(0.13)	11.5	(0.12)	44.7	(0.17)	48.4	(0.16)	6.9	(0.04)
Ireland	83.7	(3.67)	7.2	(2.68)	9.0	(2.64)	63.8	(4.21)	10.7	(2.44)	25.5	(4.10)
Italy	36.6	(2.87)	34.4	(2.91)	29.0	(2.81)	26.3	(2.70)	61.3	(2.99)	12.4	(2.16)
Korea	33.6	(3.33)	49.8	(3.75)	16.6	(3.03)	26.8	(3.76)	44.3	(4.37)	29.0	(4.18)
Lithuania	17.1	(2.61)	14.0	(2.49)	68.9	(3.26)	29.0	(3.59)	50.6	(4.08)	20.4	(3.13)
Malaysia	43.0	(3.62)	40.9	(4.00)	16.2	(2.87)	45.0	(3.71)	38.1	(3.82)	16.9	(2.61)
Malta	25.3	(0.17)	11.8	(0.11)	62.9	(0.18)	22.4	(0.18)	12.3	(0.12)	65.3	(0.20)
Mexico	22.7	(3.35)	14.7	(2.91)	62.6	(3.94)	19.2	(3.47)	20.4	(3.52)	60.5	(4.14)
Norway	29.9	(3.83)	18.3	(3.25)	51.8	(4.27)	43.3	(3.85)	25.4	(3.67)	31.3	(3.67)
Poland	14.3	(3.13)	79.4	(3.63)	6.3	(2.15)	23.5	(3.97)	71.9	(4.32)	4.6	(1.87)
Portugal	73.1	(3.52)	4.2	(1.69)	22.7	(3.20)	41.3	(4.48)	20.4	(3.53)	38.3	(4.32)
Slovak Republic	62.1	(3.85)	35.5	(3.67)	2.4	(1.53)	26.4	(4.06)	71.3	(4.22)	2.4	(1.32)
Slovenia	41.1	(3.83)	51.5	(4.06)	7.4	(2.01)	23.5	(3.35)	64.6	(4.02)	11.9	(2.65)
Spain	20.9	(3.22)	15.7	(2.71)	63.4	(3.70)	17.6	(2.77)	18.1	(2.74)	64.3	(3.60)
Turkey	50.2	(5.27)	16.2	(4.04)	33.6	(5.10)	22.3	(4.85)	69.6	(5.51)	8.1	(3.22)
TALIS average	**44.5**	**(0.73)**	**26.5**	**(0.70)**	**29.0**	**(0.62)**	**36.5**	**(0.75)**	**38.4**	**(0.76)**	**25.1**	**(0.60)**

Source: OECD, *TALIS Database.*
StatLink 📊 http://dx.doi.org/10.1787/607807256201

Table 3.7

Reasons for not participating in more professional development (2007-08)
Percentage of teachers of lower secondary education who wanted more professional development and gave the following reasons for not undertaking more

	Reason for not undertaking more professional development										
	Did not have the pre-requisites		Too expensive		Lack of employer support		Conflict with work schedule		Family responsibilities		No suitable professional development	
	%	(S.E.)	%	(S.E.)	%	(S.E.)	%	(S.E.)	%	(S.E.)	%	(S.E.)
Australia	3.2	(0.59)	32.6	(1.61)	26.5	(1.52)	61.7	(1.93)	27.6	(1.73)	40.5	(1.80)
Austria	2.6	(0.46)	18.0	(0.93)	9.3	(0.79)	41.5	(1.34)	29.0	(1.21)	64.2	(1.15)
Belgium (Fl.)	3.6	(0.86)	11.8	(1.33)	10.9	(1.40)	43.2	(1.69)	40.6	(1.70)	38.8	(1.73)
Brazil	5.1	(0.46)	51.0	(1.46)	24.6	(1.35)	57.8	(1.46)	18.4	(0.92)	27.0	(1.22)
Bulgaria	7.0	(1.61)	34.6	(2.41)	2.9	(0.47)	24.4	(1.46)	16.6	(1.22)	48.3	(2.35)
Denmark	1.8	(0.44)	29.6	(1.94)	38.3	(1.76)	23.7	(1.90)	15.4	(1.21)	42.1	(1.99)
Estonia	4.2	(0.62)	35.1	(1.59)	15.3	(1.30)	60.5	(1.65)	25.2	(1.35)	52.3	(1.61)
Hungary	5.6	(0.85)	46.9	(2.40)	23.0	(1.90)	40.3	(1.88)	24.5	(1.77)	25.9	(1.89)
Iceland	1.8	(0.70)	18.6	(1.61)	6.7	(1.18)	43.0	(2.41)	35.4	(1.99)	47.0	(2.36)
Ireland	5.5	(0.75)	12.2	(0.96)	13.9	(1.47)	42.6	(1.53)	29.4	(1.57)	45.2	(1.83)
Italy	5.1	(0.44)	23.5	(1.23)	5.8	(0.50)	43.1	(1.47)	40.8	(1.38)	47.2	(1.37)
Korea	11.9	(0.95)	19.9	(0.98)	8.7	(0.93)	73.3	(1.26)	32.7	(1.30)	42.2	(1.28)
Lithuania	7.7	(0.90)	25.7	(1.45)	15.9	(1.19)	46.7	(1.63)	26.4	(1.20)	53.2	(1.60)
Malaysia	28.4	(1.38)	22.2	(1.41)	13.7	(1.14)	58.9	(1.30)	31.3	(1.32)	45.9	(1.25)
Malta	4.7	(1.06)	18.4	(2.06)	10.2	(1.73)	38.8	(2.37)	45.4	(2.85)	40.5	(2.84)
Mexico	17.2	(1.07)	49.0	(1.48)	21.1	(1.01)	48.7	(1.31)	37.4	(1.29)	20.3	(0.97)
Norway	2.5	(0.38)	31.6	(1.36)	26.4	(1.79)	50.4	(1.44)	26.5	(1.37)	30.0	(1.36)
Poland	3.4	(0.51)	51.2	(1.72)	12.3	(1.20)	40.7	(1.90)	32.6	(1.63)	38.7	(1.84)
Portugal	6.5	(0.63)	36.3	(1.14)	10.4	(0.66)	65.5	(1.26)	35.6	(1.28)	48.2	(1.23)
Slovak Republic	9.5	(0.96)	18.8	(1.48)	12.8	(1.32)	38.2	(1.95)	20.6	(1.35)	58.0	(1.81)
Slovenia	3.7	(0.74)	35.9	(1.57)	18.2	(1.48)	47.8	(1.75)	22.3	(1.25)	32.6	(1.52)
Spain	6.7	(0.67)	19.2	(0.99)	6.3	(0.66)	50.3	(1.23)	48.4	(1.43)	38.4	(1.25)
Turkey	16.9	(2.03)	12.4	(1.48)	11.9	(1.51)	34.7	(3.47)	31.2	(2.68)	46.6	(2.22)
TALIS average	**7.2**	**(0.19)**	**28.5**	**(0.32)**	**15.0**	**(0.27)**	**46.8**	**(0.37)**	**30.1**	**(0.33)**	**42.3**	**(0.36)**

Source: OECD, *TALIS Database.*
StatLink http://dx.doi.org/10.1787/607807256201

Table 3.8

Impact of different types of professional development undertaken by teachers (2007-08)
Percentage of teachers of lower secondary education reporting that the professional development undertaken in the previous 18 months had a moderate or high impact upon their development as teachers

	Courses and workshops		Education conferences and seminars		Qualification programmes		Observation visits to other schools		Professional development network		Individual and collaborative research		Mentoring and peer observation		Reading professional literature		Informal dialogue to improve teaching	
	%	(S.E.)	%	(S.E.)	%	(S.E.)	%	(S.E.)	%	(S.E.)	%	(S.E.)	%	(S.E.)	%	(S.E.)	%	(S.E.)
Australia	78.5	(1.04)	67.6	(1.32)	78.6	(2.67)	72.2	(2.26)	73.5	(1.27)	85.8	(1.53)	72.5	(1.40)	66.4	(1.28)	86.0	(0.85)
Austria	75.7	(0.89)	55.5	(1.24)	89.0	(1.21)	61.0	(2.99)	68.6	(1.33)	88.4	(0.96)	72.7	(1.63)	82.4	(0.69)	84.9	(0.71)
Belgium (Fl.)	52.9	(1.26)	42.6	(1.82)	67.0	(2.01)	47.0	(2.84)	53.9	(1.92)	67.6	(1.52)	48.1	(2.64)	57.8	(1.20)	71.7	(1.05)
Brazil	76.1	(1.07)	72.9	(1.32)	89.9	(0.93)	67.5	(1.49)	73.4	(1.91)	80.9	(1.26)	65.8	(1.66)	82.6	(1.09)	76.5	(0.99)
Bulgaria	84.2	(1.58)	80.6	(1.67)	88.0	(2.06)	79.3	(3.00)	86.2	(1.83)	87.1	(1.70)	86.0	(1.68)	92.3	(1.21)	86.3	(1.20)
Denmark	86.0	(0.96)	82.9	(1.70)	96.8	(1.18)	83.6	(3.34)	88.1	(1.32)	94.6	(0.86)	78.7	(3.45)	84.9	(1.14)	92.8	(0.89)
Estonia	86.4	(0.74)	70.4	(1.52)	90.4	(0.99)	69.9	(1.27)	84.3	(1.06)	90.5	(1.04)	76.8	(1.58)	87.3	(0.70)	81.8	(0.94)
Hungary	86.0	(1.04)	78.2	(1.46)	93.1	(0.93)	81.4	(1.74)	84.8	(1.11)	93.8	(1.30)	91.1	(1.00)	92.6	(0.78)	92.9	(0.89)
Iceland	83.0	(1.13)	73.7	(1.75)	92.4	(1.76)	80.5	(1.37)	90.6	(0.85)	94.2	(1.70)	77.8	(2.09)	88.7	(0.97)	91.8	(0.85)
Ireland	81.9	(0.96)	74.5	(1.55)	92.5	(1.53)	81.0	(4.35)	78.7	(1.36)	86.8	(1.41)	71.3	(2.81)	71.0	(1.55)	83.0	(1.00)
Italy	81.9	(1.17)	78.5	(1.16)	86.8	(1.58)	82.6	(2.06)	86.6	(1.06)	95.1	(0.45)	86.9	(1.03)	90.9	(0.60)	90.6	(0.47)
Korea	79.2	(0.87)	75.1	(1.36)	84.2	(1.37)	65.2	(1.15)	85.4	(1.01)	89.9	(0.82)	69.5	(1.17)	77.4	(1.22)	85.8	(0.67)
Lithuania	91.4	(0.62)	83.2	(1.03)	88.2	(1.26)	90.7	(0.81)	90.0	(0.94)	91.4	(0.78)	85.2	(1.24)	96.2	(0.41)	92.0	(0.64)
Malaysia	94.4	(0.48)	89.1	(1.05)	95.0	(0.88)	87.6	(1.30)	90.3	(0.97)	88.8	(1.17)	89.9	(0.89)	86.4	(0.78)	92.2	(0.49)
Malta	73.9	(1.65)	70.0	(2.47)	94.4	(1.56)	69.8	(3.87)	75.2	(2.45)	89.8	(1.57)	67.8	(3.78)	78.1	(1.83)	84.3	(1.29)
Mexico	85.4	(0.77)	82.2	(1.54)	91.3	(1.03)	77.7	(1.65)	81.3	(1.69)	91.0	(0.69)	78.3	(1.59)	84.0	(0.98)	81.6	(0.92)
Norway	79.3	(0.96)	73.7	(1.46)	93.7	(1.24)	71.9	(2.39)	81.1	(1.83)	95.3	(1.39)	77.9	(2.62)	78.1	(0.93)	95.7	(0.44)
Poland	86.3	(0.73)	75.8	(1.31)	92.1	(0.97)	78.2	(2.29)	88.3	(0.91)	92.8	(0.90)	77.9	(1.11)	93.4	(0.49)	90.0	(0.70)
Portugal	82.8	(0.88)	73.0	(1.38)	87.0	(1.12)	67.4	(1.82)	80.7	(2.04)	94.0	(0.76)	87.6	(1.84)	78.9	(1.04)	88.1	(0.68)
Slovak Republic	75.5	(1.57)	75.9	(1.44)	83.0	(1.43)	66.0	(2.02)	78.0	(1.93)	83.8	(3.72)	78.6	(1.10)	88.8	(1.03)	85.9	(0.85)
Slovenia	83.3	(0.73)	78.6	(0.91)	80.2	(2.43)	77.3	(2.74)	64.1	(1.30)	89.9	(1.44)	76.1	(1.53)	81.5	(0.85)	87.0	(0.74)
Spain	76.5	(0.94)	71.8	(1.75)	73.1	(1.97)	76.2	(2.31)	81.5	(1.49)	89.9	(0.89)	81.1	(1.49)	74.4	(1.01)	80.2	(0.74)
Turkey	72.9	(1.78)	74.1	(1.65)	79.3	(3.77)	87.8	(1.99)	80.5	(1.43)	92.3	(2.11)	84.8	(1.77)	91.3	(1.17)	92.8	(1.01)
TALIS average	**80.6**	**(0.23)**	**73.9**	**(0.31)**	**87.2**	**(0.35)**	**74.9**	**(0.50)**	**80.2**	**(0.31)**	**89.3**	**(0.30)**	**77.6**	**(0.41)**	**82.8**	**(0.22)**	**86.7**	**(0.18)**

Source: OECD, *TALIS Database.*
StatLink http://dx.doi.org/10.1787/607807256201

CHAPTER 4

Teaching Practices, Teachers' Beliefs and Attitudes

Highlights

- Teachers are more inclined to regard students as active participants in the process of acquiring knowledge than to see the teacher's main role as the transmission of information and demonstration of "correct solutions". This is most true in northwest Europe, Scandinavia, Australia and Korea and least true in southern Europe, Brazil and Malaysia where teachers fall between the two views.

- In the classroom, teachers in all countries put greater emphasis on ensuring that learning is well structured than on student-oriented activities which give them more autonomy. Both of these teaching practices are emphasised more than enhanced learning activities such as project work. This pattern is true in every country.

- Co-operation by teachers in all countries more commonly takes the form of exchanging and co-ordinating ideas and information than direct professional collaboration such as team teaching.

- At least half of teachers in most countries spend over 80% of their lesson time on teaching and learning. However, one in four teachers in most countries lose at least 30% of their lesson time, and some lose more than half, through disruptions and administrative tasks. This is closely associated with the classroom disciplinary climate. Country and school differences in this respect are less important than differences among teachers within schools.

- Almost all Norwegian teachers report better than average relationships between teachers and students. In other countries, teacher-student relationships vary considerably. Only part of this variation is related to differences among schools. Even though teacher-student relations are often seen as a feature of schools as a whole, different teachers within schools perceive them differently.

- The average levels of job satisfaction and of teachers' belief in their own effectiveness are fairly similar across countries, although Norwegian teachers again stand out as well above average in both respects. Most differences in these job-related attitudes entail differences among teachers within countries and within schools.

- Female teachers are less likely than male teachers to see teaching as the direct transmission of knowledge and are more likely to adopt structuring and student oriented practices as well as to co-operate more with colleagues.

- Teachers who undertake professional development undertake a wider array of teaching practices and are more likely to co-operate with other teachers.

INTRODUCTION

Teachers' beliefs, practices and attitudes are important for understanding and improving educational processes. They are closely linked to teachers' strategies for coping with challenges in their daily professional life and to their general well-being, and they shape students' learning environment and influence student motivation and achievement. Furthermore they can be expected to mediate the effects of job-related policies – such as changes in curricula for teachers' initial education or professional development – on student learning. TALIS examines a variety of beliefs, practices and attitudes which previous research has shown to be relevant to the improvement and effectiveness of schools. Using representative data from 23 countries, this chapter presents a cross-cultural comparative analysis of profiles, variations and interrelationships of these aspects as they shape teachers' working environment.

The first part of the chapter describes teachers' beliefs, practices and attitudes and shows that in all participating countries certain beliefs and practices are more prominent than others. It also highlights cross-cultural differences regarding beliefs and practices, the quality of the learning environment, the strength of teachers' beliefs in their own efficacy ("self-efficacy"), and their job satisfaction. The second part of the chapter focuses on the relations between teachers' views of learning and instruction and the school as their place of work. Some findings are remarkably consistent across countries.

THEORETICAL BACKGROUND AND ANALYTICAL FRAMEWORK

TALIS examines teachers' beliefs, attitudes and practices and compares teachers, schools and countries. Although TALIS does not seek to explain student achievement or changes in achievement, student motivation or changes in motivation, it highlights factors which have been shown to be related to student outcomes.

Many studies have described aspects of teaching practice which are related to effective classroom learning and student outcomes (Brophy and Good, 1986; Wang, Haertel and Walberg, 1993). Close monitoring, adequate pacing and classroom management as well as clarity of presentation, well-structured lessons and informative and encouraging feedback – known as key aspects of "direct instruction"– have generally been shown to have a positive impact on student achievement. This is not enough, however; while the teacher provides learning opportunities, these must be recognised and utilised by the student to be effective. Motivation, goals and outcomes have to be taken into account as well. Therefore, the framework of instructional quality is broader than the direct instruction described above. Based on results from the TIMSS video study, Klieme *et al.* (2006) proposed three basic (second-order) dimensions of instructional quality: clear and well-structured classroom management (which includes key components of direct instruction), student orientation (including a supportive climate and individualised instruction), and cognitive activation (including the use of deep content, higher order thinking tasks and other demanding activities). These dimensions are to be understood as "latent" factors which are related to, but not identical with specific instructional practices (see Lipowsky *et al.*, 2008, for a theoretical foundation and an empirical test of the model). TALIS uses a domain-general version of this triarchic model, identifying structure, student orientation, and enhanced activities as basic dimensions of teaching practices.

Instructional practices, in turn, depend on what teachers bring to the classroom. Professional competence is believed to be a crucial factor in classroom and school practices (Shulman, 1987, Campbell *et al.,* 2004; Baumert and Kunter, 2006). To study this, a number of authors have used, for example, measures of the effects of constructivist compared with "reception/direct transmission" beliefs on teaching and learning, developed by Peterson *et al.* (1989). TALIS uses a domain-general version of two teaching and learning-related indices (constructivist and direct transmission) to cover teachers' beliefs and basic understanding of the nature of teaching and learning.

Teachers' professional knowledge and actual practices may differ not only among countries but also among teachers within a country. To gain an understanding of the prevalence of certain beliefs and practices it is therefore important to examine how they relate to the characteristics of teachers and classrooms. For example, previous research suggests that the beliefs and practices of female and male teachers may systematically differ (*e.g.* Singer, 1996), so that TALIS must control for gender. From the perspective of education policy, however, it is even more relevant to look at the impact on teachers' beliefs, practices and attitudes of professional background factors such as type of training, certification and professional development, subject taught, employment status (part-time versus full-time) and length of tenure. It is important to note that any of these relationships can have different causal interpretations. For example, professional development activities may change beliefs and attitudes, but participation in such activities may itself be due to certain beliefs. As a cross-sectional study, TALIS can describe such relationships, but it cannot disentangle causal direction. Some of the analyses TALIS provides on these matters are merely exploratory, because so far there is little research, for example, on beliefs and practices specific to certain subjects.

Good instruction, of course, is not determined just by the teacher's background, beliefs and attitudes; it should also be responsive to students' needs and various student, classroom and school background factors. TALIS looks at whether teaching practices "adapt" to students' social and language background, grade level, achievement level, and class size. For example studies on aptitude-treatment interactions suggest that students with low intellectual abilities profit more from structured, teacher-centred instruction, while students with high intellectual abilities may gain more from less structured and more complex instruction (Snow and Lohman, 1984). TALIS does not allow for examining whether classroom practices are adapted to individual students but instead looks at macro-adaptivity (Cronbach, 1957), *i.e.* the adaptation of teaching practices to characteristics of the class.

Teachers do not act only in the classroom where they instruct students more or less in isolation from other classes and teachers. A modern view of teaching also includes professional activities on the school level, such as co-operating in teams, building professional learning communities, participating in school development, and evaluating and changing working conditions (Darling-Hammond *et al.* 2005). These activities shape the learning environment on the school level, *i.e.* the school climate, ethos and culture, and thus directly and indirectly (via classroom-level processes) affect student learning. TALIS distinguishes between two kinds of co-operation by a school's teaching staff: exchange and co-ordination for teaching (*e.g.* exchanging instructional material or discussing learning problems of individual students) versus more general and more innovative kinds of professional collaboration (*e.g.* observing other teachers' classes and giving feedback). It is assumed that both kinds of co-operative activities will be influenced by school-level context variables such as a school's teacher evaluation policies and the school's leadership, which are covered in chapters 5 and 6 respectively of this report.

As is known from research on the effectiveness of schools (Scheerens and Bosker, 1997; Hopkins, 2005; Lee and Williams, 2006; Harris and Chrispeels, 2006), the quality of the learning environment is the factor affecting student learning and outcomes that is most readily modified, given that background variables such as cognitive and motivational capacities, socio-economic background, social and cultural capital are mostly beyond the control of teachers and schools. TALIS captures students' background by asking teachers and principals about the social composition and the relative achievement level of the student population they serve. A more important task for TALIS is to assess quality, as perceived by teachers, at the classroom as well as the school level. However, as the environment generally varies between subjects and teachers, it is not easy to identify domain-general indicators. TALIS uses *time on task* – *i.e.* the proportion of lesson time that is actually used for teaching and learning – as a basic indicator for the quality of the learning environment. Also, *classroom climate* is used because of its strong impact on cognitive as well as motivational aspects of student learning in different subjects. The method used here is adapted from PISA and focuses on the disciplinary aspect. For example, the statement "When the lesson begins, I have to wait quite a long time for the students to quiet down" indicates a low level of classroom discipline. It has been shown that classroom discipline, aggregated to the school level, is a core element of instructional quality. In PISA, it is positively related to the school's mean student achievement in many participating countries (Klieme and Rakoczy, 2003). Also, it has been shown that – unlike other features of classroom instruction – there is a high level of agreement about this indicator among teachers, students and observers (Clausen, 2002). In addition to the environment at the classroom level, *school climate* is used as an indicator for the school environment. Here, school climate is defined as the quality of social relations between students and teachers (including the quality of support teachers give to students), which is known to have a direct influence on motivational factors, such as student commitment to school, learning motivation and student satisfaction, and perhaps a more indirect influence on student achievement (see Cohen, 2006, for a review of related research). The triarchic model of instructional quality mentioned above (Klieme *et al.*, 2006; Lipowsky *et al.*, 2008; Rakoczy *et al.*, 2007) suggests specific relations between teaching practices and the two climate factors: structure-oriented teaching practices should primarily relate to high levels of classroom climate, while student-oriented practices should be linked with positive social relations.

Figure 4.1

Framework for the analysis of teaching practices and beliefs

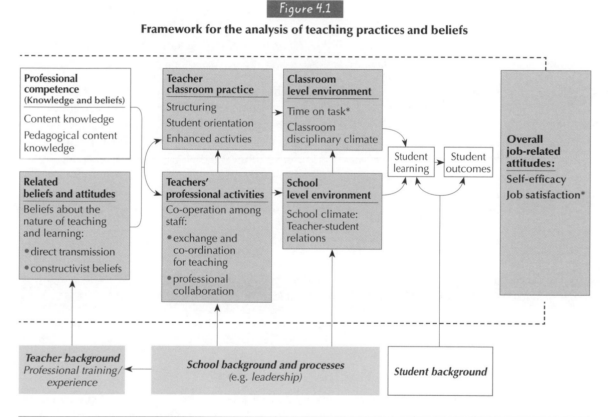

Note: Constructs that are covered by the survey are highlighted in blue; single item measures are indicated by an asterisk (*).
Source: OECD, *TALIS Database*.

TALIS does not address the ultimate effects of classroom and school-level activities and climate on student learning and outcomes. However, because TALIS studies teachers (as opposed to the effectiveness of education), teachers were asked to evaluate what they themselves do. TALIS assessed teachers' beliefs about their efficacy by adopting a construct and a related measurement that is widely used in educational research (*e.g.* Schwarzer, Schmitz and Daytner, 1999). As a second indicator, TALIS used a single item for overall job satisfaction. Research has shown that teachers' sense of their efficacy plays a crucial role in sustaining their job satisfaction (*e.g.* Caprara *et al.*, 2006). It has also been found to be associated with constructivist goals and student orientation (Wheatley, 2005) and with successful management of classroom problems and keeping students on task (*e.g.* Chacon, 2005; Podell and Soodak, 1993). Thus, previous research suggests that there are significant relations between teachers' beliefs, attitudes and practices.

In summary, TALIS is able to cover core aspects of teachers' beliefs (general pedagogical knowledge), teachers' activities (teaching practices and teachers' co-operation) as well as quality indicators at the classroom level (classroom disciplinary climate, time on task) and at the school level (quality of social relations) and general job-related attitudes. Based on previous research, these aspects are expected to be related. Figure 4.1 illustrates the choice of constructs for this chapter and their supposed interactions.

Chapter outline

The following sections of this chapter are organised along the model described in Figure 4.1. Moving from the left (general pedagogical beliefs) to the right (overall job-related attitudes), each group (box) of variables is discussed by describing country profiles and – where appropriate – comparing country means. These results are presented in the first six sections of the chapter.

The chapter then explores the associations between background factors (such as kind of training, certification and professional development, subject taught, gender, employment status, and length of tenure) and beliefs, practices and attitudes. For teaching practices, both teacher background and classroom context are taken into account: Are teaching practices "adaptive" with regard to students' social and language background, grade level, achievement level, and class size? This section also contains a first attempt to use TALIS data to understand conditions for successful schooling and teaching within countries. This involves systematic tests of the hypotheses that are implied by the model (see Figure 4.1) and previous research. Working from left to right, the relationships between beliefs, attitudes and practices and activities are tested. Ultimately, multiple regressions and multi-level models are used to attempt to understand how job-related attitudes ("self-efficacy" and job satisfaction as proximal indicators for professional success) and the perceived quality of the learning environment (classroom and school climate) relate to teachers' professional beliefs and activities. The focus is on relations and effects that hold across or in a majority of countries. Single countries or groups of countries with specific patterns are identified when they help to understand certain profiles of beliefs, practices, and attitudes in those countries.

The final section of the chapter summarises the results of the analysis and discusses some policy implications of the findings.

BELIEFS ABOUT THE NATURE OF TEACHING AND LEARNING

The beliefs about the nature of teaching and learning which are the focus of TALIS include "direct transmission beliefs about learning and instruction" and "constructivist beliefs about learning and instruction". These dimensions of these beliefs are well established in educational research at least in Western countries and have also received support elsewhere (*e.g.* Kim, 2005).

The **direct transmission view** of student learning implies that a teachers' role is to communicate knowledge in a clear and structured way, to explain correct solutions, to give students clear and resolvable problems, and to ensure calm and concentration in the classroom. In contrast, a **constructivist view** focuses on students not as passive recipients but as active participants in the process of acquiring knowledge. Teachers holding this view emphasise facilitating student inquiry, prefer to give students the chance to develop solutions to problems on their own, and allow students to play active role in instructional activities. Here, the development of thinking and reasoning processes is stressed more than the acquisition of specific knowledge (Staub and Stern, 2002).

It is important to note the difference between beliefs on the one hand, and practices, on the other. Both practices and beliefs are shaped by pedagogical and cultural traditions. They represent different though related parts of the pedagogical context for student learning.

In TALIS, beliefs about teaching were assessed on a four-point Likert scale, ranging from 1 = "strongly disagree" to 4 = "strongly agree". Across countries, the basic dimensions for teacher beliefs about instruction – the direct transmission view and the constructivist view - were identified from the survey responses. Box 4.1 lists the questionnaire items from which the two indices for teachers' beliefs about teaching were constructed (See Annex A1.1 for full details.)

Box 4.1 Teachers' beliefs about teaching

The two indices for teachers' beliefs about teaching comprise the following questionnaire items:

Direct transmission beliefs about teaching

- Effective/good teachers demonstrate the correct way to solve a problem.
- Instruction should be built around problems with clear, correct answers, and around ideas that most students can grasp quickly.
- How much students learn depends on how much background knowledge they have; that is why teaching facts is so necessary.
- A quiet classroom is generally needed for effective learning.

Constructivist beliefs about teaching

- My role as a teacher is to facilitate students' own inquiry.
- Students learn best by finding solutions to problems on their own.
- Students should be allowed to think of solutions to practical problems themselves before the teacher shows them how they are solved.
- Thinking and reasoning processes are more important than specific curriculum content.

Box 4.2 Cross-cultural validity of the indices for teachers' beliefs, practices and attitudes

The cross-cultural comparability – or "invariance" – of the indices for teaching practices, teachers' beliefs and attitudes, which are the feature of this chapter, was tested by means of confirmatory factor analysis (see Annex A1.1 and the *TALIS Technical Report* [forthcoming]).

For the indices measuring *teaching beliefs*, *classroom teaching practices* and *co-operation among teaching staff*, the analysis indicated that the country means on these indices are not directly comparable. The analysis of these indices therefore focuses more on the pattern of cross-cultural differences than on specific country-by-country comparisons. Within-country differences are examined through the calculation of ipsative scores (see Box 4.3).

For the indices measuring *classroom disciplinary climate*, *teacher self-efficacy* and *teacher-student relations* – the variables that best represent outcome variables in TALIS – although full cross-cultural comparability of the indices was not proven, the results were sufficiently close to allow an examination of the global picture of mean score differences.

As with the indices in Chapter 6, analysis was conducted to test for cross-cultural consistency of the indices on teaching practices, teachers' beliefs and attitudes (see Annex A1.1 and the *TALIS Technical Report* [forthcoming]). Box 4.2 summarises the outcomes of that analysis. For the indices on beliefs about teaching, the analysis indicated that countries' mean scores on these indices are not directly comparable. The analysis in this section therefore focuses on profiles within countries and in particular on the extent to which teachers endorse one belief over the other. To do this, teachers' responses are standardised and presented as *ipsative scores,* which describe the relative endorsement of the two indices (see Box 4.3).

Box 4.3 Computation of ipsative scores

Calculating ipsative scores is an approach to standardising individual responses to express them as preferences between two or more options and thus helps reduce the effects of response bias (Fischer, 2004). For teachers' beliefs about instruction, ipsative scores were computed by subtracting the individual mean across all of the eight items measuring teachers' beliefs from the individual mean across the four items belonging to the index *direct transmission beliefs about instruction* and also from the four items measuring *constructivist beliefs about instruction.* Thus, mean scores were calculated for both indices and corrected for the overall tendency to accept any of the belief items. The means across both indices average zero for each teacher, and therefore the country means across both indices also equal zero. The resulting score of an individual teacher is the relative endorsement of this index or the relative position of the individual on one index in relation to the other index. Positive score values indicate that one set of beliefs receives a relatively stronger support than the other.

Country differences in profiles of beliefs about instruction

In research and practice there is an ongoing debate about the effects of direct transmission versus constructivist approaches on student achievement, and about the appropriateness of constructivist approaches in non-European countries. TALIS data make it possible to conduct exploratory comparative analysis to learn whether countries differ with regard to profiles of teachers' beliefs. Differences in national cultures and pedagogical traditions suggest the possibility of differences in the pattern and strength of endorsement of the two views among countries.

Figure 4.2 shows that in all countries but Italy the average endorsement of constructivist beliefs is stronger than that of direct transmission beliefs. In most countries, therefore, teachers believe that their task is not simply to present facts and give their students the opportunity to practice, but rather that they should support students in their active construction of knowledge.

Besides this general agreement on beliefs about instruction, countries differ in the strength of teachers' endorsement of each of the two approaches. The preference for a constructivist view is especially pronounced in Austria, Australia, Belgium (Fl.), Denmark, Estonia and Iceland. Differences in the strength of endorsement are small in Brazil, Bulgaria, Italy, Malaysia, Portugal and Spain. Hence teachers in Australia, Korea, north-western Europe and Scandinavia show a stronger preference for a constructivist view than teachers in Malaysia, South America and southern Europe. Teachers in eastern European countries lie in between.

Figure 4.2

Country profiles of beliefs about the nature of teaching and learning (2007-08)
Country mean of ipsative scores

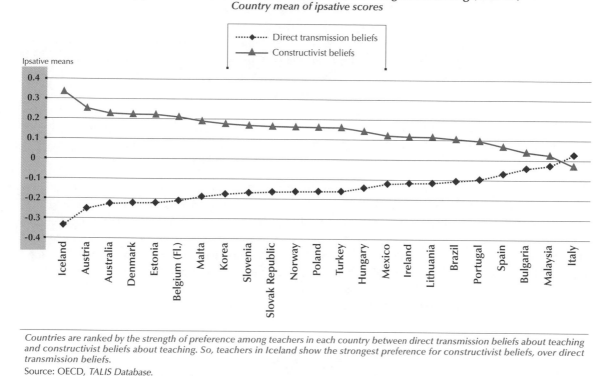

Countries are ranked by the strength of preference among teachers in each country between direct transmission beliefs about teaching and constructivist beliefs about teaching. So, teachers in Iceland show the strongest preference for constructivist beliefs, over direct transmission beliefs.
Source: OECD, *TALIS Database*.

StatLink ⬛🔗🖴 http://dx.doi.org/10.1787/607814526732

Correlations between direct transmission and constructivist beliefs

Are teachers who hold constructivist beliefs more or less likely also to hold direct transmission beliefs and vice versa? To examine the relation between the two at the level of individual teachers, correlations for the two indices were analysed by country. Based on previous research, it was expected that constructivist beliefs and direct transmission beliefs would show negative or at most zero correlations, since the two views are supposed to be contradictory in nature.

Table 4.1 shows that teachers in Australia, Austria and Iceland tend to take sides regarding their beliefs about instruction. Their endorsement of a constructivist view tends to be slightly higher when their endorsement of a direct transmission view is lower and vice versa. As described above, most of the teachers in these countries endorse constructivist beliefs considerably more strongly than direct transmission beliefs.

In Asian and Central and South American countries (Brazil, Korea, Malaysia and Mexico) there seems to be less opposition between the two approaches, and there are fairly strong positive correlations between them.

The two approaches are also quite commonly integrated in eastern and southern Europe (especially in Bulgaria, Lithuania, Poland, the Slovak Republic and Slovenia, and in Italy, Portugal, Spain and Turkey). These regions show a broadly equal endorsement of the two approaches or a moderate preference for the constructivist view and a moderately strong association between the two.

Variance distribution across levels

To what extent are teachers within schools and within countries similar as a result of their shared socialisation? This question was examined by analysing how much of the total variation in teachers' beliefs about teaching lies between countries, between schools and between teachers within schools. Results show that 25% of the variation in teachers' constructivist beliefs and more than 50% of the variation in teachers' direct transmission beliefs are accounted for by variance between countries (see Figure 4.3). These are exceptionally high percentages compared with other TALIS indices measuring teachers' beliefs and practices. This suggests that these variables are very strongly influenced by national school systems, culture and pedagogical traditions. Interestingly, for constructivist beliefs the percentage of variance is noticeably smaller on the country level, and higher on the individual level than for direct transmission beliefs. Thus, relative to the total variance of the constructs, pedagogical traditions and other cultural factors are of greater relevance for direct transmission beliefs, while there is greater variance within countries and schools for constructivist beliefs.

The variance that exists between schools represents only a small proportion of the total variance for both indices. Thus, beliefs about instruction seem to be relatively unaffected by socialisation within the school, the influence of colleagues and superiors, and other school-level factors. This may indicate that these beliefs are formed relatively early during initial education or before and remain stable over time. Stability of teachers' attitudes has been observed before (*e.g.* Nettle, 1998) and is coherent with general findings from psychology that attitudes can be quite resistant to change. It may also be that school-level variables have different effects on individual teachers depending on other personal characteristics. The large within-school variance also suggests that teachers with varying beliefs about instruction may well work side by side in the same school.

Figure 4.3

Distribution of total variance across the three levels of analysis for teachers' beliefs about instruction (2007-08)

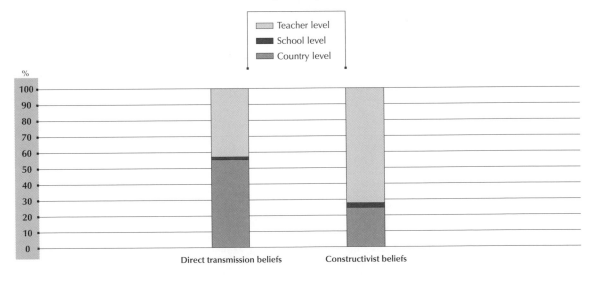

The chart analyses the variation in teachers' beliefs about instruction and indicates how much of this variation can be attributed to country characteristics (country level), school level characteristics (school level) and individual teacher characteristics (teacher level).
Source: OECD, *TALIS Database.*

StatLink ⬛🔊⬛ http://dx.doi.org/10.1787/607814526732

In summary, constructivist beliefs, which are "promoted" nowadays by most educational researchers and teacher educators, seem to receive rather strong support on average across most participating countries. However, individual teachers vary considerably, and there are huge between-country differences in terms of support for direct transmission beliefs and the extent to which they co-exist with constructivist beliefs.

CLASSROOM TEACHING PRACTICE

It has been demonstrated that quality of instruction is fundamental to student learning. For instance, Wang, Haertel and Warburg (1993) showed that classroom management and classroom interactions had effects similar in size to students' cognitive competencies and their home environment. Likewise, when reviewing contemporary research on school effectiveness, Scheerens and Bosker (1997) concluded that characteristics of instruction have a greater effect on student achievement than those of the school environment. However, researchers agree that there is no single, well-defined best way of teaching. The effectiveness of classroom practice is domain-specific as well as goal-specific; it depends on the cultural context and professional traditions. Thus, TALIS seeks to identify different profiles of teaching practices rather than a single "optimal" type of practice.

Classroom teaching practices were examined by teachers' frequency estimations on a 5-point scale, ranging from "never or hardly ever" to "in almost every lesson". Three indices were established (see Annex A1.1 for full details):

- "Structuring practices" were measured with five items, such as "I explicitly state learning goals." The other items include summary of earlier lessons, homework review, checking the exercise book, and checking student understanding during classroom time by questioning students.

- "Student-oriented practices" were measured with four items, such as "Students work in small groups to come up with a joint solution to a problem or task." The other items include ability grouping, student self-evaluation and student participation in classroom planning.

- "Enhanced activities" were also measured with four items, such as "Students work on projects that require at least one week to complete." The other items include making a product, writing an essay, and debating arguments.

Teachers were asked to report their teaching practices for a particular class that they teach in one of their main subjects fields. In order to randomise the choice of class, this "target class" was defined as the first ISCED level 2 class the teacher (typically) teaches after 11 a.m. on Tuesdays.

Country differences in profiles of classroom teaching practices

Do countries differ with regard to the profiles of their teaching practices? Comparative research, especially the TIMSS video studies, has proven that in mathematics and science lessons more "traditional" activities dominate in almost all countries (Hiebert *et al.,* 2003). Thus, it is to be expected that the dimension "structured practices" would dominate the other two dimensions in every country. However, according to previous research in comparative education (including TIMSS, PIRLS and PISA), countries have quite different profiles in terms of "alternative" or enhanced teaching practices. Groups of countries with similar cultural backgrounds and pedagogical traditions are likely to have similar profiles.

Figure 4.4 presents ipsative country means based on TALIS data. As the structure of the index did not prove to be completely invariant across countries (see Box 4.2), relative data are presented, *i.e.* scores that describe the relative importance of a dimension of teaching practices, compared to the overall emphasis of teaching practices within that country. Thus, instead of comparing country means, the figure illustrates country preferences. Ipsative scores were computed following the procedure outlined in Box 4.3, so that the individual mean score across all 13 items measuring classroom teaching practices was subtracted from each of the three index means.

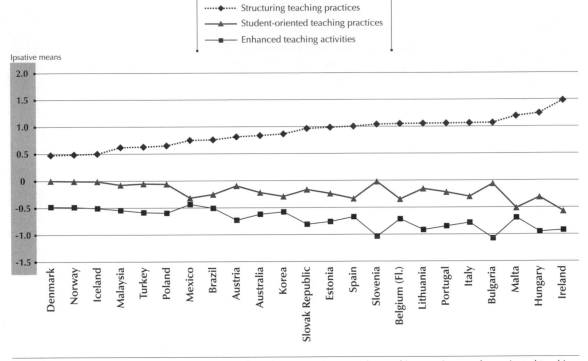

Figure 4.4

Country profiles of classroom teaching practices (2007-08)
Country mean of ipsative scores

Countries are ranked by the relative frequency with which they engage in structuring teaching practices, student-oriented teaching practices and enhanced activities. So, teachers in Denmark adopt the different practices to a fairly similar degree, while teachers in Ireland use structuring teaching practices much more than they do either student-oriented practices and enhanced activities.
Source: OECD, *TALIS Database*.

StatLink ᔕᓂ http://dx.doi.org/10.1787/607814526732

Figure 4.4 shows that, in accordance with TIMSS results, structuring practices, such as stating learning goals, summarising former lessons, homework review, checking the exercise book, and checking student understanding are the most frequently employed practices across all participating countries. The relative country means for this index are higher than those for student-oriented practices and enhanced activities in all of the countries. The predominance of structuring practices is most pronounced in Hungary, Ireland and Malta, while teachers in Denmark, Iceland and Norway report using structuring practices only slightly more frequently than the other two practices.

Enhanced activities are less frequent than student-oriented practices in all participating countries. This implies that teachers in different regions of the world on average allow student co-determination of the lesson, employ ability grouping and give students individually adapted tasks more often than they assign their student projects, debates, essays and the creation of products. Again, a general pattern of relative frequencies is observed but also cross-country differences. In Brazil, Korea, Malta and Mexico the relative average frequencies of enhanced activities and student-oriented practices are very similar. Hence, in these countries the relative frequency of enhanced activities is high compared with other countries. Relatively large differences between student-oriented and enhanced activities are found in Bulgaria and Slovenia.

In summary, the dimensions of instructional practices and the patterns of relative frequencies of classroom teaching practices are similar across countries. This is an important result and confirms previous findings of culture-general categorisation for instructional practices and routines. The size of the differences in reported frequencies of the three practices varies markedly among countries. It is, however, striking that in no country on average are student-oriented practices reported to be more frequently used than structuring practices, or in which enhanced activities are reported to be more frequently used than student-oriented practices.

It should be noted that all three of these dimensions of classroom teaching practices have been shown to be related to student outcomes, even if their correlation with outcomes is not linear and if high frequency is more meaningful for some than for others. Nevertheless, the TALIS results suggest that more use might be made of student-oriented practices and enhanced activities, especially in the countries in the right half of Figure 4.4.

Domain specificity of profiles of instructional practices

In addition to examining country profiles of instructional practices across school subjects, differences among subjects were also considered. The constructs used to measure teachers' beliefs and practices were mainly developed in the context of research on mathematics and science teaching (see Peterson *et al.*, 1989; Klieme *et al.*, 2006; Lipowsky *et al.*, 2008). TALIS makes it possible to examine the extent to which basic behavioral dimensions of instruction can be generalised across subjects. It was assumed that the same three dimensions of instructional practices are relevant for all subjects, but – given differences in content, subject matter, curriculum and specific instructional goals – differences in profiles of reported frequencies of practices were also expected. The results are illustrated in Figure 4.5.

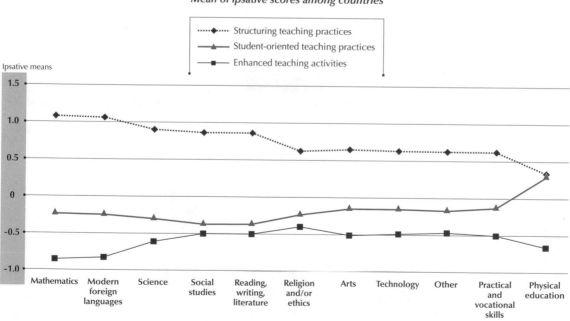

Figure 4.5

Subject profiles of classroom teaching practices (2007-08)
Mean of ipsative scores among countries

Subjects are ranked in descending order of the degree to which the use of different practices differs. Across countries, for example, mathematics teachers use structuring teaching practices much more than they do either student-oriented practices or enhanced activities.
Source: OECD, *TALIS Database*.

StatLink ⟨⟩ http://dx.doi.org/10.1787/607814526732

Analysis of the TALIS data reveals in fact that the three dimensions of instructional practices apply for all subjects (see *TALIS Technical Report* [forthcoming]). Thus, the structuring, student-oriented and enhanced activities dimensions seem appropriate to describe instruction in different domains. As expected, however, the profile of relative frequencies of instructional practices proved to be domain-specific to a certain extent. In all subjects but physical education, structuring practices are used more often than student-oriented practices, which in turn are more common than enhanced activities. In the mathematics, the foreign languages and the science classroom the predominance of structuring practices, such as checking understanding, summarising and controlling assignments, is especially strong. In the humanities, on the other hand, it is more common to assign students debates, essays, projects and work on products. Finally, teachers teaching practical and vocational skills, arts and technology report higher frequency of student-oriented practices than the other two groups. Given the more practical nature of these subjects there seems to be more scope for student co-determination of lesson content, ability grouping and individualised instruction. This is especially true for physical education classes, where teachers report student-oriented practices as often as structuring practices.

These results emphasise the importance of the humanities and creative and practical subjects, as these seem to offer learning experiences which are less often provided in mathematics, science and foreign language classes. Student-oriented practices and enhanced activities, which are more often used in the former subjects, allow students to take responsibility and to self-organise and they help develop a broad spectrum of skills that will be helpful for students' future professional lives.

Variance distribution across levels

The variance distribution across levels of analysis (Figure 4.6) shows that teaching practices – like beliefs about instruction – represent personal strategies and habits to a great extent and vary noticeably among teachers within a school. The effect of socialisation processes and other factors to which all teachers in a school are exposed is quite small (the variance between schools is only about 5%), but it is stronger for teaching practices than it is for beliefs about the nature of teaching and learning. Cultural factors and pedagogical traditions shape teaching practices significantly (variance between countries constitutes 17 to 34% of the total variance).

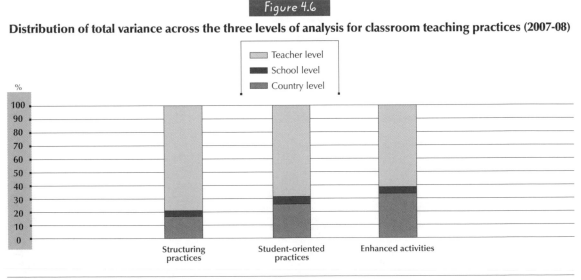

Figure 4.6

Distribution of total variance across the three levels of analysis for classroom teaching practices (2007-08)

Source: OECD, *TALIS Database.*

StatLink ⟧⟧⟧ http://dx.doi.org/10.1787/607814526732

Interestingly, countries differ especially with regard to the frequency of enhanced activities, whereas structuring activities seem to be about equally popular across countries.

Again, these results point to the significance of individual professional learning experiences and psychological processes as well as national pedagogical traditions and culture for shaping teachers' beliefs and practices, while the local context, *i.e.* professional norms and practices that are specific to schools and socialisation within a school, seems to play a relatively subordinate role.

TEACHERS' PROFESSIONAL ACTIVITIES: CO-OPERATION AMONG STAFF

The TALIS teacher questionnaire covered various aspects of *teachers' co-operation*. This co-operation implies teachers working together in groups or teams to improve educational processes and outcomes. To achieve complex objectives such as quality of education and school development requires common goals and co-operation among staff, which facilitate the co-ordination of resources and strategies of individual teachers, since no teacher can achieve such goals without at least some input from others. Furthermore, co-operation among staff creates opportunities for social and emotional support, exchange of ideas and practical advice. It can thus enhance professionalism and feelings of self-efficacy and prevent stress and "burnout" (*e.g.* Rosenholtz, 1989; Clement and Vandenberghe, 2000).

Co-operation can take various forms. It may involve administrative tasks, the teaching of students or professional development. Teachers may for example exchange instructional materials and meet regularly for discussions about individual students. More sophisticated forms of co-operation include collective learning activities such as observing others and providing feedback and engaging in professional learning activities and joint activities across classes and age groups. Steinert *et al.* (2006) showed that in Germany and Switzerland co-operative practices involving the definition of common goals and communication and co-ordination of curricula, teaching practices and marks within grades and groups of teachers of a given subject are more common than comprehensive co-ordination of instruction, didactics and diagnostics across grades and subject groups and systematic observation of instruction and the learning development of students and collaborative professional development. Furthermore, different kinds of collaboration may not have the same effects. Clement and Vandenberghe (2000) argue for example that, in order to enhance "progressive professionalism", co-operation has to encompass exchange of ideas and attitudes at a deeper level, not simply collective practical problem solving.

TALIS uses two indices to measure teachers' participation in co-operation with other staff. The index *exchange and co-ordination for teaching* consists of the following co-operative practices: exchange and discussion of teaching material, discussion of the development of individual students, attendance at team conferences, and ensuring common standards. These practices are highly correlated. Thus, teachers who exchange and discuss teaching material also engage in the other practices more often than other teachers and vice versa. Practices that form the *professional collaboration* index, like team teaching, observing other teachers to provide feedback, co-ordinating homework or activities across classes and age groups, and engaging in professional learning activities are highly correlated as well (see Annex A1.1 for full details).

Country differences in profiles of co-operation among staff

Teachers' co-operation is likely to be influenced by national pedagogical traditions, aspects of the school system and cultural dimensions, among other factors (*e.g.* Steinert *et al.*, 2006). Therefore, differences are to be expected in countries' teacher co-operation profiles. Again, relative (ipsative) scores within countries are reported (see Box 4.3).

Because of the evidence of cultural bias in the survey responses (see Box 4.2), patterns within countries are used for these indices rather than direct comparisons of country averages. Figure 4.7 shows that for all participating countries there is a considerably higher frequency of *exchange and co-ordination for teaching* than of *professional collaboration*. Thus, a majority of teachers across and within countries report exchanging and co-ordinating information and ideas on teaching and administrative issues more often than they engage jointly in professional learning activities and projects across subjects and age groups. This is in line with the research cited above by Steinert *et al.* (2006) on Germany and Switzerland, which identified different levels of co-operation, with practices summarised here as "exchange and co-ordination for teaching" being more common than those here called "professional collaboration". Interestingly, TALIS shows that these results can be generalised to a variety of countries with large cultural differences.

In addition to the general similarity of profiles, Figure 4.7 also reveals cross-country differences. In Estonia, Hungary, Korea, Lithuania, Mexico, Slovak Republic, Poland and Turkey, differences in the relative frequencies of both forms of co-operation are comparatively small. In contrast, teachers in Australia, Belgium (Fl.), Iceland, Malta, Slovenia and Spain report the basic forms of exchange and co-ordination of teaching to be noticeably more common than professional collaboration.

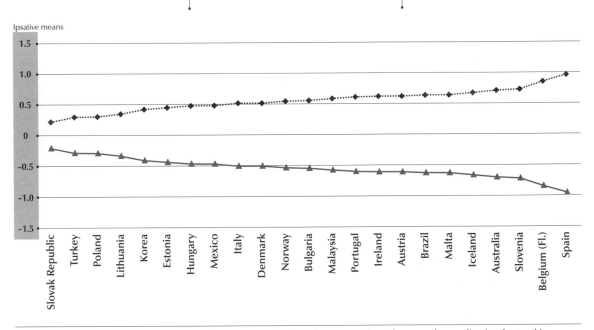

Figure 4.7

Country profiles for co-operation among staff (2007-08)
Country mean of ipsative scores

Countries are ranked in ascending order of the degree to which teachers engage in exchange and co-ordination for teaching more than professional collaboration. For example, for teachers in the Slovak Republic both types of co-operation are reported almost equally frequently, while teachers in Spain report a more common practice of exchange and co-ordination for teaching over professional collaboration.

Source: OECD, *TALIS Database*.

StatLink ⟐ http://dx.doi.org/10.1787/607814526732

Both kinds of co-operation are important practices which can enhance school development and effectiveness and ensure the professionalism and the well-being of teachers. Professional collaboration, however, is closer to the kind of co-operation that relates to more progressive forms of professionalism as discussed by Clement and Vandenberghe (2000). TALIS shows that these practices are still relatively rare compared with practices that focus on co-ordination and exchange of information and material, an indication that it may be useful to enhance and support such practices, especially in the countries depicted in the right half of Figure 4.7.

Variance distribution across levels

Do teachers within a school agree on the level of co-operation? To what extent is this actually a school-level factor, rather than a matter of individual perception and evaluation? To answer these questions the variance distribution across the three levels of analysis was examined. As one would expect, the proportion of variance at the school (and also at country) level is relatively high, compared with other indices discussed in this chapter, although teachers within the same school do not fully agree on how they co-operate. To summarise, school-level variance accounts for 9% of the total variance in *exchange and co-ordination for teaching* and for 7% of the total variance in *professional collaboration*; country-level variance accounts for 44 and 50% respectively; 47 and 43% of the total variance concerns teachers within schools (see Figure 4.8).

Figure 4.8

Distribution of total variance across the three levels of analysis for co-operation among staff (2007-08)

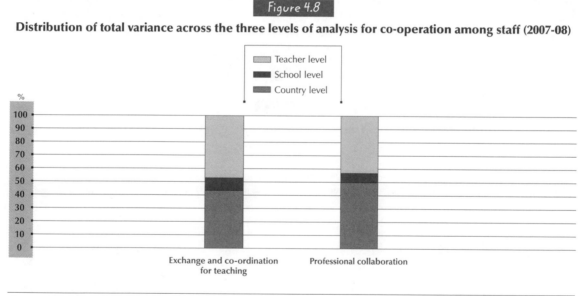

Source: OECD, *TALIS Database*.

StatLink ᘖᔊ http://dx.doi.org/10.1787/607814526732

CLASSROOM ENVIRONMENT

The classroom environment is the setting in which student learning takes place. It concerns the classroom's physical environment, the social system, the atmosphere, and norms and values (Creemers and Rezigt, 1996). Studies conducted in different regions of the world have shown that classroom climate is one of the most important predictors of student achievement (*e.g.* Brophy and Good, 1986; Mortimore *et al.*, 1988; Muijs and Reynolds, 1999; Wang, Haertel and Walberg, 1997). However, as this environment often varies between subjects and teachers, it is not easy to identify domain-general indicators. TALIS focuses on the disciplinary climate because it has a strong impact on student learning in *various* subjects (Klieme and Rakoczy, 2003; Rakoczy *et al.*, 2007), and because it has been shown that – unlike other features of classroom climate – there is a high level of agreement about this indicator among teachers, students and observers. To measure classroom disciplinary climate, TALIS asked teachers whether they had to cope with a lot of noise and interruptions during lessons and whether they find the learning atmosphere pleasant (see Annex A1.1 for full details). This measure is adapted from the PISA student questionnaire.

An additional measure of the environment at the classroom level derived from TALIS data is an index for "time on task". Teachers were asked about the percentage of time they typically spend on actual teaching and learning in the target class.[1] Time on task is a central aspect of instructional effectiveness because it provides students with a maximum opportunity to learn.

As noted in Box 4.2, country means are reported for the classroom disciplinary climate index since, although full scalar invariance was not established, the cross-country variance in the structure of the index was relatively small (see *TALIS Technical Report* [forthcoming]). Thus, small differences among countries may be due to a country-specific reporting bias, but larger differences among countries are more amenable to interpretation.

Country differences in classroom environment

As the disciplinary climate of the classroom is one of the key variables examined in Chapter 7, discussion of country comparisons at this level are deferred to that chapter. Countries' scores on the classroom disciplinary climate index are presented in Table 7.3. The index values are standardised so that the international mean is equal to zero and the international standard deviation is equal to 1. Thus a negative score indicates a less positive classroom disciplinary climate than the international average and a positive value a more positive one.

Figure 4.9

Distribution of time spent in the classroom during an average lesson (2007-08)

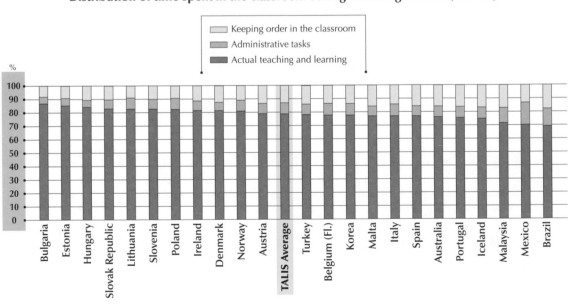

Countries are ranked in descending order of the percentage of actual teaching and learning time.
Source: OECD, *TALIS Database*.

StatLink 🔗 http://dx.doi.org/10.1787/607814526732

What proportion of lesson time is spent on actual teaching and learning in different countries? How time-consuming are administrative tasks and maintaining order in the classroom? How is the indicator for time on task distributed among teachers within countries? These questions are examined in the following section.

Figure 4.9 shows that across countries an average of 70 to 90% of lesson time is typically spent on teaching and learning. Between 5 and 17% is spent on administrative tasks and 8 to 18% on maintaining order. Country means for time on task are above 80% in Bulgaria, Denmark, Estonia, Hungary, Ireland, Lithuania, Norway, Poland, the Slovak Republic and Slovenia. Thus, relatively effective use is made of lesson time. In Brazil, Malaysia and Mexico a comparatively large proportion of time is spent on activities other than actual teaching and learning. One reason is that teachers in Brazil, Malaysia and Mexico spend more time on administrative tasks on average than teachers in other countries (13, 11 and 17%, respectively, compared to less than 9% in all other participating countries). Another important reason – at least in Brazil and Malaysia – is disruption caused by noise in the classroom. Teachers in these two countries spend on average 18 and 17%, respectively, of lesson time on maintaining order, compared to an international average of 13%. In Mexico less than 14% of lesson time is spent maintaining order in the classroom. Time spent maintaining order in the classroom is also more than 14% in Australia, Iceland, Italy, Malta, Portugal and Spain. It is less than 10% in Bulgaria, Estonia, Lithuania, and Poland.

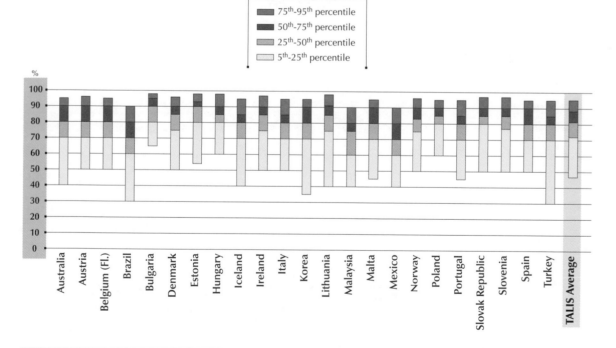

Figure 4.10

Percentiles of time on task (2007-08)

The chart shows the distribution within each country of the percentage of lesson time spent teaching and learning. So in Australia, 25% of teachers report spending at least 90% of the lesson time on teaching and learning.
Source: OECD, *TALIS Database*.

StatLink ⬛⬛ http://dx.doi.org/10.1787/607814526732

Figure 4.10 not only illustrates country differences regarding the time teachers typically spend on actual teaching and learning, it also shows the extent of within-country variation. In most participating countries, about 50% of teachers report spending at least 80% of the average lesson time on actual teaching and learning, of whom about half report spending 90% or more. Given that a certain proportion of lesson time is necessarily spent on administrative issues and maintaining order, these teachers can be said to use lesson time effectively and to maximise students' learning opportunities. Another 25% of teachers in most countries report spending at least 70% of lesson time on actual teaching and learning. For these teachers, there is some latitude for improvement, but they still reach minimum standards for effective instruction. However, in a majority of countries the self-reported time use of the remaining 25% of teachers gives cause for concern. These teachers report using less than 70% of the lesson time of an average lesson on actual teaching and learning, some even less than 50%. This indicates that in each of the participating countries, an intervention facilitating more effective use of time by about a quarter of the teachers would be advisable, to ensure that all students have an equivalent and maximum amount of learning opportunities.

Interestingly, the distribution across countries is quite similar, although there are some striking differences. On average, teachers in eastern European countries report comparatively effective use of time. Some 50% of Bulgarian and Estonian teachers report spending more than 90% of the lesson time on actual teaching and learning. In these countries, and in Hungary and Poland, few teachers report spending less than 70% of time on task. In Asian and Southern American countries, on the other hand, there is a noticeable number of outliers with a low score for this indicator. This indicates that in these countries a substantial number of teachers do not reach what may be regarded as minimum standards for undisturbed instruction.

| Figure 4.11 |

Country means for two indicators of the quality of the classroom environment (2007-08)

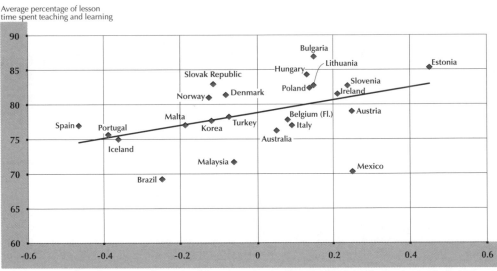

Factor scores are standardised, so that the international mean equals zero and the international standard deviation equals one (see Technical Report, *forthcoming). Thus a negative score indicates a score for classroom disciplinary climate that is below the international average. This may not necessarily indicate a poor classroom disciplinary climate.*
Source: OECD, *TALIS Database.*

StatLink ᘉᔐᏁᏦ http://dx.doi.org/10.1787/607814526732

Figure 4.11 and Table 4.2 show that, as expected, classroom disciplinary climate and time on task are related both within and between countries. The better the classroom disciplinary climate, the more time spent on actual teaching and learning. Within-country correlations between these aspects are significant in all countries, and they are 0.5 or more in most. At the country level, countries in which teachers report spending a comparatively small percentage of time on teaching and learning also have a low mean score for classroom disciplinary climate. This mainly concerns Brazil, Iceland, Korea, Malaysia, Malta, Portugal, Spain and Turkey. Likewise, countries with a high mean score for classroom disciplinary climate also have comparatively high mean scores for time on task. This is the case for Estonia and to a lesser extent for Austria, Bulgaria, Hungary, Ireland, Lithuania, Poland and Slovenia. Mexico is a notable exception in that teachers view the classroom disciplinary climate quite positively despite the low average score for time on task. As noted above, the time loss in Mexico is due less to noise and interruptions than to the fact that a large proportion of instructional time is spent on administrative activities (see Figure 4.9).

Variance distribution across levels

The variance of the constructs *classroom disciplinary climate* and *time on task* was also partitioned into three components: teacher-, school- and country-level variance. The results are illustrated in Figure 4.12. The small degree of variance among countries for these two indices is striking. For most of the other beliefs and practices discussed in this chapter, the variance between countries ranges from 20 to 60% of the total variance. For classroom disciplinary climate, it is only 4% and for time on task only 8%. Also, analysis of cross-cultural invariance demonstrates a relatively high level of cross-cultural validity for this index (see *TALIS Technical Report* [forthcoming]). Thus, classroom climate seems to be less affected by cultural and system-level influences than by beliefs about instruction and classroom teaching practices. This suggests that a positive and orderly classroom climate is a very basic aspect of instruction and school quality which is quite similar across countries.

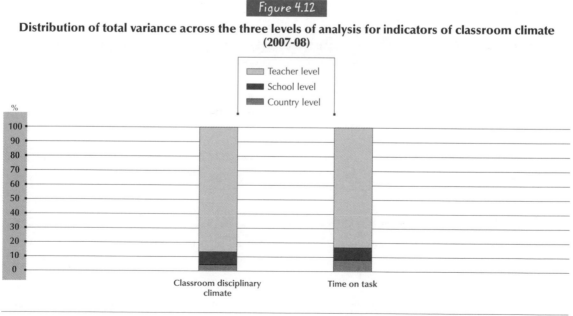

Figure 4.12

Distribution of total variance across the three levels of analysis for indicators of classroom climate (2007-08)

Source: OECD, *TALIS Database*.

StatLink http://dx.doi.org/10.1787/607814526732

Some 9% of the variance in classroom disciplinary climate and in time on task is between schools. This suggests that school-level variables have a significant influence. Yet variance within schools is much greater, amounting to 86% of total variance for classroom disciplinary climate and 83% for time on task. Thus, individual classroom and teacher characteristics and aspects of the interaction of a specific teacher with a specific class are the main factors in classroom disciplinary climate and effective time use, followed by school-level influences.

In summary, both the time spent on actual teaching and learning and the classroom disciplinary climate are of fundamental importance for effective schooling. TALIS results show that a majority of teachers in all participating countries report using lesson time effectively. Nevertheless, a considerable percentage of teachers in each of the countries, and especially in Brazil, Malaysia and Mexico, are not able to provide their students with adequate time for learning. Generally, time loss is largely due to disciplinary problems. Especially in Mexico, administrative issues also distract from actual teaching and learning. School-level factors influence classroom climate and time on task, but teachers within schools vary strongly with regard to these indicators. This suggests that in addition to background characteristics of the school, which might not be easily open to policy interventions the characteristics and competencies of individual teachers, the features of the specific class and their interaction may play a significant role. Therefore, interventions aimed at helping individual teachers improve their classroom management skills in order to prevent and cope with noise and distraction may increase learning opportunities for students.

Chapter 7 will extend this analysis by considering the classroom disciplinary climate as a key indicator of a positive learning environment and will examine the school- and teacher-level factors associated with this.

SCHOOL-LEVEL ENVIRONMENT: SCHOOL CLIMATE

The systematic study of school climate has its roots in organisational psychology and research on school effectiveness. There are various definitions of school climate. Researchers agree that school climate essentially reflects a subjective view of the learning environment at the school level (Cohen, 2006). Relevant aspects of the school environment are the physical environment, the social system, relationships between principals, teachers and students, a sense of community, teacher and student morale, norms among peers, and safety. School climate is fundamental for the quality of schooling and instruction. A growing body of research shows that school climate affects students' academic achievement and their well-being and personal and social development (*e.g.* Blum *et al.*, 2002; Rutter *et al.*, 1979). Many important aspects of the school-level environment are addressed in Chapter 5, which focuses on school evaluation and teacher appraisal and feedback. In addition, the teacher questionnaire provides an index for *school climate*, based on four items which asked teachers the extent to which they believed that students and teachers get on well together, that teachers care for students' well-being, that they are interested in what students have to say, and that students get extra assistance from the school if they need it (see Annex A1.1).

Again, mean scores cannot be compared directly, but the influence of country-specific factors on single items is comparably weak, so that it is at least possible to interpret larger differences among countries and general tendencies (see Box 4.2).

Country differences in teacher-student relations

What is the overall level of teacher-student relations reported by teachers from different countries? Do countries differ regarding the quality of teacher-student relations as perceived by teachers? Percentile bands were used to examine this question.

Figure 4.13 indicates comparatively good teacher-student relations in Austria, Iceland and Ireland. Norwegian teachers report exceptionally good teacher-student relations. On the other hand, the medians for Bulgaria, Italy, Korea, Lithuania, Malaysia and the Slovak Republic are comparatively low. Figure 4.13 also illustrates differences within countries. With regard to the spread, there are comparatively large differences between the country's teachers in Austria, Mexico and Turkey and – to a lesser degree – in Brazil, Lithuania, Poland and Spain. A small spread is found for Norway and Slovenia. Hence, in the latter countries, teachers' appraisals of teacher-student relations at their schools are relatively similar, while in the former there are more outliers, *i.e.* those who view the relationships as being quite bad or exceptionally good. In many countries the distribution is skewed to the right. Here, most teachers are concentrated in the lower part of the distribution, which denotes teacher-student relations of average quality. While quite a few teachers in each country report especially positive teacher-student relations, almost no teachers report exceptionally negative relations. Norway is the exception to this pattern, as a majority of teachers have a very positive view of teacher-student relations and differences among teachers are rather small.

Figure 4.13

Teacher-student relations: percentiles of the standardised factor scores (2007-08)

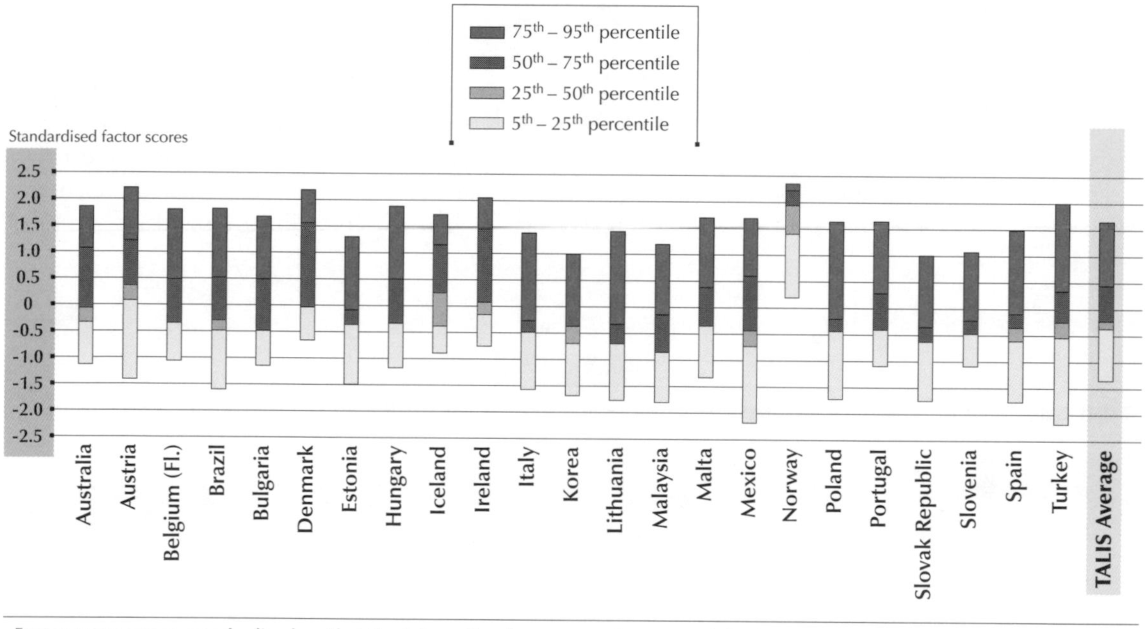

Factor scores were standardised so that the international mean equals zero and the international standard deviation equals one (see Technical Report, forthcoming). Thus a negative score indicates a score for teacher-student relations which is below the international average. This may nevertheless be indicative of positive teacher-student relations.
Source: OECD, *TALIS Database*.

StatLink ⤳ http://dx.doi.org/10.1787/607814526732

The preceding section showed that classroom disciplinary climate and time on task rank relatively high in eastern European and Scandinavian countries and in Ireland. Teacher-student relations are also described comparatively positively by teachers in Scandinavian countries (Denmark, Iceland and Norway) and Ireland, but teachers in Bulgaria, Estonia, Hungary, Lithuania, the Slovak Republic and Slovenia report less positive teacher-student relations, although they report a comparatively good classroom disciplinary climate. Classroom climate and thus maintaining order in the classroom require classroom management competencies, structure and authority. Teacher-student relations on the other hand concern the quality of the relationships, which calls for social skills, empathy and mutual respect. Both aspects of the climate within a school are important for effective student learning and development. The Scandinavian countries (Denmark, Iceland and Norway) and Ireland seem best able to prevent disruption and to encourage positive relationships at the same time.

Variance distribution across levels

Do teachers within a school agree on the quality of teacher-student relations? To what extent is this a school-level factor, rather than a matter of individual perception and evaluation? To answer these questions, the overall variance in teacher-student relations was broken down into between-country variance, between-school variance and within-school variance. Figure 4.14 shows that about 10% of the total variance is variance between schools. This is a high level compared with indices measuring teacher beliefs and practices and indicates that the quality of teacher-student relations is a school-level factor. At the same time some 65% of the total variance is within-school variance and points to significant differences in the perception of this aspect of school climate within schools. The between-country variance (25%) is of medium size compared with that of other constructs and indicates that countries differ markedly with regard to the quality of teacher-student relations as perceived by teachers.

The variance at all levels of analysis indicates that in all countries some teachers describe less favourable teacher-student relations than others. It can be assumed that these teachers' daily work is more challenging and that students at these schools may have a less favourable learning environment. These schools and teachers may need support in order to improve school climate, ensure an agreeable working climate for all teachers, and provide all students with a supportive learning environment and thus promote equity. Analysis in the next section will show that teachers working in schools with a large proportion of disadvantaged students may need special attention.

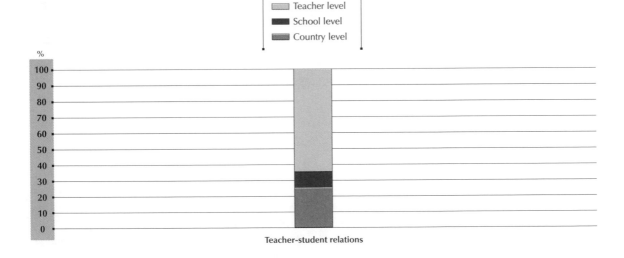

Figure 4.14

Distribution of total variance across the three levels of analysis for teacher-student relations (2007-08)

Source: OECD, *TALIS Database*.

StatLink http://dx.doi.org/10.1787/607814526732

JOB-RELATED ATTITUDES: SELF-EFFICACY AND JOB SATISFACTION

In addition to pedagogical beliefs and attitudes, the teacher questionnaire addresses job-related attitudes, namely job satisfaction (single item) and teacher "self-efficacy". Job satisfaction is a central concept in organisational and work psychology. It is assumed that job satisfaction is both affected by the work situation and influences work-related behaviour, including performance, absenteeism and turnover (Dormann and Zapf, 2001). It has been demonstrated that teachers generally have a rather positive attitude towards their job – despite the challenges of teaching – and job satisfaction usually increases with tenure, though this is partly due to the fact that dissatisfied teachers tend to drop out.

Research on self-efficacy goes back to the seminal work of Bandura, who defines self-efficacy as "a judgement of one's capability to accomplish a given level of performance" (Bandura, 1986, p. 391). In recent years it has taken a central role in educational research regarding both students and teachers. Teachers with high self-efficacy expect to succeed in teaching and to handle students well, and this influences their interpretation of successes and disappointments, the standards they set and their approaches to coping with difficult instructional situations (Bandura, 1997; Ross, 1998). Strong self-efficacy beliefs can prevent stress and burnout and teachers' self-efficacy beliefs and their job satisfaction are linked to instructional practices and student achievement (*e.g.* Ashton and Webb, 1986; Ross, 1998).

In TALIS, the teacher self-efficacy index was constructed from four items of the teacher questionnaire which asked teachers, for instance, how strongly they felt that they made an educational difference in students' lives and how well they were able to make progress with the most difficult and unmotivated students (see Annex A1.1). For this index a comparatively high level of invariance was established, but there were slight differences in the structure of the index (see Box 4.2). Thus, small differences among countries may be due to country-specific factors other than the construct of interest, but it is possible to interpret larger differences in mean scores.

Country differences in self-efficacy and job satisfaction

Country means for the self-efficacy index and for the single item measuring job satisfaction are illustrated in Figure 4.15.

Generally there are small country differences in self-efficacy and job satisfaction. Norway has an exceptionally high mean score for both self-efficacy and job satisfaction. Teachers in Austria and Belgium (Fl.) are also relatively satisfied with their job. For Hungary and the Slovak Republic, however, average job satisfaction is low compared to that of the other participating countries. Comparatively weak self-efficacy beliefs are reported by teachers in Estonia, Korea, Hungary and Spain. The distribution of country means suggests an association of both constructs on the country level. Associations between constructs on the individual teacher level are examined in the next section.

Variance distribution across levels

While self-efficacy and job satisfaction vary little at the country level, this is not the case for the school and individual teacher levels. Figure 4.16 shows that for both constructs the most variance (87 and 90%, respectively) is at the teacher level. Only 5 and 6%, respectively, of the total variance is between schools and only 8 and 4%, respectively, is variance between countries. Thus, teachers within a school vary markedly in their levels of self-efficacy and job satisfaction, while differences between schools and between countries are rather small. Furthermore, variance at the school level is relatively similar across countries. These results emphasise the psychological nature of the constructs. Across countries teachers' self-efficacy and job satisfaction mainly depend on and interact with their personality, personal experiences, competencies and attitudes. This should be considered in interventions aiming at enhancing teachers' self-efficacy. Results suggest that individualised interventions may be more effective than school or system level policies.

Figure 4.15

Country means of teacher self-efficacy and job satisfaction (2007-08)

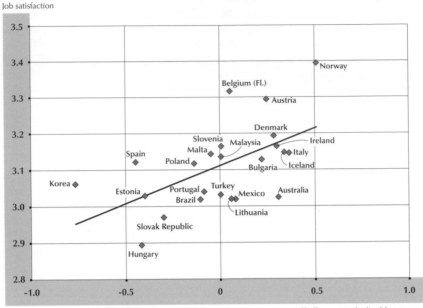

Factor scores are standardised, so that the international mean is zero and the international standard deviation equals one (see Technical Report, forthcoming). Thus a negative score indicates a score for self-efficacy that is below the international average. This may not necessarily indicate a low level of self-efficacy. The score for job satisfaction represents the extent of agreement on average with the statement "All in all I am satisfied with my job", where strongly agree = 4 points, agree = 3 points, disagree = 2 points and strongly disagree = 1 point.
Source: OECD, *TALIS Database*.

StatLink ⬛🖼️ http://dx.doi.org/10.1787/607814526732

Figure 4.16

Distribution of total variance across the three levels of analysis for self-efficacy and job satisfaction (2007-08)

- Teacher level
- School level
- Country level

Source: OECD, *TALIS Database*.

StatLink ⬛🖼️ http://dx.doi.org/10.1787/607814526732

Chapter 7 will extend this analysis by considering teachers' self-efficacy together with the classroom disciplinary climate as important factors for creating a positive learning environment and will examine factors that may be helpful in fostering this.

UNDERSTANDING TEACHERS' PROFESSIONALISM: FIRST STEPS IN LINKING THE SCHOOL CONTEXT AND TEACHERS' BELIEFS AND PRACTICES TO TEACHERS' PERCEIVED EFFICACY AND THE QUALITY OF THE LEARNING ENVIRONMENT

The preceding sections have shown that teachers' beliefs and practices and the perceived learning environment vary between countries, between schools and – most notably – within schools. This section aims at explaining the variance between and within schools. It does not report cross-country comparisons but associations between the individual background, the school context, teachers' beliefs and practices and the learning environment which are consistently found in a large number of countries. Based on the theoretical framework (Figure 4.1), the analysis starts by examining the association of teachers' background variables with teachers' beliefs and practices. It then looks at associations between classroom and school background variables and the perceived learning environment and the effects of professional development on teachers' beliefs and practices. Finally it examines associations between teachers' beliefs and, practices, the learning environment, and teachers' job satisfaction. The results will help to explore the complex relations among teachers' beliefs and practices and classroom and school variables, to see some pattern in them, and to indicate further research possibilities. The great advantage of this analysis, as compared to previous research, is to have covered in parallel 23 educational systems and cultures. The fact that a number of results are the same across countries is by no means trivial; it can help identify issues that educational policy needs to deal with in all countries and internationally. Some implications for policy making are discussed in the final section.

The results presented in the remainder of this chapter are generated from a series of statistical regressions analyses (see Box 4.4). Tables 4.3 to 4.14 highlight the variables that were statistically significant in these regressions, with a plus sign indicating a significant positive relation and a minus sign indicating a significant negative relation. Where no significant relation was found, the cell in the table is blank. Tables containing the regression coefficients are available on line.

Significance of context and background variables

Effects of individual characteristics of teachers on their beliefs, attitudes and practices

As outlined earlier in the analytical framework, teachers' beliefs and practices are expected to be associated with their background characteristics, especially with their professional education. Regression analysis reported in this section examines these associations. Effects of gender, subject taught in the target class,[1] experience and level of education (a Master's degree or higher versus a lower level qualification) on beliefs, attitudes and practices are analysed. Results are listed in Table 4.3. Multiple regressions in this subsection only consider the individual level and were computed for each country separately. But, as the primary focus of this chapter is on cross-cultural effects, effects that are significant in more than half of countries are indicated in the tables.

Table 4.3 shows the presence of a few cross-culturally consistent net effects of background variables on teachers' beliefs and practices. In a majority of participating countries, female teachers endorse direct transmission beliefs less strongly than male teachers. They also report greater use of structuring and student-oriented practices than their male colleagues. Also according to their self-reports, they are more often involved in co-operative activities. This suggests female teachers' greater professionalism and motivation even controlling for the subject taught, professional experience and level of education. Differences between both groups are quite small, but they are significant and relatively consistent across countries. Thus, interventions aimed at promoting modern beliefs about instruction and modern professional practices might best explicitly target male teachers.

Box 4.4 **Description of regression analysis**

Regression analysis enables the estimation of the effects of one or more predictor (or independent) variables on dichotomous or continuous predicted (or dependent) variables. Regression analysis was carried out for each country separately, as prior analysis showed noticeable differences in regression coefficients between countries. The same background variables were included as control variables in each of the models. These variables were the teacher's gender, years of experience, subject taught (two dummy variables were created for this: "maths/science" versus other subjects and "humanities" versus other subjects), and level of education (a Master's degree or higher versus a lower level qualification). After analysing this background model, the predictor variables considered to be relevant based on theoretical considerations were added. Thus, in each of the models net effects are reported instead of gross effects.

Notes on the interpretation of results of regression analysis with cross-sectional data

To examine relations between background variables, beliefs and practices, multiple regressions were used which take the complex sample design of TALIS into account. Note that with cross-sectional data such as the TALIS data, no direction of impact can be established. Thus, it is not possible to decide empirically between, for example, a model that describes school climate as dependent on teacher practices and a model that describes teacher practices as dependent on school climate. The perspective taken, *i.e.* the choice of predicted and predictor variables, is based on purely theoretical considerations, as laid out in the analytical framework. When the notion of "effects" is used, it is used in a technical manner: An "effect" is a statistical parameter that describes the linear relation between a "predicted" variable (*e.g.* job satisfaction) and a "predictor" variable (*e.g.* participation in professional development activities), taking effects of individual and school background as well as other "predictor" variables into account. Thus, the "effects" reported are statistical net effects which do not imply any causality. In the example, a significant effect of professional development on job satisfaction would not imply that the former is a cause for the latter; in fact, causality may work in the opposite direction, and in many cases the cross-sectional "effects" identified will be based on complex mutual dependencies among the various phenomena the model addresses.

Annex A1.4 provides a fuller technical description and specifications of the variables used.

The subject taught in the target class also has significant and cross-culturally consistent net effects, especially on teaching practices, but also on beliefs about instruction and the classroom disciplinary climate. First, constructivist beliefs are more prevalent among maths and science teachers than among teachers of other subjects. As detailed earlier in the chapter, mathematics and science teachers report more structuring practices and less student-oriented practices and enhanced activities. Humanities teachers also report more structuring and less student-oriented practices than teachers teaching creative and practical subjects or physical education. These results highlight the subject specificity of classroom teaching practices and beliefs about instruction. In a majority of countries teachers of different subjects are at least partly educated and socialised in homogeneous groups by subject. But there also appears to be a difference in the appropriateness of certain practices for different subjects. These differences might explain some of the domain specificity of beliefs and practices. The subject is also associated with classroom disciplinary climate, but these effects are not consistent across countries. However, in a majority of countries, mathematics teachers exhibit lower self-efficacy than teachers teaching creative and practical subjects. Mathematics teachers have to communicate complex concepts, and indifference to, or even fear of, mathematics is quite widespread. Thus, mathematics teachers might need special support to develop skills for gaining students' interest in mathematics and improving their understanding of the subject. To arouse students' interest in mathematics, it might be promising to use more student-oriented techniques and enhanced activities, which teachers of this subject currently use less often than other teachers.

Years of professional experience has a significant net effect on teaching practices, both forms of co-operation and collaboration among staff, classroom disciplinary climate and self-efficacy in more than half of the countries, but most of these effects are not cross-culturally consistent. In about half of the countries, teachers with more experience report using structuring practices more often. Both indices on participation in co-operative activities are positively associated with on-the-job experience in about half of the countries. When examined at the country level, these effects are not only inconsistent across countries, they are also relatively small. However, for classroom disciplinary climate and self-efficacy, consistent effects are found. In a majority of countries experienced teachers report a better classroom climate and in about half of the countries their self-efficacy beliefs are stronger than those of less experienced teachers. Either experienced teachers develop strategies for effective classroom management or they progressively lower their standards. Either way, this finding might reassure young teachers experiencing disciplinary problems in their classrooms and insecurity regarding their competence. It might of course also be due to turnover of teachers with less effective strategies for instruction and coping with the everyday challenges of their job.

Finally, controlling for other teacher background variables, no differences were found regarding their beliefs and practices between teachers with an ISCED 5A Master's degree or a PhD and those with a lower level qualification. Thus, the length of university education and socialisation do not seem to significantly influence teachers' beliefs and practices.

Effects of classroom background variables on teaching practices

In addition to associations of teachers' beliefs and practices with teachers' background variables, effects of characteristics of the target class[1] on teaching practices were also analysed. The results, which are informative about the macro-adaptivity of instructional approaches, are summarised in Table 4.4.

Across countries there are some consistent, but rather weak effects of classroom background variables. The percentage of students with a mother tongue different from the language of instruction is positively associated with student-oriented practices. Teachers teaching a class in which more than 10% of students have a mother tongue different from the language of instruction, report using strategies such as work in small groups, ability grouping, individualised tasks and student participation in lesson planning more often than teachers teaching a class with a smaller proportion of second-language learners. This can be viewed as a kind of macro-adaptivity. Positive associations are less frequent between the language composition of the class and structuring practices or enhanced activities.

The data indicate that, in a majority of countries, teachers are also responsive to the average ability of their classes. Teachers who perceive their students to have high ability as compared with other students of the same age use more student-oriented practices and more enhanced activities than teachers with students who have low ability. Again, this can be viewed as evidence of some macro-adaptivity of instruction. High-ability classes tend to get more varied and probably more demanding learning opportunities than low-ability classes. The effects on structuring practices are rather heterogeneous and only significant in a few countries. However, considered as a whole, the results imply that the *relative* importance of structuring practices (as opposed to student-oriented practices and enhanced activities) is greater for those who are in greater need of structured instruction, as found in previous research.

Table 4.4 further shows that in about half of the countries the larger the target class the less frequently teachers employ student-oriented practices. It seems that – at least in these countries – the higher the number of students in a class, the more difficult it becomes to respond to individual students' needs. (Note that this holds even when the effects of level of ability and proportion of second language learners are controlled for, because the results are based on multiple regression analysis.) Associations of class size with structuring practices and enhanced activities are largely non-significant.

Effects of the school context on teacher-student relations

Teacher-student relations, as one aspect of school climate, can be expected to depend not only on the individual characteristics of the different actors within a school and on the school processes, but also on the external context. Therefore, this section examines the effects of different aspects of the school context on school climate at the school level. The following context variables were considered: private versus public management of the school; whether the school is located in a city or in a town, hamlet, village or rural area; the social background of the students (the school average of teachers' estimation of the percentage of students whose parents have completed ISCED level 3 [upper secondary education] or higher in the target classes in a school); and teachers' estimation of the average ability of students compared with students of the same age at the school level. Multiple multilevel regressions were used for this analysis (see Annex A1.4 for details). All effects were examined at the school level. At the same time teacher characteristics (gender, years of experience as a teacher, level of education and subject taught in the target class) were controlled for at the individual level. It should be noted that, once again, all these conditions are entered at once into the statistical model, so that the effects reported here are pure or "net" effects.

In almost half of the countries fewer than 10% of the sampled teachers work in private schools. For these countries differences between private and public schools were not analysed. In most of the other countries teachers working for private schools report significantly better teacher-student relations than teachers working for public schools – even when controlling for the social background of the students (Table 4.5). The social background on the other hand has a significant (net) effect in Australia, Belgium (Fl.), Brazil, Denmark, Hungary, Iceland and Italy. In these countries, teacher-student relations are considered more positive by teachers working for schools with a high proportion of students whose parents have at least completed ISCED level 3 (upper secondary education). Student composition in terms of ability is also associated with teacher-student relations in about half of the countries. Teachers perceive relations between students and teachers as better when the students at their schools have higher ability. School size is another important predictor of teacher-student relations. Large schools seem to provide less opportunity for teachers and students to develop positive relationships. Significant effects are found even when the management of the school, students' social background and average ability, and the size of the community in which the school is located in are controlled for.

Finally, whether the school is located in a city or not is not an important predictor for teacher-student relations at the school level. Significant net effects are found for Estonia, Hungary, Ireland, Malaysia and the Slovak Republic. In Estonia, Hungary, Ireland and the Slovak Republic teachers working in schools located in a city report better teacher-student relations. In Malaysia the opposite is true.

These results suggest a lack of equity across countries. Teachers and students at large public schools with a high percentage of students from a disadvantaged social background and with students of low average ability have to cope with a noticeably less favourable working and learning environment. This can be challenging and stressful for teachers and hinder effective schooling, thereby widening the gap in student performance.

Effects of professional development activities

Most professional development activities are aimed at changing teachers' knowledge and beliefs and instructional practices. This subsection examines the extent to which participation in professional development activities is associated with direct transmission and constructivist beliefs, with structuring and student-oriented practices and enhanced activities, and with co-operation among staff. Four different indicators of professional development were analysed: number of days of professional development activities during the last 18 months, participation in workshops or courses, mentoring, and networks for professional development. When interpreting any of the effects, it should be noted that all other features of professional development are controlled for. For example, the effect of days of professional development is the "net" effect that results when the *kind* of activity (as operationalised by the three dummy variables for participation in workshops or courses, mentoring, and networks for professional development) is controlled for. In addition, teacher background variables – gender, subject taught in the target class, experience and level of education – are controlled for.

Table 4.6 shows only a few significant net effects of professional development on teachers' beliefs about instruction. The direction of those effects, however, is quite consistent. If professional learning activities have any effect on teacher beliefs, it is in the direction of stronger constructivist and weaker direct transmission beliefs.

Table 4.7, which shows the relation between professional activities and teaching practices, allows for drawing some general conclusions:

- Professional development is generally associated with more (reported) use of specific instructional practices. There is not a single significantly negative cell in the table. This means that teachers who engage in professional learning tend to use specified practices more often.[2]

- The *kind* of professional development a teacher participates in is more important than the amount of time invested. The net effects of days of professional development are small and only significant in a few countries, whereas indicators of participation in networks and mentoring (and in some countries also in workshops and/ or courses) have significant and stronger net associations with teaching practices in a majority of countries.

- Professional development activities that take place at regular intervals and involve teachers in a rather stable social and collaborative context (*i.e.* networks or mentoring) have a significantly stronger association with teaching practices than regular workshops and courses.

- Student-oriented practices and enhanced activities are more strongly associated with professional development than structuring practices. Net effects of indicators of attendance at professional development activities are stronger and significant in a larger number of countries for student-oriented practices and enhanced activities than for structuring practices.

It should be noted that, although teacher background variables (gender, experience, level of education and subject taught in the target class) are controlled for, the associations found here should not be interpreted as causal effects of professional development on the respective teaching practices. Rather, in every case alternate interpretations are possible and cannot be ruled out on the basis of TALIS data. Results may indicate that professional development – particularly mentoring and networks for professional development – are effective in instructing and inspiring teachers to use modern and multifaceted practices, especially student-oriented practices and enhanced activities. But it may just as well be that teachers who report using student-oriented practices and enhanced activities relatively often are generally more motivated to learn and apply innovative teaching strategies and thus engage in more professional development.

In many countries, professional development is more and more implemented at the school level, with in-house training addressing the teaching staff as a group rather than individual teachers. It is thought that – besides changing teachers' personal beliefs and individual practices directly – professional development can help foster collaboration and co-operation among teachers and have indirect effects on beliefs and practices and a more general impact on school quality. Table 4.8 provides data that help judge the realisation of this goal.

In fact, all kinds of professional development activities are positively associated with both kinds of co-operation among staff, even if teacher background variables are controlled for. The effects are noticeably strong for professional development networks and mentoring activities. Of course, these are forms of collaborative learning, but the results indicate that participation in such networks is associated with other forms of collaboration as well.

Effects of beliefs on instructional practices

Are teachers' beliefs and self-reported teaching practices associated and are the associations the same across participating countries? Based on previous research, "constructivist" beliefs were expected to be correlated with student-oriented practices and/or enhanced learning activities. This hypothesis was examined with multiple regression analysis.

In all of the participating countries except Bulgaria, Malaysia and Turkey, significant relations between beliefs and practices were observed when controlling for teacher background characteristics and other beliefs (Table 4.9). For student-oriented practices and enhanced activities, the expected predictive pattern was found in 18 and 16 countries, respectively. Both kinds of activities are related to constructivist beliefs rather than direct transmission beliefs. In some countries, however, both belief indices have the same predictive power for teaching practices, though in Korea the profile of effects is reversed. This is also evidence that the beliefs and practices indices may have slightly different meanings in different cultures.

For structuring practices as a predicted (or dependent) variable, results are mixed. In only a handful of countries are these practices tied to direct transmission beliefs rather than constructivist beliefs. In Korea and Poland it is the constructivist rather than the direct transmission view that is associated with structuring practices. It seems that, by and large, structuring practices are less strongly related to teachers' beliefs than other kinds of practices.

The importance of teachers' beliefs for teaching practices has been subject to discussion. While many authors report positive associations, others conclude that there is no direct link (e.g. Levitt, 2001; Wilcox-Herzog, 2002). There is an important difference between abstract and concrete beliefs, and the latter have greater relevance for action. Beliefs measured in TALIS are not domain-specific and are quite general in nature. Still, largely significant – although rather weak – correlations with teaching practices are found across countries. Constructivist beliefs are associated with more frequent use of practices that aim at creating a stimulating, challenging and individually adapted learning environment supportive of students' construction of knowledge.

Effects of instructional practices on classroom disciplinary climate

As outlined earlier, teaching practices are seen as one means of positively influencing the classroom learning environment. Structuring and student-oriented practices are expected to help maintain student discipline, student attention and collaboration. Therefore these two variables are expected to have positive effects on the classroom disciplinary climate. Enhanced activities may not need the same types of disciplinary climate to be successfully completed by students. Enhanced activities require – among other things – self-reliance, structure, time management and stamina, but a quiet and orderly classroom climate may be less important than for reception-oriented, teacher-centred instruction, which primarily involves listening to the teacher and responding to his/her questions. Furthermore, group work and the need for discussion and advice may even lead to a certain level of disruption when students are assigned enhanced activities. Thus, this variable was not expected to be associated with the disciplinary aspects of classroom climate. Again multiple regressions at the individual teacher/classroom level were used.

If all three kinds of practices are considered at the same time, teachers' structuring classroom practices turn out to be a relatively better predictor of classroom disciplinary climate, as hypothesised above. Table 4.10 shows that in about half of the participating countries, teachers who more often summarise the previous lesson, state learning goals and check student understanding also report a better learning atmosphere in the classroom, less noise and fewer distractions. Clarity and structure seem to help maintain students' attention and a positive disciplinary climate; conversely, a poor climate might restrict the use of effective teaching practices. Net effects of student-oriented teaching practices are also significant in eleven countries. These practices, such as individualised tasks, student co-determination of the lesson and group work, also seem either to help to create a positive learning environment or to be used more often in classes with a good classroom climate. Enhanced activities were not expected to be associated with the classroom climate, and in fact significant net effects are only found for six countries, five of these being negative.

Chapter 7 will take a more extensive look at the factors that are associated with the disciplinary climate of the classroom, including aspects from the other chapters of the report alongside the indices of teaching practices that have been considered in this chapter. This will show, for instance, how teaching practices relate to the classroom disciplinary climate once a wider range of variables are taken into account.

Effects of teachers' co-operation on teacher-student relations

Associations between co-operation by teachers and teacher-student relations were examined, but only at the teacher level. The issue was whether individual teachers who participate in more co-operative professional activities involving other teachers also have a more positive perception of teacher-student relations than teachers who participate less frequently in such activities. Results are presented in Table 4.11.

Table 4.11 shows that, across countries, teachers who co-operate more often with other teachers also have a more positive view of teacher-student relations at their school. However, if the two measures of participation in co-operative activities are introduced jointly as predictors of perceived teacher-student relations, only the effects of exchange and co-ordination for teaching are positive and significant across participating countries, when controlling for a variety of teacher background and school context variables. This is in line with theoretical expectations, because exchange and co-ordination for teaching is closer to classroom interactions with students than professional collaboration, which is more related to teachers' individual development as professionals. Both kinds of judgements about the quality of relationships within a school – co-operation among staff and teacher-student relations – can be seen as important aspects of a general school quality that are shown to be interrelated, suggesting that they may also be addressed jointly in school development programmes.

Determinants of teachers' job satisfaction

As a final step in connecting the conditions and possible consequences of teachers' beliefs and practices, the focus turns to the extreme right of the model set out in Figure 4.1. Here, the analysis seeks to understand how teachers' job satisfaction is related to teachers' beliefs about instruction, their practices and professional activities, and climate factors. These are used as predictors at both the individual and school levels. As in all other regressions reported in this chapter, individual level background variables were controlled for. A similar analysis of the effects on self-efficacy, the other indicator at the far right of the theoretical model outlined in Figure 4.1, will be examined in Chapter 7.

Tables 4.12 and 4.13 show that teachers' perceptions of the classroom and school climate and their self-efficacy seem to be the most important predictors of job satisfaction. Teachers reporting higher self-efficacy also report higher job satisfaction. Significant and comparably strong net effects are found across all countries, even though teacher background variables, teachers' professional practices and the perception of the learning environment are controlled for. Moreover, across all countries, teachers who perceive their classes as having a positive disciplinary climate also feel more satisfied with their job than teachers who evaluate the classroom climate less positively. Even controlling for this factor, in a majority of countries, the second factor of school climate, namely teacher-student relations, has a significant (net) effect at the individual level. In other words, when teachers view the relations between teachers and students more positively, their job satisfaction is greater. However, at the school level, net effects of classroom climate and teacher-student relations are only significant in a few countries (Table 4.13). This indicates that the climate at the school level does not have an additional effect on job satisfaction. It is not the more objective aggregate measure of climate that affects teachers' job satisfaction; instead, it seems that within each school teachers who get along well with their colleagues and students are also more satisfied with their job. Thus, the association seems to be mainly based on individuals' perceptions and evaluative processes.

In a majority of countries teachers' beliefs and classroom teaching practices are unrelated to job satisfaction, when all other variables are controlled for. Neither strong followers of constructivism nor those that hold a direct transmission view are more satisfied with their jobs. Job satisfaction seems neither to be affected by nor to influence the frequency with which structuring and student-oriented practices and enhanced activities are used.

CONCLUSIONS AND IMPLICATIONS FOR POLICY AND PRACTICE

Figure 4.1 illustrates the variety of teacher beliefs, attitudes and practices measured by TALIS. The postulated relations of these constructs with the perceived quality of the learning environment and teachers' job satisfaction are by and large found across countries, confirming their relevance for teachers and schooling. An important policy issue is therefore, how to further facilitate these aspects of teachers' effectiveness. TALIS provides some suggestions.

Teachers generally support modern constructivist beliefs about instruction, but there is scope for strengthening this support

Key results:

- Teachers across countries are more likely to express support for a "constructivist" view of teaching with the teacher as facilitator than to regard the teacher as a direct transmitter of knowledge (Figure 4.2).

- This is most true in northwest Europe, Scandinavia, Australia and Korea. It is least true in Italy and Malaysia, where the level of teachers' support for the two views is much closer.

Discussion

Throughout the world educationalists and teacher instructors promote constructivist views about instruction. While most teachers agree, their preferences, influenced by individual characteristics, vary greatly within each country and school. If policy seeks to support constructivist positions, a promising strategy might be to enhance the systematic construction of knowledge about teaching and instruction in teachers' initial education and professional development. Interventions may be especially important for experienced teachers and for those who teach subjects other than mathematics.

Special attention is needed in countries in which many teachers who express support for a constructivist view, which may be perceived as being in style and thus socially desirable, also accept a direct transmission view. Especially in Brazil, Korea, Malaysia and Mexico, where the two views are correlated, it may help to raise awareness of the difference between these positions in the course of teacher education. It is, therefore, a good sign – even though the correlations are rather weak – that professional development is positively associated with constructivist beliefs and negatively with direct transmission beliefs across countries.

A further argument in favour of enhancing constructivist beliefs is that they are found to be associated with more varied instructional practices. This is important as TALIS results show that modern student-oriented practices and enhanced activities, which offer students specific learning opportunities which facilitate both cognitive and non-cognitive outcomes, are generally less often used than structuring practices.

It would, however, be wrong simply to introduce constructivism. Teachers need to be convinced that they can be successful in communicating deep content and in involving students in cognitively demanding activities, thereby following constructivist principles, while maintaining a positive disciplinary climate and providing student-oriented support. None of the basic dimensions of educational quality can be dispensed with. Fostering constructivist beliefs and enhanced activities is an important goal for professional development, but care should be taken to emphasise broad teaching practices, including structured teaching and self-regulatory learning. Depending on cultural traditions, and also on the stages of the learning process, various approaches should be applied to suit the circumstances. An example is starting a lesson with more direct teaching and gradually creating more open learning situations (fading), while working in a more structured way with weaker students.

Teachers need to use a wider range of instructional strategies and techniques

Key results

- Of the three teaching practices identified in TALIS, teachers were most likely to adopt structuring of lessons, followed by student-oriented practices and finally enhanced learning activities such as project work. This order applies in every country (Figure 4.4).

- In the humanities and the more practical and creative subjects, enhanced activities are more frequent than average, and in mathematics, structuring is the most common practice (Figure 4.5).

Discussion

The aspect which most differentiates teaching styles in different countries is the use of a variety of enhanced learning activities – the least common of the three instructional approaches identified by TALIS. In particular in countries where these activities are relatively less frequently used, it seems advisable to help teachers of all subjects, but especially those teaching mathematics and science, to acquire and implement a wider variety of modern instructional strategies.

Results concerning the frequency of different teaching practices also emphasise the importance of maintaining a broad curriculum, so that in subjects where enhanced activities are more common, students experience greater participation, autonomy and responsibility.

All three of these practices have been shown to play an important role in successful teaching and learning, and each deserves support. TALIS shows that structuring and student-oriented practices tend to be associated with a pleasant, orderly classroom climate, which in turn tends to go together with teacher self-efficacy and job satisfaction.

Professional development might be one way to boost teachers' use of student-oriented practices and enhanced activities. This applies particularly to development activities involving stable professional relationships with other teachers, such as networks for teacher development and mentoring.

In many participating countries, teachers tend to adapt their instructional practices to the overall characteristics of their students. Enhanced activities are more often used in classes with students with higher average ability. In classes with a high proportion of students with a migration background or a minority status – as indicated by a first language other than the language of instruction – more student-oriented practices are used. Such adaptation may be encouraged, as it helps provide students with appropriate levels of cognitive challenge and supportive practices. However, to work towards equality of learning opportunities, teacher education and professional development need to find new ways of expanding the use of enhanced activities for all students, independent of their ability. For example, peer learning and peer tutoring can improve learning outcomes, especially for students with learning difficulties (Topping, 2005).

TALIS results also show that across countries fewer student-oriented practices are used in larger classes. This suggests that larger class sizes limit the possibility to be responsive to each individual student.

There is scope to improve teachers' effectiveness by extending teacher co-operation and linking this to an improved school climate

Key results

- Teacher co-operation more often takes the form of exchanging and co-ordinating ideas and information than direct professional collaboration such as team teaching (Figure 4.7).
- Teachers who attend more professional development, especially in a co-operative context, are more likely to be involved in co-operative teaching (Table 4.8).
- Female teachers and experienced teachers engage in such collaboration most frequently (Table 4.3).

Discussion

Research has shown teacher co-operation to be an important engine of change and quality development in schools. However, the more reflective and intense professional collaboration, which most enhances modernisation and professionalism, is the less common form of co-operation. This creates a clear case for extending such activities, although they can be very time-consuming. It might therefore be helpful to provide teachers with some scheduled time or salary supplement to encourage them to engage in them. It may also be worth focusing such incentives on men and young professionals who participate least in co-operative teaching.

TALIS shows that teachers who exchange ideas and information and co-ordinate their practices with other teachers also report more positive teacher-student relations at their school. Thus, it may be reasonable to encourage teachers' co-operation in conjunction with improving teacher-student relations, as these are two sides of a positive school culture. Positive teacher-student relations are not only a significant predictor of student achievement, they are also closely related to teachers' job satisfaction – at least at the individual teacher level. This result emphasises the role of teachers' positive evaluations of the school environment for effective education and teacher well-being. Efforts to improve school climate are particularly important in larger public schools attended by students with low average ability, since all these factors are associated with a poorer school climate.

Support of teachers' classroom management techniques and a positive attitude towards the job

Key results

- One teacher in four in most countries loses at least 30% of the lesson time, and some lose more than half, in disruptions and administrative tasks (Figure 4.10).
- This is closely associated with classroom disciplinary climate, which varies more among individual teachers than among schools (Figures 4.11, 4.12).

Discussion

Several studies have shown that the classroom disciplinary climate affects student learning and achievement. TALIS supports this view by showing that disciplinary issues in the classroom limit the amount of students' learning opportunities. The classroom climate is also associated with individual teachers' job satisfaction.

Thus a positive learning environment is not only important for students, as is often emphasised, but also for teachers. Across all participating countries it therefore seems advisable to work on enhancing teachers' classroom management techniques. The results suggest that in most schools at least some teachers need extra support, through interventions that consider teachers' individual characteristics and competences and the features of individual classes. The same holds true for policies aiming at enhancing teacher self-efficacy beliefs and job satisfaction, as these variables were also shown to be strongly influenced by teachers' individual characteristics.

ADDITIONAL MATERIAL

The following additional material relevant to this chapter is available on line at:

StatLink ⬛ℐ⬛ http://dx.doi.org/10.1787/607814526732

Notes

1. The target class was defined as the first ISCED level 2 class that the teacher (typically) teaches after 11 a.m. on Tuesdays.

2. Professional development might also sensitise teachers to differences between instructional practices. Therefore the significant effects of networks for professional development and mentoring might not be indicative of a higher frequency of the different practices, but rather of a higher awareness of own use of instructional strategies. But as teachers' instructional strategies are likely to be intentional and goal-oriented, this interpretation seems unlikely.

Table 4.1

Correlation between direct transmission and constructivist beliefs about teaching (2007-08)

Teachers of lower secondary education

	Correlation coefficient (r_{xy})
Australia	-0.08
Austria	-0.24
Belgium (Fl.)	0.17
Brazil	0.65
Bulgaria	0.67
Denmark	0.14
Estonia	0.03
Hungary	0.29
Iceland	-0.18
Ireland	0.20
Italy	0.44
Korea	0.67
Lithuania	0.37
Malaysia	0.98
Malta	0.28
Mexico	0.74
Norway	0.14
Poland	0.31
Portugal	0.35
Slovak Republic	0.41
Slovenia	0.39
Spain	0.39
Turkey	0.79

▓ Statistically significant at the 5% level.
Source: OECD, *TALIS Database*.
StatLink http://dx.doi.org/10.1787/607814526732

Table 4.2

Correlation between time on task[1] and classroom disciplinary climate (2007-08)

Teachers of lower secondary education

	Correlation coefficient (r_{xy})	(S.E.)
Australia	0.63	(0.019)
Austria	0.56	(0.014)
Belgium (Fl.)	0.54	(0.018)
Brazil	0.31	(0.022)
Bulgaria	0.50	(0.021)
Denmark	0.57	(0.024)
Estonia	0.62	(0.017)
Hungary	0.61	(0.020)
Iceland	0.48	(0.029)
Ireland	0.65	(0.015)
Italy	0.46	(0.018)
Korea	0.21	(0.018)
Lithuania	0.35	(0.018)
Malaysia	0.36	(0.024)
Malta	0.58	(0.026)
Mexico	0.20	(0.027)
Norway	0.56	(0.018)
Poland	0.46	(0.024)
Portugal	0.59	(0.016)
Slovak Republic	0.49	(0.020)
Slovenia	0.51	(0.019)
Spain	0.61	(0.014)
Turkey	0.41	(0.029)

▓ Statistically significant at the 5% level.
1. Percentage of classroom time spent on teaching and learning.
Source: OECD, *TALIS Database*.
StatLink http://dx.doi.org/10.1787/607814526732

Table 4.3

Relationship between teacher characteristics and teachers' beliefs, attitudes and practices and the learning environment (2007-08)

Significant variables in the multiple regressions of teachers' characteristics with teachers' beliefs, attitudes and practices and the learning environment, teachers of lower secondary education

Example: In more than half of the TALIS countries, female teachers are less likely than male teachers to hold direct transmission beliefs about teaching, controlling for variables listed.

Predicted variables	Predictor variables:				
	Female	Teacher of Mathematics/ Science	Teacher of Humanities	Years of experience as a teacher	Highest level of qualification[1]
Direct transmission beliefs about teaching	–				
Constructivist beliefs about teaching		+			
Structuring teaching practices	+	+	+	+	
Student-oriented teaching practices	+	–	–	+	
Enhanced activities		–	–	–	
Exchange and co-ordination for teaching	+			+	
Professional collaboration	+		–	+	
Classroom disciplinary climate		+		+	
Teacher-student relations					
Self-efficacy		–		+	
Job satisfaction					

Note: Positive relationships that are significant in more than half of the countries are indicated by a "+", while negative relationships that are significant in more than half of the countries are indicated by a "–". Otherwise the cells are left blank. Significance was tested at the 5% level.
1. ISCED 5A Master degree or higher compared with lower-level qualifications.
Source: OECD, *TALIS Database*.
StatLink http://dx.doi.org/10.1787/607814526732

Table 4.4

Relationship between classroom context and teaching practices (2007-08)[1]

Significant variables in the multiple regressions of aspects of classroom context with indices for teaching practice, teachers of lower secondary education[2]

Example: In Australia, teachers are likely to use structuring teaching practices to a greater degree in classes with higher percentages of students with a mother tongue different from the language of instruction, allowing for teacher background characteristics.

	Structuring teaching practices			Student-oriented teaching practices			Enhanced activities		
	Dependent on:			Dependent on:			Dependent on:		
	Class size	Average ability of students in the class[3]	Students with a mother tongue different from the language of instruction[4]	Class size	Average ability of students in the class[3]	Students with a mother tongue different from the language of instruction[4]	Class size	Average ability of students in the class[3]	Students with a mother tongue different from the language of instruction[4]
Australia			+			+			+
Austria				–				+	+
Belgium (Fl.)	–	+		–		+	–		
Brazil		+	+		+	+		+	+
Bulgaria	–	+	+	–	+	+		+	
Denmark								+	
Estonia			+	–	+	+		+	
Hungary				–		+			+
Iceland						+			
Ireland	–			–					
Italy	–			–			–	+	
Korea		+	+	–	+	+	–	+	+
Lithuania			+	–	+	+		+	+
Malaysia		+			+			+	
Malta				–					
Mexico		+			+	+		+	+
Norway	–			–			–		
Poland	+				+	+	+	+	+
Portugal			–	–	+		–	+	
Slovak Republic			+		+	+		+	+
Slovenia					+			+	+
Spain									
Turkey			5		+	5		+	5

1. Controlling for teacher gender, years of experience, highest level of education and subject taught in the target class.

2. Variables where a significant positive relationship was found are indicated by a "+" while those where a significant negative relationship was found are shown with a "–". Cells are blank where no significant relationship was found. Significance was tested at the 5% level.

3. Average ability estimated by the teacher relative to students of the same grade/year level generally.

4. "Less than 10%" or "10% or more".

5. In Turkey questions concerning the language of the student were not administered.

Source: OECD, *TALIS Database.*

StatLink http://dx.doi.org/10.1787/607814526732

Table 4.5

Relationship between school context and teacher-student relations (2007-08)[1]

Significant variables in the multiple multi-level regressions of school context variables and the teacher-student relations index at the school level, teachers of lower secondary education[2]

Example: In Australia, teachers working in private schools report better teacher-student relations than in public schools, after controlling for other variables.

| | Teacher-student relations | | | | |
| | Dependent on: | | | | |
	Private school	City location of school	School size (Total pupil enrolment)	Social background of students[5]	Average ability of students: school level[6]
Australia	+			+	
Austria	+		−		+
Belgium (Fl.)			−	+	+
Brazil			−	+	+
Bulgaria	3				+
Denmark	+		−	+	
Estonia	3	+	−		+
Hungary	+	+		+	−
Iceland	3	4	−	+	
Ireland		+			
Italy	3		−	+	
Korea			−		
Lithuania	3				
Malaysia	3	−	−		+
Malta		4	−		
Mexico			−		+
Norway	3		−		
Poland	3		−		+
Portugal	+		−		+
Slovak Republic		+	−		
Slovenia	3		−		
Spain	+				+
Turkey	+		−		+

1. Controlling for teacher gender, years of experience, level of education and subject taught in the target class.

2. Variables where a significant positive relationship was found are indicated by a "+" while those where a significant negative relationship was found are shown with a "−". Cells are blank where no significant relationship was found. Significance was tested at the 5% level.

3. Less than 10% of teachers report to work in a private school.

4. Less than 10% of the schools are in cities or large cities.

5. Based on teachers' estimation of the education level of students' parents aggregated to the school level.

6. Teachers' estimation of the average ability of students in their class relative to students of the same grade/year level generally, aggregated to the school level.

Source: OECD, *TALIS Database.*

StatLink ⬛🔗 http://dx.doi.org/10.1787/607814526732

Table 4.6

Relationship between teachers' professional development activities and their teaching beliefs about instruction (2007-08)[1]

Significant variables in the multiple regressions of aspects of teachers' professional development with indices for teachers' teaching beliefs about instruction, teachers of lower secondary education[2]

Example: In Australia, teachers held direct transmission beliefs about instruction less strongly, the more days of professional development they had taken part in.

	Direct transmission beliefs about instruction				Constructivist beliefs about instruction			
	Dependent on:				Dependent on:			
	Days of professional development taken by the teacher	Participation in workshops/ courses	Participation in networks	Participation in mentoring activities	Days of professional development taken by the teacher	Participation in workshops/ courses	Participation in networks	Participation in mentoring activities
Australia	−	−			+	+		
Austria	−	−			+	+		
Belgium (Fl.)		−						
Brazil								
Bulgaria		−		+				
Denmark								
Estonia	−	−	+		+			+
Hungary	−					+		+
Iceland	−	−			+	+		
Ireland	−	−						
Italy			−	+	+	+		+
Korea				+	+	+		
Lithuania					+		+	
Malaysia								
Malta								
Mexico					+			
Norway	−	−	−					
Poland		−					+	
Portugal								
Slovak Republic								
Slovenia	−				+			
Spain		+				+	+	
Turkey								

1. Controlling for teacher gender, years of experience, level of education and subject taught in the target class.

2. Variables where a significant positive relationship was found are indicated by a "+" while those where a significant negative relationship was found are shown with a "−". Cells are blank where no significant relationship was found. Significance was tested at the 5% level.

Source: OECD, *TALIS Database*.

StatLink ⟨⟩ http://dx.doi.org/10.1787/607814526732

Table 4.7

Relationship between teachers' professional development activities and teaching practices (2007-08)[1]
Significant variables in the multiple regressions of aspects of teachers' professional development and teaching practice indices, teachers of lower secondary education[2]

Example: In Australia, teachers engaged more frequently in structuring teaching practices, the more days of professional development they had taken after controlling for other variables listed.

	Structuring teaching practices				Student-oriented teaching practices				Enhanced activities			
	Dependent on:				Dependent on:				Dependent on:			
	Days of professional development taken by the teacher	Participation in workshops/courses	Participation in networks	Participation in mentoring activities	Days of professional development taken by the teacher	Participation in workshops/courses	Participation in networks	Participation in mentoring activities	Days of professional development taken by the teacher	Participation in workshops/courses	Participation in networks	Participation in mentoring activities
Australia	+		+	+			+	+			+	+
Austria				+	+		+	+	+		+	+
Belgium (Fl.)	+	+	+	+			+	+	+		+	+
Brazil	+		+	+			+	+	+		+	+
Bulgaria		+		+	+		+	+				+
Denmark	+				+			+	+			+
Estonia			+	+			+	+	+		+	+
Hungary	+	+	+		+	+	+	+	+	+	+	+
Iceland	+				+			+	+			+
Ireland			+		+			+				+
Italy	+				+	+	+	+	+	+	+	+
Korea			+	+	+		+	+	+		+	+
Lithuania		+	+	+			+	+			+	+
Malaysia			+				+	+			+	+
Malta			+	+		+	+	+			+	+
Mexico			+	+			+	+			+	+
Norway							+	+			+	+
Poland			+	+	+		+		+		+	+
Portugal	+	+		+	+	+	+	+	+	+	+	+
Slovak Republic			+	+			+	+		+	+	
Slovenia		+			+	+	+	+	+			+
Spain	+	+			+	+	+	+	+	+	+	+
Turkey	+		+	+	+		+	+	+		+	

1. Controlling for teacher gender, years of experience, level of education and subject taught in the target class.
2. Variables where a significant positive relationship was found are indicated by a "+" while those where a significant negative relationship was found are shown with a "–". Cells are blank where no significant relationship was found. Significance was tested at the 5% level.

Source: OECD, *TALIS Database*.
StatLink http://dx.doi.org/10.1787/607814526732

Table 4.8

Relationship between teachers' professional development activities and teacher co-operation (2007-08)[1]

Significant variables in the multiple regressions of aspects of teachers' professional development and indices of teacher co-operation, teachers of lower secondary education[2]

Example: In Australia, teachers engaged more frequently in exchange and co-ordination for teaching with their colleagues the more days of professional development they had taken part in, after controlling for other variables listed.

	Exchange and co-ordination for teaching				Professional collaboration			
	Dependent on:				Dependent on:			
	Days of professional development taken by the teacher	Participation in workshops/ courses	Participation in networks	Participation in mentoring activities	Days of professional development taken by the teacher	Participation in workshops/ courses	Participation in networks	Participation in mentoring activities
Australia	+	+	+	+	+		+	+
Austria	+		+	+	+		+	+
Belgium (Fl.)	+	+	+	+	+	+	+	+
Brazil	+	+		+	+	+	+	+
Bulgaria			+	+	+	+	+	+
Denmark	+		+	+	+		+	+
Estonia	+	+	+	+	+	+	+	+
Hungary	+	+	+	+	+	+	+	+
Iceland	+	+	+	+	+	+	+	+
Ireland		+	+	+	+	+	+	+
Italy		+	+	+		+	+	+
Korea	+		+	+	+	+	+	+
Lithuania	+	+	+	+	+	+	+	+
Malaysia	+	+	+	+	+		+	+
Malta			+	+			+	+
Mexico		+	+	+		+	+	+
Norway		+	+	+		+	+	+
Poland		+	+	+	+	+	+	+
Portugal		+	+	+		+	+	+
Slovak Republic		+	+	+	+	+	+	+
Slovenia	+	+		+	+	+	+	+
Spain		+	+	+		+	+	+
Turkey	+		+	+	+		+	+

1. Controlling for teacher gender, years of experience, level of education and subject taught in the target class.

2. Variables where a significant positive relationship was found are indicated by a "+" while those where a significant negative relationship was found are shown with a "–". Cells are blank where no significant relationship was found. Significance was tested at the 5% level.

Source: OECD, *TALIS Database.*
StatLink http://dx.doi.org/10.1787/607814526732

Table 4.9

Relationship between teachers' beliefs about instruction and teaching practices (2007-08)[1]

Significant variables in the multiple regressions of the indices for teachers' beliefs about instruction and the indices for teaching practices, teachers of lower secondary education[2]

Example: In Australia, the stronger teachers' beliefs in the direct transmission approach to teaching, the more frequently they engaged in structuring teaching practices, after controlling for other variables listed.

| | Structuring teaching practices | | Student-oriented teaching practices | | Enhanced activities | |
| | Dependent on: | | Dependent on: | | Dependent on: | |
	Direct transmission beliefs about instruction	Constructivist beliefs about instruction	Direct transmission beliefs about instruction	Constructivist beliefs about instruction	Direct transmission beliefs about instruction	Constructivist beliefs about instruction
Australia	+	+		+	+	+
Austria	+	+		+	+	+
Belgium (Fl.)	+	+	+	+	+	+
Brazil	+		+		+	
Bulgaria				+		+
Denmark	+			+		+
Estonia	+	+	+	+	+	+
Hungary	+	+		+		+
Iceland	+	+		+	+	+
Ireland	+			+		+
Italy	+	+		+	+	+
Korea		+	+	–	+	–
Lithuania	+	+	+	+	+	
Malaysia	+					
Malta	+					
Mexico	+		+	+	+	+
Norway	+	+		+		+
Poland		+		+		+
Portugal	+	+		+		+
Slovak Republic	+	+	+	+	+	
Slovenia	+	+		+		+
Spain	+	+		+	+	+
Turkey						

1. Controlling for teacher gender, years of experience, level of education and subject taught in the target class.

2. Variables where a significant positive relationship was found are indicated by a "+" while those where a significant negative relationship was found are shown with a "–". Cells are blank where no significant relationship was found. Significance was tested at the 5% level.

Source: OECD, *TALIS Database*.

StatLink ⏋ http://dx.doi.org/10.1787/607814526732

Table 4.10

Relationship between teaching practices and classroom disciplinary climate (2007-08)[1]

Significant variables in the multiple regressions of the indices for teaching practices and the index for classroom disciplinary climate, teachers of lower secondary education[2]

Example: In Australia, the more frequently teachers engaged in structuring teaching practices, the better they reported the classroom disciplinary climate to be.

| | Classroom disciplinary climate | | |
| | Dependent on: | Dependent on: | Dependent on: |
	Structuring teaching practices	Student-oriented teaching practices	Enhanced activities
Australia	+	+	
Austria		+	−
Belgium (Fl.)	+		
Brazil	+	+	−
Bulgaria	+		
Denmark	+		
Estonia		+	
Hungary			
Iceland			
Ireland	+		
Italy	+		+
Korea	+		
Lithuania		+	−
Malaysia	−	+	−
Malta			
Mexico	+		
Norway			
Poland		+	
Portugal	+	+	
Slovak Republic		+	
Slovenia		+	
Spain	+		
Turkey		+	−

1. Controlling for teacher gender, years of experience, level of education and subject taught in the target class, class size, average ability of the students and percentage of students with a mother tongue different from the language of instruction as estimated by the teachers.

2. Variables where a significant positive relationship was found are indicated by a "+" while those where a significant negative relationship was found are shown with a "−". Cells are blank where no significant relationship was found. Significance was tested at the 5% level.

Source: OECD, *TALIS Database*.

StatLink ▒▒▒ http://dx.doi.org/10.1787/607814526732

Table 4.11

Relationship between teacher co-operation and teacher-student relations (2007-08)[1]

Significant variables in the multiple regressions of the indices for teacher co-operation and the index for teacher-student relations, teachers of lower secondary education[2]

Example: In Australia, the more frequently teachers engaged in exchange and co-ordination for teaching with their colleagues, the better they reported the teacher-student relations to be.

| | Teacher-student relations | |
| | Dependent on: | |
	Exchange and co-ordination for teaching	Professional collaboration
Australia	+	
Austria	+	–
Belgium (Fl.)	+	
Brazil	+	+
Bulgaria	+	
Denmark		
Estonia	+	
Hungary	+	
Iceland	+	
Ireland	+	
Italy	+	
Korea	+	+
Lithuania	+	
Malaysia	+	
Malta	+	
Mexico	+	
Norway		+
Poland	+	
Portugal	+	
Slovak Republic	+	+
Slovenia	+	
Spain	+	
Turkey	+	

1. Examined at the teacher level, controlling for teacher gender, years of experience, level of education and subject taught in the target class, private versus public management of schools, size of the community in which the school is located, average social status of student and average ability of the students estimated by the teachers.

2. Variables where a significant positive relationship was found are indicated by a "+" while those where a significant negative relationship was found are shown with a "–". Cells are blank where no significant relationship was found. Significance was tested at the 5% level.

Source: OECD, *TALIS Database*.
StatLink ⫸ http://dx.doi.org/10.1787/607814526732

Table 4.12

Relationship between teachers' beliefs about instruction, classroom teaching practices, the learning environment, self-efficacy, and teachers' job satisfaction (2007-08)[1]

Significant variables in the multiple multi-level regressions of the indices for teachers' beliefs about instruction, classroom teaching practices, the learning environment, self-efficacy and teachers' job satisfaction, teachers of lower secondary education[2]

Example: In Belgium (Fl), the more strongly teachers held direct transmission beliefs, the less positve they reported their job satisfaction.

| | Job satisfaction | | | | | | | |
| | Dependent on: | | | | | | | |
	Direct transmission beliefs about teaching	Constructivist beliefs about teaching	Structuring teaching practices	Student-oriented teaching practices	Enhanced activities	Classroom disciplinary climate	Teacher-student relations	Teacher's self-efficacy
Australia						+	+	+
Austria						+	+	+
Belgium (Fl.)	–					+	+	+
Brazil		–	+			+	+	+
Bulgaria	+					+	+	+
Denmark						+	+	+
Estonia						+	+	+
Hungary	+					+	+	+
Iceland						+	+	+
Ireland						+	+	+
Italy						+	+	+
Korea		+				+	+	+
Lithuania		+		+		+	+	+
Malaysia						+	+	+
Malta						+	+	+
Mexico						+	+	+
Norway			–			+	+	+
Poland						+	+	+
Portugal	+	–	+			+	+	+
Slovak Republic	+					+	+	+
Slovenia			–			+	+	+
Spain	+		+			+	+	+
Turkey	+					+	+	+

1. Controlling for teacher gender, years of experience, level of education and subject taught in the target class and classroom disciplinary climate and student-teacher relations at the school level.

2. Variables where a significant positive relationship was found are indicated by a "+" while those where a significant negative relationship was found are shown with a "–". Cells are blank where no significant relationship was found. Significance was tested at the 5% level.

Source: OECD, *TALIS Database.*
StatLink ᐧᐧ http://dx.doi.org/10.1787/607814526732

Table 4.13

Relationship between school-level classroom disciplinary climate, teacher-student relations and job satisfaction (2007-08)[1]

Significant variables in the multiple multi-level regressions of the indices for classroom disciplinary climate, teacher-student relations and teachers' job satisfaction, teachers of lower secondary education[2]

	Example: In Australia, the more postive the classroom disciplinary climate reported by teachers, the more positive was teachers' reports of job satisfaction.	
	Job satisfaction	
	Dependent on:	
	Classroom disciplinary climate[3]	Teacher-student relations[3]
Australia	+	
Austria		+
Belgium (Fl.)		
Brazil	+	
Bulgaria		
Denmark	+	
Estonia	+	
Hungary		
Iceland		
Ireland		
Italy		
Korea		
Lithuania		
Malaysia		−
Malta	+	
Mexico		
Norway		
Poland		+
Portugal		
Slovak Republic		
Slovenia	+	
Spain		
Turkey		

1. Controlling for teacher gender, years of experience, level of education and subject taught in the target class and teachers' beliefs about instruction, classroom teaching practices, the learning environment, and self-efficacy at the individual teacher level .

2. Variables where a significant positive relationship was found are indicated by a "+" while those where a significant negative relationship was found are shown with a "−". Cells are blank where no significant relationship was found. Significance was tested at the 5% level.

3. Measured at the school level.

Source: OECD, *TALIS Database.*

StatLink ⬛⬛ http://dx.doi.org/10.1787/607814526732

CHAPTER 5

School Evaluation, Teacher Appraisal and Feedback and the Impact on Schools and Teachers

Highlights

• Appraisal and feedback have a strong positive influence on teachers and their work. Teachers report that it increases their job satisfaction and, to some degree, their job security, and it significantly increases their development as teachers.

• The greater the emphasis on specific aspects of teacher appraisal and feedback, the greater the change in teachers' practices to improve their teaching. In some instances, more emphasis in school evaluations on certain aspects of teaching is linked to an emphasis on these aspects in teacher appraisal and feedback which, in turn, leads to further changes in teachers' reported teaching practices. In these instances, the framework for the evaluation of education appears to be operating effectively.

• A number of countries have a relatively weak evaluation structure and do not benefit from school evaluations and teacher appraisal and feedback. For example, one-third or more of teachers work in schools in Austria (35%), Ireland (39%) and Portugal (33%) that had no school evaluation in the previous five years. In addition, on average across TALIS countries, 13% of teachers did not receive any appraisal or feedback in their school. Large proportions of teachers are missing out on the benefits of appraisal and feedback in Italy (55%), Portugal (26%), and Spain (46%).

• Most teachers work in schools that offer no rewards or recognition for their efforts. Three-quarters reported that they would receive no recognition for improving the quality of their work. A similar proportion reported they would receive no recognition for being more innovative in their teaching. This says little for a number of countries' efforts to promote schools as centres of learning that foster continual improvements.

• Most teachers work in schools that do not reward effective teachers and do not dismiss teachers who perform poorly. Three-quarters of teachers reported that, in their schools, the most effective teachers do not receive the most recognition. A similar proportion reported that, in their schools, teachers would not be dismissed because of sustained poor performance.

INTRODUCTION

The framework for evaluation of education in schools and for appraisal and feedback of teachers are key TALIS concerns. Evaluation can play a key role in school improvement and teacher development (OECD, 2005). Identifying strengths and weaknesses, making informed resource allocation decisions, and motivating actors to improve performance can help achieve policy objectives such as school improvement, school accountability and school choice. Data were collected from school principals and teachers on these and related issues, including the recognition and rewards that teachers receive. Analysis of the data has produced a number of important findings for all stakeholders.

Data from teachers and school principals show that school evaluations can affect the nature and form of teacher appraisal and feedback which can, in turn, affect what teachers do in the classroom. An opportunity therefore exists for policy makers and administrators to shape the framework of evaluation to raise performance and to target specific areas of school education. In particular, TALIS data indicate that opportunities exist to better address teachers' needs for improving their teaching in the areas of teaching students with special learning needs and teaching in a multicultural setting (see also Chapter 3).

In addition, teachers report that the current framework for evaluation lacks the necessary support and incentives for their development and that of the education they provide to students. They report few rewards for improvements or innovations and indicate that in their school, the most effective teachers do not receive the greatest recognition. Opportunities to strengthen the framework for evaluating school education in order to reap the benefits of evaluation therefore appear to exist in most, if not all, education systems. Teachers report that the appraisal and feedback they receive is beneficial, fair and helpful for their development as teachers. This provides further impetus to strengthen and better structure both school evaluations and teacher appraisal and feedback.

The first section discusses the nature and impact of school evaluations across TALIS countries. It focuses on the frequency of evaluation, particularly in countries where schools are rarely, if ever, evaluated, and on the objectives of these evaluations. This is followed by a discussion of teacher appraisal and feedback with special attention to its frequency and focus. The outcomes and impacts of teachers' appraisal and feedback are then discussed in the following sections. Teacher appraisal and feedback in the broader context of school development is then analysed. The links between school evaluations, teacher appraisal and feedback, and impacts on teachers and their teaching are then discussed and concluding comments and key policy implications are then presented.

Analyses presented in this chapter (and throughout this report) and the discussion of the main findings are tempered somewhat by the nature of the TALIS data. It should be noted that, since TALIS is a cross-sectional study, it is not prudent to make sweeping causal conclusions, particularly about the impact on student performance as this is not measured in the TALIS programme. Care must therefore be taken in interpreting results where the long-term impact on student performance cannot be ascertained.

Framework for evaluating education in schools: data collected in TALIS

The role of school evaluation has changed in a number of countries in recent years. Historically, it focused on monitoring schools to ensure adherence to procedures and policies and attended to administrative issues (OECD, 2008d). The focus in a number of countries has now shifted to aspects of school accountability and school improvement. Moreover, in some systems, school performance measures and other school evaluation information are published to promote school choice (Plank and Smith, 2008; OECD, 2006a). An additional factor driving the development of the framework for evaluating education in schools, and of school evaluation in particular, is the recent increase in school autonomy in a number of educational systems (OECD, 2008a).

A lessening of centralised control can lead to an increase in monitoring and evaluation to ensure adherence to common standards (Caldwell, 2002). Moreover, greater school autonomy can lead to more variation in practices as schools are able to choose and refine the practices that best suit their needs. Such variation, and its impact on performance, may need to be evaluated not only to ensure a positive impact on students and adherence to various policy and administrative requirements but also to learn more about effective practices for school improvement. This is particularly important in view of the greater variation in outcomes and achievement among schools in some education systems than in others (OECD, 2007; OECD, 2008a).

School evaluation with a view to school improvement may focus on providing useful information for making and monitoring improvements and can support school principals and teachers (van de Grift and Houtveen, 2006). Appraisal of teachers and subsequent feedback can also help stakeholders to improve schools through more informed decision making (OECD, 2005). Such improvement efforts can be driven by objectives that consider schools as learning organisations which use evaluation to analyse the relationships between inputs, processes and, to some extent, outputs in order to develop practices that build on identified strengths and address weaknesses that can facilitate improvement efforts (Caldwell and Spinks, 1998).

Holding agents accountable for public resources invested and the services provided with such resources is an expanding feature of Government reform in a number of countries (*e.g.* Atkinson, 2005; Dixit, 2002; Mante and O'Brien, 2002). School accountability, which often focuses on measures of school performance, can be an aspect of this accountability and can drive the development of school evaluations (Mckewen, 1995). School accountability can also be part of a broader form of political accountability which holds policy makers accountable through the evaluation of their decision-making and market-based accountability that focuses on the public evaluating different uses of public resources (Ladd and Figlio, 2008). School accountability may also be an important element of standards-based reforms which emphasise standards in teaching practices or the entire school education system. The framework for evaluating education in schools can also be used to drive efforts aimed at teacher accountability. Recently, such reforms have tended to concentrate on student performance standards (Bourque, 2005). School evaluations and teacher appraisal and feedback can focus on such standards, the extent to which they are met, and the methods employed to reach, meet, or exceed them. Identifying and setting standards can also have implications for teachers' professional development, which, in turn, can be oriented to help teachers to better achieve them (OECD, 2005).

When families are free to choose among various schools, school choice can be an important focus of the evaluation of school education. Information about schools helps parents and families decide which school is likely to best meet their child's needs (Glenn and de Groof, 2005). Improved decision-making can increase the effectiveness of the school system as the education offered by diverse schools is better matched to the diverse needs of parents and families if they are free and able to choose between schools (Hoxby, 2003). The effects of more informed school choice depend upon factors such as the type of information available and parents' and families' access to that information (Gorard, Fitz and Taylor, 2001). In some education systems, the results of school evaluations are therefore made available to the public to drive school accountability and improve school choice. For example, in Belgium (Fl.), current information on school evaluations is available on a central website and earlier school reports can be requested by families that are choosing a school for their child (OECD, 2008a).

Data collected in TALIS

Figure 5.1 depicts the framework for evaluating education in schools and the main areas on which data from teachers and school principals were collected. It reflects previous research on the role of evaluation in the development of schools and teachers and on the design of such evaluations to meet education objectives (OECD, 2008d; Sammons *et al.*, 1994; Smith and O'Day, 1991). This framework often begins with direction from the central administrative and policy-making body (Webster, 2005; Caldwell, 2002). In most education systems it is the Government Ministry responsible for school education that sets regulatory and procedural requirements for schools and teachers. Policy makers may set performance standards and implement specific measures which should be, along with other factors, the focus of school evaluations (Ladd, 2007). These may include student performance standards and objectives, school standards, and the effective implementation of particular programmes and policies (Hanushek and Raymond, 2004). A focus on a specific aspect of evaluation, such as teacher appraisal and feedback, may have a flow-on effect on the school and its practices, as teachers are the main actors in achieving school improvement and better student performance (O'Day, 2002). However, for evaluations to be effective their objectives should be aligned with the objectives and incentives of those who are evaluated (Lazear, 2000). To the extent that evaluations of organisations and appraisals of employees create incentives, the evaluations and appraisals need to be aligned so that employees have the incentive to focus their efforts on factors important to the organisation (OECD, 2008d). The extent of this effect can depend on the focus in the school evaluation and the potential impact upon schools (Odden & Busch, 1998). It may also affect the extent to which teacher appraisal and feedback is emphasised within schools (Senge, 2000). However, it is important to recognise that TALIS does not collect information about the objectives, regulations and procedures developed and stated by policy makers in each education system. Data collected in TALIS are at the school and teacher level from school principals and teachers and therefore focus on the final three aspects of the evaluative framework of school education depicted in Figure 5.1.

TALIS collected data on school evaluations from school principals. The data include the frequency of school evaluations, including school self-evaluations, and the importance placed upon various areas. Data were also obtained on the impacts and outcomes of school evaluations, with a focus on the extent to which these outcomes affect the school principal and the school's teachers. TALIS also collected data from teachers on the focus and outcomes of teacher appraisal and feedback. This information makes it possible to see the extent to which the focus of school evaluations is reflected in teacher appraisal and feedback.

Both school evaluation and teacher appraisal and feedback should aim to influence the development and improvement of schools and teachers. Even a framework for evaluation based on regulations and procedural requirements would focus on maintaining standards that ensure an identified level of quality of education. TALIS therefore collected information on changes in teaching practices and other aspects of school education subsequent to teacher appraisal and feedback. According to the model depicted in Figure 5.1, a focus in school evaluations on specific areas which reflect stated policy priorities should also be a focus of teacher appraisal and feedback. This should in turn affect practices in those areas. Considering that TALIS does not collect information on student outcomes, teachers' reports of changes in teaching practices are used to assess the impact of the framework of evaluation. In addition, teachers' reports of their development needs provide further information on the relevance and impact of this framework on teachers' development.

Data were also collected from teachers on the role of appraisal and feedback in relation to rewards and recognition within schools. The focus on factors associated with school improvement and teachers' development included teachers' perceptions of the recognition and rewards obtained for their effectiveness and innovation in teaching.

In gathering data in TALIS, the following definitions were applied:

• School evaluation refers to an evaluation of the whole school rather than of individual subjects or departments.

• Teacher appraisal and feedback occurs when a teacher's work is reviewed by either the school principal, an external inspector or the teacher's colleagues. This appraisal can be conducted in ways ranging from a more formal, objective approach (*e.g.* as part of a formal performance management system, involving set procedures and criteria) to a more informal, more subjective approach (*e.g.* informal discussions with the teacher).

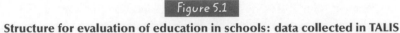

Figure 5.1

Structure for evaluation of education in schools: data collected in TALIS

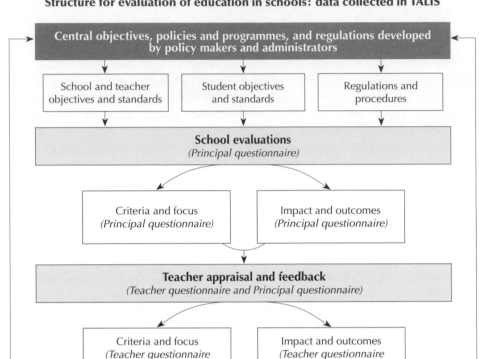

Source: OECD.

StatLink 🔗 http://dx.doi.org/10.1787/607856444110

NATURE AND IMPACT OF SCHOOL EVALUATIONS

TALIS provides information on the frequency of school self-evaluations and external school evaluations (*e.g.* those conducted by a school inspector or an agent from a comparable institution) and on the areas covered by such evaluations. School principals were asked to rate the importance of 17 items ranging from measures of student performance to student discipline and behaviour. Data were also obtained on the influence of evaluations upon important aspects which can affect schools and teachers, such as an impact on the school budget, performance feedback, and teachers' remuneration. In addition, data were obtained from school principals regarding the publication of information on school evaluations.[1]

Frequency of school evaluations

The frequency of school evaluations provides an initial indication of both the breadth of the evaluation of education in schools and the place of school evaluations in the framework of evaluation. Distinctions between external and internal evaluations identify the actors involved and the interaction between schools and a centralised decision-making body. As Table 5.1 shows, countries differ considerably in this respect. One-third or more of teachers worked in schools whose school principal reported no internal or external school evaluations in the previous five years in Austria (35%), Ireland (39%), and Portugal (33%). This also was the case for around one-quarter of teachers in Denmark and Spain and around one-fifth in Brazil, Bulgaria and Italy. Clearly, these countries have relatively little in the way of a framework for school evaluation. However, in Ireland and Italy policies are being implemented to increase the frequency and reach of school evaluations but at the time of the survey these policies were not yet fully in place.

In contrast, in a number of countries teachers worked in schools with at least one evaluation over the previous five years. In Australia, Brazil, Bulgaria, Hungary, Italy, Korea, Lithuania, Malaysia, Malta, Mexico, Poland, the Slovak Republic, Slovenia and Turkey, at least half of teachers worked in schools whose school principal reported at least an annual school evaluation (either an external evaluation or a school self-evaluation). This is an interesting finding for Brazil, Bulgaria and Italy where the frequency of school evaluations is particularly varied. In each of these countries, over half of teachers work in schools with at least annual evaluations but also around one-fifth work in schools that had had no evaluation in the previous five years. Over three-quarters of teachers in Lithuania, Malaysia and the Slovak Republic worked in schools whose school principal reported having annual or more frequent evaluations (Source: OECD, *TALIS Database.*). This represents a stark contrast with schools with no evaluations in the previous five years.

School evaluations conducted by an external inspectorate or equivalent agency were slightly less frequent than school self-evaluations. Eighty per cent of teachers worked in schools whose school principal reported a school self-evaluation in the previous five years compared to some 70% who worked in schools whose school principal reported an external inspection (Table 5.1). This indicates that in some countries, systems of school evaluation are more internally driven. As an example, around half of teachers in Malta worked in schools whose school principal reported an external evaluation but 90% worked in schools where the school principal reported having a school self-evaluation in the previous five years. Denmark, Italy, Lithuania, the Slovak Republic and Slovenia also had relatively fewer external evaluations than self-evaluations.

Across TALIS countries there was little difference in the frequency of external evaluations between public schools and Government-dependent and independent schools (Source: OECD, *TALIS Database.*). In general, there do not appear to be separate requirements for the public and private school sectors, as there is little difference in the frequency of external evaluations in most countries. However, in Hungary, Korea and Spain, public schools have significantly less frequent external evaluations than other schools, although the difference is less marked in Korea. In contrast, public schools in Australia were more likely than other schools to have had at least annual external evaluations.

The frequency of school self-evaluations also does not vary significantly between school sectors across TALIS countries. Exceptions are public schools in Belgium (Fl.) and Italy, which have more frequent self-evaluations than other schools. In Hungary and Spain the reverse is true: the frequency of school self-evaluations is significantly greater for private schools. Among schools that had not conducted either an internal or external evaluation in the previous five years, there was also little difference between school sectors in most countries. However, in Belgium (Fl.) public schools were more likely to have undertaken an evaluation in the previous five years, whereas in Spain public schools were less likely to have done so (Source: OECD, *TALIS Database.*). It should be noted that a number of countries do not have sufficiently large numbers of private schools to make meaningful comparisons.

An important finding is that in a number of countries a substantial proportion of schools only conducted self-evaluations. They include Austria (22% of teachers worked in schools that conducted a self-evaluation but no external evaluation during the previous five years), Denmark (27%), Italy (40%), Lithuania (34%), Malta (46%), Norway (17%), the Slovak Republic (17%) and Slovenia (24%). As Table 5.1 shows, several of these countries have relatively low levels of external evaluations of schools. This indicates the lack of a formal framework requiring schools to be evaluated annually by an external inspector. The fact that these schools conducted self-evaluations in the absence of strict regulatory requirements demonstrates that school principals and teachers consider evaluation a valuable tool for internal development even if policy makers in these countries may not have imposed it. Such schools appear to be leading the development of this aspect of evaluation of school education and provide an opportunity to learn from their example.

Focus of school evaluations

School principals were asked to rate the importance of 17 potentially important areas in evaluations undertaken in the previous five years. Given that these areas (see Table 5.1a) would generally be considered important for students' education, it is not surprising that most teachers worked in schools whose school principals considered them to be of moderate or high importance in school evaluations conducted at their school. However, while most of the criteria were considered important, the greatest proportion of teachers worked in schools where the school principal reported that relations between teachers and students were of moderate or high importance, and teaching in a multicultural setting the lowest.

Given the relatively even spread across countries in the importance accorded to each item, it is interesting to analyse differences within countries. Therefore, a high focus on particular items in, for example, Spain is discussed below relative to the importance of other items in Spain rather than in other countries. This also helps account for national differences in the social desirability of responses. As an example, some three-quarters or more teachers in Australia work in schools where their school principal rated all of the items as being of moderate or high importance, except for student feedback on teaching at the school, teaching in a multicultural setting, and inferences drawn from a direct appraisal of classroom teaching. Differences in the importance of various items show some interesting country trends which are discussed below.

Table 5.1a distinguishes between three categories of student outcomes in school evaluations: student test scores, retention and pass rates, and a category described as other learning outcomes. Interestingly, school principals in some countries reported that specific types of student outcomes were emphasised more than others in school evaluations. Comparing student outcomes criteria, student test scores were the most important criteria in seven TALIS countries (Bulgaria, Malaysia, Malta, Norway, Poland, the Slovak Republic and Turkey). Retention and pass rates of students was the most important in eight TALIS countries (Belgium (Fl.), Brazil, Estonia, Ireland, Italy, Mexico, Portugal and Spain) while in nine TALIS countries the category "other student learning outcomes" was considered the most important evaluative measure of student outcomes (Australia, Austria, Denmark, Hungary, Iceland, Korea, Lithuania, Malta and Slovenia) (Table 5.1a).

Comparing the other criteria, feedback from parents and students were considered to be of somewhat relatively low importance according to school principals in a number of TALIS countries. Student feedback about the teaching they received was rated of relatively low importance in Australia, Bulgaria, Hungary, Ireland, Malta and Slovenia where it was one the three lowest rated criteria for school evaluations (measured as the percentage of teachers whose school principal considered it to be of moderate or high importance). However, this does not necessarily mean that the role of students is disregarded, as relations between teachers and students were in the three highest rated criteria in each of these countries except Bulgaria. Feedback from parents was the top rated criteria for school evaluations in Iceland and Italy and the lowest rated criteria in Brazil and Bulgaria (Table 5.1a).

Given the resources devoted to teachers' professional development and its importance in school development, it is interesting that it was in the three highest rated criteria in Belgium (Fl.), Bulgaria, Estonia, Ireland, Korea, Lithuania and Slovenia and was one of the three lowest rated criteria Austria and Italy. This is particularly significant in light of the discussion of this issue in Chapter 3. In addition, teachers who work well with the school principal and their colleagues was the highest rated criteria in Korea, Malaysia and Slovenia (Figure 5.2).

Criteria of school evaluations (2007-08)

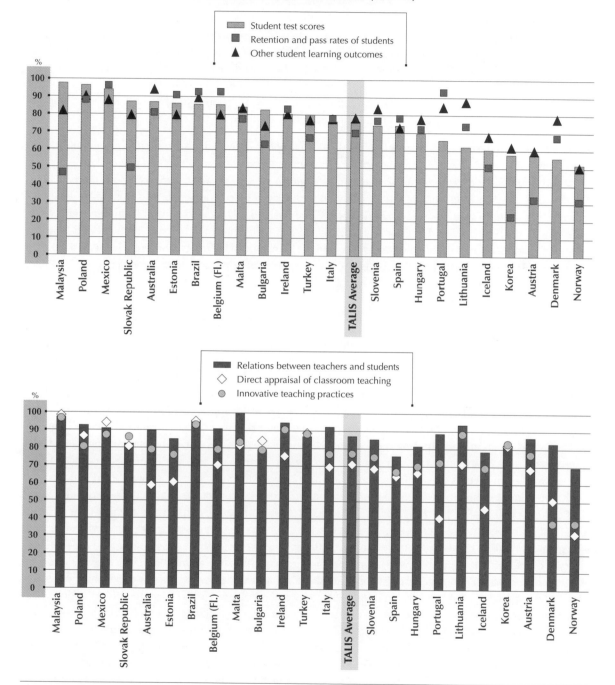

Percentage of teachers of lower secondary education whose school principal reported that this criteria were considered with high or moderate importance in school self-evaluations or external evaluations.

Countries are ranked in descending order of the importance of student test scores in school evaluations.

Source: OECD, Table 5.1a.

StatLink http://dx.doi.org/10.1787/607856444110

Central to teachers' ability to educate students is their knowledge of their main subject fields and of instructional practices. These were considered to be of high importance in school evaluations in Hungary and Mexico but of relatively low importance in Spain where they were the two lowest rated criteria for school evaluations. This may reflect the comparatively little evaluation of teachers and schools in Spain (see Tables 5.1 and 5.3). A further key aspect of teaching is the importance accorded to innovative teaching practices. This was not in the two highest rated criteria for school evaluations in any TALIS country but was in the two lowest rated criteria in Denmark and Poland. Other important aspects of teachers' work include classroom management skills and student discipline and behaviour. These were generally considered to be of relatively high importance in school evaluations. Student discipline was the top rated criteria in Malta and Norway and teachers' classroom management was the top rated criteria in Bulgaria and Turkey (Table 5.1a).

An indication of the extent to which school evaluations emphasise evaluating teaching is the importance of direct appraisal of classroom teaching. Direct appraisals of teaching are considered valuable tools in a number of schools and education systems (OECD, 2008d; Malone, 2002). They can be viewed as complementary to student outcome data in evaluating school education. However, school principals in a number of countries reported that school evaluations gave relatively low emphasis to this method of evaluating teachers' work. On average, teachers in Australia, Estonia, Hungary, Ireland, Italy, Lithuania, Norway, Portugal and Slovenia worked in schools whose school principal reported this as being one of the three lowest rated criteria for school evaluations. However, direct appraisal of teachers was one of the top three highest rated criteria in Brazil, Bulgaria, Malaysia and Turkey.

Teaching in a multicultural setting was the lowest rated criteria for school evaluations on average across TALIS countries and also specifically in Australia, Belgium (Fl.), Estonia, Hungary, Iceland, Lithuania, Malta, Poland, the Slovak Republic and Slovenia. A relatively low emphasis was also given to teaching students with special learning needs on average across TALIS countries except in Estonia, Ireland and the Slovak Republic where it was one of the two highest rated criteria. Intuitively, teaching in a multicultural setting would not be an important factor in school evaluations if the school was not multicultural to an extent that affects teaching and learning. However, this may be an issue for countries with a large and growing proportion of students with an immigrant background (OECD, 2008b). Indeed, teachers' reports of the proportion of students they teach whose linguistic background is different from the language of instruction indicate that school evaluations may not sufficiently emphasise a potentially important aspect of teachers' work. Across TALIS countries, similar proportions of teachers worked in schools where their school principals reported their school evaluations considered teaching in a multi-cultural setting to be of no, low, or high importance regardless of the linguistic diversity in teachers' classrooms (Source: OECD, *TALIS Database.*). However there were exceptions to the average pattern, as in some countries there was a greater emphasis on teaching in a multi-cultural setting in evaluations of schools with greater linguistic diversity. School evaluations that appear to recognise the need to adapt to the linguistic diversity of the student population were more common in Australia, Austria, Belgium (Fl.), Denmark, Norway and, to a lesser extent, Portugal. As an example, in Australia, among teachers who reported teaching classes in which 60% or more of the students had a linguistic background other than the language of instruction, 43% worked in schools that gave high importance in school evaluations to teaching in a multicultural setting. This contrasts with an overall Australian average of only 15% of teachers who worked in schools that gave this high importance. This relationship is also evident in Bulgaria, where teaching in a multicultural setting had relatively high importance in school evaluations in schools with high levels of linguistic diversity but little importance in schools with a more linguistically homogenous student population (Source: OECD, *TALIS Database.*).

The relatively minor focus on teaching in a multicultural setting in school evaluations may be a problem if teachers report the need for improvements in their teaching in a multicultural setting (see Chapter 3). A comparison of the importance of the items included in school evaluations and teachers' professional development needs shows that evaluations might be better structured to address areas in which teachers report the need for further development. For teaching in a multicultural setting, there is a quantitatively small but statistically significant relationship between the emphasis on teaching in a multicultural setting in school evaluations and teachers' professional development needs in this area. A positive relationship may indicate that the school evaluations are designed in a manner that recognises the importance of teaching in a multicultural setting for teachers in these schools and that teachers' initial education and professional development were inadequate to properly address this issue.

On average across TALIS countries, 14% of teachers reported a high level of need for professional development for teaching in a multicultural setting (Table 3.4).[2] One-quarter of these teachers worked in schools whose school principal reported that teaching in a multicultural setting was either not considered in their school evaluations or had low importance. A further 33% of teachers reported having a moderate level of need for professional development in this area, and of these teachers, 28% worked in schools where again it was either not considered or considered to have low importance in school evaluations. Iceland, Ireland and Korea have larger proportions of teachers who reported higher levels of professional development needs in this area; a substantial proportion of these teachers worked in schools where teaching in a multicultural setting was either not considered or considered of low importance in school evaluations. This situation may be exacerbated in schools reporting a lack of school evaluations. In contrast, in Malaysia over three-quarters of teachers who reported a high level of development need in this area worked in schools that gave teaching in a multicultural setting moderate or high importance in their school evaluations (Source: OECD, TALIS Database.). This may be an indication that school evaluations are targeted to address teachers' development needs or issues that coincide with those needs. There is, in any case, a clear opportunity to restructure school evaluations to better address this issue in schools where teachers see a moderate or high need for further professional development in this area. This opportunity is even greater in education systems that consider improving the teaching and learning offered in schools serving multicultural populations to be of great importance.

Across TALIS countries, teachers with more linguistically diverse classrooms did not report a stronger need for professional development for teaching in a multicultural setting. However, there were strong positive relationships in Austria, Belgium (Fl.) and Denmark and a slightly weaker positive relationship in Bulgaria and Slovenia. In these countries, teachers' needs for professional development for teaching in a multicultural setting were greater for teachers in more linguistically diverse classrooms. Importantly, in these countries, as well as in Australia, Norway and the Slovak Republic, school evaluations are more likely to focus on teaching in a multicultural setting if teachers report having a moderate or high need for further development in this area and have linguistically diverse classrooms (Source: OECD, TALIS Database.). School evaluations appear to be better targeted in these countries to the needs of teachers and the linguistic diversity of their students.

Influence of school evaluations

To better understand the role of school evaluations in the framework for evaluating education in schools, school principals were asked to identify the level of influence of school evaluations in six areas. If school evaluations are to have an impact on school principals and teachers, and ultimately on student learning, they will have to have an effect on the functioning of schools and potentially on the development of school principals and teachers. The greater the potential impact of a school evaluation the greater the potential impact on the education offered by schools. Table 5.2 shows that school evaluations generally have a high or moderate level of influence on performance appraisal and feedback but relatively less on financial matters. These school-level data support the system-level data collected from OECD countries (OECD, 2008a).

More than eight teachers in ten worked in schools whose school principal reported that school evaluations had a high or moderate effect on performance feedback to their school (Table 5.2).[3] Over three-quarters of teachers worked in schools whose school principal also reported a high or moderate effect on the appraisal of the school management's performance. Slightly fewer teachers (71%) worked in schools whose school principal reported this effect on the appraisal of teachers' performance in their school and on the assistance provided to teachers to improve their teaching skills (70%). Except in Denmark, Iceland and Spain a large proportion of teachers worked in schools whose school principal reported that school evaluations had a high or moderate effect on performance feedback to the school.

Unlike the appraisal of school management and feedback to schools, school evaluations had little influence on the school budget. Across TALIS countries, less than half of teachers worked in schools whose school principal reported that school evaluations had a moderate or high influence on the school budget (Table 5.2). However, differences among countries range from three-quarters of teachers in Australia and Korea to less than 20% in Austria, Iceland, Poland and the Slovak Republic. It should be noted that influence on the school budget can be interpreted in two ways. It may represent a change in the level of funding received by schools from the Government or other sources, or it may represent a change in the internal allocation of the budget. In Italy, for example, a school evaluation cannot lead to a change in the funds provided to schools by the Government. It is therefore assumed that when Italian school principals reported that the evaluation had an effect on the school budget, this meant that it affected internal decisions regarding allocation. This may be linked to the school self-evaluations which have been promoted by the Italian Ministry to improve the decision making, operation and effectiveness of schools[4] (see Table 5.1).

Information collected on the impact of school evaluations on teachers focuses on the impact on the appraisal of their performance, the assistance they receive to improve their teaching, and their remuneration and bonuses. Over 70% of teachers' school principals reported that school evaluations had a moderate or high influence on appraisals of teachers' performance (Table 5.2). However, countries differed widely in this respect; substantially more teachers worked in schools where this had a relatively greater influence in school evaluations in Brazil, Malaysia, Mexico, and Poland. Some 70% of teachers worked in schools whose school principal reported that evaluations had a moderate or high influence on the assistance provided to teachers to improve their teaching skills. It was reported to be high in Australia, Brazil, Korea, Malaysia, Malta, Mexico, the Slovak Republic and Slovenia but relatively low in Denmark and Iceland.

School evaluations had substantially less influence on teachers' remuneration and bonuses, with just over one-quarter of teachers working in schools whose school principal reported a moderate or high influence (Table 5.2). Furthermore, they had very little influence in a number of countries; less than 10% of teachers worked in schools whose school principal reported a high or moderate influence in Australia, Austria, Belgium (Fl.), Denmark, Ireland, Norway, Portugal and Spain. They had a greater influence in Brazil, Hungary, Italy, Malaysia, Mexico, Poland and the Slovak Republic.

Publication of information on school evaluations

Publication of measures of school performance has been a contentious policy issue in a number of countries. On the one hand, there is evidence of positive benefits on student performance. For example, PISA shows publication of school results to be positively associated with performance, even after discounting for other factors, including students' social background (OECD, 2007). On the other hand, teachers in some systems take a negative view of publication of the performance measures or information on evaluations (Bethell, 2005). The publication of information on school evaluations is generally considered useful for policies and programmes aimed at school accountability, yet information on school performance can also help parents and families choose the school their child will attend (Gorard, Fitz and Taylor, 2001). In some countries, it may reflect views on freedom of information or be a response to regulatory requirements (OECD, 2008a).

Decisions to publish this information should not be viewed as necessarily imposed top-down. Schools themselves may also publish school results either at the national or local level if they find this will help their school. They may believe that it can lead to school improvements, or they may desire to share information with the local community. Some private schools may be required to publish information on their schools as part of a network of private schools.

Table 5.2a shows that just over half of teachers in TALIS countries worked in schools whose school principal reported that the results of their school evaluations were published. This result does not differentiate between external evaluations and school self-evaluations. There were large discrepancies in the extent to which this information was published across countries. In Poland and Turkey, less than 20% of teachers worked in schools whose school principal reported that this information was published, whereas in Denmark over 80% of teachers worked in such schools. Of greater importance from a policy perspective are the clear discrepancies within countries. Except in federal countries, where differences between states or regions are to be expected, a national policy to publish this information should affect most, if not all, of the country's schools. Except for a few countries, such as Denmark, this was clearly not the case. Therefore, individual schools, local communities, or municipalities must make these decisions. The publication of information on school evaluations in tables that compare schools is uncommon except in Brazil, Denmark and Mexico. This also suggests that the publication of information is decided by individual schools, which lack data for other schools to make comparative tables.

There may be some misunderstanding about the extent of Government involvement in the publication of comparative tables. School principals were asked if these tables were compiled by Governments. Positive responses were received in countries with no Government policy in this area. However, comparative tables have sometimes been published in the media, and the information has become widely known. Hence, even in the absence of Government policy, the ability of the media to make these comparisons may have led school principals to assume Government involvement. This is potentially an important lesson for Governments regarding the information they make publicly available and their efforts to control the use of this information.

FORM OF TEACHER APPRAISAL AND FEEDBACK

This section focuses on the form of teacher appraisal and feedback. It concentrates initially on the frequency of appraisal and feedback and whether it is internally or externally provided. The criteria for teacher appraisal and feedback are the same as those discussed for school evaluations and include information on student outcomes, direct appraisals of teaching, feedback from stakeholders, professional development, and a variety of teaching and school activities. It therefore provides information not only on the focus of teacher appraisal and feedback within schools but also on the links with school evaluations.

Frequency of appraisal and feedback

Frequency of teachers' appraisal and feedback is a starting point for analysis of these issues. It provides a measure of the extent to which this plays a role in teachers' development and in communication among colleagues within schools. It may also provide an indication of the extent to which teachers' co-operation and collective responsibility for students' education are present in schools. Importantly, it identifies teachers who received no appraisal or feedback about their work as teachers. Insofar as appraisal and feedback are considered beneficial for teachers and the education students receive, this is an important indicator for understanding more about teachers' careers, their development and ways to raise school effectiveness.

Data were obtained on the appraisal and feedback teachers received in their school. Table 5.3 shows that a distinction was made between the frequency of appraisal and feedback and its source: the school principal; other teachers or members of the school management team; or an external (to the school) individual or body.

Appraisal and feedback were received more often from within the school than from an external source. Just over half of teachers had not received any appraisal or feedback from an external source (*e.g.* a school inspector). In fact, over three-quarters of teachers in Norway and Portugal did not receive appraisal or feedback from an external agent. In Italy, external teacher appraisal and feedback is virtually non-existent. These three countries also have a large proportion of teachers working in schools whose school principal reported that they had not received an external school evaluation in the previous five years (Table 5.1).

Thirteen per cent of teachers in TALIS countries did not receive any feedback or appraisal of their work in their school (Figure 5.3). Clearly, the evaluative element of these teachers' work was minimal in these cases. As Table 5.3 shows, a substantial proportion of teachers received no appraisal or feedback from any source in some countries, including Ireland (26%), Italy (55%), Portugal (26%) and Spain (46%). Teachers in these countries with relatively weak evaluation frameworks are not receiving the potential benefits of appraisal and feedback. Moreover, teacher appraisal and feedback can be an effective policy lever for developing specific aspects of education targeted by policy makers and administrators.

Teachers were asked about the appraisal and feedback they had received in their school. However, as some teachers were new to their school, they may not have been there long enough to receive the normal appraisal and feedback, or conversely, they may receive substantial appraisal and feedback because they are new. Of the teachers who received no appraisal or feedback, just under one-quarter were in their first year and 37% were in their first two years at the school (Source: OECD, *TALIS Database*.). In comparison, the TALIS average is 12 and 11% of teachers in their first and second year, respectively. However, the relationship between the frequency of teachers' appraisal and feedback and the number of years of teaching at the school is not linear.

Figure 5.3

**Teachers who received no appraisal or feedback
and teachers in schools that had no school evaluation in the previous five years (2007-08)**

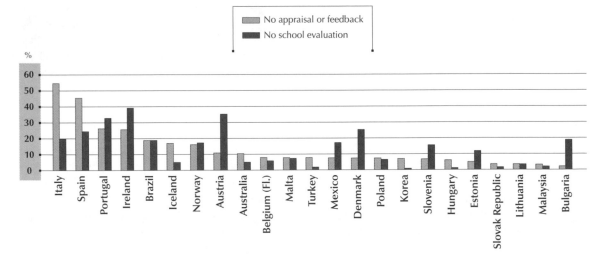

Countries are ranked in descending order of the percentage of teachers who have received no appraisal or feedback.
Source: OECD, Tables 5.1 and 5.3.

StatLink ⟪⟫ http://dx.doi.org/10.1787/607856444110

Teachers in their first two years were more likely either to have received no appraisal and feedback or to have received very frequent appraisal and feedback (more than once per month). Policy makers and administrators wishing to encourage more appraisal and feedback for teachers new to a school may wish to encourage or implement effective school mentoring and induction programmes (Rockoff, 2008). In Mexico and Malta, teachers in their first two years at a school are significantly more likely to have more appraisal and feedback in schools with formal induction processes. For example, among teachers in Mexico who had received no appraisal or feedback in their school, 72% were in schools that had no formal induction process; over half of all Mexican teachers work in schools without a formal induction process. However, across TALIS countries, there is no quantitatively important relationship between the frequency of appraisal and feedback for teachers in their first two years at a school and the presence of a mentoring programme (Source: OECD, *TALIS Database.*). This indicates that mentoring programmes may need to be adapted if their purpose is to provide more appraisal and feedback to new teachers. Mentoring programmes may of course have objectives unrelated to consistent teacher appraisal and feedback, but this goes against the general impression of the nature and purpose of mentoring and induction programmes (OECD, 2005: Ingersoll & Smith, 2004; Serpell, 2000).

As Figure 5.3 indicates, teachers working in schools that had no school evaluations over the previous five years were less likely to receive appraisal or feedback. For example, in Korea, in schools that had not conducted or participated in a school evaluation during the previous five years, 18% of teachers had also never received any appraisal or feedback at that school. Only 7% of teachers had not if the school had conducted or been subject to an evaluation (Source: OECD, *TALIS Database.*). This offers further evidence that school evaluations can be an essential component of an evaluative framework which can foster and potentially shape teacher appraisal and feedback. Policy makers may also be able to alter the framework and requirements of school evaluations to better shape the appraisal and feedback received by teachers.

Focus of appraisal and feedback

Policy makers and administrators attempting to shape and develop the evaluation of school education would naturally consider the focus of teacher appraisal and feedback important in terms of providing incentives and shaping teachers' actions within schools. TALIS obtained information from teachers on the importance of 17 items in the appraisal and feedback they had received at their school. These are the same as those discussed for school evaluations and include: various student performance measures; feedback from parents and students; teaching practices and requirements; teachers' knowledge and understanding of their main subject field and instructional practices; relations with students; findings from direct appraisals of classroom teaching; professional development; and, teachers' handling of student discipline and behaviour problems. Given the relatively even spread across countries in the importance given to each item, it is interesting to again analyse differences within countries. Therefore, the discussion below focuses on differences within each country so that a high focus on particular criteria in, for example, Austria is discussed relative to the importance placed on other items in Austria rather than on its importance in other countries. This also helps take into account national differences in the social desirability of responses.

Given the importance of these aspects of school education, it is not surprising that most were considered to be of fairly high importance. As Table 5.4 shows, the areas considered by most teachers to be of moderate or high importance were relations between teachers and students; knowledge and understanding of instructional practices; classroom management; and knowledge and understanding of teachers' main instructional fields (approximately 80% on average for each of these items across TALIS countries). In comparison, substantially fewer teachers reported that teaching students with special needs, the retention and pass rates of students and teaching in a multicultural setting were of moderate or high importance in their appraisal and feedback. Yet, even with their comparably lower rating (57, 56 and 45%, respectively), a number of teachers participating in appraisal and feedback still reported that these had moderate or high importance in the appraisal and feedback they received. The importance of selected items is illustrated in Figure 5.4.

Certain elements of teaching and teachers' work in the classroom were understandably considered important elements of appraisal and feedback. In fact, across TALIS countries, the quality of teachers' relations with students was the most important item as measured by the percentage of teachers who considered it to have moderate or high importance. This is an important finding as it emphasises the importance accorded to teacher-student relations in school education and also because of the relatively lesser importance given to feedback from students (on average across TALIS countries, 73% of teachers rated it as of high or moderate importance in their appraisal and feedback).While teacher-student relations were considered to be of prime importance across TALIS countries, measurement of these relations in teachers' appraisal and feedback did not depend entirely on student opinion and feedback. It is therefore assumed that other methods were used to determine the state of these relations. Another area of relatively high importance in assessing teaching and teachers' work is direct appraisal of classroom teaching. This is a clear and visible element of a system of appraisal and feedback within schools and of moderate or high importance in the appraisals and feedback of, on average, just under three-quarters of teachers. It was in the top three rated criteria (measured by the percentage of teachers rating it as of moderate or high importance in their teacher appraisal and feedback) in Austria, Belgium (Fl.) and the Slovak Republic. Yet, it was the second lowest rated criteria in Portugal.

Countries vary substantially in the emphasis on student outcomes in teachers' appraisal and feedback. Three aspects were considered: student test scores; students' retention and pass rates; and other student learning outcomes. On average across TALIS countries, the retention and pass rates of students was the second lowest rated criteria in teacher appraisal and feedback and was the lowest rated criteria in Austria and Italy. Student test scores were also not given a high priority in teacher appraisal and feedback in a number of TALIS countries. It was one of the three lowest rated criteria in Denmark, Hungary and Italy. There are often substantial differences in the importance placed upon these three measures of student outcomes within countries: for example, in Denmark student test scores and the retention and pass rates of students were considered to be of moderate or high importance by just over one-quarter of teachers but other student learning outcomes were of considerably more importance to teacher appraisal and feedback with just fewer than half of Danish teachers reporting it to be of moderate or high importance. Feedback from stakeholders (*e.g.* students and parents) can be useful for teachers and for those responsible for appraising teachers but was rated relatively lowly on average across TALIS countries. Student feedback on the education they receive was the second highest rated criteria in Iceland and Portugal but was the lowest rated criteria in Spain. Feedback from parents was one of the lowest three rated criteria in Belgium (Fl.), Brazil, Bulgaria, Mexico and Turkey.

Given the importance of professional development in some education systems it is important to clarify the role of appraisal and feedback not only in identifying development needs but also in assessing the impact of professional development on the work of teachers within schools. It is clear that while it is of moderate or high importance in the appraisal and feedback of the majority of teachers across TALIS countries, it was not in the five highest rated criteria of any TALIS country. Moreover, it was one of the lowest three rated criteria in teacher appraisal and feedback in Australia, Austria, Hungary, Ireland, Malta, the Slovak Republic and Spain. A broader view of professional development activities encompasses non-formal activities and the learning that takes place when working with peers and colleagues. Teachers' work with the school principal and colleagues in their school had moderate or high importance in the appraisal and feedback of a large percentage of teachers across TALIS countries. It was one of the top three highest rated criteria in Belgium (Fl.), Denmark, Iceland, Norway and Portugal.

Given teachers' roles in schools and their positions as educators, it is perhaps not surprising that for over three-quarters of teachers their knowledge and understanding of their main subject fields and of instructional practices in these fields was of moderate or high importance in the appraisal and feedback they receive. This was considered one of the most important items in teachers' appraisal and feedback across TALIS countries. Knowledge and understanding of their main subject fields was one of the two most important criteria in Australia, Brazil,

Bulgaria, Hungary, Lithuania, Malaysia and Mexico. Similarly, knowledge and understanding of instructional practices in their main subject fields was one of the two most important criteria for teacher appraisal and feedback in Estonia, Hungary, Malaysia, Mexico, the Slovak Republic and Slovenia.

Other issues concerning classroom teaching are student discipline and classroom management practices. Both were of importance in teachers' appraisal and feedback. Teachers' classroom management was the highest rated criteria in teacher appraisal and feedback in Bulgaria, Korea and Turkey. Student discipline was the highest rated criteria in Poland and Spain.

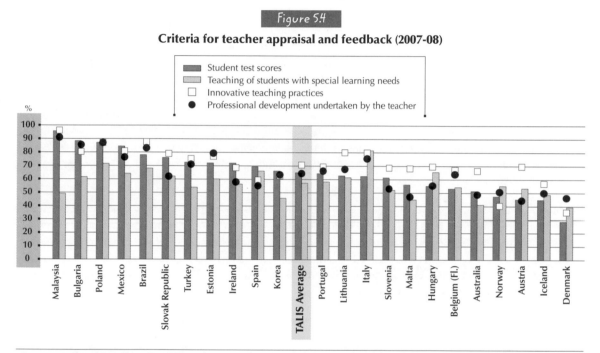

Figure 5.4

Criteria for teacher appraisal and feedback (2007-08)

Percentage of teachers of lower secondary education who reported that these criteria were considered with high or moderate importance in the appraisal and/or feedback they received.
Countries are ranked in descending order of the importance of student test scores in teacher appraisal and feedback.
Source: OECD, Table 5.4.

StatLink ⟶ http://dx.doi.org/10.1787/607856444110

Teaching in a multicultural setting and teaching students with special learning needs

A number of countries have concerns about the performance of students from immigrant backgrounds and those with special learning needs (OECD, 2008b; OECD 2006b). Teachers may have to use teaching methods that adapt to meet these needs. It is therefore somewhat surprising that the importance of teaching in a multicultural setting and teaching students with special learning needs were reported by a comparatively low percentage of teachers as being of moderate or high importance in their appraisal and feedback. On average across TALIS countries, teaching in a multicultural setting was the lowest rated criteria in teacher appraisal and feedback and was the lowest rated criteria in 16 TALIS countries (Australia, Belgium (Fl.), Denmark, Estonia, Hungary, Iceland, Ireland, Korea, Lithuania, Malta, Norway, Poland, Portugal, the Slovak Republic, Slovenia, and Turkey). In a similar vein, teaching students with special learning needs was one of the lowest three rated criteria in teacher appraisal and feedback in 13 TALIS countries (Australia, Brazil, Bulgaria, Estonia, Ireland, Lithuania, Malaysia, Malta, Mexico, Poland, Portugal, Slovenia and Turkey).

This may be a concern for policy makers in countries where the policy emphasis on these issues is not matched by their importance in the system of teacher appraisal and feedback. However, if teachers do not consider teaching in a multicultural setting or teaching students with special learning needs to be important, a problem may not exist. To better understand this issue, analysis focused on:

• The importance accorded to these issues in teachers' appraisal and feedback.

• The extent of teachers' professional development needs in these areas.

• The linguistic background reported in teachers' classrooms.

Teaching in a multicultural setting and teaching students with special learning needs were reported by teachers to be given relatively less importance in their appraisal and feedback. For teachers who do not teach students with these needs or backgrounds or who consider this not important to their teaching or their development as teachers, this is to be expected. However, although these areas received little emphasis in appraisal and feedback, reports on teachers' professional development needs show that a substantial proportion had development needs in these areas. This is a particularly worrying finding if teachers' appraisal and feedback is considered important to their continuing development. It suggests that their needs are not being met in a potentially important area. Analysis of teachers' reports of the linguistic background of students also shows that this is not an issue of these teachers teaching in front of homogenous classes. If this had been the case, it would be understandable that the appraisal and feedback teachers received did not focus on either teaching in a multi-cultural setting or teaching students with special learning needs.

Chapter 3 in fact indicates that many teachers had professional development needs in these areas. Across TALIS countries, three-quarters of teachers had moderate or high development needs for teaching students with special learning needs and 47% for teaching in a multicultural setting. Of these teachers, 22% did not receive any appraisal or feedback and therefore did not receive any professional development in these areas as a result of these activities. This was particularly apparent in Italy, where 53% of teachers with moderate or high development needs in these areas had not received any appraisal or feedback, and in Spain (45%).

Among teachers with moderate or high development needs in these areas and who received some appraisal or feedback, little or no consideration was often given to these areas. Just over one-third (35%) of teachers with moderate or high needs for teaching students with special learning needs received appraisal or feedback which gave little or no importance to this area. This was particularly apparent in Australia, Denmark and Malta where it was the case for 56% of these teachers. For teaching students in a multicultural setting, 32% of teachers with moderate or high development needs received appraisal or feedback which gave little or no importance to this issue. In a number of countries, the mismatch between teachers' development needs and the focus of appraisal and feedback was more pronounced. Over half of teachers in Australia (53%), Denmark (61%), Iceland (69%), Ireland (58%), Korea (58%), Malta (65%), Norway (70%) and Slovenia (58%) who reported moderate or high development needs for teaching in a multicultural setting received appraisal or feedback that gave little or no importance to this aspect of teaching (Source: OECD, *TALIS Database*.). It should be noted when interpreting the data that the proportion of teachers with these needs varies in these countries. In addition, there is no substantial difference in the reported linguistic diversity of teachers' classes for teachers with moderate or high development needs for teaching in a multicultural setting and teachers overall.

OUTCOMES OF APPRAISAL AND FEEDBACK OF TEACHERS

The following discussion of the outcomes of teacher appraisal and feedback focuses upon relatively direct outcomes, including monetary rewards and career advancement, teachers' development needs, and a variety of non-monetary rewards. Additional aspects discussed are the actions taken by school principals when specific weaknesses are identified. Seven specific outcomes that reward and/or affect teachers and their work were identified as possibly stemming from teacher appraisal and feedback: a change in salary; a financial bonus or another kind of monetary reward; opportunities for professional development; a change in the likelihood of career advancement; public recognition from the school principal and other colleagues; changes in work responsibilities that makes teachers' jobs more attractive; and a role in school development initiatives. These are presented in Table 5.5 which shows the percentage of teachers reporting changes in these outcomes following appraisal or feedback. In interpreting the data it should be kept in mind that the percentages only represent teachers who received appraisal or feedback in their school.

The data suggest that teachers' appraisal and feedback have relatively minor direct outcomes. In most TALIS countries, appraisal and feedback have little financial impact and are not linked to career advancement. On average across TALIS countries, 9% of teachers reported that appraisal or feedback had a moderate or large impact upon their salary and fewer than 11% reported that it had an impact on a financial bonus or another kind of monetary reward. However, there are stronger links to teacher salaries in a few countries. In Bulgaria (26%), Malaysia (33%), and the Slovak Republic (20%), between one-fifth and one-third of teachers indicate that appraisal and feedback led to a moderate or a large change in their salary. Similarly, teachers in Bulgaria, Estonia, Hungary, Lithuania, Malaysia, Poland, the Slovak Republic and Slovenia were more likely to report a link between appraisal and feedback and a bonus or other monetary reward (Table 5.5). Broadly speaking, it may be said that linking appraisal and feedback to teachers' monetary compensation was considerably more common in central and eastern European TALIS countries than in other TALIS countries.

Direct monetary impacts, such as bonuses, may be coupled with longer-term monetary outcomes through career advancement. Again, most teachers reported that appraisal and feedback led to a small or no change in their likelihood for career advancement. This indicates a strictly structured career path with little or no relationship to teachers' appraisal and feedback. Exceptions are found in Brazil, Malaysia, Mexico, Poland, the Slovak Republic and Slovenia. It is interesting that countries in which more teachers reported direct monetary impacts generally also reported a greater impact upon career advancement. However, in Bulgaria and Estonia tight promotion and career structures may prevent any effect on career advancement but direct financial rewards are possible. A number of countries that report low levels of direct monetary outcomes report a somewhat greater likelihood of an impact on career advancement. Teachers in Australia, Brazil, Ireland, Malaysia, Malta, Mexico, Poland, Portugal, Spain and Turkey report greater likelihood of an impact on career advancement than of direct monetary outcomes; in this case any monetary consequence would be of a long-term nature. That said, as shown in Table 5.5, the proportion of teachers in a number of countries reporting a moderate or large impact upon career advancement is still relatively low (16%).

A far more common outcome of teachers' appraisal and feedback is some form of public recognition either from the school principal or from teachers' colleagues. Thirty-six per cent of teachers said that their appraisal and feedback had led to a moderate or large change in the recognition they received from their school principal and/or colleagues within the school (Table 5.5). Public recognition is a clear incentive and a non-monetary outcome which highlights the role of teacher appraisal and feedback in rewarding quality teaching. Unfortunately, while it was more common than monetary outcomes, recognition was still not very frequent and clearly in many TALIS countries there are weak links between appraisal and feedback and both monetary and non-monetary outcomes.

A key feature of systems of appraisal and feedback is to provide a mechanism for assessing and improving the performance of staff. A number of development mechanisms can result from identifying specific needs, creating development opportunities within and beyond the school, and rewarding teachers for enhanced performance (OECD, 2005). Teachers reported on three development outcomes from teacher appraisal and feedback: opportunities for professional development, changes in work responsibilities that make their job more attractive;

and obtaining a role in school development initiatives. On average across TALIS countries, just fewer than one-quarter of teachers reported that appraisal and feedback led to a moderate or a large change in their opportunities for professional development. The largest proportions were in Bulgaria (42%), Estonia (36%), Lithuania (42%), Malaysia (51%), Poland (38%) and Slovenia (36%). Slightly more teachers reported an impact on changes in their work responsibilities and 30% on their role in school development initiatives (Table 5.5).

An important issue is whether teacher appraisal and feedback mechanisms can assume a developmental role or should be viewed more strictly in terms of rewarding performance. Such outcomes are not mutually exclusive, as a reward linked to teacher appraisal and feedback does not preclude development outcomes. In fact, a greater percentage of teachers report a moderate or strong link between their appraisal and feedback and changes in work responsibilities that make their jobs more attractive in Brazil, Lithuania, Malaysia and Mexico, where teachers' remuneration is also more likely to be linked to appraisal and feedback. Few teachers report a strong link in Australia, Austria, Belgium (Fl.), Denmark, Ireland, Malta, Norway and Spain (Table 5.5). For these countries, teacher appraisal and feedback may be a rather benign activity, and, in Austria, Denmark, Ireland and Spain was also reflected in low rates of school evaluations (Figure 5.5 and Table 5.1).

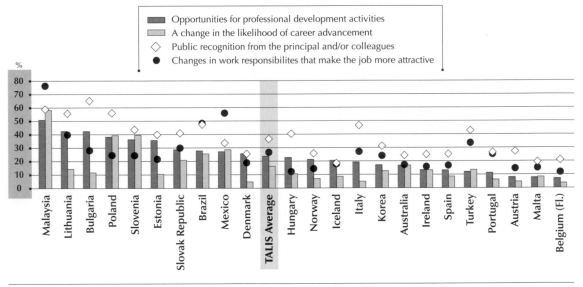

Figure 5.5

Impact of teacher appraisal and feedback (2007-08)

Legend:
- Opportunities for professional development activities
- A change in the likelihood of career advancement
- ◇ Public recognition from the principal and/or colleagues
- ● Changes in work responsibilites that make the job more attractive

Percentage of teachers of lower secondary education who reported that the appraisal and/or feedback they received led to a moderate or large change in these aspects of their work and careers.
Countries are ranked in descending order of changes in teachers' opportunities for professional development activities.
Source: OECD, Table 5.5.

StatLink ᴍᴤᴨ http://dx.doi.org/10.1787/607856444110

Actions following the identification of weaknesses in teacher appraisal

An essential aspect of any form of appraisal or feedback is the identification of strengths and weaknesses and taking steps to build on the former and correct the latter. Information was collected from school principals on actions taken when weaknesses are identified as a result of teachers' appraisal. Data collected focused on the extent of communication with the teacher; whether it is used to establish a development or training plan for the teacher; the relationship with a broader evaluation framework; and whether there is a financial impact for teachers.

The information collected in an appraisal of teachers' work can serve a number of purposes. It can be discussed with the teacher to communicate a judgement about their work and performance, it can be communicated to other bodies or institutions outside of the school, or it can be kept by the school principal to inform his/her own judgements. Informing external institutions may be part of regulatory requirements concerning the appraisal of teachers' work or of a broader regulatory structure concerning teachers' careers and their work. External communication may also indicate a more bureaucratic structure or top-down management practices than communication to the teacher.

As Table 5.6 shows, most school principals reported the outcome of teacher appraisals to the teacher, with 62% of teachers working in schools whose school principal reported that they always report the outcome of an appraisal that identifies weaknesses to the teacher (and a further 26% of teachers work in schools where the school principal reported doing so most of the time). This was the case in Australia (75% of teachers worked in schools whose school principal reported doing this all of the time), Austria (81%), Belgium (Fl.) (75%), Bulgaria (81%), Estonia (76%), Hungary (82%), Poland (96%) and the Slovak Republic (76%). However, some countries do not communicate the results of appraisals to teachers. For example, 32% of teachers in Korea worked in schools whose school principal reported that they never report the outcome to the teacher. In Turkey just fewer than one-quarter of teachers worked in schools whose school principal reported that they either never or only sometimes reported the outcome to the teacher. This may indicate poor communication between school principals and teachers. In most cases teacher appraisals (and the results) remain within the school. Across TALIS countries, nearly 90% of teachers worked in schools whose school principal reported that they never (51%) or only sometimes (37%) report underperformance to another body for action. Such reporting procedures are more common in Austria (21% of teachers' school principals report underperformance to another body to take action most of the time or always), Brazil (27%), and Malta (21%). It is particularly common in Mexico, where 47% of teachers worked in schools whose school principal said they report underperforming teachers to another body most of the time or always.

In a number of countries, using appraisal and feedback to establish a development or training plan for teachers to address weaknesses in their teaching is less common than simply reporting these identified weaknesses to the teacher (Table 5.6). This indicates that teacher appraisal is either not linked to professional development or that professional development is not common (either may be a concern if teachers' professional development is considered useful). Up to one-quarter of teachers worked in schools whose school principal reported that they never establish a development plan if an appraisal identifies weaknesses in Austria (23%), Estonia (11%), Hungary (12%), Ireland (19%), Korea (17%), Norway (20%), Poland (11%), Portugal (14%), the Slovak Republic (13%) Slovenia (16%) and Spain (22%) (Table 5.6). The use of teacher appraisal and feedback for professional development appears to be prevalent in certain countries. In Australia (58%) and Mexico (35%) at least one-third of teachers had school principals who reported that they always establish a development plan. Moreover, in some countries it is common to discuss measures to remedy weaknesses with teachers: over three-quarters of teachers in Hungary (81%), Lithuania (76%) and Poland (83%) worked in schools whose school principal reported that they always discussed these measures with the teachers concerned.

It is clear that for the vast majority of teachers, the results of appraisal and feedback are not used to impose material sanctions. On average across TALIS countries over 85% of teachers worked in schools whose school principal reported that a material sanction is never imposed when a teacher appraisal identifies a weakness. However, a greater percentage of teachers in Estonia (24%), Hungary (38%), Poland (28%) and the Slovak Republic (87%) work in schools where the school principal reported that this happened at least sometimes. While still not a common practice in these countries, this indicates a framework that links appraisal and feedback to salaries and financial rewards. It may also indicate a stronger link between appraisal and feedback and teachers' careers.

IMPACT OF TEACHER APPRAISAL AND FEEDBACK

The impact of appraisal and feedback is complementary to the direct outcomes discussed above but here the focus is on less tangible impacts, such as teachers' job satisfaction, effect on their teaching, and broader school development. To better illustrate these issues, the discussion begins with teachers' perception of the nature of their appraisal and feedback.

As Table 5.7 shows, on average across TALIS countries, teachers who received appraisal and feedback had a positive view of the process and its connection to their work and their careers. Overall, teachers considered the appraisal and feedback they received to be a fair assessment of their work and to have a positive impact upon their job satisfaction and, to a lesser degree, job security (Table 5.7a). This is an important finding given the negative connotations that may be associated with the introduction of a teacher appraisal system. TALIS provides, for the first time, international data from representative samples of countries that show that systems of appraisal and feedback have a positive impact on teachers.

Feelings of insecurity, fear and reduced appreciation of work can occur when a new or enhanced appraisal system is introduced in an organisation (Saunders, 2000). An emphasis on accountability can be assumed in some instances to imply strict and potentially punitive measures and thus have a negative impact upon teachers, their appreciation of their jobs and work as teachers (O'Day, 2002). In some respects, this appears to have been expected in some education systems that introduced new systems of teacher appraisal and accountability (Bethell, 2005). The results presented here do not show that a system of teacher appraisal and feedback will have a negative impact upon teachers. Specific systems can have negative impacts and considerable research has been conducted into the negative consequences of systems that misalign incentives and rewards (Lazear, 2000). A wide range of systems in TALIS countries emphasise different outcomes and different aspects of teachers' work. Yet, the great majority of teachers in these varied systems consider the appraisal and feedback they receive to be beneficial to their work as teachers, to be fair, and to increase both job satisfaction and, to a lesser degree, job security. In fact, given the benefits of systems of appraisal and feedback, the greatest concern may be in countries that lack such systems. Moreover, it appears that very few systems fully exploit the potential positive benefits of systems of teacher appraisal and feedback and provide teachers with these benefits.

Teachers' perceptions of the fairness of appraisal and feedback

Teachers' perceptions of the appraisal and feedback they receive is likely to be shaped by the degree to which they consider it a fair and just assessment of their work. It may be assumed that teachers who do not consider their appraisal and feedback a fair assessment of their work would also have a negative view of other aspects of its impact and role within their school. Impressions of fairness are also linked to indicators of the extent to which the outcomes and incentives of an appraisal and feedback system are properly aligned with teachers' work, what they consider to be important in their teaching, and the school's organisational objectives. For example, if teachers are appraised and receive feedback on a particularly narrow set of criteria or on a particular outcome measure which they feel does not fully or fairly reflect their work, a measure of the fairness of the system should highlight this problem.

Table 5.7 shows that 63% of teachers agreed and 20% strongly agreed that the appraisal and feedback they received was a fair assessment of their work. However, there were notable perceptions of a lack of fairness in some countries. A substantial proportion of teachers either strongly disagreed or disagreed that the appraisal and feedback was fair in Korea (9% strongly disagreed and 38% disagreed), and Turkey (12 and 23%, respectively). As detailed in Table 5.7a, very few teachers reported a negative impact upon their job security. In fact, 34% considered that it led to either a small or large increase in job security. In addition, over half reported either a small or large increase in their job satisfaction. Appraisal and feedback may therefore be considered to have a positive impact on aspects of teachers' careers.

Similar to the overall findings of teachers' perceptions of the fairness of the appraisal and feedback they received, on average across TALIS countries, over three-quarters of teachers also agreed or strongly agreed that their appraisal and feedback was helpful in the development of their work as teachers (Table 5.7). This is further evidence of the benefits of appraisal and feedback. However, over 40% of teachers reported that they did not receive suggestions for improving aspects of their work (Table 5.7). Contrasting these two findings suggest that feedback may be helpful in the sense that it highlights teachers' strengths and weaknesses even if it does not contain suggestions for addressing weaknesses or building on strengths.

The positive impact teachers perceive that appraisal and feedback has on their work is important given that, on average across TALIS countries, 13% of teachers reported receiving no appraisal or feedback in their school. These teachers may be missing out on the benefits of appraisal and feedback both for themselves and for their schools, and on commensurate developmental opportunities. This may be a bigger concern in some countries than in others. A number of TALIS countries have a large proportion of teachers who received no appraisal or feedback in their school (see Table 5.3). This was apparent in Ireland (26% of teachers have not received appraisal or feedback from any source in their school) and Portugal (26%) where over one-quarter of teachers have not received any appraisal or feedback in their school and particularly in Italy (55%) and Spain (46%) where around one-half of teachers have not received any appraisal or feedback. Policy makers looking to further develop systems of teacher appraisal and feedback will be interested to learn that of those teachers who received appraisal and feedback in Italy and Portugal the percentage who considered it helpful was above the TALIS average. In these countries with a less well-developed system of teacher appraisal and feedback, the benefits for those teachers it does reach seem to be considerable. This appears to be a clear signal to policy makers that appraisal and feedback can improve the working lives of teachers and school effectiveness.

Impact of appraisal and feedback on teaching and teachers' work

Teachers' views on their appraisal and feedback offer important insights into the nature and use of feedback systems in schools and a context for discussion of the impact upon teaching and teachers' work. Information was obtained on the extent to which the appraisal and feedback teachers received led to changes in eight aspects of their work: classroom management practices; knowledge and understanding of teachers' main subject field; knowledge and understanding of instructional practices in their main subject field; a development or training plan to improve their teaching; teaching students with special learning needs; handling of student discipline and behaviour problems; teaching students in a multicultural setting; and the emphasis on improving student test scores.

Table 5.8 shows that between 22 and 41% of teachers reported a moderate or large change in each of these aspects following the appraisal and the feedback they received. Appraisal and feedback thus has a positive impact not only on teachers' job satisfaction but also on their teaching and their jobs as teachers. Overall, the greatest impacts are on the emphasis on improving student test scores; classroom management practices; understanding of instructional practices; and knowledge and development or training plans. These facets of teachers' work and careers reflect positive developmental features of teacher appraisal and feedback and support teachers' perceptions of the nature of the appraisal and feedback they receive (see Table 5.7). In Hungary, Iceland and Korea, the greatest impact of teacher appraisal and feedback was on teachers' development or training plans. However, taking an average of the responses on each outcome, only in Brazil, Bulgaria, Malaysia and Mexico did the majority of teachers report that appraisal and feedback led to moderate or large changes in these aspects of their work. It is therefore clear that in most countries, further work is required to better target teacher appraisal and feedback to specific measures and/or to take measures to strengthen the system of teacher appraisal and feedback.

Appraisal and feedback has the greatest impact on teachers' emphasis on student test scores. Just over 40% of teachers considered that appraisal and feedback led to a moderate or large change in this aspect of their work (Table 5.8). Teachers in Australia, Brazil, Bulgaria, Ireland, Italy, Malaysia, Malta, Mexico, Poland, Portugal,

Slovenia and Turkey reported the greatest impact in this area (measured as the percentage of teachers that considered that appraisal and feedback led to a moderate or large change in this aspect of their work). For over one-third of teachers, appraisal and feedback led to a moderate or a large change in their classroom management practices and teachers reported this as one of the two largest impacts upon aspects of their work in Australia, Austria, Belgium (Fl.), Brazil, Bulgaria, Hungary, Ireland, Mexico, Norway, Slovenia and Spain. Similar proportions of teachers reported moderate or large changes in their knowledge and understanding of their main subject field and of instructional practices in that subject field. Teachers in Spain reported a particularly weak impact on these aspects of their work which is commensurate with the low importance they received for teacher appraisal and feedback. Knowledge and understanding of instructional practices had the greatest impact in Austria, Estonia, Lithuania and the Slovak Republic.

Appraisal and feedback had the least impact on teaching students in a multicultural setting which, as noted, was not an important criterion in the appraisal and feedback received by most teachers. This may explain why it had the least impact on this aspect of teachers' work in over two-thirds of TALIS countries. Findings were similar for the impact on teaching students with special learning needs and the explanation may also be the same. For policy makers wishing to emphasise these aspects of teaching and schooling, this is a potentially important finding. Appraisal and feedback had a greater impact on teachers' handling of student discipline and behaviour problems and was particularly strong in Denmark, Norway and Spain relative to the impact on other aspects of teachers' work in these countries (Figure 5.6).

Figure 5.6

Impact of teacher appraisal and feedback upon teaching (2007-08)

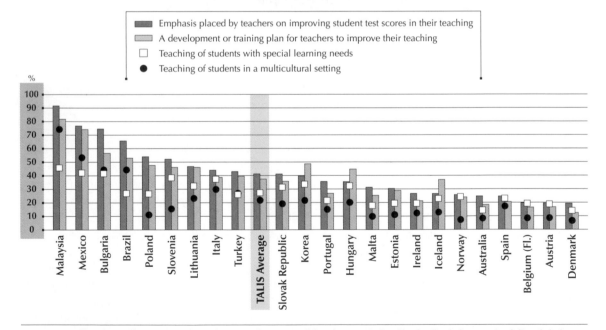

Percentage of teachers of lower secondary education who reported that the appraisal and/or feedback they received directly led to or involved moderate or large changes in these aspects of teaching.

Countries are ranked in descending order of changes in the emphasis placed by teachers on improving student test scores in their teaching.

Source: OECD, Table 5.8.

StatLink ⬛🔗 http://dx.doi.org/10.1787/607856444110

TEACHER APPRAISAL AND FEEDBACK AND SCHOOL DEVELOPMENT

Table 5.9 presents teachers' views on their school's system of appraisal and feedback and various issues of school development, incentives and career structures within schools, and the recognition accorded teachers for their work. It provides a worrying picture of the careers and working lives of teachers for those who believe in providing incentives and recognising achievement, for those wishing to promote effective learning networks within schools, and for the broad objectives of continually increasing school effectiveness. Systems of appraisal and feedback generally did not recognise teachers' efforts and successes, reward effective teachers and effective teaching practices, or provide incentives to teachers. Teachers in TALIS countries generally did not receive recognition for their work and reported that if they increased their efforts and effectiveness they would not receive more recognition. Most teachers reported that successful and effective teaching is not rewarded and that the recognition that is given in their school does not go to the teachers who most deserve it.

Just fewer than three-quarters of teachers reported working in schools that do not reward (in either monetary or non-monetary terms) the most effective teachers (Table 5.9). Such a result may not be unexpected for purely monetary returns. However, recognition other than financial rewards is an important aspect of the TALIS analysis and is covered in the questionnaires completed by teachers and school principals. The lack of this broader recognition shows that teachers' workplaces offer little incentive for more effective teaching. This was the situation for the great majority of teachers in a number of countries and for over 90% in Australia, Belgium (Fl.), Ireland and Spain. This finding is reinforced by the fact that a similar proportion of teachers report that they would receive no monetary or non-monetary reward if they improve the quality of their teaching or are more innovative in their teaching.[5] This again points to the lack of incentives for teachers and may affect schools' culture and work practices. This is particularly important given that efforts to improve schools rely on improving the quality of teaching. These figures indicate that efforts to treat schools as learning organisations which continually refine their teaching methods to improve student learning have not been successful in providing commensurate recognition or incentives for teachers.

Given the lack of recognition for teachers and their work, it is important to consider their beliefs about colleagues who are under performing within schools. If teachers who are more effective or more innovative are not recognised, what is the situation for teachers who underperform? Over three-quarters of teachers in TALIS countries reported that their school principal does not take steps to alter the monetary rewards of a persistently underperforming teacher (Table 5.9). This is not surprising in light of the lack of a link between appraisal and feedback and monetary outcomes in most countries and the reports of school principals discussed previously. Moreover, not all education systems grant school principals the authority to make such changes. Across TALIS countries, just over one-quarter of teachers agreed that in their school teachers would be dismissed for sustained poor performance. In most countries teachers reported that sustained poor performance would not lead to dismissal. This was particularly true in Austria (89% strongly disagreed or disagreed), Ireland (89%), Korea (90%), Norway (89%), Slovenia (91%), Spain (85%) and Turkey (89%) (Figure 5.7). However, in some countries a substantial proportion of teachers agreed or strongly agreed with the statement that their school principal does take steps to alter the monetary rewards of a persistently underperforming teacher, particularly in Bulgaria (44%), Hungary (41%), Malaysia (47%), Mexico (35%), Poland (31%), the Slovak Republic (51%) and Slovenia (45%) (Table 5.9).

Given the lack of action against underperforming teachers, it is important that most teachers across TALIS countries thought that in their school sustained or persistent underperformance would not be tolerated by the rest of the staff. However, over one-third thought that poor performance would be tolerated, and in Australia, Austria, Denmark, Ireland, Korea, Malaysia, Malta and Norway over 40% of teachers agreed or strongly agreed that this was the situation. It is clear therefore that a lack of recognition for effectiveness is linked in many schools to an inability or unwillingness to take action for underperforming teachers.

Perception of teachers of appraisal and feedback and its impact in their school (2007-08)

Teachers will be dismissed because of sustained poor performance in their school

Teachers whose school principal takes steps to alter the monetary rewards of a persistently underperforming teacher

Teachers who would receive increased monetary or non-monetary rewards if they are more innovative in their teaching

Teachers who would receive increased monetary or non-monetary rewards if they improve the quality of their teaching

Malaysia
Bulgaria
Poland
Italy
Slovak Republic
Hungary
Mexico
Slovenia
Turkey
Lithuania
TALIS Average
Estonia
Brazil
Portugal
Iceland
Malta
Austria
Korea
Spain
Denmark
Australia
Ireland
Norway
Belgium (Fl.)

% 100   80   60   40   20   0   20   40   60   80   100 %

Percentage of teachers of lower secondary education who agree of strongly agree with these statements about aspects of appraisal and/or feedback in their school.

Countries are ranked in descending order of the percentage of teachers reporting they would receive increased monetary or non-monetary rewards for improving the quality of their teaching.

Source: OECD, Table 5.9.

StatLink ⟡⟡⟡ http://dx.doi.org/10.1787/607856444110

A key question regarding underperformance is how it is measured and how information is obtained to determine a teacher's level of performance. It is difficult to take steps when decision makers cannot obtain or properly measure information about performance. It is therefore important that across TALIS countries 55% of teachers agree that their school principal has effective methods to determine whether teachers perform well or badly. This is an important finding given the difficulty of determining teachers' performance. However, more than 60% of teachers disagreed with this statement in Denmark, Iceland, Ireland, Korea, Norway and Spain (Table 5.9).

Forty-four per cent of teachers agreed with the statement that teachers' work is reviewed merely to fulfil an administrative requirement. This is a finding that could be used to support the claim that appraisal and feedback had a positive impact upon many teachers, but it also shows that for many teachers this is mainly an administrative exercise. Just fewer than half of teachers reported that the review of teachers' work has little impact on how teachers act in the classroom. However, 60% of teachers reported that a development or training plan is used in their schools to improve their work as a teacher. This is a positive sign if such plans have a positive effect. However, in Austria and Korea over two-thirds of teachers disagreed that this occurred (Table 5.9).

LINKS ACROSS THE FRAMEWORK FOR EVALUATING EDUCATION IN SCHOOLS

The framework for evaluating education in schools involves the evaluation and appraisal of actors and institutions within the school education system. To maintain standards and improve performance, evaluations must assess performance in the areas of the system considered most important. It may include assessments of inputs, processes and outcomes. To affect school performance, the evaluations carried out under this framework must affect, either directly or indirectly, the actors who most influence performance. In school education, these actors are school principals and teachers.

To achieve the greatest impact, the focus of school evaluation should either be linked to or have an effect on the focus of teacher appraisal and feedback. The factors considered important for evaluating the performance of schools should be the same as those for evaluating the actors who most influence that performance. Thus, teacher appraisal and feedback should have the same, or similar, focus as school evaluation. For example, if an objective of school education is to raise student's retention and pass rates, school performance should be evaluated on these outcomes and on the input and process measures linked to student retention. In turn, teachers' appraisal and feedback should also focus on these measures. If teachers are appraised on the basis of measures distinct from or even orthogonal to those on which schools are evaluated, the incentives of key actors are misaligned. This can create a mismatch of incentives and objectives that can lead teachers to pursue objectives contrary to those of the school.

A key assumption here is that both the system of school evaluation and teacher appraisal and feedback have as their objective to maintain standards and improve performance. If not, these links need not exist. Benefits from the synergies between school evaluation and teacher appraisal and feedback are of prime importance if, however, the objective of such systems is to improve school performance. For policy makers and administrators, such synergies are of particular importance if the system of school evaluation is more policy malleable than the system of teacher appraisal and feedback. This may be the case if teacher appraisal and feedback is more commonly administered at the school level and school evaluations are more commonly centrally administered or if the criteria of such evaluations are set centrally. TALIS data show that most teacher appraisal and feedback is conducted within the school either by the school principal or teachers' colleagues but that school evaluations are frequently conducted by an external institution (Tables 5.1 and 5.3). Data collected from national Governments shows that over half of OECD countries have requirements concerning school self-evaluation which indicate some centrally administered control over the process (OECD, 2008a).

Box 5.1 Path analysis methodology

To better understand the relationships between several sets of teacher and school principal variables, a number of path analysis models were fitted to the TALIS data. In particular, the investigation covered the nature of the relationship between the importance of certain elements to school evaluation and teacher appraisal and feedback; the changes in teaching resulting from the appraisal and feedback regarding these elements; and how all of these variables related to changes in professional development needs. It was hypothesised that the more important selected aspects were to school evaluations, the more important they would be to teacher appraisal and feedback. Subsequently, it was reasoned that an increased importance of the select elements in school evaluations and teacher appraisal and feedback would be associated with changes in teaching practices and might also be reflected in teachers' professional development needs.

Variables

The variables chosen for analysis were taken from the teacher and school principal questionnaires and are listed below. To fit the models to the TALIS data, the response option "I don't know" was excluded. This exclusion added to the overall missing rate. It should also be noted that only teachers who received appraisal and fee dback were included in the path models. This should be considered when interpreting the results of the analysis.

Topic	Importance to school evaluation	Importance to teacher appraisal and feedback	Changes in teaching due to appraisal and feedback	Professional development needs
Teaching students with special learning needs	School principal questionnaire	Teacher questionnaire	Teacher questionnaire	Teacher questionnaire
Teaching in a multicultural setting	School principal questionnaire	Teacher questionnaire	Teacher questionnaire	Teacher questionnaire
Teachers' classroom management	School principal questionnaire	Teacher questionnaire	Teacher questionnaire	Teacher questionnaire
Student discipline and behaviour	School principal questionnaire	Teacher questionnaire	Teacher questionnaire	Teacher questionnaire
Teachers' knowledge and understanding of main subject	School principal questionnaire	Teacher questionnaire	Teacher questionnaire	Teacher questionnaire
Teachers' knowledge and understanding of instructional practices in main subject field	School principal questionnaire	Teacher questionnaire	Teacher questionnaire	Teacher questionnaire

Models

The path analyses, estimated in Mplus, adhered to the cross-cultural equivalence and scaling undertaken and detailed in Chapter 4. In addition, CFI, RMSEA, and SRMR were used as fit statistics. All dependent variables were treated as multivariate normal in these models as the skewness and kurtosis generally did not exceed acceptable limits (Bolen, 1989; Schumacker and Lomax, 2004). The models' fit to the data, including the hypothesised direction of the relations, are presented in Figures 5.6 - 5.11. The numbers on the figures represent the magnitude of the correlations between the variables. For each aspect analysed, an international model was fit to the data. In general, all of the international models exhibited a good fit with the exception of the path model for teaching in a multicultural setting, which had marginally good fit (CFI = 0.91; RMSEA = 0.06; SRMR = 0.05).

Path analysis was undertaken to examine the links between the criteria for school evaluation and the criteria for teacher appraisal and feedback and their impact on teachers' work. Links to teachers' professional development needs were also examined. They showed that in some systems appraisal and feedback and its impacts are linked to teachers' professional development needs. In these instances, aspects of teachers' work identified as important in their appraisal and feedback are more likely to be areas in which teachers consider that they have professional development needs.

Path analysis measures the relationships between particular variables. It was conducted on the relationships between the importance of various criteria in school evaluations; the importance of those criteria in teacher appraisal and feedback; the extent to which appraisal and feedback led to changes in teachers' work and practices in these areas; and, teachers' professional development needs in these areas. Six areas were chosen for the analysis: teaching students with special learning needs; teaching in a multicultural setting; teachers' classroom management; teachers' knowledge and understanding of instructional practices in their main subject fields; teachers' handling of student discipline and behaviour problems; and, teachers' knowledge and understanding of their main subject field. Box 5.1 provides some technical details on the path analysis undertaken. The results are presented in Figure 5.8 to Figure 5.13 (the numbers in the figures represent the magnitude of the correlation between the variables). Results for each country are presented in Table 5.10 (available on line).

The six path models shown in Figures 5.8 to 5.13 highlight links between school evaluation, teacher appraisal and feedback, and the reported impacts and links to teachers' professional development needs. These links differ across education systems and also in intensity between each of the six areas. The correlations in the path analyses presented in the below Figures represent those for the international models that include all TALIS countries. All of the correlations were statistically significant for the international models. However, in the path analyses modelled for each TALIS country, not all correlations were statistically significant (see Table 5.10 available on line).

Teaching students with special learning needs and teaching in a multicultural setting are two aspects of teaching that are highlighted in the TALIS analyses. First, teachers have significant professional development needs in these areas relative to other aspects of teaching (see Chapter 3). Second, both of these aspects are considered of relatively low importance both in school evaluations and in teacher appraisal and feedback.

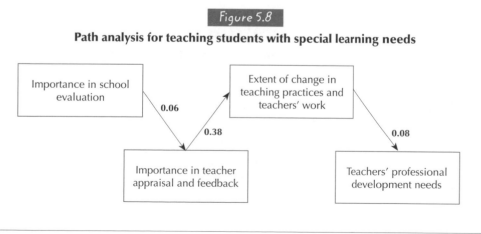

Figure 5.8

Path analysis for teaching students with special learning needs

Source: OECD, *TALIS Database*.

StatLink ᵐˢᵖ http://dx.doi.org/10.1787/607856444110

Figure 5.9

Path analysis for teaching in a multicultural setting

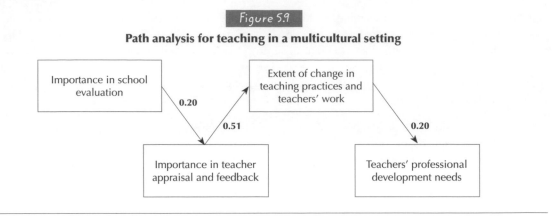

Source: OECD, *TALIS Database*.

StatLink http://dx.doi.org/10.1787/607856444110

Figure 5.10

Path analysis for teachers' classroom management

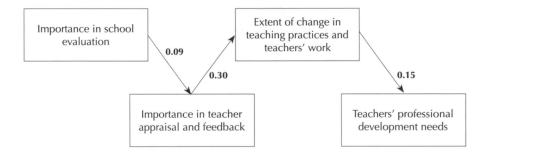

Source: OECD, *TALIS Database*.

StatLink http://dx.doi.org/10.1787/607856444110

Figure 5.11

Path analysis for teachers' handling of student discipline and behaviour problems

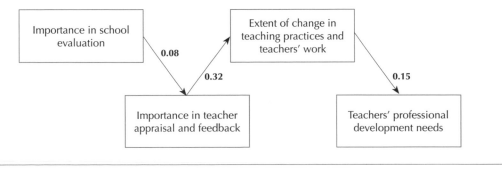

Source: OECD, *TALIS Database*.

StatLink http://dx.doi.org/10.1787/607856444110

 Creating Effective Teaching and Learning Environments: First Results from TALIS – ISBN 978-92-64-05605-3

Path analysis for teachers' knowledge and understanding of main subject field

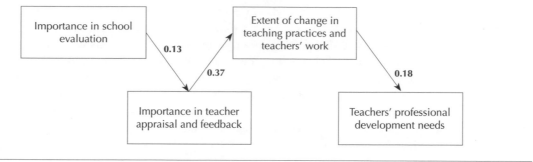

Source: OECD, *TALIS Database.*

StatLink ⛓ http://dx.doi.org/10.1787/607856444110

Path analysis for teachers' knowledge and understanding of instructional practices in their main subject field

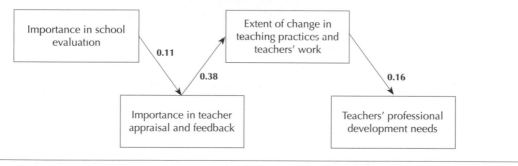

Source: OECD, *TALIS Database.*

StatLink ⛓ http://dx.doi.org/10.1787/607856444110

Given this mismatch between teachers' development needs and the framework for evaluating education in schools, it is important to understand the links that might facilitate policy development in these areas. As Figures 5.8 and 5.9 indicate, the greater the emphasis placed on these areas in school evaluations the greater the emphasis placed on them in teacher appraisal and feedback. When greater emphasis is placed on teaching students with special learning needs in school evaluations, greater emphasis is placed upon this in teacher appraisal and feedback in Austria, Bulgaria, Denmark, Hungary, Lithuania, Norway, Poland, Portugal, the Slovak Republic and Spain (see Table 5.10 available on line). The size of this relationship is particularly large in Austria, Lithuania and the Slovak Republic. For teaching in a multicultural setting the relationship between the importance in school evaluation and in teacher appraisal and feedback is larger and significant in 14 TALIS countries, and is larger in Belgium (Fl.), Bulgaria, Denmark and Norway.

The link between the importance of these aspects in teacher appraisal and feedback and the extent to which it led to changes in teachers' practices is significant for every TALIS country. The greater the importance accorded to these aspects of teaching in teachers' appraisal and feedback, the greater the change in their teaching practices. The effect is larger for teaching in a multicultural setting, but is still significant and quantitatively important for teaching students with special learning needs. In fact, the relationships for both of these aspects of teaching are statistically significant and quantitatively important in each TALIS country. In most TALIS countries, changes in these aspects of teaching are significantly correlated with greater professional development needs in these areas. Teachers who are changing their practices consider that they have further development needs. For teaching students with special learning needs this is statistically significant and quantitatively important in all countries except Brazil, Ireland, Malta, Mexico, Spain and Turkey. For teaching in a multicultural setting, this is statistically significant and quantitatively important for all countries except Malta and Turkey. Except for these countries, changes in teaching practices following teachers' appraisal and feedback do not appear sufficient to overcome the need for further professional development in these areas. This indicates that teachers respond positively to appraisal and feedback but cannot access the required professional development to meet their needs. This may be due to a lack of professional development overall or what is available may not be targeted to meet teachers' needs and expectations.

In general, the same relationship holds with regard to teachers' classroom management practices. In every country except Malta, the more important classroom management is to teacher appraisal, the more teachers change their classroom management practices following appraisal. In every country except Brazil and Italy, changes in classroom management significantly predict increased professional development needs in this area. However, except in Estonia, Italy and Norway, there is no significant link between the importance of teachers' classroom management practices in school evaluations and its importance in teacher appraisal and feedback. The scenario is similar for teachers' handling of student discipline and behaviour problems. Again, except in Estonia, Poland, Spain and Turkey there is no significant link between the importance of this aspect of teaching in school evaluations and in teacher appraisal and feedback. However, in all TALIS countries except Malta, the greater the importance of this aspect of teaching in teacher appraisal and feedback, the greater the change in teaching practices. In all TALIS countries except Brazil, greater changes in teachers' handling of student discipline and behaviour problems are significantly correlated with greater need for professional development in this area.

More changes take place in teachers' knowledge and understanding of their main subject fields and in their instructional practices when greater emphasis is placed on these areas in teacher appraisal and feedback. These relationships are statistically significant in all TALIS countries. In addition the greater the changes made following appraisal and feedback the greater the professional development needs. With respect to teachers' knowledge and understanding of their main subject field, this relationship is statistically significant and quantitatively important for all TALIS countries except Turkey. The relationship between the importance accorded to these aspects of teachers' work in school evaluations and in teacher appraisal and feedback is less strong. It is statistically significant with respect to teachers' knowledge and understanding of their main subject field only in Lithuania and Spain, and statistically significant with respect to teachers' knowledge and understanding of instructional practices in their main subject field only in Austria, Estonia, Hungary and Korea.

Path analysis identifies the strength of the links between school evaluation, teacher appraisal and feedback, its impact, and teachers' professional development needs for each of the six aspects of teaching identified above. A clear finding is that the greater the importance given to an area of teaching in teacher appraisal and feedback, the greater the impact on teaching. While the overall level of change reported by teachers following their appraisal and feedback is not necessarily substantial, this may be due to the relatively weak or imprecise appraisal and feedback that many teachers may have received. Given the positive relationship between the importance given to aspects of teachers' work in their appraisal and feedback and the changes resulting from this appraisal and feedback, the positive benefits of teacher appraisal and feedback become clearer. Not only are appraisal and feedback linked to greater job satisfaction and teachers' beliefs regarding their overall development, but the stronger the emphasis on particular aspects of teachers' appraisal and feedback, the greater the reported influence on teachers' work within schools.

This has important policy implications for targeting specific aspects of school education. If a particular aspect needs to be improved, the framework of evaluation can be modified to emphasise this aspect. Given the links between school evaluations, teacher appraisal and feedback, and changes in teaching practices discussed here, a policy lever exists to address aspects of school education that may not be sufficiently targeted under general education policies.

CONCLUSIONS AND IMPLICATIONS FOR POLICY AND PRACTICE

The findings discussed in this Chapter have multiple implications, for teaching, for schools and for the structure of teachers' careers. They include the following:

Teacher appraisal and feedback has a positive impact on teachers

Key results:

Teachers generally report that:

- Appraisal and feedback are fair and useful to their development as teachers.
- Appraisal and feedback increases their job satisfaction and to a lesser degree their job security.

Discussion

For policy makers, administrators, school principals and teachers, these findings highlight a dual benefit of appraisal and feedback, both to teachers personally and to the development of their teaching.

Positive impacts on job satisfaction and, to a lesser extent, job security are important, given that the introduction of systems of teacher appraisal can be met with criticism and potential negative reactions, especially where it is linked to accountability (Table 5.7a). The TALIS findings not only allay fears of teachers that such systems will be damaging, but show that in practice teachers find their outcomes to be positive.

Moreover, teacher reports that appraisal and feedback has contributed to their development as teachers suggest that such systems contribute to school improvement (Table 5.7). Numerous initiatives developed by policy makers aiming to lift school improvement have had teacher development at the core (OECD, 2005). Strengthening the system of teacher appraisal and feedback can, according to teachers' reports of their impact, develop teaching skills within schools.

These findings are of greater importance if it is considered that the system of appraisal and feedback in schools could be strengthened, in a number of ways. Greater emphasis upon the framework for evaluating education in schools could strengthen links between school evaluations and teacher appraisal and feedback. The results of appraisal could be used more directly to plan professional development of individual teachers. And policy measures to emphasise teacher appraisal and feedback in the career structure of teachers may better instil the benefits of appraisal and feedback within schools. Closer links with career progression could have the added benefit of addressing what teachers report as a severe lack of recognition for their development, and a problem with teachers' rewards not being properly linked to their effectiveness.

School evaluation and teacher appraisal and feedback are relatively rare in a number of education systems, and do not always have consequences for teachers

Key results

- One in five teachers work in a school that had not conducted a self-evaluation in the last five years, and just under one in three in a school that has not had an external evaluation (Table 5.1).

- Thirteen per cent of teachers have received no appraisal and feedback upon their work as teachers. In Ireland and Portugal it is over one in four, and in Italy and Spain it is around one half (Table 5.3).

- Teachers' remuneration is linked to school evaluations for only one-quarter of teachers and to teacher appraisal and feedback to fewer than one in ten. Fewer than 4 in 10 teachers work in schools where school evaluations are linked to the school budget (Table 5.5).

- For only one in six teachers is appraisal and feedback linked to their career advancement and to fewer than one in four to professional development (Tables 5.2 and 5.5).

- Nearly half of teachers think that their school principals do not use effective methods to determine teacher performance within their school (Table 5.9).

Discussion

These results show that opportunities for strengthening school evaluation and teacher appraisal and feedback are particularly great in some countries, while across countries there are opportunities for strengthening the evaluative framework of school education.

Increased frequency of evaluations and of teacher appraisal and feedback could be facilitated and encouraged within schools or regulations put in place to ensure they occur. The focus of the evaluative framework could be improved to better identify education objectives and particular policies and programmes that can be highlighted in school evaluations and teacher appraisal and feedback. In most education systems, there is not a clear focus on specific aspects of school education or teaching in these activities. Rather, the emphasis was relatively evenly spread over virtually all of the 17 criteria included in the TALIS analysis, the exceptions to this being teaching students with special learning needs and teaching in a multicultural setting (Table 5.4).

Strengthening linkages with rewards and career progression would address the fact that most teachers feel that effective and innovative teaching are not being recognised. Three quarters of teachers across TALIS countries reported that the most effective teachers in their school do not receive the greatest monetary or non-monetary rewards. As a consequence, they believe that they would not themselves gain such rewards were they to improve their teaching. They report a lack of any links between their personal development, their effectiveness, and the recognition they receive (Table 5.9).

Linking recognition and rewards to teacher effectiveness is not just a matter of carrying out appraisals but also of school leaders adopting effective methods of identifying good performance. In some cases where there are no methods to identify good performance, this is because there is little or no appraisal and feedback, but in others, it is a matter of finding ways of using the information gained. The fact that nearly four times as many teachers say that their principal does not identify effective teaching as say that they have not recently been appraised is an indicator of the need for follow through (Table 5.3 and Table 5.9).

Teachers reported that they would receive little, if any, recognition for improving their teaching, as teacher effectiveness is not linked to the recognition and rewards they receive

Key results

- Three-quarters of teachers report that they would receive no recognition for improving the quality of their teaching (Table 5.9).

- Three-quarters of teachers report that they would receive no recognition for being more innovative in their teaching (Table 5.9).

- Three-quarters of teachers report that the most effective teachers in their school do not receive the greatest monetary and non-monetary rewards (Table 5.9).
- Only just over one-quarter of teachers report that in their school, teachers will be dismissed because of sustained poor performance (Table 5.9).

Strengthening the evaluative framework requires linkages between school evaluation and teacher appraisal and feedback on the one hand and teachers' rewards and recognition on the other. In particular, there are substantial opportunities for strengthening – in many cases actually creating – links between teacher appraisal and feedback and the rewards and recognition teachers receive. These links are relatively weak, as reflected in teachers' reports of the lack of incentives in their careers and the lack of rewards and recognition for teacher effectiveness.

Teachers currently have few incentives, in terms of recognition and rewards, to improve their teaching. Yet, teachers' effectiveness is central to efforts to improve schools and raise student performance. In addition, school improvement efforts are increasingly viewed in the context of schools as learning organisations in which teaching practices are adapted and improved to better meet student needs and improve the education they receive (O'Day, 2002; Senge, 2000). However, teachers report that they have no incentives to participate actively in such efforts. Three-quarters of teachers report that they would receive no recognition for increasing the quality of their teaching or becoming more innovative in their teaching (Table 5.9).

Most teachers are faced with a career lacking these incentives which flows through schools so that teachers see colleagues whom they consider to be relatively ineffective receive greater recognition than their more effective colleagues. Three-quarters of teachers across TALIS countries report that the most effective teachers in their school do not receive the greatest monetary and non-monetary rewards (Table 5.9). Further evidence of the lack of sufficient links between the evaluation framework and teachers' recognition is the fact that over three-quarters of teachers report that their school principal does not take steps to alter the monetary rewards of a persistently underperforming teacher. This inaction is magnified in career structures that reward experience over effectiveness and in such cases further reward persistently underperforming teachers.

A system that better links teacher appraisal and feedback to teachers' rewards and the recognition they receive should help overcome these problems. A lack of incentives that recognise effectiveness coupled with the rewarding of ineffectual teachers shows that the framework of evaluation and of teacher appraisal and feedback is not effective. It is either not properly assessing teachers' work or effectiveness or it does not link the system of rewards to teachers' effectiveness. Evidence from TALIS indicates that both should be of concern for policy makers.

School evaluations can be structured so that they and teacher appraisal and feedback lead to developments in particular aspects of school education

Key results

- Teachers report that the greater the emphasis placed on a specific aspect of their teaching in their appraisal and feedback, the greater the resultant changes in that aspect of their teaching (Figure 5.8 – Figure 5.13).
- In some instances the greater the emphasis placed on aspects of a school's evaluation, the greater the focus on that aspect in the appraisal and feedback received by teachers (Figure 5.8 – Figure 5.13).

Discussion

The school evaluative framework is often policy malleable so that not only can the strength of the evaluative framework be altered but also its focus. The criteria by which schools are evaluated and teachers are appraised and receive feedback should be aligned with the objectives of the system of school education. These objectives may relate to aspects of student performance, teacher development, specific teaching practices, the maintenance of specific standards and procedures, and a variety of aspects of the work of teachers and school principals.

Aligning criteria for school evaluation with those for teacher appraisal and feedback would emphasise the importance of policy objectives at the school level and could give teachers and school principals an incentive to meet such objectives.

Teachers have reported that the greater the emphasis placed on a specific aspect of their teaching in the appraisal and feedback they receive, the greater the subsequent changes in their teaching. In addition, in some instances the greater the emphasis placed on aspects of a school's evaluation, the stronger the focus in teachers' appraisal and feedback (Figure 5.8 – Figure 5.13). The link between elements of the evaluation framework facilitates policy makers' efforts to shape the framework to influence teachers' work. For example, setting a particular focus on an area of teaching or student outcomes and emphasising the impact that this can have on schools can lead to greater emphasis on this area in teacher appraisal and feedback which, in turn, increases the changes in teachers' work and teaching practices. The availability of this policy lever emphasises the importance of appraisal and feedback to administrators, school principals and teachers.

In what ways might such influence be wielded? Teaching students with special learning needs and teaching in a multicultural setting were given relatively low importance in school evaluations and teacher appraisal and feedback (Table 5.1a and Table 5.4). If these are considered priority areas, then there are opportunities for increasing their focus in the evaluative framework, particularly as teachers report they have unmet developmental needs in these areas.

A growing focus in a number of countries has been the methods and policy initiatives implemented to address disparities in education outcomes between schools and specific groups of students (OECD, 2007). This has often emphasised disparities between specific migrant groups and students with specific learning requirements (OECD 2008b). In this context, it is important for policy makers that teachers reported the greatest need for professional development in the area of teaching students with special learning needs (Table 3.4). This has been discussed in Chapter 3, and greater emphasis on special needs in the evaluative framework for school education could help address the shortfalls identified in that chapter. At the same time, teachers who teach linguistically diverse classrooms and have professional development needs for teaching in a multicultural setting may also benefit from more evaluation and feedback in these areas than they now receive.

ADDITIONAL MATERIAL

The following additional material relevant to this chapter is available on line at:
StatLink ⟶ http://dx.doi.org/10.1787/607856444110

Table 5.10   Path analysis: Country results (2007-08)

Notes

1. Given the time constraints for developing a workable questionnaire that was not overly burdensome for respondents, school principals were asked only once for information on the criteria and impact of school evaluations. Therefore, this information does not, in the main, distinguish between school self-evaluations compared to external evaluations.

2. This issue is explored in further detail and with a different methodology in the forthcoming OECD report, Teacher Education for Diversity.

3. It is important to note that this figure only includes school principals who reported having a school evaluation at some time in the previous five years. It does not include the 14% who reported no school evaluation over the previous five years. For example, in Austria, Ireland, Italy and Portugal a large proportion of schools did not conduct or participate in such evaluations (see Table 5.1).

4. While external school evaluations are relatively uncommon in Italy, the Italian Ministry of Education has made it compulsory for schools that want to receive additional resources from the EU structural funds to participate in the "School Service Evaluation" survey, co-ordinated by the National Institute of Evaluation, which collects data on many aspects of schools.

5. It should be noted that TALIS did not seek to define innovative or effective teaching for respondents. Therefore, teachers' reports in these areas represent their opinions of what is and is not innovative and effective teaching and teachers.

Table 5.1

Frequency and type of school evaluations (2007-08)

Percentage of teachers of lower secondary education working in schools where school evaluations were conducted with the following frequency over the last five years

| | Frequency of school self-evaluations over the last five years | | | | | | | | | |
| | Never | | Once | | 2-4 times | | Once per year | | More than once per year | |
	%	(S.E.)	%	(S.E.)	%	(S.E.)	%	(S.E.)	%	(S.E.)
Australia	6.8	(2.87)	25.3	(3.89)	14.1	(3.17)	50.0	(4.16)	3.7	(1.73)
Austria	41.7	(3.59)	28.2	(2.94)	17.7	(2.91)	11.3	(2.11)	1.1	(0.63)
Belgium (Fl.)	22.0	(3.91)	33.4	(4.04)	30.9	(4.93)	12.9	(2.59)	0.7	(0.71)
Brazil	24.4	(2.61)	10.2	(1.67)	16.5	(2.23)	33.2	(3.29)	15.7	(2.70)
Bulgaria	22.0	(3.65)	12.6	(3.16)	11.4	(3.30)	34.5	(6.15)	19.5	(3.98)
Denmark	32.4	(4.12)	15.1	(4.01)	19.8	(3.92)	25.4	(3.84)	7.3	(2.60)
Estonia	23.9	(3.50)	26.7	(3.50)	19.5	(3.41)	28.4	(3.62)	1.6	(1.13)
Hungary	4.7	(1.92)	11.7	(2.46)	23.1	(3.22)	41.2	(6.51)	19.3	(6.36)
Iceland	11.3	(0.14)	30.9	(0.15)	26.3	(0.17)	28.9	(0.12)	2.6	(0.12)
Ireland	56.5	(5.06)	25.2	(4.52)	7.6	(2.52)	8.2	(2.87)	2.5	(1.73)
Italy	21.2	(2.84)	10.2	(1.81)	19.7	(2.63)	43.9	(3.20)	5.1	(1.50)
Korea	6.5	(2.26)	10.9	(2.70)	26.7	(3.41)	26.8	(3.80)	29.2	(3.32)
Lithuania	3.7	(1.40)	7.9	(2.03)	9.4	(2.53)	67.8	(3.54)	11.2	(2.42)
Malaysia	2.1	(0.98)	2.2	(0.96)	19.9	(2.70)	50.7	(3.36)	25.1	(3.08)
Malta	10.1	(0.13)	10.2	(0.09)	30.5	(0.15)	48.6	(0.20)	0.6	(0.00)
Mexico	20.4	(4.00)	9.5	(2.47)	17.1	(2.86)	32.4	(3.93)	20.6	(3.55)
Norway	25.5	(4.08)	14.3	(3.35)	18.7	(3.32)	33.5	(4.13)	7.9	(2.36)
Poland	10.4	(2.56)	13.8	(2.95)	24.2	(3.92)	34.2	(3.80)	17.5	(2.97)
Portugal	47.9	(3.97)	19.3	(3.56)	13.3	(2.95)	13.0	(3.10)	6.4	(2.14)
Slovak Republic	1.6	(0.79)	5.4	(2.00)	8.3	(2.36)	70.5	(3.34)	14.3	(2.88)
Slovenia	19.9	(2.97)	15.9	(2.91)	12.1	(2.59)	45.2	(3.84)	6.9	(1.86)
Spain	31.1	(3.31)	18.1	(2.74)	13.7	(2.39)	32.4	(3.72)	4.7	(1.80)
Turkey	18.0	(4.43)	16.5	(4.73)	20.9	(3.74)	30.7	(4.58)	13.9	(2.90)
TALIS average	**20.2**	**(0.65)**	**16.2**	**(0.62)**	**18.3**	**(0.63)**	**34.9**	**(0.78)**	**10.3**	**(0.55)**

| | Frequency of external evaluations over the last five years | | | | | | | | | | No evaluation from any source over the last five years | |
| | Never | | Once | | 2-4 times | | Once per year | | More than once per year | | | |
	%	(S.E.)	%	(S.E.)	%	(S.E.)	%	(S.E.)	%	(S.E.)	%	(S.E.)
Australia	21.2	(3.43)	36.2	(4.06)	29.7	(4.03)	10.7	(2.28)	2.2	(1.31)	5.0	(2.30)
Austria	58.3	(3.37)	22.9	(3.09)	9.0	(1.89)	6.4	(1.78)	3.4	(1.22)	35.2	(3.49)
Belgium (Fl.)	10.4	(2.82)	54.6	(4.38)	32.7	(3.71)	1.9	(0.96)	0.4	(0.41)	5.8	(2.19)
Brazil	24.3	(2.64)	14.2	(2.56)	21.3	(2.59)	24.9	(2.99)	15.3	(2.50)	18.9	(2.42)
Bulgaria	29.4	(4.50)	30.4	(3.86)	15.9	(3.49)	14.0	(3.17)	10.4	(5.71)	18.8	(3.43)
Denmark	53.0	(4.31)	22.4	(4.36)	10.9	(2.97)	11.5	(2.83)	2.2	(1.62)	25.4	(4.03)
Estonia	27.5	(3.94)	47.8	(4.22)	18.4	(3.43)	4.4	(1.72)	1.8	(0.84)	11.8	(2.76)
Hungary	12.4	(2.47)	20.9	(2.81)	38.2	(6.36)	23.2	(6.93)	5.2	(1.47)	1.2	(0.67)
Iceland	18.0	(0.11)	56.3	(0.20)	22.5	(0.18)	0.7	(0.00)	2.5	(0.08)	5.0	(0.09)
Ireland	56.9	(5.16)	36.5	(5.05)	5.2	(2.11)	1.4	(1.41)	0.0	(0.00)	39.1	(4.91)
Italy	60.7	(3.15)	11.3	(2.16)	14.6	(2.37)	12.3	(2.29)	1.1	(0.66)	19.8	(2.76)
Korea	3.0	(1.53)	26.3	(3.65)	41.0	(4.22)	10.6	(2.27)	19.1	(3.20)	0.9	(0.88)
Lithuania	37.1	(3.50)	25.1	(3.06)	20.6	(3.12)	8.4	(1.66)	8.9	(2.59)	3.4	(1.35)
Malaysia	7.8	(2.00)	11.4	(2.27)	25.3	(3.12)	22.9	(3.17)	32.7	(3.51)	2.1	(0.98)
Malta	53.9	(0.24)	38.8	(0.25)	6.3	(0.08)	1.0	(0.00)	0.0	(0.00)	7.4	(0.13)
Mexico	21.1	(4.05)	11.0	(2.54)	20.0	(3.41)	20.0	(3.20)	27.9	(4.09)	17.1	(3.82)
Norway	35.6	(4.44)	34.9	(4.49)	21.2	(3.78)	5.9	(2.17)	2.5	(1.44)	17.2	(3.64)
Poland	13.6	(3.07)	51.5	(4.14)	20.1	(3.53)	12.8	(2.83)	1.9	(1.33)	6.5	(2.39)
Portugal	49.1	(4.34)	29.9	(4.10)	18.2	(3.11)	2.1	(1.18)	0.6	(0.65)	32.8	(3.32)
Slovak Republic	18.1	(3.73)	56.0	(4.28)	15.7	(3.53)	6.8	(1.78)	3.3	(1.45)	1.6	(0.79)
Slovenia	40.1	(3.89)	34.2	(3.78)	16.0	(2.95)	7.8	(2.20)	1.9	(1.11)	15.5	(2.81)
Spain	38.5	(3.67)	27.2	(3.79)	19.7	(3.27)	13.8	(2.90)	0.8	(0.76)	24.5	(3.14)
Turkey	8.5	(3.53)	8.0	(3.82)	28.5	(3.88)	37.6	(5.16)	17.4	(4.50)	1.8	(1.07)
TALIS average	**30.4**	**(0.72)**	**30.8**	**(0.74)**	**20.5**	**(0.70)**	**11.4**	**(0.58)**	**7.0**	**(0.48)**	**13.8**	**(0.56)**

Source: OECD, *TALIS Database.*
StatLink ᵐᵖ http://dx.doi.org/10.1787/607856444110

Table 5.1a (1/2)

Criteria of school evaluations (2007-08)

Percentage of teachers of lower secondary education whose school principal reported that the following criteria were considered with high or moderate importance in school self-evaluations or external evaluations

	Student test scores		Retention and pass rates of students		Other student learning outcomes		Student feedback on the teaching they receive		Feedback from parents		How well teachers work with the principal and their colleagues	
	%	(S.E.)	%	(S.E.)	%	(S.E.)	%	(S.E.)	%	(S.E.)	%	(S.E.)
Australia	86.9	(3.12)	81.9	(3.62)	94.8	(2.14)	69.0	(4.13)	88.3	(2.92)	79.5	(4.02)
Austria	57.7	(5.01)	33.3	(4.40)	60.7	(4.24)	81.2	(3.01)	83.4	(2.88)	76.3	(3.65)
Belgium (Fl.)	85.6	(3.03)	93.8	(1.82)	80.4	(3.40)	72.4	(3.97)	71.5	(4.51)	92.3	(2.48)
Brazil	85.7	(2.67)	93.7	(1.70)	90.1	(2.58)	88.0	(2.56)	83.9	(2.87)	95.5	(0.91)
Bulgaria	82.8	(3.25)	64.2	(4.78)	74.3	(7.50)	60.3	(4.74)	45.2	(5.76)	78.0	(4.05)
Denmark	55.8	(5.77)	68.4	(4.59)	78.7	(5.31)	69.6	(3.94)	58.5	(5.58)	65.6	(6.07)
Estonia	86.2	(2.94)	91.9	(2.40)	80.3	(3.58)	80.7	(2.78)	73.7	(4.12)	83.0	(3.27)
Hungary	69.7	(4.26)	73.1	(3.82)	78.3	(3.10)	68.3	(3.88)	83.5	(3.15)	79.9	(3.21)
Iceland	60.5	(0.20)	51.7	(0.23)	68.5	(0.15)	60.2	(0.19)	88.8	(0.12)	87.0	(0.18)
Ireland	80.5	(4.91)	84.2	(4.67)	80.9	(5.07)	55.8	(6.80)	76.1	(5.77)	82.3	(5.17)
Italy	76.3	(3.47)	78.8	(3.11)	78.3	(3.09)	80.0	(3.07)	93.1	(1.99)	91.2	(2.03)
Korea	57.8	(4.27)	23.7	(3.97)	62.6	(3.99)	70.8	(3.64)	80.1	(3.20)	87.3	(2.76)
Lithuania	62.1	(3.75)	74.8	(3.77)	88.2	(2.22)	88.7	(2.25)	87.9	(2.58)	85.7	(2.62)
Malaysia	97.7	(1.10)	47.7	(3.98)	82.6	(2.65)	87.1	(2.54)	86.0	(2.40)	98.7	(0.90)
Malta	84.3	(0.13)	78.4	(0.20)	84.3	(0.20)	68.0	(0.22)	89.8	(0.19)	90.2	(0.14)
Mexico	94.0	(1.80)	97.3	(1.28)	88.6	(3.10)	84.8	(3.05)	74.7	(3.97)	89.2	(2.69)
Norway	52.0	(4.95)	32.1	(4.90)	51.2	(4.99)	50.3	(4.79)	65.1	(4.55)	64.9	(4.89)
Poland	96.5	(1.40)	89.0	(2.68)	91.0	(2.33)	89.8	(2.29)	93.5	(2.02)	93.6	(2.02)
Portugal	65.9	(4.72)	94.2	(2.19)	85.2	(3.52)	73.5	(4.73)	78.3	(4.45)	79.8	(3.85)
Slovak Republic	87.2	(2.96)	50.5	(4.85)	80.1	(3.68)	65.7	(4.21)	55.6	(4.69)	81.5	(3.70)
Slovenia	74.2	(3.81)	77.8	(3.36)	84.2	(3.03)	67.5	(4.27)	82.5	(3.12)	88.6	(2.49)
Spain	74.1	(4.14)	79.2	(3.84)	73.4	(3.99)	60.4	(4.94)	67.1	(4.50)	69.8	(4.16)
Turkey	80.1	(5.50)	68.0	(6.55)	77.6	(5.45)	81.2	(4.13)	70.7	(4.25)	86.3	(4.16)
TALIS average	**76.2**	**(0.77)**	**70.8**	**(0.77)**	**78.9**	**(0.79)**	**72.7**	**(0.79)**	**77.3**	**(0.79)**	**83.7**	**(0.70)**

	Direct appraisal of classroom teaching		Innovative teaching practices		Relations between teachers and students		Professional development undertaken by teachers		Teachers' classroom management		Teachers' knowledge and understanding of their main subject field(s)	
	%	(S.E.)	%	(S.E.)	%	(S.E.)	%	(S.E.)	%	(S.E.)	%	(S.E.)
Australia	58.8	(4.50)	78.6	(4.00)	89.7	(2.92)	87.3	(3.18)	79.6	(3.85)	76.5	(4.17)
Austria	68.5	(3.78)	76.5	(3.09)	86.4	(2.79)	53.5	(4.33)	74.9	(4.02)	68.8	(4.09)
Belgium (Fl.)	70.4	(4.09)	78.9	(4.14)	90.9	(2.53)	94.9	(1.83)	72.8	(4.37)	79.3	(3.83)
Brazil	95.4	(1.25)	92.8	(1.62)	95.6	(1.18)	90.8	(1.94)	93.5	(1.88)	93.6	(1.82)
Bulgaria	84.3	(3.75)	78.6	(4.87)	79.3	(4.13)	85.1	(3.82)	89.5	(3.22)	81.1	(4.38)
Denmark	50.8	(5.36)	37.5	(6.04)	83.1	(4.84)	73.7	(4.93)	62.5	(5.35)	67.0	(5.61)
Estonia	60.7	(4.31)	75.7	(4.14)	85.0	(3.10)	87.1	(2.86)	82.8	(2.92)	78.5	(3.58)
Hungary	66.3	(3.96)	69.7	(4.28)	81.5	(3.27)	77.0	(3.52)	71.5	(3.93)	84.3	(2.67)
Iceland	46.1	(0.21)	68.8	(0.20)	78.5	(0.12)	74.0	(0.19)	56.6	(0.22)	40.2	(0.21)
Ireland	75.7	(5.69)	90.3	(3.85)	94.5	(2.89)	93.2	(2.91)	93.1	(2.95)	90.5	(3.71)
Italy	69.5	(3.74)	76.4	(3.20)	92.3	(2.30)	75.7	(3.10)	81.0	(3.01)	82.1	(2.98)
Korea	81.9	(3.50)	82.6	(3.27)	82.5	(3.13)	86.5	(2.93)	81.6	(3.57)	76.5	(3.49)
Lithuania	71.3	(4.15)	88.0	(2.83)	93.7	(2.01)	93.0	(1.96)	84.7	(2.97)	83.5	(3.23)
Malaysia	98.6	(0.82)	96.4	(1.26)	97.3	(1.20)	96.3	(1.46)	98.5	(0.83)	97.7	(1.12)
Malta	81.7	(0.19)	83.1	(0.12)	100.0	(0.00)	83.5	(0.17)	92.0	(0.03)	86.3	(0.18)
Mexico	94.4	(2.14)	86.9	(2.85)	90.9	(2.43)	88.3	(2.27)	95.7	(1.69)	96.8	(1.45)
Norway	31.7	(4.67)	37.4	(4.95)	69.6	(4.58)	65.4	(4.49)	68.6	(4.15)	61.4	(4.53)
Poland	86.7	(2.85)	80.2	(3.36)	92.7	(2.64)	86.7	(3.33)	88.0	(3.13)	88.6	(2.85)
Portugal	40.8	(5.71)	71.8	(4.56)	88.7	(2.95)	72.7	(4.20)	72.5	(4.93)	75.4	(4.08)
Slovak Republic	80.8	(3.70)	85.7	(2.94)	82.2	(3.62)	80.4	(3.68)	70.6	(3.88)	68.0	(4.38)
Slovenia	68.7	(4.16)	74.8	(3.77)	85.3	(3.17)	86.6	(2.89)	82.3	(3.53)	78.2	(3.73)
Spain	64.4	(4.64)	66.5	(4.34)	75.8	(3.80)	57.0	(4.47)	72.3	(4.06)	55.9	(4.77)
Turkey	88.9	(4.29)	87.8	(4.02)	86.8	(4.03)	86.8	(3.70)	92.2	(3.28)	89.7	(3.64)
TALIS average	**71.1**	**(0.81)**	**76.7**	**(0.76)**	**87.1**	**(0.63)**	**81.5**	**(0.67)**	**80.7**	**(0.71)**	**78.2**	**(0.73)**

Note: Only includes those teachers working in schools that had a school evaluation sometime in the previous 5 years.
Source: OECD, *TALIS Database*.
StatLink http://dx.doi.org/10.1787/607856444110

Table 5.1a (2/2)

Criteria of school evaluations (2007-08)

Percentage of teachers of lower secondary education whose school principal reported that the following criteria were considered with high or moderate importance in school self-evaluations or external evaluations

	Teachers' knowledge and understanding of instructional practices in their main subject field(s)		Teaching of students with special learning needs		Student discipline and behaviour		Teaching in a multicultural setting		Extra-curricular activities with students (e.g. school plays and performances, sporting activities)	
	%	(S.E.)	%	(S.E.)	%	(S.E.)	%	(S.E.)	%	(S.E.)
Australia	70.8	(3.98)	79.8	(3.97)	88.0	(3.01)	41.9	(5.11)	77.0	(4.04)
Austria	65.6	(4.17)	58.6	(3.74)	66.1	(3.84)	35.7	(4.62)	74.5	(3.54)
Belgium (Fl.)	79.8	(3.88)	72.9	(4.71)	66.5	(4.17)	35.3	(4.41)	62.9	(4.83)
Brazil	92.4	(1.82)	84.6	(2.73)	89.5	(2.03)	86.8	(2.33)	89.2	(2.04)
Bulgaria	83.3	(4.58)	57.3	(6.86)	82.5	(4.08)	62.2	(5.66)	82.8	(4.29)
Denmark	52.9	(6.48)	65.8	(4.39)	76.3	(4.90)	43.9	(6.12)	48.8	(6.34)
Estonia	84.3	(3.33)	94.7	(2.17)	76.3	(3.48)	39.9	(4.14)	84.8	(3.04)
Hungary	81.5	(3.25)	70.8	(5.09)	78.2	(3.52)	51.5	(5.11)	75.5	(2.94)
Iceland	48.8	(0.21)	85.8	(0.10)	83.7	(0.08)	34.7	(0.16)	39.5	(0.23)
Ireland	91.6	(3.88)	97.5	(1.99)	91.9	(3.53)	62.9	(5.69)	85.6	(3.89)
Italy	79.9	(3.17)	87.7	(2.52)	87.3	(2.52)	77.0	(3.39)	84.4	(3.09)
Korea	78.6	(3.33)	58.8	(4.21)	81.7	(3.22)	38.0	(4.19)	66.2	(3.63)
Lithuania	86.5	(3.08)	90.9	(2.45)	81.3	(3.26)	53.8	(4.37)	85.9	(3.20)
Malaysia	98.3	(0.90)	71.1	(3.36)	97.4	(1.23)	85.6	(2.65)	93.9	(1.85)
Malta	85.2	(0.21)	83.5	(0.21)	100.0	(0.00)	40.9	(0.24)	88.3	(0.09)
Mexico	92.8	(2.19)	72.5	(4.07)	92.7	(2.12)	80.4	(3.45)	84.6	(3.06)
Norway	48.0	(4.51)	65.2	(4.27)	76.3	(3.63)	27.6	(4.53)	12.3	(3.61)
Poland	86.6	(3.04)	86.8	(2.98)	96.3	(2.16)	48.5	(5.56)	94.7	(1.89)
Portugal	78.4	(3.49)	80.7	(4.49)	80.4	(3.82)	57.9	(5.11)	83.3	(3.59)
Slovak Republic	76.1	(4.10)	85.7	(2.70)	82.7	(3.72)	42.9	(4.92)	78.8	(3.70)
Slovenia	82.5	(3.45)	82.6	(3.47)	81.7	(3.30)	44.0	(4.91)	77.7	(3.57)
Spain	51.9	(4.48)	72.0	(3.91)	79.8	(3.51)	56.5	(4.99)	67.1	(4.28)
Turkey	86.0	(4.17)	70.2	(5.54)	86.0	(3.26)	68.2	(5.23)	76.7	(5.68)
TALIS average	**77.5**	**(0.75)**	**77.2**	**(0.79)**	**83.6**	**(0.67)**	**52.9**	**(0.94)**	**74.5**	**(0.75)**

Note: Only includes those teachers that work in schools that had a school evaluation sometime in the previous 5 years.

Source: OECD, *TALIS Database*.

StatLink ᴍꜱᴘ http://dx.doi.org/10.1787/607856444110

Table 5.2

Impacts of school evaluations upon schools (2007-08)

Percentage of teachers of lower secondary education whose school principal reported that school evaluations (external or self-evaluations) had a high or moderate level of influence on the following

	Level of school budget or its distribution within schools		Performance feedback to the school		Performance appraisal of the school management		Performance appraisal of teachers		Assistance provided to teachers to improve their teaching		Teachers' remuneration and bonuses	
	%	(S.E.)	%	(S.E.)	%	(S.E.)	%	(S.E.)	%	(S.E.)	%	(S.E.)
Australia	76.4	(3.85)	96.2	(1.72)	88.5	(3.01)	64.9	(4.39)	86.8	(2.97)	5.1	(2.18)
Austria	12.0	(2.81)	76.2	(3.66)	62.0	(3.95)	63.1	(3.92)	64.1	(3.89)	4.5	(2.13)
Belgium (Fl.)	37.7	(4.43)	94.3	(1.97)	79.1	(3.45)	73.8	(3.74)	78.0	(3.79)	2.6	(1.39)
Brazil	55.4	(3.46)	86.0	(2.80)	89.1	(2.33)	92.2	(1.55)	87.0	(2.18)	41.2	(3.51)
Bulgaria	23.3	(7.20)	72.5	(5.23)	73.7	(5.47)	77.5	(4.96)	58.0	(4.95)	28.5	(7.20)
Denmark	22.3	(4.54)	52.9	(5.94)	58.5	(5.42)	32.5	(5.60)	44.3	(4.64)	9.0	(3.43)
Estonia	23.1	(3.67)	80.3	(3.44)	73.1	(4.06)	63.9	(3.79)	54.9	(4.63)	28.0	(3.59)
Hungary	28.1	(5.16)	75.4	(3.44)	78.5	(3.14)	76.1	(3.46)	68.7	(4.02)	48.9	(3.78)
Iceland	18.4	(0.17)	61.1	(0.18)	52.8	(0.16)	44.9	(0.18)	43.2	(0.20)	13.1	(0.11)
Ireland	36.7	(6.99)	87.0	(4.18)	86.1	(4.16)	66.7	(6.07)	74.0	(5.16)	1.2	(0.89)
Italy	67.4	(3.54)	90.1	(2.38)	83.1	(2.79)	78.5	(3.28)	78.3	(2.95)	40.5	(3.75)
Korea	73.6	(4.09)	91.5	(2.39)	93.7	(2.10)	73.8	(3.23)	80.2	(3.12)	27.5	(3.60)
Lithuania	24.1	(3.25)	84.4	(2.99)	87.8	(2.53)	83.6	(3.11)	77.8	(3.68)	16.3	(3.13)
Malaysia	88.2	(2.49)	97.4	(1.13)	97.5	(1.25)	96.7	(1.44)	91.1	(2.01)	68.9	(3.41)
Malta	53.8	(0.24)	92.4	(0.11)	88.1	(0.10)	87.6	(0.12)	82.4	(0.14)	16.7	(0.18)
Mexico	45.1	(5.02)	81.1	(3.40)	89.3	(2.43)	91.1	(2.15)	85.2	(3.04)	50.0	(4.66)
Norway	26.8	(4.25)	78.3	(4.25)	60.8	(4.64)	43.1	(4.52)	61.2	(4.40)	7.5	(1.24)
Poland	18.7	(3.47)	75.5	(3.71)	87.9	(3.04)	88.5	(3.11)	57.9	(4.63)	40.7	(4.65)
Portugal	35.8	(5.36)	91.6	(2.92)	91.1	(3.06)	57.3	(5.28)	55.1	(5.40)	2.6	(1.54)
Slovak Republic	19.6	(3.79)	78.6	(2.99)	57.2	(3.86)	81.9	(3.38)	80.6	(3.78)	79.8	(3.33)
Slovenia	24.5	(3.71)	85.1	(3.17)	85.5	(2.92)	69.4	(3.94)	80.9	(3.45)	36.3	(4.31)
Spain	22.2	(3.51)	60.4	(4.21)	61.3	(4.61)	43.6	(4.57)	53.0	(4.04)	9.1	(2.34)
Turkey	39.8	(6.21)	81.9	(4.68)	86.0	(4.11)	85.0	(4.29)	73.5	(4.67)	22.9	(4.23)
TALIS average	**38.0**	**(0.90)**	**81.3**	**(0.71)**	**78.7**	**(0.72)**	**71.1**	**(0.79)**	**70.3**	**(0.79)**	**26.1**	**(0.71)**

Note: Only includes those teachers working in schools that had a school evaluation sometime in the previous 5 years.

Source: OECD, *TALIS Database*.

StatLink ᴍꜱᴘ http://dx.doi.org/10.1787/607856444110

Table 5.2a

Publication of school evaluations (2007-08)

Percentage of teachers of lower secondary education in schools where school evaluations were published or used in comparative tables

	School evaluation results were published		Results used in school performance tables	
	%	(S.E.)	%	(S.E.)
Australia	75.7	(3.85)	23.3	(3.97)
Austria	38.9	(4.20)	12.9	(2.99)
Belgium (Fl.)	76.8	(3.15)	29.7	(4.44)
Brazil	56.6	(3.15)	61.2	(3.30)
Bulgaria	23.8	(6.94)	34.7	(5.09)
Denmark	84.5	(4.04)	54.8	(5.19)
Estonia	68.2	(4.03)	24.8	(3.29)
Hungary	72.6	(5.11)	34.0	(3.69)
Iceland	79.0	(0.15)	47.4	(0.17)
Ireland	64.9	(7.15)	8.1	(2.69)
Italy	44.2	(3.85)	19.9	(3.15)
Korea	69.0	(3.65)	26.0	(3.72)
Lithuania	33.7	(3.82)	28.6	(2.97)
Malaysia	50.7	(3.57)	40.1	(3.42)
Malta	41.6	(0.20)	0.0	(0.00)
Mexico	74.9	(3.87)	71.0	(3.99)
Norway	58.2	(4.71)	15.4	(3.69)
Poland	17.0	(3.51)	29.2	(4.46)
Portugal	63.2	(4.79)	23.5	(4.46)
Slovak Republic	75.3	(3.73)	29.7	(3.61)
Slovenia	41.7	(4.41)	6.0	(1.76)
Spain	40.9	(4.31)	32.1	(4.29)
Turkey	19.4	(4.12)	8.0	(2.29)
TALIS average	**55.3**	**(0.88)**	**28.7**	**(0.74)**

Note: Only includes those teachers that work in schools that had a school evaluation sometime in the previous 5 years.

Source: OECD, *TALIS Database*.

StatLink ⟨ᵣᵉ⟩ http://dx.doi.org/10.1787/607856444110

Table 5.3 (1/2)

Frequency and source of teacher appraisal and feedback (2007-08)

Percentage of teachers of lower secondary education who reported having received appraisal and/or feedback on their work with the following frequency from the following sources

	Appraisal and/or feedback received from the principal about the teacher's work in the school															
	Never		Less than once every two years		Once every two years		Once per year		Twice per year		3 or more times per year		Monthly		More than once per month	
	%	(S.E.)	%	(S.E.)	%	(S.E.)	%	(S.E.)	%	(S.E.)	%	(S.E.)	%	(S.E.)	%	(S.E.)
Australia	30.1	(1.49)	14.6	(0.90)	5.4	(0.57)	19.1	(1.21)	9.0	(0.70)	13.3	(0.89)	3.8	(0.53)	4.7	(0.67)
Austria	18.0	(0.85)	19.4	(0.75)	9.6	(0.55)	19.6	(0.91)	11.2	(0.60)	15.2	(0.64)	4.0	(0.36)	2.8	(0.33)
Belgium (Fl.)	19.1	(1.05)	24.0	(0.97)	10.0	(0.67)	25.2	(1.16)	9.9	(0.68)	8.4	(0.87)	1.9	(0.27)	1.4	(0.23)
Brazil	28.4	(1.30)	5.0	(0.49)	2.0	(0.21)	18.3	(1.05)	8.5	(0.67)	17.6	(1.14)	11.5	(0.77)	8.7	(0.73)
Bulgaria	4.1	(0.38)	5.9	(0.53)	3.3	(0.57)	26.5	(2.51)	22.4	(2.50)	22.7	(1.71)	8.4	(1.87)	6.7	(1.65)
Denmark	14.2	(1.16)	9.2	(0.96)	8.9	(0.91)	37.5	(1.59)	8.5	(0.87)	16.0	(1.31)	2.7	(0.46)	3.0	(0.50)
Estonia	13.9	(0.94)	10.1	(0.79)	6.9	(0.50)	29.4	(0.91)	14.1	(0.65)	17.1	(0.76)	4.8	(0.48)	3.7	(0.45)
Hungary	9.3	(1.08)	6.5	(0.61)	3.8	(0.77)	23.9	(2.54)	20.3	(1.61)	23.3	(1.41)	6.6	(0.73)	6.3	(1.30)
Iceland	23.3	(1.30)	6.2	(0.69)	4.1	(0.57)	22.0	(1.08)	14.6	(1.16)	16.0	(0.97)	6.6	(0.61)	7.3	(0.77)
Ireland	43.3	(1.37)	11.8	(0.90)	2.6	(0.37)	15.4	(0.91)	7.8	(0.63)	12.6	(0.84)	3.5	(0.42)	2.9	(0.47)
Italy	59.7	(1.36)	4.1	(0.37)	1.4	(0.21)	10.9	(0.79)	6.9	(0.60)	9.9	(0.75)	4.4	(0.56)	2.8	(0.42)
Korea	15.0	(0.82)	7.0	(0.57)	2.6	(0.29)	36.2	(0.93)	12.2	(0.68)	13.0	(0.70)	8.3	(0.57)	5.5	(0.53)
Lithuania	11.5	(0.86)	7.3	(0.57)	4.2	(0.44)	22.5	(0.97)	14.0	(0.81)	23.7	(0.98)	10.0	(0.65)	6.9	(0.57)
Malaysia	10.9	(0.91)	4.7	(0.51)	2.3	(0.27)	21.7	(1.14)	13.3	(0.98)	25.4	(1.21)	8.0	(0.76)	13.8	(1.60)
Malta	17.1	(1.38)	8.3	(1.03)	4.6	(0.72)	26.7	(1.59)	13.0	(1.05)	19.6	(1.36)	4.5	(0.66)	6.1	(0.87)
Mexico	16.9	(1.05)	2.7	(0.33)	1.4	(0.24)	15.8	(1.06)	11.4	(0.65)	21.8	(1.18)	19.1	(1.15)	10.7	(0.76)
Norway	26.2	(1.34)	12.8	(0.80)	5.4	(0.61)	28.2	(1.30)	9.4	(0.89)	11.1	(0.74)	3.8	(0.43)	3.1	(0.47)
Poland	9.6	(0.73)	22.5	(1.11)	9.0	(0.82)	23.9	(1.03)	15.6	(0.87)	14.0	(1.05)	2.9	(0.35)	2.4	(0.43)
Portugal	38.8	(1.44)	8.4	(0.58)	2.5	(0.38)	16.8	(0.89)	6.7	(0.53)	16.8	(0.77)	4.5	(0.45)	5.4	(0.74)
Slovak Republic	7.8	(0.89)	4.0	(0.48)	2.1	(0.27)	15.3	(1.07)	17.7	(0.91)	27.5	(1.08)	16.0	(1.23)	9.5	(1.00)
Slovenia	9.0	(0.89)	7.2	(0.63)	6.7	(0.53)	30.7	(1.17)	15.3	(0.70)	22.5	(0.93)	6.5	(0.62)	2.0	(0.27)
Spain	59.8	(1.43)	5.0	(0.56)	0.8	(0.17)	11.6	(0.79)	3.4	(0.39)	13.2	(0.86)	2.8	(0.37)	3.5	(0.46)
Turkey	20.6	(1.26)	4.9	(0.71)	4.4	(0.72)	27.7	(1.16)	18.0	(1.79)	12.0	(1.65)	8.0	(1.33)	4.4	(0.63)
TALIS average	**22.0**	**(0.24)**	**9.2**	**(0.15)**	**4.5**	**(0.11)**	**22.8**	**(0.27)**	**12.3**	**(0.21)**	**17.1**	**(0.22)**	**6.6**	**(0.16)**	**5.4**	**(0.16)**

Source: OECD, *TALIS Database*.

StatLink ⟨ᵣᵉ⟩ http://dx.doi.org/10.1787/607856444110

Table 5.3 (2/2)

Frequency and source of teacher appraisal and feedback (2007-08)

Percentage of teachers of lower secondary education who reported having received appraisal and/or feedback on their work with the following frequency from the following sources

	Appraisal and/or feedback received from other teachers or members of the school management team about the teacher's work in the school															
	Never		Less than once every two years		Once every two years		Once per year		Twice per year		3 or more times per year		Monthly		More than once per month	
	%	(S.E.)	%	(S.E.)	%	(S.E.)	%	(S.E.)	%	(S.E.)	%	(S.E.)	%	(S.E.)	%	(S.E.)
Australia	14.8	(0.86)	11.5	(0.76)	3.9	(0.45)	16.9	(1.05)	10.7	(0.75)	20.4	(1.18)	10.8	(0.71)	10.9	(0.87)
Austria	34.8	(0.89)	10.3	(0.48)	4.1	(0.34)	7.9	(0.45)	7.8	(0.49)	19.0	(0.69)	9.1	(0.43)	7.0	(0.52)
Belgium (Fl.)	41.9	(1.58)	10.4	(0.61)	3.1	(0.35)	11.0	(0.73)	6.7	(0.53)	14.5	(1.05)	7.0	(0.49)	5.5	(0.46)
Brazil	29.5	(1.23)	4.0	(0.45)	1.6	(0.24)	13.5	(0.89)	8.5	(0.83)	17.3	(0.86)	14.4	(0.94)	11.3	(0.69)
Bulgaria	21.5	(1.97)	9.5	(1.24)	3.5	(0.48)	21.5	(2.39)	11.3	(1.25)	15.4	(2.51)	8.5	(1.19)	8.8	(1.63)
Denmark	21.3	(1.32)	6.9	(0.63)	1.7	(0.33)	9.7	(0.85)	8.7	(0.82)	27.4	(1.25)	12.5	(0.85)	11.7	(0.93)
Estonia	9.5	(0.76)	6.6	(0.56)	3.8	(0.37)	21.6	(0.86)	12.2	(0.65)	27.1	(0.81)	10.7	(0.69)	8.6	(0.55)
Hungary	13.3	(1.21)	8.5	(0.67)	2.3	(0.35)	19.5	(2.07)	17.2	(1.03)	22.6	(1.00)	8.2	(0.67)	8.3	(1.01)
Iceland	29.2	(1.40)	7.4	(0.70)	2.6	(0.39)	6.7	(0.73)	7.2	(0.74)	18.0	(1.10)	12.6	(1.00)	16.3	(1.04)
Ireland	52.3	(1.16)	7.5	(0.67)	2.0	(0.30)	7.4	(0.63)	5.8	(0.64)	16.1	(0.80)	5.3	(0.53)	3.5	(0.42)
Italy	68.2	(1.08)	2.9	(0.32)	0.9	(0.14)	5.4	(0.36)	4.5	(0.41)	8.5	(0.55)	4.4	(0.43)	5.2	(0.69)
Korea	17.2	(0.83)	7.5	(0.53)	3.3	(0.39)	24.8	(0.96)	10.4	(0.58)	12.9	(0.68)	13.0	(0.55)	10.9	(0.66)
Lithuania	5.9	(0.54)	4.4	(0.42)	2.4	(0.33)	15.1	(0.73)	13.3	(0.70)	30.9	(0.99)	17.9	(0.84)	10.2	(0.72)
Malaysia	7.2	(0.51)	4.2	(0.39)	2.0	(0.23)	16.0	(0.93)	21.9	(1.35)	25.8	(1.08)	9.2	(0.89)	13.6	(1.19)
Malta	24.9	(1.53)	5.8	(0.78)	2.5	(0.61)	19.2	(1.45)	10.7	(1.04)	19.4	(1.34)	9.6	(0.97)	7.9	(0.82)
Mexico	34.1	(1.18)	2.5	(0.30)	1.8	(0.28)	10.4	(0.69)	10.2	(0.87)	16.4	(0.97)	15.5	(0.99)	9.1	(0.92)
Norway	28.1	(0.94)	11.1	(0.76)	2.0	(0.31)	10.2	(0.74)	6.4	(0.56)	17.3	(0.96)	12.6	(0.76)	12.4	(0.84)
Poland	30.0	(1.19)	11.7	(0.76)	5.3	(0.48)	15.4	(0.79)	9.0	(0.61)	15.8	(0.88)	7.4	(0.72)	5.5	(0.55)
Portugal	31.4	(1.31)	5.1	(0.48)	1.6	(0.23)	9.5	(0.63)	6.3	(0.45)	23.5	(1.05)	11.0	(0.76)	11.6	(0.88)
Slovak Republic	9.8	(0.77)	3.5	(0.40)	2.1	(0.34)	11.7	(0.93)	12.7	(1.01)	27.6	(1.22)	16.2	(1.03)	16.5	(1.07)
Slovenia	26.5	(1.01)	8.4	(0.55)	4.4	(0.41)	13.6	(0.71)	9.4	(0.51)	22.8	(0.93)	9.4	(0.62)	5.6	(0.44)
Spain	58.5	(1.22)	4.1	(0.41)	0.9	(0.17)	7.3	(0.66)	3.1	(0.37)	15.1	(0.83)	5.0	(0.39)	6.1	(0.48)
Turkey	47.5	(1.55)	4.5	(0.82)	2.1	(0.64)	12.2	(1.31)	10.2	(1.44)	9.9	(1.04)	7.8	(1.46)	5.9	(1.04)
TALIS average	**28.6**	**(0.25)**	**6.9**	**(0.13)**	**2.6**	**(0.08)**	**13.3**	**(0.22)**	**9.7**	**(0.17)**	**19.3**	**(0.23)**	**10.4**	**(0.17)**	**9.1**	**(0.18)**

	Appraisal and/or feedback received from an external individual or body (e.g. external inspector) about the teacher's work in the school																Not received appraisal or feedback from any source	
	Never		Less than once every two years		Once every two years		Once per year		Twice per year		3 or more times per year		Monthly		More than once per month			
	%	(S.E.)	%	(S.E.)	%	(S.E.)	%	(S.E.)	%	(S.E.)	%	(S.E.)	%	(S.E.)	%	(S.E.)	%	(S.E.)
Australia	73.8	(1.39)	12.3	(0.90)	3.0	(0.49)	5.4	(0.63)	2.1	(0.37)	2.2	(0.40)	0.6	(0.17)	0.6	(0.25)	10.4	(0.79)
Austria	42.5	(1.07)	31.5	(0.88)	8.3	(0.48)	8.5	(0.49)	3.6	(0.32)	3.9	(0.31)	0.9	(0.16)	0.8	(0.16)	10.9	(0.58)
Belgium (Fl.)	39.9	(2.02)	41.2	(1.42)	7.6	(0.77)	7.4	(0.77)	1.7	(0.26)	1.4	(0.26)	0.4	(0.13)	0.3	(0.12)	8.0	(0.67)
Brazil	57.2	(1.35)	4.9	(0.52)	2.3	(0.28)	18.6	(1.20)	4.5	(0.56)	6.6	(0.65)	3.9	(0.64)	2.1	(0.30)	18.9	(1.06)
Bulgaria	20.9	(2.20)	30.2	(1.96)	10.9	(1.02)	27.5	(1.66)	6.1	(1.34)	3.4	(1.19)	0.5	(0.12)	0.6	(0.23)	2.1	(0.29)
Denmark	69.7	(1.51)	9.2	(1.34)	1.9	(0.35)	5.7	(0.62)	4.8	(0.58)	5.3	(0.58)	1.5	(0.32)	2.0	(0.59)	7.4	(0.93)
Estonia	36.7	(1.22)	36.9	(1.09)	7.0	(0.54)	11.5	(0.66)	2.9	(0.32)	3.4	(0.35)	1.0	(0.19)	0.6	(0.16)	4.9	(0.61)
Hungary	51.4	(3.48)	29.4	(2.72)	4.1	(0.65)	10.0	(0.99)	1.9	(0.29)	2.2	(0.34)	0.6	(0.33)	0.4	(0.12)	6.1	(1.00)
Iceland	69.6	(1.39)	8.1	(0.90)	1.8	(0.39)	5.7	(0.64)	3.3	(0.49)	5.6	(0.62)	3.5	(0.57)	2.5	(0.43)	17.0	(1.05)
Ireland	53.0	(1.72)	32.3	(1.39)	4.9	(0.55)	6.5	(0.59)	1.0	(0.25)	1.6	(0.27)	0.4	(0.12)	0.4	(0.16)	25.7	(1.13)
Italy	90.3	(0.77)	2.3	(0.31)	0.8	(0.31)	2.7	(0.38)	0.9	(0.16)	1.7	(0.26)	0.7	(0.31)	0.5	(0.16)	54.6	(1.26)
Korea	31.0	(1.11)	12.1	(0.75)	7.3	(0.45)	29.3	(0.92)	14.6	(0.82)	4.5	(0.39)	0.8	(0.21)	0.4	(0.16)	7.1	(0.56)
Lithuania	34.1	(1.34)	21.4	(0.86)	9.2	(0.71)	18.7	(1.04)	6.4	(0.47)	6.0	(0.52)	2.7	(0.34)	1.4	(0.22)	3.5	(0.45)
Malaysia	32.9	(1.30)	15.2	(0.78)	5.4	(0.53)	22.7	(0.94)	11.6	(0.95)	10.9	(1.12)	0.9	(0.23)	0.3	(0.08)	3.2	(0.35)
Malta	44.4	(1.73)	13.8	(1.26)	7.7	(0.85)	19.3	(1.38)	7.8	(0.92)	5.7	(0.85)	0.4	(0.16)	0.9	(0.34)	7.8	(0.95)
Mexico	24.7	(1.37)	4.4	(0.40)	2.6	(0.34)	22.9	(1.18)	16.7	(1.12)	21.6	(1.29)	5.2	(0.66)	1.8	(0.29)	7.5	(0.68)
Norway	77.8	(1.08)	11.8	(0.94)	1.3	(0.26)	4.2	(0.41)	2.1	(0.37)	2.1	(0.34)	0.5	(0.14)	0.3	(0.10)	16.2	(0.89)
Poland	60.5	(1.07)	28.6	(0.92)	4.0	(0.45)	4.6	(0.52)	1.2	(0.24)	0.6	(0.15)	0.3	(0.10)	0.2	(0.07)	7.4	(0.62)
Portugal	84.0	(1.02)	7.7	(0.64)	2.0	(0.26)	4.2	(0.64)	0.9	(0.25)	0.9	(0.22)	0.2	(0.09)	0.1	(0.04)	26.3	(1.25)
Slovak Republic	33.3	(1.68)	43.6	(1.34)	8.2	(0.68)	9.3	(0.90)	2.3	(0.28)	1.9	(0.29)	0.9	(0.24)	0.4	(0.16)	3.6	(0.48)
Slovenia	57.5	(1.19)	25.6	(0.98)	3.9	(0.42)	7.5	(0.58)	2.2	(0.28)	2.6	(0.39)	0.6	(0.15)	0.2	(0.11)	6.7	(0.74)
Spain	65.7	(1.45)	10.4	(0.63)	3.7	(0.35)	13.1	(0.91)	3.5	(0.53)	2.7	(0.54)	0.5	(0.14)	0.4	(0.17)	45.5	(1.37)
Turkey	14.2	(1.29)	4.8	(0.64)	17.1	(1.95)	37.7	(1.85)	21.8	(1.91)	2.3	(0.85)	1.6	(1.21)	0.4	(0.16)	7.8	(0.65)
TALIS average	**50.7**	**(0.33)**	**19.0**	**(0.24)**	**5.4**	**(0.14)**	**13.2**	**(0.20)**	**5.4**	**(0.15)**	**4.3**	**(0.13)**	**1.2**	**(0.08)**	**0.8**	**(0.05)**	**13.4**	**(0.18)**

Source: OECD, *TALIS Database.*
StatLink http://dx.doi.org/10.1787/607856444110

Table 5.4 (1/2)

Criteria for teacher appraisal and feedback (2007-08)

Percentage of teachers of lower secondary education who reported that the following criteria were considered with high or moderate importance in the appraisal and/or feedback they received

	Student test scores		Retention and pass rates of students		Other student learning outcomes		Student feedback on the teaching they receive		Feedback from parents		How well they work with the principal and their colleagues	
	%	(S.E.)	%	(S.E.)	%	(S.E.)	%	(S.E.)	%	(S.E.)	%	(S.E.)
Australia	51.4	(1.58)	51.8	(1.61)	62.1	(1.42)	58.4	(1.87)	54.7	(1.59)	69.7	(1.27)
Austria	45.2	(1.26)	19.7	(0.95)	51.5	(1.02)	70.9	(1.03)	73.4	(0.93)	73.7	(0.91)
Belgium (Fl.)	53.2	(1.76)	52.0	(1.64)	47.9	(1.49)	59.1	(1.43)	51.4	(1.65)	78.3	(1.17)
Brazil	78.0	(1.25)	78.4	(1.17)	84.1	(0.97)	88.4	(0.87)	76.7	(1.22)	87.9	(0.83)
Bulgaria	88.4	(2.26)	72.6	(2.87)	78.5	(2.36)	81.0	(2.19)	64.2	(1.75)	85.5	(1.76)
Denmark	28.6	(1.74)	25.3	(1.43)	44.5	(1.73)	60.7	(1.49)	56.4	(1.75)	70.0	(1.64)
Estonia	72.1	(1.42)	65.8	(1.35)	77.4	(1.00)	79.2	(1.24)	71.7	(1.28)	75.0	(1.00)
Hungary	55.2	(1.61)	56.8	(1.66)	71.3	(1.28)	67.2	(1.95)	72.6	(1.33)	76.4	(1.67)
Iceland	44.9	(2.02)	40.3	(1.77)	52.8	(1.99)	78.6	(1.50)	76.3	(1.65)	77.8	(1.54)
Ireland	72.0	(1.51)	70.9	(1.70)	67.7	(1.70)	59.4	(1.51)	66.8	(1.41)	74.0	(1.23)
Italy	62.5	(1.77)	59.8	(1.61)	82.5	(1.19)	85.9	(1.21)	89.2	(0.96)	89.6	(0.89)
Korea	66.3	(1.15)	32.4	(1.04)	59.2	(1.05)	62.2	(1.16)	56.1	(1.08)	64.4	(1.08)
Lithuania	62.8	(1.19)	50.9	(1.40)	74.0	(1.12)	82.3	(0.89)	80.1	(0.89)	78.8	(0.83)
Malaysia	95.7	(0.39)	57.0	(2.32)	91.0	(0.51)	94.1	(0.43)	83.9	(0.85)	94.3	(0.47)
Malta	56.2	(2.01)	55.4	(2.01)	64.3	(1.63)	71.3	(1.81)	70.2	(1.87)	77.6	(1.81)
Mexico	84.5	(0.93)	86.6	(0.88)	77.9	(1.18)	82.9	(1.08)	66.7	(1.36)	75.3	(1.15)
Norway	47.3	(1.63)	41.6	(1.50)	55.8	(1.47)	59.9	(1.56)	68.2	(1.24)	79.3	(1.18)
Poland	87.2	(0.99)	66.2	(1.15)	84.6	(1.05)	82.8	(1.20)	86.6	(0.99)	89.3	(0.85)
Portugal	64.4	(1.51)	75.2	(1.10)	71.0	(1.44)	82.7	(1.02)	73.3	(1.49)	80.5	(1.01)
Slovak Republic	76.0	(1.19)	48.8	(1.73)	68.0	(1.16)	81.7	(0.96)	70.4	(1.34)	74.2	(1.57)
Slovenia	61.4	(1.33)	45.6	(1.29)	61.6	(1.27)	60.3	(1.31)	59.8	(1.21)	73.1	(1.12)
Spain	69.5	(1.43)	73.9	(1.35)	66.5	(1.59)	54.9	(1.74)	59.7	(1.34)	60.8	(1.65)
Turkey	72.6	(1.72)	65.9	(2.37)	79.2	(2.18)	71.7	(1.72)	61.5	(2.13)	75.7	(1.98)
TALIS average	**65.0**	**(0.32)**	**56.2**	**(0.34)**	**68.4**	**(0.30)**	**72.8**	**(0.29)**	**69.1**	**(0.29)**	**77.5**	**(0.27)**

	Direct appraisal of classroom teaching		Innovative teaching practices		Relations with students		Professional development undertaken		Classroom management		Knowledge and understanding of their main subject field(s)	
	%	(S.E.)	%	(S.E.)	%	(S.E.)	%	(S.E.)	%	(S.E.)	%	(S.E.)
Australia	59.9	(1.43)	66.5	(1.53)	80.1	(1.23)	48.8	(1.58)	69.8	(1.21)	72.4	(1.25)
Austria	77.6	(0.84)	69.8	(0.94)	85.7	(0.65)	44.5	(0.89)	77.7	(0.62)	76.4	(0.90)
Belgium (Fl.)	77.5	(1.03)	67.2	(1.34)	82.5	(0.95)	63.9	(1.59)	74.4	(1.09)	73.3	(1.35)
Brazil	90.1	(0.60)	87.7	(0.81)	93.7	(0.55)	83.1	(1.02)	89.6	(0.75)	92.5	(0.52)
Bulgaria	88.9	(0.96)	80.4	(1.64)	90.1	(1.12)	85.5	(1.45)	92.1	(0.93)	91.4	(1.05)
Denmark	40.7	(1.75)	35.7	(2.07)	75.7	(1.24)	46.4	(1.81)	61.6	(1.47)	47.1	(1.88)
Estonia	78.2	(1.16)	77.0	(1.01)	90.4	(0.60)	79.4	(0.91)	86.1	(0.85)	86.0	(0.85)
Hungary	80.2	(1.25)	69.6	(1.35)	80.2	(1.78)	55.5	(1.48)	82.1	(0.93)	89.7	(0.87)
Iceland	44.1	(1.92)	57.0	(1.86)	84.0	(1.42)	50.0	(1.88)	66.6	(1.78)	66.4	(1.82)
Ireland	69.5	(1.45)	68.6	(1.40)	86.1	(1.15)	58.0	(1.63)	84.7	(1.34)	82.4	(1.16)
Italy	79.9	(1.15)	79.9	(1.30)	94.7	(0.67)	75.5	(1.33)	94.6	(0.63)	92.2	(0.74)
Korea	67.8	(0.95)	62.6	(1.06)	69.8	(0.99)	63.5	(1.07)	74.3	(0.93)	64.8	(1.05)
Lithuania	80.1	(0.90)	80.0	(0.98)	89.8	(0.70)	67.7	(1.10)	81.3	(0.89)	89.8	(0.72)
Malaysia	96.3	(0.36)	96.2	(0.34)	96.6	(0.35)	91.0	(0.61)	96.6	(0.33)	97.8	(0.25)
Malta	77.1	(1.68)	68.2	(1.92)	84.2	(1.34)	47.1	(1.86)	83.1	(1.33)	78.4	(1.61)
Mexico	86.6	(0.84)	80.9	(1.10)	84.9	(0.86)	76.4	(1.11)	79.2	(1.20)	88.1	(0.78)
Norway	48.4	(1.45)	40.4	(1.65)	86.2	(0.98)	50.8	(1.56)	73.5	(1.12)	72.1	(1.14)
Poland	94.3	(0.66)	87.1	(0.86)	94.8	(0.52)	87.0	(0.92)	91.3	(0.67)	94.6	(0.66)
Portugal	55.3	(1.65)	69.4	(1.46)	90.9	(0.68)	66.4	(1.36)	76.4	(1.24)	78.6	(1.14)
Slovak Republic	83.3	(0.98)	79.0	(1.11)	83.3	(1.18)	62.1	(1.48)	72.6	(1.25)	82.7	(1.01)
Slovenia	76.1	(1.11)	68.7	(1.23)	80.7	(0.91)	53.2	(1.41)	68.7	(1.29)	78.0	(1.03)
Spain	62.0	(1.51)	59.5	(1.82)	75.8	(1.57)	55.3	(1.73)	75.7	(1.35)	65.6	(1.68)
Turkey	75.3	(1.70)	75.3	(1.69)	79.1	(1.65)	71.1	(2.20)	82.0	(1.40)	79.0	(1.90)
TALIS average	**73.5**	**(0.26)**	**70.7**	**(0.29)**	**85.2**	**(0.22)**	**64.5**	**(0.30)**	**79.7**	**(0.23)**	**80.0**	**(0.25)**

Note: Only includes those teachers who received appraisal or feedback.
Source: OECD, *TALIS Database*.
StatLink http://dx.doi.org/10.1787/607856444110

Table 5.4 (2/2)

Criteria for teacher appraisal and feedback (2007-08)

Percentage of teachers of lower secondary education who reported that the following criteria were considered with high or moderate importance in the appraisal and/or feedback they received

	Knowledge and understanding of instructional practices in their main subject field(s)		Teaching of students with special learning needs		Student discipline and behaviour		Teaching in a multicultural setting		Extra-curricular activities with students (e.g. school performances, sporting activites)	
	%	(S.E.)	%	(S.E.)	%	(S.E.)	%	(S.E.)	%	(S.E.)
Australia	66.7	(1.40)	41.2	(1.87)	63.1	(1.46)	29.1	(1.62)	51.7	(1.61)
Austria	71.8	(1.00)	53.5	(0.97)	77.3	(0.71)	33.7	(1.31)	65.0	(1.01)
Belgium (Fl.)	72.5	(1.22)	54.3	(1.58)	64.9	(1.24)	31.6	(1.92)	52.0	(1.34)
Brazil	91.1	(0.65)	68.0	(1.40)	88.0	(0.89)	76.5	(1.27)	81.2	(1.09)
Bulgaria	90.5	(1.54)	61.7	(1.94)	85.8	(2.36)	68.9	(2.27)	83.0	(2.00)
Denmark	41.1	(2.08)	39.5	(1.79)	56.3	(1.58)	22.9	(1.70)	42.5	(1.77)
Estonia	87.0	(0.93)	60.2	(1.39)	84.5	(0.75)	33.9	(1.88)	69.8	(0.94)
Hungary	89.0	(1.20)	65.5	(2.31)	81.7	(1.15)	52.0	(2.16)	73.4	(1.30)
Iceland	62.4	(1.98)	48.8	(1.86)	68.2	(1.57)	22.9	(1.87)	25.9	(1.89)
Ireland	80.1	(1.28)	56.4	(1.91)	79.9	(1.42)	40.1	(2.19)	63.5	(1.48)
Italy	90.3	(0.97)	81.5	(1.21)	92.5	(0.75)	70.6	(1.65)	77.9	(1.34)
Korea	68.1	(0.96)	45.8	(1.18)	68.7	(1.13)	31.8	(1.10)	37.1	(0.98)
Lithuania	88.0	(0.71)	61.4	(1.36)	80.5	(1.00)	48.9	(1.76)	73.5	(1.03)
Malaysia	97.5	(0.28)	49.2	(2.29)	94.8	(0.46)	81.9	(1.50)	81.4	(0.92)
Malta	73.4	(1.79)	44.9	(1.96)	79.5	(1.71)	32.6	(2.01)	61.3	(1.88)
Mexico	87.7	(0.92)	64.2	(1.56)	85.5	(0.84)	67.8	(1.37)	66.2	(1.48)
Norway	63.1	(1.27)	55.2	(1.15)	72.6	(1.02)	21.0	(1.53)	22.3	(1.28)
Poland	94.7	(0.57)	71.5	(1.77)	95.1	(0.58)	40.0	(1.71)	80.3	(0.95)
Portugal	78.9	(1.19)	58.2	(1.63)	80.2	(1.29)	47.9	(1.51)	72.9	(1.23)
Slovak Republic	83.9	(0.97)	62.2	(1.56)	80.6	(0.98)	44.0	(1.68)	65.6	(1.36)
Slovenia	79.3	(0.98)	52.1	(1.45)	65.2	(1.12)	27.1	(1.51)	58.6	(1.34)
Spain	63.4	(1.58)	66.2	(1.67)	79.1	(1.26)	56.0	(1.76)	59.8	(1.58)
Turkey	77.6	(2.00)	54.0	(2.32)	74.5	(1.99)	53.6	(1.68)	67.6	(2.05)
TALIS average	**78.2**	**(0.27)**	**57.2**	**(0.35)**	**78.2**	**(0.26)**	**45.0**	**(0.36)**	**62.3**	**(0.30)**

Note: Only includes those teachers who received appraisal or feedback.

Source: OECD, *TALIS Database*.

StatLink ⌐Π╗ http://dx.doi.org/10.1787/607856444110

Table 5.5

Outcomes of teacher appraisal and feedback (2007-08)

Percentage of teachers of lower secondary education who reported that the appraisal and/or feedback they received led to a moderate or large change in the following aspects of their work and careers

	A change in salary		A financial bonus or another kind of monetary reward		A change in the likelihood of career advancement		Public recognition from the principal and/or their colleagues		Opportunities for professional development activities		Changes in work responsibilites that make the job more attractive		A role in school development initiatives (e.g. curriculum development group)	
	%	(S.E.)	%	(S.E.)	%	(S.E.)	%	(S.E.)	%	(S.E.)	%	(S.E.)	%	(S.E.)
Australia	5.6	(0.53)	1.6	(0.26)	16.9	(0.80)	24.1	(0.99)	16.7	(1.03)	17.4	(0.96)	24.1	(1.03)
Austria	1.1	(0.18)	1.7	(0.20)	4.7	(0.39)	27.1	(0.88)	8.0	(0.51)	14.7	(0.63)	17.2	(0.70)
Belgium (Fl.)	0.4	(0.11)	0.1	(0.06)	3.7	(0.37)	20.7	(0.92)	7.1	(0.57)	11.9	(0.74)	10.1	(0.86)
Brazil	8.2	(0.77)	5.5	(0.55)	25.6	(1.16)	47.8	(1.22)	27.8	(1.18)	47.7	(1.42)	41.6	(1.43)
Bulgaria	26.2	(1.70)	24.2	(2.12)	11.6	(0.93)	64.9	(1.56)	42.4	(2.85)	28.2	(1.58)	49.5	(1.86)
Denmark	2.2	(0.50)	2.7	(0.53)	4.7	(1.13)	25.3	(1.49)	25.6	(1.43)	19.0	(1.61)	16.3	(1.23)
Estonia	14.3	(0.72)	19.8	(1.13)	10.5	(0.63)	39.6	(1.23)	35.6	(1.30)	21.7	(0.82)	31.3	(0.94)
Hungary	9.4	(0.92)	25.1	(1.62)	10.7	(0.76)	40.2	(1.42)	22.8	(1.05)	12.3	(0.81)	28.7	(1.42)
Iceland	7.5	(0.76)	9.3	(0.98)	8.6	(0.93)	18.3	(1.44)	20.5	(1.28)	18.1	(1.37)	19.2	(1.29)
Ireland	3.5	(0.44)	1.4	(0.40)	13.3	(1.09)	24.8	(1.10)	13.4	(1.00)	16.0	(1.11)	23.2	(1.29)
Italy	2.0	(0.35)	4.0	(0.47)	4.9	(0.53)	46.4	(1.40)	19.2	(1.30)	27.1	(1.34)	38.3	(1.51)
Korea	5.2	(0.49)	8.3	(0.56)	12.7	(0.78)	31.0	(1.19)	17.1	(0.91)	24.1	(0.91)	24.9	(1.02)
Lithuania	17.3	(0.94)	22.0	(1.31)	14.3	(0.89)	55.4	(1.11)	42.4	(1.13)	39.9	(1.06)	42.8	(1.20)
Malaysia	33.0	(1.36)	29.0	(1.30)	58.2	(1.39)	58.6	(1.33)	50.8	(1.39)	76.4	(0.92)	64.1	(1.22)
Malta	1.7	(0.46)	1.2	(0.36)	8.2	(0.89)	19.3	(1.47)	7.8	(1.07)	15.1	(1.40)	16.7	(1.29)
Mexico	10.6	(0.72)	7.3	(0.60)	28.6	(1.25)	33.4	(1.30)	27.2	(1.07)	55.9	(1.35)	34.4	(1.42)
Norway	7.0	(0.78)	3.0	(0.41)	6.9	(0.61)	25.6	(1.09)	21.3	(1.00)	14.5	(0.79)	22.4	(0.98)
Poland	14.5	(0.88)	26.5	(1.19)	39.2	(1.17)	55.7	(1.22)	38.2	(1.19)	24.6	(1.13)	42.1	(1.21)
Portugal	1.7	(0.29)	0.6	(0.14)	6.2	(0.66)	26.3	(1.11)	11.3	(0.82)	25.3	(1.26)	25.3	(1.10)
Slovak Republic	19.7	(1.17)	37.3	(1.50)	20.8	(1.05)	40.7	(1.47)	28.7	(1.20)	30.0	(1.00)	35.9	(1.20)
Slovenia	14.2	(0.78)	19.4	(1.12)	39.4	(1.16)	43.3	(1.29)	36.2	(1.26)	24.5	(1.04)	28.7	(1.01)
Spain	1.8	(0.34)	1.6	(0.36)	8.6	(0.76)	25.1	(1.27)	13.2	(0.94)	16.9	(1.01)	20.7	(1.38)
Turkey	2.2	(0.49)	3.6	(0.85)	13.5	(1.15)	42.6	(2.13)	12.1	(1.35)	33.7	(1.69)	24.4	(1.87)
TALIS average	**9.1**	**(0.16)**	**11.1**	**(0.20)**	**16.2**	**(0.19)**	**36.4**	**(0.27)**	**23.7**	**(0.26)**	**26.7**	**(0.24)**	**29.6**	**(0.26)**

Note: Only includes those teachers who received appraisal or feedback.

Source: OECD, *TALIS Database*.

StatLink ⫘ http://dx.doi.org/10.1787/607856444110

Table 5.6 (1/3)

Actions undertaken following the identification of a weakness in a teacher appraisal (2007-08)

Percentage of teachers of lower secondary education whose school principal reported that the following occurs if an appraisal of teachers' work identifies a specific weakness

| | The principal ensures that the outcome is reported to the teacher | | | | | | | |
| | Never | | Sometimes | | Most of the time | | Always | |
	%	(S.E.)	%	(S.E.)	%	(S.E.)	%	(S.E.)
Australia	0.0	(0.00)	3.1	(1.54)	21.6	(3.33)	75.2	(3.54)
Austria	0.4	(0.41)	3.7	(1.27)	15.1	(2.49)	80.8	(2.64)
Belgium (Fl.)	0.8	(0.58)	1.9	(1.20)	21.9	(3.35)	75.3	(3.41)
Brazil	0.0	(0.00)	10.0	(2.24)	26.3	(3.00)	63.7	(3.28)
Bulgaria	0.7	(0.74)	0.6	(0.48)	17.9	(3.63)	80.7	(3.75)
Denmark	0.9	(0.94)	15.7	(3.97)	27.9	(4.38)	55.5	(4.67)
Estonia	0.5	(0.46)	8.4	(2.27)	15.6	(3.01)	75.5	(3.28)
Hungary	0.4	(0.44)	2.1	(1.30)	15.3	(2.54)	82.2	(2.95)
Iceland	3.1	(0.01)	9.2	(0.14)	39.4	(0.22)	48.2	(0.21)
Ireland	3.5	(2.06)	11.5	(3.30)	25.5	(5.15)	59.4	(5.28)
Italy	3.7	(1.42)	10.5	(2.51)	27.5	(3.53)	58.4	(4.12)
Korea	31.7	(4.00)	53.8	(4.27)	13.7	(2.52)	0.8	(0.80)
Lithuania	0.5	(0.49)	2.0	(1.08)	33.1	(3.69)	64.5	(3.80)
Malaysia	0.5	(0.52)	14.3	(2.54)	38.4	(3.59)	46.8	(3.92)
Malta	0.2	(0.00)	1.3	(0.00)	32.8	(0.17)	65.7	(0.17)
Mexico	0.8	(0.83)	2.2	(1.15)	38.7	(4.16)	58.3	(4.25)
Norway	2.6	(1.47)	12.5	(3.27)	41.7	(5.39)	43.2	(5.00)
Poland	0.0	(0.00)	0.4	(0.39)	4.0	(1.62)	95.7	(1.67)
Portugal	0.5	(0.53)	14.5	(3.55)	24.5	(3.75)	60.6	(4.49)
Slovak Republic	0.0	(0.00)	5.7	(2.04)	18.3	(3.48)	76.0	(3.81)
Slovenia	0.0	(0.00)	3.2	(1.18)	24.6	(3.62)	72.2	(3.45)
Spain	4.1	(1.96)	12.0	(3.04)	24.7	(4.06)	59.2	(4.92)
Turkey	3.7	(2.10)	20.6	(5.90)	45.1	(6.02)	30.6	(5.61)
TALIS average	**2.6**	**(0.26)**	**9.5**	**(0.53)**	**25.8**	**(0.75)**	**62.1**	**(0.78)**

| | The principal ensures that measures to remedy the weakness in their teaching are discussed with the teacher | | | | | | | |
| | Never | | Sometimes | | Most of the time | | Always | |
	%	(S.E.)	%	(S.E.)	%	(S.E.)	%	(S.E.)
Australia	0.0	(0.00)	4.0	(1.97)	30.4	(4.02)	65.6	(4.23)
Austria	0.4	(0.41)	3.1	(1.28)	23.6	(2.85)	72.8	(2.99)
Belgium (Fl.)	0.0	(0.00)	2.9	(1.40)	29.1	(3.83)	68.0	(3.91)
Brazil	0.0	(0.00)	3.1	(1.16)	32.3	(3.17)	64.7	(3.25)
Bulgaria	0.0	(0.00)	0.9	(0.53)	29.5	(4.24)	69.7	(4.27)
Denmark	0.0	(0.00)	10.7	(3.32)	28.3	(5.03)	61.0	(5.16)
Estonia	0.0	(0.00)	9.9	(2.27)	25.4	(3.51)	64.7	(3.90)
Hungary	0.0	(0.00)	1.3	(0.69)	17.9	(3.33)	80.8	(3.43)
Iceland	0.7	(0.00)	5.5	(0.14)	46.4	(0.19)	47.3	(0.19)
Ireland	2.2	(1.40)	12.8	(3.32)	30.1	(5.42)	54.9	(5.34)
Italy	3.3	(1.38)	7.8	(2.21)	30.1	(3.81)	58.9	(3.78)
Korea	6.5	(2.24)	63.7	(4.03)	24.7	(3.45)	5.1	(1.81)
Lithuania	0.0	(0.00)	0.3	(0.33)	23.4	(3.42)	76.3	(3.41)
Malaysia	0.5	(0.52)	13.0	(2.46)	35.9	(3.72)	50.6	(3.83)
Malta	0.0	(0.00)	1.1	(0.03)	24.6	(0.15)	74.3	(0.15)
Mexico	0.5	(0.49)	5.8	(1.84)	39.8	(4.11)	54.0	(4.18)
Norway	2.0	(1.46)	17.8	(3.57)	47.8	(5.31)	32.4	(4.97)
Poland	0.0	(0.00)	0.0	(0.00)	16.6	(3.13)	83.4	(3.13)
Portugal	0.0	(0.00)	16.9	(3.56)	26.0	(4.45)	57.1	(4.75)
Slovak Republic	0.0	(0.00)	3.8	(1.57)	22.7	(3.76)	73.5	(4.02)
Slovenia	0.0	(0.00)	4.9	(1.54)	30.7	(3.56)	64.5	(3.63)
Spain	5.3	(2.14)	9.6	(2.79)	36.9	(4.36)	48.2	(5.05)
Turkey	1.2	(1.20)	18.1	(4.10)	54.8	(5.34)	25.9	(4.17)
TALIS average	**1.0**	**(0.18)**	**9.4**	**(0.48)**	**30.7**	**(0.81)**	**58.9**	**(0.81)**

Source: OECD, *TALIS Database.*
StatLink http://dx.doi.org/10.1787/607856444110

Table 5.6 (2/3)

Actions undertaken following the identification of a weakness in a teacher appraisal (2007-08)

Percentage of teachers of lower secondary education whose school principal reported that the following occurs if an appraisal of teachers' work identifies a specific weakness

	The principal, or others in the school, establishes a development or training plan for the teacher to address the weakness in their teaching							
	Never		Sometimes		Most of the time		Always	
	%	(S.E.)	%	(S.E.)	%	(S.E.)	%	(S.E.)
Australia	0.0	(0.00)	7.1	(2.41)	35.5	(4.49)	57.5	(4.58)
Austria	23.1	(3.15)	37.1	(3.00)	29.5	(2.90)	10.3	(1.91)
Belgium (Fl.)	3.3	(1.38)	40.3	(4.55)	40.5	(4.64)	15.8	(3.06)
Brazil	8.3	(1.97)	28.2	(3.26)	33.4	(2.83)	30.1	(3.09)
Bulgaria	9.0	(3.04)	34.7	(3.45)	43.1	(5.06)	13.2	(3.40)
Denmark	7.6	(2.91)	37.3	(4.59)	34.3	(5.39)	20.8	(4.46)
Estonia	10.6	(2.51)	41.4	(3.87)	30.1	(3.87)	17.8	(3.18)
Hungary	12.4	(3.17)	35.9	(3.67)	31.9	(4.12)	19.8	(4.12)
Iceland	9.5	(0.16)	19.2	(0.17)	53.2	(0.20)	18.0	(0.14)
Ireland	18.9	(4.29)	30.1	(4.77)	31.7	(5.24)	19.3	(3.90)
Italy	7.8	(1.94)	31.4	(3.63)	37.7	(4.10)	23.0	(3.61)
Korea	17.1	(3.19)	53.1	(3.95)	26.9	(3.64)	2.8	(1.42)
Lithuania	0.5	(0.39)	20.0	(3.18)	53.9	(3.96)	25.6	(3.53)
Malaysia	1.8	(0.91)	27.8	(3.37)	39.9	(3.33)	30.4	(3.17)
Malta	7.5	(0.09)	42.1	(0.23)	30.0	(0.20)	20.5	(0.18)
Mexico	4.2	(1.44)	21.1	(3.28)	40.0	(4.27)	34.7	(4.51)
Norway	20.4	(3.56)	42.2	(4.62)	28.0	(4.60)	9.4	(3.15)
Poland	11.1	(2.99)	21.4	(3.57)	41.4	(4.14)	26.0	(3.51)
Portugal	13.6	(3.12)	29.4	(4.19)	35.6	(4.35)	21.3	(3.99)
Slovak Republic	12.9	(2.85)	45.1	(4.64)	32.4	(4.29)	9.6	(2.62)
Slovenia	16.0	(3.07)	47.5	(4.22)	27.6	(3.47)	9.0	(2.13)
Spain	21.8	(3.59)	32.1	(4.30)	30.2	(4.36)	16.0	(3.73)
Turkey	4.4	(2.18)	34.7	(5.38)	38.1	(4.97)	22.7	(4.11)
TALIS average	**10.5**	**(0.54)**	**33.0**	**(0.79)**	**35.9**	**(0.85)**	**20.6**	**(0.70)**

	The principal, or others in the school, imposes material sanctions on the teacher (e.g. reduced annual increases in pay)							
	Never		Sometimes		Most of the time		Always	
	%	(S.E.)	%	(S.E.)	%	(S.E.)	%	(S.E.)
Australia	91.9	(2.15)	4.4	(1.95)	2.0	(1.15)	1.7	(1.33)
Austria	98.8	(0.73)	1.2	(0.73)	0.0	(0.00)	0.0	(0.00)
Belgium (Fl.)	99.4	(0.42)	0.3	(0.30)	0.0	(0.00)	0.3	(0.29)
Brazil	93.5	(1.60)	2.7	(0.80)	1.2	(0.46)	2.6	(1.33)
Bulgaria	81.2	(3.33)	16.5	(3.19)	1.5	(0.92)	0.7	(0.46)
Denmark	94.9	(2.09)	4.2	(1.88)	1.0	(0.94)	0.0	(0.00)
Estonia	75.9	(3.59)	23.1	(3.52)	0.5	(0.52)	0.5	(0.47)
Hungary	61.6	(6.54)	33.0	(6.51)	3.5	(1.39)	1.8	(1.18)
Iceland	95.4	(0.02)	4.6	(0.02)	0.0	(0.00)	0.0	(0.00)
Ireland	99.1	(0.92)	0.9	(0.92)	0.0	(0.00)	0.0	(0.00)
Italy	96.4	(1.49)	3.6	(1.49)	0.0	(0.00)	0.0	(0.00)
Korea	84.1	(3.10)	12.0	(2.77)	2.5	(1.24)	1.4	(1.00)
Lithuania	87.7	(2.58)	12.0	(2.56)	0.0	(0.00)	0.3	(0.29)
Malaysia	85.4	(2.76)	10.7	(2.39)	0.7	(0.46)	3.2	(1.37)
Malta	91.9	(0.15)	8.1	(0.15)	0.0	(0.00)	0.0	(0.00)
Mexico	82.0	(3.39)	12.1	(2.70)	3.8	(1.74)	2.1	(1.14)
Norway	95.0	(1.70)	5.0	(1.70)	0.0	(0.00)	0.0	(0.00)
Poland	71.9	(3.95)	18.3	(3.36)	8.2	(2.61)	1.6	(1.02)
Portugal	98.6	(0.84)	1.4	(0.84)	0.0	(0.00)	0.0	(0.00)
Slovak Republic	12.9	(2.78)	70.8	(4.05)	14.3	(3.32)	2.0	(1.03)
Slovenia	88.1	(2.69)	9.8	(2.40)	2.1	(1.20)	0.0	(0.00)
Spain	98.3	(1.17)	1.7	(1.17)	0.0	(0.00)	0.0	(0.00)
Turkey	94.7	(1.85)	3.5	(1.37)	0.4	(0.27)	1.4	(1.19)
TALIS average	**86.0**	**(0.54)**	**11.3**	**(0.52)**	**1.8**	**(0.24)**	**0.9**	**(0.16)**

Source: OECD, *TALIS Database*.
StatLink ᴴᴴᴴ http://dx.doi.org/10.1787/607856444110

Table 5.6 (3/3)

Actions undertaken following the identification of a weakness in a teacher appraisal (2007-08)

Percentage of teachers of lower secondary education whose school principal reported that the following occurs if an appraisal of teachers' work identifies a specific weakness

	The principal, or others in the school, report the underperformance to another body to take action (e.g. governing board, local authority, school inspector)							
	Never		Sometimes		Most of the time		Always	
	%	(S.E.)	%	(S.E.)	%	(S.E.)	%	(S.E.)
Australia	31.1	(4.11)	52.7	(5.00)	5.2	(1.70)	11.0	(2.89)
Austria	26.8	(3.27)	52.3	(3.74)	15.7	(2.48)	5.3	(1.55)
Belgium (Fl.)	18.8	(3.70)	65.3	(4.39)	8.3	(2.34)	7.7	(2.07)
Brazil	35.7	(2.99)	37.0	(3.38)	13.2	(2.48)	14.1	(2.69)
Bulgaria	50.8	(4.19)	42.0	(4.32)	5.0	(1.74)	2.2	(1.00)
Denmark	73.5	(4.58)	24.5	(4.52)	1.0	(1.00)	1.0	(0.98)
Estonia	68.2	(3.88)	28.1	(3.84)	2.1	(0.88)	1.6	(0.64)
Hungary	71.9	(5.19)	21.8	(4.98)	5.4	(2.17)	0.8	(0.62)
Iceland	45.2	(0.20)	39.7	(0.20)	9.6	(0.11)	5.5	(0.08)
Ireland	56.0	(5.12)	31.9	(4.53)	5.7	(2.36)	6.4	(2.44)
Italy	61.7	(3.75)	35.7	(3.72)	1.6	(0.98)	0.9	(0.71)
Korea	59.2	(4.27)	34.9	(3.99)	4.6	(1.72)	1.4	(1.00)
Lithuania	46.9	(3.38)	47.9	(3.41)	3.4	(0.89)	1.7	(0.88)
Malaysia	33.1	(3.24)	50.0	(3.45)	9.4	(2.17)	7.4	(2.11)
Malta	15.9	(0.11)	63.3	(0.20)	15.7	(0.16)	5.1	(0.13)
Mexico	22.6	(3.34)	30.7	(3.74)	23.3	(3.80)	23.5	(3.73)
Norway	60.0	(4.02)	35.0	(4.31)	5.0	(2.76)	0.0	(0.00)
Poland	68.9	(4.00)	24.9	(3.73)	5.0	(1.94)	1.2	(1.22)
Portugal	63.8	(4.28)	32.5	(4.43)	1.0	(0.78)	2.7	(1.61)
Slovak Republic	77.6	(3.96)	21.0	(3.99)	0.4	(0.29)	1.0	(0.74)
Slovenia	88.9	(2.52)	10.5	(2.43)	0.0	(0.00)	0.7	(0.67)
Spain	45.1	(4.51)	40.6	(5.06)	8.2	(2.66)	6.1	(2.23)
Turkey	51.3	(5.63)	35.1	(5.33)	7.5	(2.87)	6.1	(1.80)
TALIS average	**51.0**	**(0.81)**	**37.3**	**(0.83)**	**6.8**	**(0.41)**	**4.9**	**(0.35)**

	The principal ensures that the teacher has more frequent appraisals of their work							
	Never		Sometimes		Most of the time		Always	
	%	(S.E.)	%	(S.E.)	%	(S.E.)	%	(S.E.)
Australia	3.2	(1.77)	38.9	(4.66)	37.0	(5.03)	20.8	(3.87)
Austria	11.1	(2.33)	36.3	(2.88)	37.4	(3.41)	15.2	(2.12)
Belgium (Fl.)	3.0	(1.39)	39.9	(4.41)	43.3	(4.12)	13.8	(4.26)
Brazil	8.4	(2.24)	32.0	(3.19)	30.0	(3.08)	29.6	(3.53)
Bulgaria	0.3	(0.19)	11.7	(2.53)	69.9	(4.39)	18.1	(3.64)
Denmark	5.3	(2.40)	42.9	(4.95)	34.7	(4.81)	17.1	(4.31)
Estonia	4.4	(1.61)	55.6	(4.18)	32.8	(3.86)	7.2	(2.18)
Hungary	3.5	(1.81)	15.5	(2.58)	57.3	(4.59)	23.8	(4.64)
Iceland	14.6	(0.16)	53.5	(0.20)	27.9	(0.18)	4.0	(0.06)
Ireland	33.9	(4.89)	38.6	(5.27)	16.6	(4.05)	11.0	(3.42)
Italy	10.9	(2.38)	33.4	(3.60)	42.8	(3.98)	12.9	(2.82)
Korea	30.4	(3.90)	53.9	(3.97)	13.4	(2.71)	2.3	(1.33)
Lithuania	0.2	(0.20)	17.7	(2.67)	66.2	(3.62)	15.9	(2.80)
Malaysia	0.5	(0.52)	18.7	(2.90)	49.5	(3.52)	31.2	(3.53)
Malta	5.2	(0.08)	46.3	(0.21)	40.2	(0.19)	8.2	(0.14)
Mexico	3.1	(1.47)	16.6	(3.19)	50.4	(3.93)	29.9	(4.07)
Norway	9.9	(2.57)	52.0	(5.57)	34.4	(4.96)	3.7	(1.91)
Poland	5.1	(2.60)	20.6	(3.69)	53.0	(4.27)	21.3	(3.98)
Portugal	11.6	(3.02)	43.5	(4.62)	34.9	(4.79)	10.0	(2.81)
Slovak Republic	0.5	(0.49)	23.5	(3.38)	61.0	(3.82)	15.0	(2.94)
Slovenia	8.4	(2.28)	35.2	(3.40)	44.8	(3.82)	11.6	(2.10)
Spain	26.4	(4.13)	35.4	(4.47)	28.8	(4.28)	9.3	(2.83)
Turkey	7.7	(3.44)	30.6	(6.06)	44.4	(5.45)	17.3	(4.46)
TALIS average	**9.0**	**(0.50)**	**34.5**	**(0.80)**	**41.3**	**(0.83)**	**15.2**	**(0.67)**

Source: OECD, *TALIS Database*.
StatLink ⬛⬛ http://dx.doi.org/10.1787/607856444110

Table 5.7

Teacher perceptions of the appraisal and/or feedback they received (2007-08)

Percentage of teachers of lower secondary education who reported the following about the appraisal and/or feedback they had received in their school

| | Appraisal and/or feedback contained a judgment about the quality of the teacher's work | | Appraisal and/or feedback contained suggestions for improving certain aspects of teacher's work | | Appraisal and/or feedback was a fair assessment of their work as a teacher in this school | | | | | | | | Appraisal and/or feedback was helpful in the development of their work as a teacher in this school | | | | | | | |
| | | | | | Strongly disagree | | Disagree | | Agree | | Strongly agree | | Strongly disagree | | Disagree | | Agree | | Strongly agree | |
	%	(S.E.)	%	(S.E.)	%	(S.E.)	%	(S.E.)	%	(S.E.)	%	(S.E.)	%	(S.E.)	%	(S.E.)	%	(S.E.)	%	(S.E.)
Australia	68.1	(1.36)	55.4	(1.28)	4.4	(0.51)	10.1	(0.73)	66.7	(1.05)	18.8	(0.94)	6.2	(0.60)	18.8	(1.15)	60.0	(1.17)	14.9	(0.87)
Austria	79.4	(0.67)	41.4	(1.09)	3.8	(0.30)	9.3	(0.57)	47.9	(0.83)	39.0	(0.84)	11.7	(0.64)	20.9	(0.81)	46.1	(1.00)	21.3	(0.80)
Belgium (Fl.)	77.3	(0.90)	64.9	(1.19)	3.0	(0.38)	9.0	(0.61)	57.2	(1.22)	30.8	(1.30)	4.2	(0.45)	13.4	(0.67)	60.4	(1.12)	22.0	(1.07)
Brazil	75.0	(1.23)	66.1	(1.65)	5.2	(0.72)	14.8	(0.96)	63.3	(1.20)	16.7	(0.91)	4.4	(0.64)	10.8	(0.76)	63.8	(1.44)	21.0	(1.18)
Bulgaria	92.5	(0.85)	70.2	(2.21)	2.1	(0.39)	6.9	(0.64)	64.8	(1.24)	26.2	(1.58)	2.4	(0.42)	6.8	(0.66)	67.4	(1.38)	23.4	(1.69)
Denmark	69.6	(1.70)	36.0	(1.67)	4.3	(0.65)	10.0	(0.97)	65.3	(1.55)	20.5	(1.25)	6.0	(0.71)	17.7	(0.95)	61.6	(1.30)	14.7	(1.08)
Estonia	83.4	(0.90)	58.2	(1.17)	2.5	(0.31)	10.9	(0.70)	68.9	(1.02)	17.7	(0.91)	6.8	(0.59)	22.9	(1.02)	59.1	(1.12)	11.2	(0.70)
Hungary	79.1	(1.33)	59.0	(2.01)	2.6	(0.43)	10.7	(0.72)	65.0	(1.15)	21.7	(1.14)	3.7	(0.48)	11.8	(0.95)	64.8	(1.06)	19.6	(1.47)
Iceland	63.7	(1.73)	29.9	(1.39)	6.8	(0.78)	12.6	(1.00)	58.9	(1.67)	21.7	(1.34)	9.3	(0.95)	19.2	(1.26)	59.3	(1.81)	12.2	(1.11)
Ireland	69.7	(1.40)	40.3	(1.72)	3.5	(0.49)	8.6	(0.73)	67.6	(1.33)	20.3	(1.13)	4.8	(0.56)	16.4	(0.89)	62.7	(1.29)	16.1	(1.10)
Italy	68.5	(1.42)	55.9	(1.67)	2.8	(0.40)	10.8	(0.84)	77.1	(1.02)	9.3	(0.80)	3.3	(0.41)	13.5	(1.02)	71.6	(1.43)	11.6	(0.96)
Korea	64.2	(1.12)	64.7	(0.99)	9.2	(0.61)	38.1	(1.03)	51.3	(1.10)	1.4	(0.29)	9.8	(0.64)	36.9	(1.00)	51.5	(1.15)	1.8	(0.27)
Lithuania	88.4	(0.82)	69.8	(1.19)	1.1	(0.27)	6.0	(0.48)	74.9	(0.81)	18.0	(0.91)	2.0	(0.31)	8.5	(0.52)	70.1	(0.95)	19.4	(0.93)
Malaysia	94.8	(0.46)	93.1	(0.53)	1.2	(0.17)	9.4	(0.65)	76.9	(0.97)	12.5	(0.89)	0.8	(0.13)	6.1	(0.49)	70.3	(1.11)	22.8	(1.17)
Malta	85.4	(1.34)	62.0	(1.63)	3.3	(0.67)	11.0	(1.24)	66.8	(1.72)	18.9	(1.32)	3.4	(0.75)	17.2	(1.53)	63.5	(1.81)	15.9	(1.29)
Mexico	72.8	(1.01)	77.5	(1.05)	6.2	(0.62)	13.6	(0.86)	54.9	(1.24)	25.4	(1.12)	5.3	(0.49)	9.2	(0.84)	52.6	(1.19)	32.9	(1.28)
Norway	61.8	(1.49)	28.2	(1.27)	6.0	(0.54)	10.0	(0.81)	46.7	(1.25)	37.4	(1.40)	9.9	(0.75)	15.1	(0.96)	54.3	(1.15)	20.7	(1.12)
Poland	88.8	(0.77)	59.1	(1.64)	2.0	(0.30)	4.4	(0.51)	62.3	(1.32)	31.3	(1.28)	2.2	(0.30)	8.9	(0.72)	68.0	(1.20)	20.9	(1.07)
Portugal	77.4	(1.03)	56.1	(1.45)	4.2	(0.54)	14.4	(0.92)	66.7	(1.15)	14.8	(0.85)	4.8	(0.58)	12.7	(0.77)	68.5	(1.22)	14.0	(1.01)
Slovak Republic	87.2	(1.01)	65.0	(1.34)	3.0	(0.40)	15.8	(0.85)	69.0	(1.28)	12.2	(0.97)	3.9	(0.48)	18.1	(1.17)	67.1	(1.26)	10.9	(0.86)
Slovenia	75.3	(0.96)	61.6	(1.30)	2.5	(0.36)	9.0	(0.59)	73.0	(1.03)	15.5	(0.91)	3.7	(0.45)	14.6	(0.79)	68.8	(1.09)	12.9	(0.92)
Spain	42.1	(1.46)	60.4	(1.40)	8.9	(0.92)	16.6	(1.07)	60.2	(1.35)	14.3	(0.96)	9.4	(0.84)	20.3	(1.24)	57.7	(1.46)	12.6	(0.96)
Turkey	53.8	(1.99)	58.7	(2.02)	12.3	(1.20)	23.2	(1.81)	50.9	(2.05)	13.6	(0.89)	10.1	(1.25)	25.4	(1.43)	51.7	(1.74)	12.8	(1.29)
TALIS average	**74.7**	**(0.26)**	**58.0**	**(0.31)**	**4.4**	**(0.12)**	**12.4**	**(0.18)**	**63.3**	**(0.27)**	**19.9**	**(0.22)**	**5.6**	**(0.13)**	**15.9**	**(0.20)**	**61.8**	**(0.27)**	**16.8**	**(0.23)**

Note: Only includes those teachers who received appraisal or feedback.

Source: OECD, *TALIS Database*.

StatLink ⟲ http://dx.doi.org/10.1787/607856444110

Table 5.7a

Teacher perceptions of the personal impact of teacher appraisal and feedback (2007-08)

Percentage of teachers of lower secondary education who reported the following changes following the appraisal and/or feedback they received in their school

	Change in their job satisfaction										Change in their job security									
	A large decrease		A small decrease		No change		A small increase		A large increase		A large decrease		A small decrease		No change		A small increase		A large increase	
	%	(S.E.)	%	(S.E.)	%	(S.E.)	%	(S.E.)	%	(S.E.)	%	(S.E.)	%	(S.E.)	%	(S.E.)	%	(S.E.)	%	(S.E.)
Australia	3.3	(0.43)	6.3	(0.58)	48.1	(1.31)	34.2	(1.11)	8.3	(0.67)	1.4	(0.32)	2.3	(0.38)	76.3	(1.03)	12.7	(0.76)	7.4	(0.71)
Austria	2.2	(0.26)	3.8	(0.35)	53.5	(0.90)	27.1	(0.84)	13.4	(0.65)	1.0	(0.16)	0.9	(0.15)	83.0	(0.80)	9.0	(0.61)	6.1	(0.41)
Belgium (Fl.)	2.5	(0.38)	4.7	(0.41)	51.4	(1.43)	29.9	(1.28)	11.5	(0.77)	1.0	(0.21)	1.5	(0.21)	68.3	(1.45)	15.9	(0.96)	13.3	(0.80)
Brazil	2.7	(0.48)	5.3	(0.57)	33.5	(1.43)	36.4	(1.15)	22.1	(1.25)	1.5	(0.38)	2.5	(0.29)	58.5	(1.50)	22.1	(1.14)	15.3	(0.94)
Bulgaria	3.7	(0.64)	4.0	(0.51)	34.8	(2.53)	41.7	(2.84)	15.8	(1.29)	1.1	(0.17)	2.2	(0.56)	37.3	(2.51)	40.7	(2.57)	18.6	(1.68)
Denmark	1.3	(0.31)	3.5	(0.47)	51.3	(1.52)	35.1	(1.38)	8.8	(0.93)	0.7	(0.25)	1.3	(0.30)	81.9	(1.41)	11.2	(1.41)	5.0	(0.81)
Estonia	3.1	(0.40)	6.3	(0.52)	37.8	(1.12)	45.0	(1.26)	7.9	(0.57)	3.2	(0.36)	7.3	(0.54)	42.5	(1.07)	36.9	(1.11)	10.2	(0.63)
Hungary	0.9	(0.21)	4.4	(0.43)	42.0	(1.08)	44.3	(1.41)	8.4	(0.95)	1.9	(0.28)	4.2	(0.50)	61.5	(1.42)	21.5	(0.82)	11.0	(1.18)
Iceland	2.8	(0.53)	3.6	(0.59)	39.7	(1.47)	29.8	(1.31)	24.1	(1.34)	1.6	(0.39)	2.4	(0.50)	51.1	(1.68)	21.1	(1.33)	23.7	(1.43)
Ireland	1.6	(0.35)	4.3	(0.56)	43.8	(1.64)	40.0	(1.64)	10.2	(0.81)	0.7	(0.21)	1.3	(0.27)	81.6	(1.17)	11.6	(0.91)	4.8	(0.53)
Italy	1.1	(0.23)	2.7	(0.62)	47.9	(1.38)	35.3	(1.21)	13.0	(1.05)	1.0	(0.23)	1.6	(0.34)	76.9	(1.21)	14.2	(0.99)	6.2	(0.65)
Korea	3.3	(0.46)	8.8	(0.60)	52.8	(1.09)	32.2	(1.10)	2.9	(0.31)	2.6	(0.39)	7.0	(0.53)	59.1	(1.17)	28.8	(1.05)	2.5	(0.32)
Lithuania	2.0	(0.25)	4.9	(0.43)	38.4	(0.99)	40.2	(0.98)	14.4	(0.93)	1.5	(0.19)	4.6	(0.45)	45.7	(1.03)	33.8	(0.92)	14.4	(0.86)
Malaysia	1.2	(0.21)	2.5	(0.28)	13.0	(0.84)	49.3	(1.16)	34.1	(1.16)	0.7	(0.16)	1.9	(0.45)	29.5	(1.88)	41.5	(1.47)	26.4	(1.06)
Malta	3.2	(0.65)	5.7	(0.92)	38.5	(1.77)	38.7	(1.81)	13.9	(1.35)	1.1	(0.42)	2.6	(0.60)	74.5	(1.61)	16.8	(1.38)	4.9	(0.80)
Mexico	1.8	(0.29)	4.7	(0.50)	16.4	(0.75)	42.5	(1.08)	34.6	(1.28)	1.6	(0.31)	3.3	(0.41)	26.1	(0.90)	32.4	(1.16)	36.6	(1.28)
Norway	1.2	(0.27)	2.8	(0.41)	46.3	(1.35)	43.6	(1.23)	6.1	(0.54)	0.8	(0.18)	1.8	(0.35)	69.8	(1.22)	19.2	(1.03)	8.4	(0.75)
Poland	1.9	(0.30)	3.0	(0.32)	36.2	(1.20)	36.1	(1.20)	22.8	(1.00)	1.6	(0.25)	2.3	(0.35)	55.2	(1.21)	23.2	(0.98)	17.8	(0.96)
Portugal	3.9	(0.48)	5.8	(0.56)	42.1	(1.27)	38.2	(1.16)	10.1	(0.76)	2.1	(0.35)	2.9	(0.42)	77.7	(1.26)	13.3	(1.00)	4.0	(0.49)
Slovak Republic	2.9	(0.48)	5.9	(0.59)	42.5	(1.14)	38.3	(1.23)	10.3	(0.77)	1.6	(0.33)	3.3	(0.37)	58.7	(1.22)	25.8	(1.24)	10.7	(0.77)
Slovenia	0.7	(0.15)	2.6	(0.29)	40.7	(1.08)	44.2	(1.10)	11.8	(0.64)	0.9	(0.21)	3.3	(0.41)	62.1	(1.02)	24.2	(0.93)	9.6	(0.61)
Spain	3.5	(0.43)	6.9	(0.64)	50.6	(1.44)	30.5	(1.28)	8.5	(0.69)	2.2	(0.39)	3.3	(0.47)	72.5	(1.16)	15.3	(1.05)	6.8	(0.72)
Turkey	6.9	(0.82)	8.2	(0.94)	47.0	(2.83)	24.9	(2.29)	12.9	(1.25)	2.6	(0.61)	4.4	(0.67)	75.1	(1.45)	10.3	(1.25)	7.6	(1.06)
TALIS average	**2.5**	**(0.09)**	**4.8**	**(0.11)**	**41.2**	**(0.30)**	**37.3**	**(0.30)**	**14.2**	**(0.20)**	**1.5**	**(0.06)**	**3.0**	**(0.09)**	**61.9**	**(0.29)**	**21.8**	**(0.25)**	**11.8**	**(0.19)**

Note: Only includes those teachers who received appraisal or feedback.

Source: OECD, *TALIS Database*.

StatLink http://dx.doi.org/10.1787/607856444110

Table 5.8

Impact of teacher appraisal and feedback upon teaching (2007-08)

Percentage of teachers of lower secondary education who reported that the appraisal and/or feedback they received directly led to or involved moderate or large changes in the following

	Classroom management practices		Knowledge or understanding of the teacher's main subject field(s)		Knowledge or understanding of instructional practices		A teacher development or training plan to improve their teaching		Teaching of students with special learning needs		Student discipline and behaviour problems		Teaching of students in a multicultural setting		The emphasis placed on improving student test scores in teaching	
	%	(S.E.)	%	(S.E.)	%	(S.E.)	%	(S.E.)	%	(S.E.)	%	(S.E.)	%	(S.E.)	%	(S.E.)
Australia	24.1	(1.09)	19.4	(0.95)	22.1	(1.21)	18.4	(1.13)	14.2	(1.07)	21.0	(1.12)	8.1	(0.90)	24.7	(1.25)
Austria	21.9	(0.79)	16.4	(0.73)	24.9	(0.96)	16.7	(0.73)	18.6	(0.73)	20.4	(0.72)	8.3	(0.63)	19.5	(0.70)
Belgium (Fl.)	20.5	(0.69)	16.7	(0.87)	20.1	(0.84)	16.4	(0.76)	19.1	(0.87)	20.1	(0.76)	8.2	(0.64)	19.6	(0.89)
Brazil	60.1	(1.26)	59.9	(1.46)	59.2	(1.39)	52.9	(1.52)	26.8	(1.17)	53.7	(1.20)	44.0	(1.34)	65.6	(1.25)
Bulgaria	68.4	(2.47)	58.8	(2.35)	62.2	(2.75)	56.5	(1.85)	41.5	(2.48)	63.3	(1.48)	44.1	(1.95)	74.5	(2.27)
Denmark	18.2	(1.13)	10.9	(1.26)	11.1	(1.27)	12.4	(1.31)	13.9	(1.09)	19.5	(1.45)	6.3	(0.79)	19.3	(1.24)
Estonia	30.3	(0.81)	32.7	(1.02)	35.7	(0.96)	28.9	(0.99)	19.4	(0.83)	26.9	(0.89)	10.8	(0.81)	30.4	(1.09)
Hungary	36.2	(1.09)	24.3	(1.32)	32.2	(1.53)	44.7	(1.58)	32.2	(2.01)	32.4	(1.19)	19.8	(0.95)	35.4	(1.18)
Iceland	24.0	(1.34)	20.3	(1.42)	23.0	(1.32)	36.9	(1.52)	22.8	(1.33)	30.0	(1.28)	12.6	(1.02)	26.6	(1.40)
Ireland	25.2	(1.28)	18.7	(0.91)	24.5	(1.30)	21.3	(1.33)	19.3	(1.20)	23.4	(1.34)	12.0	(1.09)	26.7	(1.04)
Italy	33.4	(1.38)	32.2	(1.58)	38.8	(1.43)	38.7	(1.47)	37.2	(1.57)	36.9	(1.43)	29.5	(1.40)	44.0	(1.78)
Korea	36.0	(1.03)	45.1	(1.01)	48.1	(1.03)	48.6	(1.02)	33.5	(1.00)	47.0	(1.01)	21.4	(0.84)	39.7	(1.09)
Lithuania	39.4	(1.13)	50.1	(1.21)	54.2	(1.23)	46.1	(1.16)	32.2	(1.23)	43.7	(1.30)	23.0	(1.22)	46.7	(1.22)
Malaysia	86.7	(0.68)	88.5	(0.62)	89.2	(0.68)	81.6	(0.91)	45.7	(1.96)	83.9	(0.77)	73.9	(1.39)	91.5	(0.61)
Malta	24.6	(1.50)	20.0	(1.34)	21.5	(1.44)	25.3	(1.92)	17.7	(1.50)	25.7	(1.67)	9.6	(1.04)	31.3	(1.78)
Mexico	74.8	(1.09)	69.1	(1.38)	71.3	(1.26)	74.1	(1.11)	42.0	(1.32)	67.1	(1.33)	53.1	(1.38)	76.7	(1.14)
Norway	28.5	(1.23)	23.0	(1.19)	21.1	(1.11)	24.0	(1.18)	24.2	(1.03)	28.6	(1.30)	7.0	(0.63)	25.7	(1.15)
Poland	45.5	(1.14)	31.3	(1.16)	38.2	(1.39)	47.6	(1.26)	26.4	(1.82)	31.9	(1.04)	10.8	(0.92)	53.9	(1.15)
Portugal	22.4	(1.29)	18.8	(1.22)	23.0	(1.17)	26.8	(1.20)	21.4	(1.12)	26.9	(1.26)	14.7	(0.98)	35.5	(1.26)
Slovak Republic	36.4	(1.15)	42.8	(1.21)	44.8	(1.15)	35.7	(1.22)	31.3	(1.39)	40.9	(1.11)	18.9	(1.00)	41.1	(1.50)
Slovenia	47.6	(1.08)	34.8	(1.09)	44.0	(1.10)	46.1	(1.12)	38.3	(1.08)	45.8	(1.15)	15.2	(1.00)	52.1	(1.13)
Spain	25.2	(1.48)	12.5	(0.94)	16.6	(1.11)	20.5	(1.34)	22.9	(1.36)	27.2	(1.15)	17.0	(1.19)	24.6	(1.29)
Turkey	35.2	(1.22)	33.3	(1.30)	36.3	(1.88)	39.4	(2.09)	25.9	(1.60)	40.0	(1.71)	26.7	(1.28)	43.0	(1.62)
TALIS average	**37.6**	**(0.26)**	**33.9**	**(0.26)**	**37.5**	**(0.28)**	**37.4**	**(0.28)**	**27.2**	**(0.29)**	**37.2**	**(0.26)**	**21.5**	**(0.23)**	**41.2**	**(0.27)**

Note: Only includes those teachers who received appraisal or feedback.

Source: OECD, *TALIS Database*.

StatLink http://dx.doi.org/10.1787/607856444110

CHAPTER 5 SCHOOL EVALUATION, TEACHER APPRAISAL AND FEEDBACK AND THE IMPACT ON SCHOOLS AND TEACHERS

Table 5.9

Teacher appraisal and feedback and school development (2007-08)

Percentage of teachers of lower secondary education who agree or strongly agree with the following statements about aspects of appraisal and/or feedback in their school

	In this school, the school principal takes steps to alter the monetary rewards of a persistently underperforming teacher		In this school, the sustained poor performance of a teacher would be tolerated by the rest of the staff		In this school, teachers will be dismissed because of sustained poor performance		In this school, the principal uses effective methods to determine whether teachers are performing well or badly		In this school, a development or training plan is established for teachers to improve their work as teachers	
	%	(S.E.)	%	(S.E.)	%	(S.E.)	%	(S.E.)	%	(S.E.)
Australia	7.1	(0.72)	42.8	(1.50)	29.2	(1.61)	48.7	(1.54)	54.5	(1.73)
Austria	7.6	(0.45)	40.8	(0.97)	11.5	(0.73)	46.2	(1.12)	21.2	(0.99)
Belgium (Fl.)	5.9	(0.51)	25.9	(1.13)	43.6	(1.63)	49.5	(1.53)	45.1	(1.54)
Brazil	24.0	(1.15)	30.4	(1.12)	30.2	(1.52)	57.7	(1.42)	70.9	(1.41)
Bulgaria	44.0	(2.30)	11.0	(1.17)	64.7	(2.41)	83.4	(1.32)	77.4	(2.25)
Denmark	6.6	(0.80)	40.7	(1.74)	35.0	(1.76)	37.8	(1.77)	54.4	(1.58)
Estonia	13.4	(0.91)	18.2	(0.93)	29.7	(1.16)	50.5	(1.66)	64.0	(1.40)
Hungary	40.7	(2.03)	32.6	(1.76)	34.3	(1.71)	61.4	(2.23)	71.9	(2.60)
Iceland	28.5	(1.40)	31.9	(1.34)	35.5	(1.32)	38.2	(1.49)	45.4	(1.46)
Ireland	5.6	(0.59)	58.9	(1.32)	10.9	(1.06)	39.1	(1.61)	51.9	(1.69)
Italy	26.4	(0.88)	28.0	(1.00)	27.3	(1.02)	68.1	(1.13)	71.9	(1.14)
Korea	13.3	(0.71)	47.3	(0.98)	10.1	(0.71)	31.9	(1.17)	31.3	(1.15)
Lithuania	27.0	(1.19)	20.2	(0.86)	60.2	(1.03)	70.3	(1.15)	90.7	(0.73)
Malaysia	47.4	(1.65)	52.8	(1.28)	17.7	(0.94)	75.0	(1.26)	89.4	(0.71)
Malta	13.3	(1.19)	41.9	(1.69)	24.7	(1.24)	56.0	(1.46)	60.4	(1.65)
Mexico	34.5	(1.31)	17.7	(1.09)	28.9	(1.30)	88.8	(0.80)	69.0	(1.43)
Norway	7.5	(0.59)	58.2	(1.15)	10.7	(0.88)	27.6	(1.33)	42.4	(1.41)
Poland	31.3	(1.37)	26.5	(1.17)	34.2	(1.22)	75.1	(1.34)	78.8	(1.24)
Portugal	22.4	(0.85)	20.0	(0.99)	27.2	(1.10)	57.2	(1.30)	49.3	(1.52)
Slovak Republic	50.8	(1.36)	34.9	(1.39)	42.4	(1.70)	64.3	(1.64)	73.6	(1.39)
Slovenia	44.8	(1.37)	35.0	(1.18)	8.9	(0.74)	64.3	(1.29)	67.4	(1.27)
Spain	12.3	(0.76)	36.3	(1.14)	15.1	(0.94)	35.5	(1.25)	53.6	(1.67)
Turkey	17.4	(1.48)	24.6	(1.17)	10.3	(1.09)	46.8	(1.66)	38.8	(2.21)
TALIS average	**23.1**	**(0.25)**	**33.8**	**(0.26)**	**27.9**	**(0.27)**	**55.4**	**(0.30)**	**59.7**	**(0.32)**

	In this school, the most effective teachers receive the greatest monetary or non-monetary rewards		In this school, if I improve the quality of my teaching I will receive increased monetary or non-monetary rewards		In this school, if I am more innovative in my teaching I will receive increased monetary or non-monetary rewards		In this school, the review of teacher's work is largely done to fulfill administrative requirements		In this school, the review of teacher's work has little impact upon the way teachers teach in the classroom	
	%	(S.E.)	%	(S.E.)	%	(S.E.)	%	(S.E.)	%	(S.E.)
Australia	9.2	(0.65)	8.2	(0.67)	9.0	(0.72)	63.4	(1.54)	61.4	(1.42)
Austria	10.9	(0.64)	11.6	(0.58)	13.8	(0.66)	44.5	(0.96)	58.9	(0.82)
Belgium (Fl.)	5.0	(0.44)	4.1	(0.34)	4.2	(0.37)	37.9	(1.48)	44.4	(1.35)
Brazil	13.2	(0.90)	18.2	(0.94)	20.0	(0.90)	45.6	(1.17)	35.9	(1.33)
Bulgaria	50.5	(2.83)	53.8	(1.70)	56.0	(1.74)	29.4	(1.85)	33.4	(1.31)
Denmark	15.0	(1.32)	8.3	(0.92)	9.0	(0.92)	48.1	(1.84)	60.8	(1.72)
Estonia	37.9	(1.59)	25.1	(1.17)	21.2	(1.12)	27.8	(1.18)	43.4	(1.09)
Hungary	45.0	(1.51)	44.3	(1.66)	42.1	(1.74)	24.4	(2.32)	40.2	(1.38)
Iceland	18.1	(1.08)	17.4	(1.00)	17.4	(1.03)	45.8	(1.41)	55.8	(1.37)
Ireland	7.5	(0.66)	6.6	(0.63)	7.0	(0.60)	52.8	(1.28)	60.2	(1.38)
Italy	42.6	(1.34)	48.8	(1.38)	48.7	(1.35)	32.8	(1.19)	40.9	(1.01)
Korea	10.0	(0.65)	11.2	(0.63)	11.8	(0.64)	60.5	(0.92)	51.9	(1.12)
Lithuania	36.3	(1.36)	27.7	(1.23)	26.6	(1.19)	48.9	(1.35)	54.9	(1.16)
Malaysia	53.1	(1.28)	56.9	(1.20)	55.1	(1.14)	50.6	(1.23)	34.7	(1.32)
Malta	10.2	(1.20)	12.3	(1.15)	12.6	(1.25)	58.3	(1.51)	51.8	(1.63)
Mexico	26.9	(1.20)	42.7	(1.28)	39.6	(1.40)	50.2	(1.67)	45.3	(1.34)
Norway	11.5	(0.81)	6.3	(0.70)	11.5	(0.87)	43.4	(1.24)	64.9	(1.09)
Poland	59.1	(1.52)	52.1	(1.35)	46.7	(1.25)	41.8	(1.53)	37.0	(1.45)
Portugal	11.0	(0.75)	17.8	(1.01)	17.4	(1.07)	47.9	(1.13)	55.3	(1.17)
Slovak Republic	48.6	(1.97)	47.0	(1.77)	48.4	(1.74)	33.8	(1.34)	54.5	(1.47)
Slovenia	42.2	(1.45)	31.4	(1.23)	35.8	(1.37)	37.5	(1.16)	55.5	(1.23)
Spain	7.3	(0.59)	10.8	(0.78)	11.3	(0.78)	48.7	(1.10)	62.2	(1.18)
Turkey	31.2	(2.08)	31.4	(2.24)	32.6	(2.08)	45.3	(2.04)	42.9	(2.40)
TALIS average	**26.2**	**(0.28)**	**25.8**	**(0.25)**	**26.0**	**(0.25)**	**44.3**	**(0.30)**	**49.8**	**(0.29)**

Source: OECD, *TALIS Database*.
StatLink ᴍᴤᴸ http://dx.doi.org/10.1787/607856444110

CHAPTER 6

Leading to Learn: School Leadership and Management Styles

Highlights

- Some principals in every country have adopted the "instructional leadership" styles which are central to today's paradigm of effective school leadership.

- However, the prevalence of such practices varies greatly by country and they are much more in evidence in some countries such as Brazil, Poland and Slovenia than they are in others, such as Estonia and Spain.

- Across TALIS countries, a significant number of principals employ both instructional and administrative leadership styles.

- Greater autonomy for the school principal in decision making about schools is not related to either management style.

- In more than half of the TALIS countries, schools with more pronounced instructional leadership tend to link teacher appraisals with teachers' participation in professional development. Also in many TALIS countries, schools whose principals are instructional leaders are more likely to take account of innovative teaching practices in the appraisal of teachers.

- In almost three-quarters of TALIS countries, principals who adopt an instructional leadership style tend to develop professional development programmes for instructionally weak teachers.

- In more than one quarter of TALIS countries, teachers whose school principal adopts a more pronounced instructional leadership style are more likely to engage in collaborative activities with their colleagues.

- In contrast, variations in principals' use of an administrative leadership style are unrelated to classroom practices, pedagogical beliefs and attitudes, or to the amount of professional development teachers receive.

INTRODUCTION

Teachers teach and work in schools that are usually administered by managers, often known as principals or headmasters. School administration is itself often part of larger administration units. The conditions of teachers' working life are influenced by the administration and leadership provided by principals, and it is widely assumed that school leadership directly influences the effectiveness of teachers and the achievement outcomes of students (*e.g.* Hallinger and Murphy, 1986; OECD, 2001; Pont, Nusche and Moorman, 2008).

In OECD countries as elsewhere in the world, school leaders face challenges due to rising expectations for schools and schooling in a century characterised by technological innovation, migration and globalisation. As countries aim to transform their educational systems to prepare all young people with the knowledge and skills needed in this changing world, the roles of school leaders and related expectations have changed radically. They are no longer expected merely to be good managers; effective school leadership is increasingly viewed as key to large-scale education reform and to improved educational outcomes.

Since at least 2001, with its series of reports, *What Works in Innovation in Education*, produced by the Centre for Educational Research and Innovation, the OECD has recognised the significant challenges faced by principals and school managers in member countries (OECD, 2001). As countries increasingly turn to improving education to address an ever more complex world, many governments give school leadership more responsibility for implementing and managing significantly more demanding education programmes. Globalisation and widespread immigration mean that children, youth and their families represent an increasingly challenging clientele for schools in many countries. Also, the standards to which schools must perform and the accountability required of management raise expectations regarding school leadership to an unprecedented level.

A recent OECD report, *Improving School Leadership*, summarises the changing landscape of schools and their management over recent decades (Pont, Nusche and Moorman, 2008, p. 6):

> *In this new environment, schools and schooling are being given an ever bigger job to do. Greater decentralisation in many countries is being coupled with more school autonomy, more accountability for school and student results, and a better use of the knowledge base of education and pedagogical processes. It is also being coupled with broader responsibility for contributing to and supporting the schools' local communities, other schools and other public services.*

This report argues that to meet the educational needs of the 21st century the principals in primary and secondary schools must play a more dynamic role and become far more than an administrator of top-down rules and regulations. Schools and their governing structures must let school leaders lead in a systematic fashion and focus on the instructional and learning processes and outcomes of their schools.

These recommendations flow from a field of education that has recently experienced a fundamental change in its philosophy of administration and even in its conception of schools as organisations. A significant research literature also indicates that what the public and other stakeholders of schools want as learning outcomes for students can only be achieved if school leadership is adapted to a new model (Pont, Nusche and Moorman, 2008). These changes are directly relevant to the working lives, professional development, instructional practices, pedagogical beliefs and attitudes and the appraisal and feedback of secondary school teachers, all of which were measured in the TALIS survey.

From bureaucratic administrator to leader for learning

Changes in school administration over recent decades are part of a larger trend in the management of public service organisations that can be characterised as the decline of older public administrative models and the rise of a new public management (NPM) model. The ideas and research findings behind the NPM model in public services – flatter management structures, market-like mechanisms, decentralisation, customer orientation and evidence-based improvement of services – have significantly changed the approach to organisational management (*e.g.* Barzelay, 2001; Jones, Schedler and Wade 1997; Sahlin-Andersson, 2000; Schedler and Proeller, 2000). The effectiveness of these changes is still debated in education research and policy circles, but it is clear that these ideas, and the debate surrounding them, have changed the terms of management.

Perhaps the most salient change in attitudes about school management created by the NPM trend is the centring of the principal's activity and behaviour on what is referred to as "instructional leadership" (Wiseman, 2002, 2004a). The term "instructional leader" has been explicitly promoted for principals since the beginning of the effective schools movement around 1980 in the United States (Blumberg and Greenfield, 1980; Bossert *et al.*, 1981) and continues to lead ideas about how principals will meet the educational challenges of the new century (*e.g.* Heck, Larsen and Marcoulides, 1990; Duke, 1987; Kleine-Kracht, 1993; Boyd, 1996; Hallinger and Murphy, 1986; Lemahieu, Roy and Foss, 1997; Reitzug, 1997; Blase and Blase, 1998; Fullan, 2000).

During the 1980s, the educational research and policy communities specifically encouraged principals to emphasise activities that would enhance or benefit classroom instruction and learning (*e.g.* National Commission on Excellence in Education, 1983). Increasingly, this means that as managers of organisations whose formal or official functions are instruction and learning, principals are responsible and accountable for school outputs such as student achievement. In particular, proponents of instructional leadership suggest that principals are the most effective of all potential instructional leaders because they are situated within the school context, unlike upper-level administrators in ministries. A package of reforms being developed by a number of OECD countries includes recommendations for greater professionalisation and specialty training for school managers with greater on-the-job managerial accountability for learning outcomes (Pont, Nusche and Moorman, 2008).

Along with the emphasis on accountability, the decentralisation of school management and the devolution of educational control have increased throughout much of the world (Baker and LeTendre, 2005). Less centralised control has meant more responsibility for a broader range of aspects of school management at the school level. For better or worse, this trend translates into a more complex school governance environment in many countries.

These ideas and the associated research on school leadership have led to reforms of the principal's role in many countries, from an emphasis on administration in terms of the school's compliance with bureaucratic procedures to an expanded role which combines administration with instructional leadership (OECD, 2001; Pont, Nusche and Moorman, 2008). This expanded role focuses strongly on the principal's management of the school's teachers and their teaching.

Goals of the TALIS survey of principals

In each TALIS country, schools and schooling have specific characteristics. School management is shaped by these characteristics, which potentially influence every aspect of a teacher's job and professional development. At the same time, there are global trends towards similarity in schooling and its management across countries (Baker and LeTendre, 2005). For the first time, the TALIS survey of principals provides rich information on the management behaviour and style of principals in secondary schools in 23 countries on four continents. The questionnaire was designed to answer three broad questions:

- In an era of accountability and devolution of authority in education, what are the salient dimensions of the management behaviour and style of secondary school principals?
- To what degree have recent trends in school leadership penetrated countries' educational systems?
- How are school leadership styles associated with the management of teachers, across the three main areas of TALIS: *i)* teachers' professional development; *ii)* teachers' practices, beliefs and attitudes; and *iii)* teachers' appraisal and feedback?

Chapter outline

The chapter begins with a description of school management behaviour based on the reports of the principals of schools providing lower secondary education in TALIS countries. It describes this behaviour on the basis of five indices (or dimensions) of management derived from a statistical analysis of principals' responses, which are then summarised as two main management styles – instructional leadership and administrative leadership – on the basis of which principals are compared. The two styles are not mutually exclusive and in fact the TALIS data demonstrate that a number of principals use both styles to a considerable degree. The section concludes by analysing these management styles according to the characteristics of schools and of the principals themselves.

The chapter then examines the relation between management styles and five aspects of teachers' work taken from Chapter 4: *i)* beliefs about the nature of teaching and learning; *ii)* teachers' classroom practices; *iii)* teachers' professional activities; *iv)* teachers' classroom environment and school climate; and *v)* teachers' attitudes towards their job.

The next two sections examine, in turn, the links between school management and teachers' appraisal and feedback, the theme of Chapter 5, and the links with teachers' professional development, the theme of Chapter 3. The final section summarises these findings and draws implications for school management.

SALIENT DIMENSIONS OF SECONDARY SCHOOL MANAGEMENT BEHAVIOUR OF SCHOOL PRINCIPALS

The questionnaire for school principals was constructed with the aid of experts on school administration and organisational reform and research. Various instruments were adopted for assessing the managerial behaviour of secondary school principals and new items were also developed. The final questionnaire included 35 items on the management behaviour of principals. Using techniques of modern item response modelling and factor analysis (described in the *TALIS Technical Report* [forthcoming]), five indices of management behaviour were constructed from the responses of 4 665 school principals in the 23 countries. These indices and the specific survey questions on which they are based are displayed in Table 6.1.

As with the indices in Chapter 4, analysis was conducted to test for cross-cultural consistency of the five indices of management behaviour (See Annex A1.1 and the *TALIS Technical Report*). As this analysis indicated that countries' mean scores on these indices may not be directly comparable, analysis in this chapter focuses more on broad comparisons against the international means. Nevertheless, care in interpretation is necessary. The analysis therefore focuses more on the pattern of cross-cultural differences than on specific country-by-country comparisons of the index scores.

Management behaviour

1. Management for school goals – *explicit management via the school's goals and curriculum development*

Principals scoring high on this index frequently take actions to manage schooling operations in accordance with the school's goals, with direct emphasis on ensuring that teachers' instruction in classrooms aims to achieve these goals. These principals also tend to use student performance levels and examination results to set goals and promote curricular developments. They endeavour to ensure clarity within the school about the responsibility for co-ordinating the curriculum. Principals scoring high on this index also report that they frequently make sure that teachers' professional development activities are aligned with school goals and curricular objectives.

As Table 6.2 shows, there is considerable variation as principals in Hungary, Poland and Slovenia are notably above the TALIS mean, while those in Austria, Denmark, Italy and Spain, among others, are notably below. On average, principals in 10 countries are significantly above the TALIS average on this index, while 10 countries are below it. Also on average, principals in Estonia, Lithuania and Mexico are at the TALIS mean.

2. Instructional management – actions to improve teachers' instruction

Principals scoring high on this index frequently work with teachers to improve weaknesses and address pedagogical problems, and also to solve problems with teachers when there are challenges to learning in a particular classroom. Also, they often inform teachers about possibilities to update their curricular knowledge and instructional skills. Finally, these principals report being vigilant about disruptive student behaviour in classrooms. In general, principals scoring high on this index spend significant amounts of their managerial time in attempting to improve classroom instruction.

On average, principals in 10 countries, including Brazil, Denmark and Malta, are above the TALIS mean and 10, including Estonia, Malaysia and the Slovak Republic, are below it (Table 6.2).

3. Direct supervision of instruction in the school – actions to directly supervise teachers' instruction and learning outcomes

Principals who score high on this index frequently use direct observation of teachers' pedagogical practices and also make frequent suggestions to teachers on how to improve instruction in classrooms. These principals also frequently monitor students' academic efforts and work.

There is again considerable variation among countries on this index (Table 6.2). On average in 11 countries, including Brazil, Poland and Slovenia, principals undertake more direct supervision of instruction than the TALIS average. Another 11 countries, including Denmark, Ireland and Portugal, are below the TALIS average; only Australia is at the TALIS average.

4. Accountable management – managing accountability to shareholders and others

Principals scoring high on this index see their role as making the school accountable internally and to stakeholders outside the school. Their role is to ensure that ministry-approved instructional approaches are explained to new teachers and that all teachers are held accountable for improving their teaching skills. These principals also focus on convincing students' parents of the need for new ideas and procedures at the school.

On average, principals in 10 countries, most markedly in Bulgaria, Malaysia and Norway, are above the TALIS mean on this index and 10 are below (Table 6.2).

5. Bureaucratic management – management actions mostly aimed at bureaucratic procedures

Principals scoring high on this index report that it is important for them to ensure that everyone in the school follows the official rules. They see their role as being significantly involved in dealing with problems in the scheduling of teachers and courses and in ensuring adequate administrative procedures and reporting to higher authorities. These principals also focus on creating an orderly and task-oriented atmosphere in the school.

The pattern across countries on this index is slightly different (Table 6.2). In just eight countries, including Bulgaria, Malaysia and Turkey, principals score above the TALIS average, in five countries they are at the TALIS average, and in ten they are below it. On average, principals in Australia, Denmark and Iceland are among the least involved with this type of management.

Management styles and school leadership

The five behavioral indices cover a significant range of principals' management actions. To further summarise their behaviour, two management styles – *instructional leadership* and *administrative leadership* – were defined (Figure 6.1). They characterise more comprehensively principals' approach to their leadership approach.

Principals scoring high for the first management style are significantly involved in what is referred to in the research literature on school management as an *instructional leadership style*. This index was derived by averaging the indices for the first three management behaviours, *management for school goals, instructional management* and *direct supervision of instruction in the school*.

The second management style can be best referred to as an *administrative leadership style* and was derived by averaging the indices for the management behaviours *accountable management* and *bureaucratic management*. This style of management focuses on administrative tasks, enforcing rules and procedures, and accountability.

Figure 6.1

Composition of the indices for instructional and administrative leadership

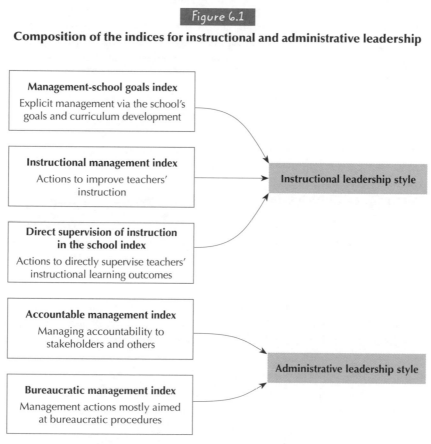

Source: OECD, *TALIS Database.*

StatLink ⬛📊 http://dx.doi.org/10.1787/608025205225

The two styles are not necessarily mutually exclusive, even though they are sometimes portrayed as such in the research literature on school leadership (*e.g.* Hallinger and Murphy, 1986). This point is reinforced by the idea of an evolution of school leadership and a move from competent administration to school management which includes an emphasis on instructional leadership and a stronger focus on student learning. Also, as the results below indicate, a number of principals use both styles to a considerable degree. So while these styles help to capture the underlying approaches that principals take to their job, particularly concerning teachers, they need not be mutually exclusive in practice.

The recent OECD report, *Improving School Leadership*, recommends that effective school management generally comes from engagement in instructional leadership (Pont, Nusche and Moorman, 2008). At the same time, effective leadership also involves administrative accountability and a workable bureaucracy. The question that arises is the extent to which these two management styles have been embraced by the TALIS countries' school leadership. Three notable findings address this question.

First, as Table 6.3 indicates, while some principals in each TALIS country adopt an instructional leadership style, there is significant variation in its use across TALIS countries. In other words, the ideas and behaviour related to instructional management are evident to varying degrees in all TALIS countries, at least according to principals' self-reports. Even the countries with the lowest average use of instructional leadership, such as Austria, Estonia and Spain, have principals that focus on this style of management.

Second, the TALIS countries fall into two roughly equal groups in terms of the emphasis on instructional leadership. In 10 countries, including Brazil, Poland and Slovenia, principals on average engage in an instructional leadership style above the overall TALIS average. Principals in the 13 other TALIS countries are less involved in this management style than the overall average.

Third, it is interesting that in countries in which principals are on average more involved in instructional leadership, they do not neglect administrative leadership. Obviously the principal's task in most schools in most countries involves actions and priorities from both management styles, and individual principals may be high on one and low on the other, or high on both, or low on both. In practice each of the two styles involves activities and priorities that can be helpful in managing schools. The TALIS results show in fact that a significant group of principals employs both styles, as shown by the positive association between them: about one-fifth of the difference among principals in each style is related (r= .44, p<.0001).

To demonstrate this, Figure 6.2 plots the TALIS countries' means on the two management styles. Seven countries fall into the upper right quadrant where on average principals are highly involved in both instructional *and* administrative leadership. At the other end in the lower left quadrant are nine countries where on average principals are only moderately involved in both management styles. Malta and Poland are the only two countries in which principals are on average more involved in instructional than in administrative leadership, while the opposite applies in Ireland, Malaysia and Norway. Lastly, in three countries principals are on average at the OECD average for administrative leadership, but in two of these, the Slovak Republic and Slovenia, they are more involved in instructional leadership while in Portugal they are less involved in instructional leadership.

Management styles and decision making

Pont, Nusche and Moorman (2008) also considers that effective instructional leadership in schools requires some degree of administrative autonomy in decision making about key components of inputs to the instructional process. The TALIS questionnaire asked principals about the degree to which they had significant input into decisions about teachers, instruction, school resources and curriculum. While there is interesting variation across countries, decision-making autonomy is unrelated to either management style, as is clear from the distribution of countries with greater principal involvement in decision making (gray points in Figure 6.2) and those with lower involvement (blue points in Figure 6.2).

School principals according to their management styles (2007-08)

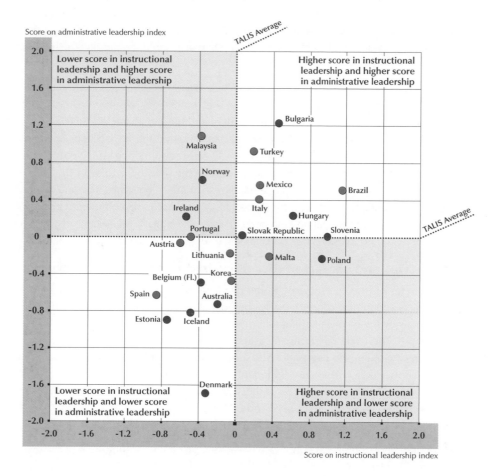

Countries in gray have a higher than average principal involvement in decision making, while countries in blue have a lower than average involvement.

Source: OECD, TALIS Database.

StatLink http://dx.doi.org/10.1787/608025205225

Management styles and characteristics of principals and schools

Are management styles of principals related to their qualities as professionals and to the characteristics of the schools they administer? Research on leadership of formal organisations in general, and in schools specifically, finds contrasting evidence on this question (e.g. Wiseman, 2004a, 2004b). Some research suggests that the professional characteristics of leaders and the qualities of the organisations they lead help determine their management styles, while an equally sizable research literature suggests the opposite. The TALIS questionnaire asked principals a series of questions about their professional standing and about the qualities of their school. These associations are summarised in Tables 6.12 and 6.13.

The results presented in this section and the section following, are generated from a series of statistical regression analyses which examine the relation between a number of predictor (or independent) variables and a predicted (or dependent) variable (see Annex A1.4 for technical details and specifications of the variables). Tables 6.4 to 6.13 highlight the variables that were statistically significant in these regressions, with a plus sign indicating a significant positive relationship and a minus sign indicating a significant negative relationship. Where no significant relationship was found, the cell in the table is left blank. Tables containing the regression coefficients are available on the TALIS website.

Interestingly, the TALIS results find little association between characteristics of principals and either their management behaviours or overall styles. By and large the associations are more evident in the instructional leadership style than in the administrative leadership style, and no one characteristic is consistently associated with either management style across all TALIS countries. As shown in the first sections of Table 6.12 and 6.13, neither the principals' educational level nor the number of years they have been principals is consistently related to their position on either the management behaviour indices or the style indices. For each of these variables there is positive relation with the style of leadership in a handful of countries but a negative one in a handful of others. The same is true for the public or private school sector, the size of the school's community, and the student/teacher ratio. Nevertheless, one trend is evident: in Belgium (Fl.), Estonia, Hungary, Malaysia, Norway, Poland, Spain and Turkey, female principals tend to use an instructional leadership style more than male principals.

Management styles and characteristics of evaluations of school performance

Are management styles of principals related to the characteristics of evaluations of the school's performance and principals' beliefs about instruction? In many countries school reforms to improve teachers' instruction and student learning focus on the idea of aligning school management with clear indicators of instructional practice and student outcomes. The TALIS questionnaire asked the sampled principals about the characteristics of their school's evaluation, including the degree to which there are both internal and external evaluations, which indicators of the school's performance are important in evaluations, and the extent to which the outcome of the school evaluation influence the appraisal of the school management or of teachers. These associations are summarised in the third sections of Tables 6.12 and 6.13.

In eight countries – Belgium (Fl.), Bulgaria, Estonia, Korea, Mexico, Norway, Portugal and Turkey – principals in schools in which indicators of teachers' innovative teaching practices are important to the evaluations tend to take an instructional leadership style of management.

There are also some mixed patterns. For example, in Australia, Austria, Belgium (Fl.), Brazil, Korea, Malta and Norway, principals have a more pronounced instructional leadership style in schools where internal (self-evaluation) evaluations are more frequent, but the opposite is true in Denmark, Lithuania, Malaysia and Spain. Similar, but weaker, associations are found between the characteristics of school evaluations and principals who adopt an administrative leadership style.

One clear trend concerns the relation between principals' beliefs about approaches to teaching and their leadership style. Instructional leadership is used in nine countries in which principals have a more constructivist belief about instruction. In countries in which principals believe that the task of teaching is to support students in their active construction of knowledge, they are also more likely to demonstrate instructional leadership. However, in 14 countries there is a similarly positive association between more administrative leadership and constructivist beliefs about instruction.

ASPECTS OF TEACHERS' WORK AND SCHOOL MANAGEMENT

This section examines the relation between the management styles of principals and five aspects of teachers' work described in Chapter 4.

For each aspect of teachers' work, the same model is estimated to examine the relation with principals' management styles. The model statistically controls for a number of teachers' professional and personal characteristics: gender, level of experience as a teacher, educational training, permanency of their teaching position, number of hours they teach, how many schools they teach in, and how much administrative work they undertake. Estimated for each country, this basic statistical model represents the main components of the teacher's professional background and summary conditions of their position within their school. Added to this basic model are the degrees to which the school's principal engages in instructional and administrative leadership styles.

As described below, the level of a principal's use of the instructional leadership style is in some cases associated with the school's teachers' beliefs, practices, professional activities, classroom environments and job-related attitudes, while the use of an administrative leadership style is usually less related to these variables. The associations tend to be moderate in size and are statistically significant net of the influences of the teacher's personal, professional background and working conditions. It should be pointed out that, since TALIS is a cross-sectional study, it is not prudent to draw sweeping causal conclusions from such results. That is, one should not assume from these findings that an association means that management style causes teachers' beliefs, practices and so forth. Such associations are necessary, but not sufficient, to draw causal conclusions, but at the very least it can be concluded that across TALIS countries, secondary school principals who have an instructional leadership style tend to work with certain types of teachers.

Beliefs about the nature of teaching and learning

In Chapter 4 two indices were developed to summarise teacher beliefs and attitudes towards pedagogy: constructivist beliefs about instruction and direct transmission beliefs about instruction. Constructivist beliefs are characterised by a view of the teacher as a facilitator of learning who gives more autonomy to students; a direct transmission view sees the teacher as the instructor who provides information and demonstrates solutions. Are principals' management styles related to teachers' pedagogical beliefs?

As displayed in Table 6.4 the first notable finding is that in most countries the degree to which a principal manages the school according to either leadership style is unrelated to the school's teachers' pedagogical beliefs and attitudes.

Net of the other factors about teachers' professional background and the basic conditions of their position within their school, it is only in Malta that principals with a more instructional leadership style tend to work with teachers who believe in a constructivist approach to instruction and learning, while the opposite is true in Iceland. These teachers see their role as more of a facilitator of students' own inquiry. They believe in encouraging independent problem solving on the part of students and also that general thinking and reasoning skills are more important than specific curricular content.

In contrast, teachers who believe strongly in direct transmission of instruction may be characterised as having more traditional attitudes towards classroom instruction. These teachers value instruction that is built around problems for students to solve which have clear and correct answers and are within the grasp of the learners. They see the teacher's main role in problem solving as demonstrating the correct procedure. These teachers tend to hold firm to the belief that teaching facts is necessary as this is how students accumulate knowledge. Lastly, these teachers believe that a quiet classroom is most conducive to learning. Interestingly, as for constructivist teachers, there is no association in most TALIS countries between either of the two leadership styles and belief in this more traditional approach to instruction and pedagogy. This finding is not necessarily surprising given the results in Chapter 4 indicating that across a number of TALIS countries there are teachers who hold both strong constructivist and direct transmission beliefs about instruction and learning. In Belgium (Fl.), Hungary and Portugal a more pronounced instructional leadership style is associated with beliefs in direct transmission instruction; in Estonia and Iceland a more pronounced administrative leadership style is associated with these beliefs.

Classroom practices of teachers

The range of instructional practices reported on by teachers is summarised on three indices for structuring practices, student-oriented practices and enhanced learning activities. As described in Chapter 4, structuring practices include such activities as stating learning goals, summarising former lessons, checking students' understanding and reviewing homework. Student-oriented practices involve students working in groups, grouping students by ability and differentiating the tasks they are set and the involvement of students in planning classroom activities. Enhanced learning activities for instance have students working on projects, holding debates and making a product. Are principal management styles related to what teachers do in the classroom?

As Table 6.5 shows, as in the case of beliefs, the degree to which a principal manages the school according to a more administrative leadership style is not directly related in most countries to any of the three classroom practices of teachers; the same is also generally true for an instructional leadership style. Among the few cases where significant relations are evident, administrative leadership is more likely than instructional leadership to be associated with all three teaching practices in Iceland and Malta. Conversely, in Italy instructional leadership is more likely to go hand in hand with greater degrees of student-oriented and enhanced learning activities.

Teachers' professional activities

In Chapter 4, teachers' co-operative professional behaviour in TALIS countries is captured by exchange/co-ordination for teaching and professional collaboration. Are principals' management styles related to how teachers co-operate with each other for effective instruction?

As Table 6.6 indicates, teachers' collaborative behaviour is related to management styles in a number of countries. In Hungary, Iceland, Lithuania, Malaysia, Mexico and Poland, where principals use an instructional leadership style of management, teachers are more likely to co-operate and work together in groups or teams for job-related purposes such as administrative tasks, the actual teaching of students or professional development. Other than in Mexico and with the addition of Norway, the same is true for more complex forms of professional collaboration: collective learning activities such as observing and critiquing other teachers' instruction and team teaching of courses. In neither case is the level of administrative leadership associated with teachers' professional activities.

Teachers' classroom environment and school climate for learning

TALIS teachers were asked about the usual classroom environment in terms of the degree of disruptive behaviour and lack of attention by students and also about the amount of time they usually allocate to actual instruction as opposed to classroom management. They were also asked about the types of support they gave students to help them learn. Chapter 4 described the three elements used to summarise the learning environment: classroom disciplinary climate, time on task, and teacher-student relations. Are school management styles associated with classroom and school environments that are conducive to learning?

The first column in Table 6.7 shows that in most TALIS countries the classroom disciplinary climate is not associated with either leadership style, after controlling for certain background characteristics of the principal and the school. The same is true for time on task (second column). However, in Denmark, Hungary, Iceland, Malta, Mexico and Portugal, schools with principals who adopt more of an instructional leadership style tend to have more positive relations between teachers and students, net of other factors regarding the school and the teacher.

Teachers' attitudes towards their job

Chapter 4 also described teachers' level of job satisfaction and their sense of self-efficacy in terms of helping students to learn. Are these attitudes towards their job related to principals' management styles?

Table 6.8 shows that teachers in Estonia, Hungary, Malta and Turkey are more satisfied with their job in schools whose principal employs an instructional leadership style of management. At the same time, teachers' job satisfaction is unrelated to administrative leadership in most countries. In Hungary, Malta, Portugal and Spain teachers who see themselves as successful with students learning work in schools where the principal has a more pronounced instructional leadership style.

TEACHER APPRAISAL AND FEEDBACK AND SCHOOL MANAGEMENT

Chapter 5 describes the frequency, use and consequences of appraisals of teachers' work. This section examines the relation between principals' management styles and three aspects of teacher appraisals: importance of appraisal criteria, objectives of the appraisal, and feedback and consequences of the appraisal. The results in Chapter 5 come from teachers' reports about appraisals. Principals were asked similar questions and the results are used here for principals in schools in which teacher appraisals take place regularly.

For each indicator about the teacher appraisal process, the same model is estimated to examine the relation with principals' management styles in each country. The model statistically controls for a number of professional and personal characteristics of principals and characteristics of their schools: gender, level of experience as a principal, educational training, the number of schools they administer, average class size, student/teacher ratio, public/private status of the school and the type of school community. This basic statistical model covers the main components of the principal's professional background and summary conditions of schools in the principal's country. Added to this basic model are the degrees to which the school's principal engages in instructional and administrative leadership styles. The caveat about drawing causal conclusions from cross-sectional data mentioned applies here as well.

Learning outcomes, teachers' practices and professional development as appraisal criteria

TALIS principals were asked about the importance of various aspects of the schooling and teaching process for use in appraisals. The review of research on teacher appraisals in Chapter 5 identifies three criteria that are crucial for maintaining and increasing effective instruction: student learning outcomes, innovative teaching and teacher's participation in professional development. Is the level of importance accorded to these criteria in teacher appraisals related to school management styles? Since these aspects of teaching are closer to school managerial processes, there are generally more associations between them and principals' leadership styles than for teachers' beliefs and practices.

As the first column of Table 6.9 indicates, higher levels of an instructional leadership style are associated with the use of student test scores as an evaluation criterion for the appraisal of teachers in Austria, Belgium (Fl), Bulgaria, Mexico, Norway, Portugal and Spain. A positive relation between an administrative leadership style and use of test scores for appraisals is found only in Austria, Denmark, Estonia and Iceland. In Portugal and Slovenia, student test scores are less likely to be used when the principal adopts a more administrative leadership style. The associations in these countries are net of characteristics of principals, schools and the community the school serves.

As shown in the second column of Table 6.9, similar results are found for the use of retention and pass rates of students for teacher appraisals. In Austria, Hungary, Ireland, Mexico, Portugal, Slovenia and Spain, the use of an instructional leadership style by principals is associated with the use of these student performance measures. However, in Denmark and Norway, an administrative leadership style is associated with the use of this criterion.

The third column of the table shows that in more than half of the TALIS countries (Brazil, Bulgaria, Estonia, Hungary, Iceland, Ireland, Lithuania, Malta, Mexico, the Slovak Republic, Slovenia, Spain and Turkey) when a principal uses a more pronounced instructional leadership style, teacher appraisals are based on the teacher's use of professional development. The association is strong in a number of cases. Only in Austria, Brazil, Estonia and Portugal does more administrative leadership go hand in hand with the use of this criterion.

Objectives of the appraisal

Chapter 5 found two contrasting objectives of teacher appraisals. One is the improvement of teachers' practices, and the other is external bureaucratic accountability. TALIS principals were asked to what degree these two types of objectives were important in the school's teacher appraisal process. Are these objectives related to school management styles?

The fourth set of columns of Table 6.9 shows that in ten countries (Australia, Estonia, Hungary, Iceland, Korea, Lithuania, Mexico, Poland, Slovenia and Turkey) principals who adopt instructional leadership manage schools in which the objective of appraisals is to improve teacher practices; administrative leadership is associated with this appraisal objective in only two countries. In most countries neither leadership style is associated with the importance school leaders attach to informing higher administrative levels of the outcome of teacher appraisals (last two columns of Table 6.9).

Feedback and consequences of the appraisal

Chapter 5 showed that effective appraisals provide good feedback and can help teachers to improve their teaching practices. Are feedback and its consequences related to management styles?

The first relevant finding is that in most countries the use of either self-evaluation or external evaluation are only weakly related to principals' leadership styles, in part because such evaluations are fairly widespread in most countries (Table 6.14). However, there is some indication that both kinds of evaluations are linked to both styles. In particular, in almost half of the countries, those schools whose principals have a more pronounced instructional leadership style are more likely to have conducted a self-evaluation in the previous five years.

The level of administrative leadership is not associated with the amount of feedback received by teachers, but in schools with more instructional leadership there is more feedback given to teachers[1].

Principals were also asked about various scenarios involving feedback and its consequences following an appraisal of a teacher with weak instructional skills. Three scenarios were proposed: *i)* the principal and others develop a training programme to address the teacher's weaknesses; *ii)* the appraisal outcome is reported to other parts of the school system for action; and *iii)* the principal imposes material sanctions on the teacher.

As shown in Table 6.10, in 17 countries, net of other factors in the model, principals with an instructional leadership style report significantly more often that they would develop a professional development programme to improve the instructional practices of the weak teacher. Neither leadership style is strongly related to the use of material sanctions or corrective actions external to the school.

Teachers' professional development

Chapter 3 describes the extent of teachers' professional development. The relation between management styles and two indicators of teachers' participation in professional development are examined here: the number of days of teachers' professional development over the previous 18 months and whether or not they would have liked more.

For each indicator, the teacher model is estimated for each country to examine the relation with principals' management styles, controlling for a number of professional and personal characteristics of teachers: gender, level of experience as a teacher, educational training, permanency of their teaching position, how many schools they teach in, and size of the community of the school.

As Table 6.11 indicates, in most TALIS countries neither leadership style is related to the number of days of professional development completed or to teachers' satisfaction with the number of professional development days that they received. There is some relation in a few countries but no consistent pattern. For instance, in Bulgaria, Iceland, Malta and Slovenia, the degree of unsatisfied demand for professional development was greater in schools with a stronger administrative leadership style, but this was also the case in Hungary, Iceland, Malta and Turkey in schools with a strong instructional leadership style.

CONCLUSIONS AND IMPLICATIONS FOR POLICY AND PRACTICE

In an era of accountability and devolution of authority in education, this chapter has considered five dimensions of the management behaviour and style of secondary school principals. Three of these are closely aligned with new ideas about school management and recent recommendations of the OECD. One concerns principals' actions for managing the school along clearly stated goals based on student learning and performance objectives. Second is management of the instructional quality of teachers in the school. Third is management that includes direct supervision of instructional quality and feedback to teachers. These three dimensions of management behaviours form the *instructional leadership style*.

The two remaining dimensions of managerial behaviour represent more traditional school administration. The first is principals' actions related to accountability regarding the school's performance and administration within the education system. The second involves actions taken with regard to scheduling of teachers and courses and the enforcement of school policies and procedures. These two dimensions of management behaviour form the *administrative leadership style*.

Figure 6.3

Effects of greater use of instructional or administrative leadership styles
Effects that are evident in at least one-quarter of the TALIS countries[1]

Leadership style	Effects	Number of countries
Instructional leadership	Greater degree of collaboration among teachers, both for exchange and co-ordination for teaching and more sophisticated professional collaboration	6
	Better teacher-student relations	6
	Greater recognition given to student test scores or other student outcome measures in teacher appraisals or feedback	7
	Greater recognition given to teachers' participation in professional development activities in teacher appraisals or feedback	13
	Greater recognition given to teachers' innovative teaching practices in teacher appraisals or feedback	10
	A development plan is established to address weaknesses following a teacher appraisal	17
Administrative leadership	No effects are consistently evident in at least one-quarter of TALIS countries.	

1. Results from multi-level linear regressions, controlling for teachers' gender, level of education, years of experience, community of the school, permanent employee, and work in other schools.
Source: OECD, *TALIS Database*.

StatLink ⟨ms⟩ http://dx.doi.org/10.1787/608025205225

The chapter has examined how these styles of leadership vary from country to country and how they relate to the work of teachers. Figure 6.3 summarises the relations that are most commonly found in the participating countries. The following conclusions can be drawn:

New trends in school leadership are evident to varying degrees in countries' educational systems

Key results:

- In 10 countries, principals use instructional leadership more; in the other 13 they use it less (Table 6.3).
- A sizeable group of principals combine instructional leadership with administrative leadership (Table 6.3).
- Leadership style is unrelated to autonomy in decision making (Figure 6.2).

Discussion

These findings suggest that the instructional leadership paradigm has made some progress in all countries, but much more in some than in others. It also challenges two common assumptions about the spread of such leadership. First, it is not necessarily an alternative to administrative leadership, and an effective principal is likely to display elements of both styles. Second, simply devolving responsibilities to schools does not necessarily trigger a change in leadership style. This points to the need for active interventions to develop the skills and practices of individual principals. It should not be assumed that structural changes in national administrative systems will automatically result in a desired form of leadership.

While neither leadership style is consistently associated with teachers' beliefs and practices, there is evidence to suggest that instructional leadership is related to important aspects of the management of effective instruction in schools

Key results

- In most countries, principals' leadership style has limited direct association with teachers' beliefs and practices or with the amount of professional development teachers receive, after other factors are controlled for (Tables 6.4, 6.5 and 6.11).

- However, more pronounced instructional leadership is associated with managerial aspects of teaching, such as the use of effective and supportive teacher appraisals and feedback processes to improve instruction (Table 6.9).

- In many TALIS countries an instructional leadership style is associated with schools that make more frequent use of an appraisal process aimed at student learning outcomes and at teachers' use of professional development. It is also associated with adopting specific professional development plans tailored to help weaker teachers to improve their teaching practices (Tables 6.9 and 6.10).

Discussion

The use of instructional leadership by principals is associated with aspects of the management of instruction that is in line with recent research and policy recommendations for developing teachers in schools. Supportive appraisals and feedback from which teachers can judge and improve their professional practices is a crucial part of effective teacher management. Similarly, aligning teacher appraisals with student achievement outcomes is a sound managerial practise to focus teachers' efforts on what really counts in the educational process. The same is true for recognising the use of professional development of teachers in the appraisal of teachers' work. Finally, school leadership that develops professional development plans to fit individual teachers' needs, as assessed by appraisals, completes the managerial process for supporting effective teachers. The fact that in a number of countries, principals who employ a significant level of instructional leadership run schools with this kind of process for appraising and developing instruction points to possible benefits to national school systems in training principals to use instructional leadership techniques.

The lack of strong relations between school leadership behaviour and teachers' practices, beliefs and attitudes (after other factors are controlled for) is an interesting finding. It is consistent with other research that shows the impact of school leadership to be indirect and mitigated through the actions of teachers and others. To some extent the finding also echoes the analysis in Chapter 4 which showed that, in the main, teachers' practices, beliefs and attitudes vary to a far greater extent among a country's teacher population generally than between teachers in different schools. Such individuality among teachers illustrates a challenge for school leaders to address the needs of a heterogeneous group of teachers in seeking to achieve common school goals.

It should also be noted that TALIS focuses on secondary school teachers and principals, the former of which are likely to be subject specialist and will develop specific attitudes and practises within their academic field.

Given this, principals' management styles in secondary education may be expected to have less of an influence on teachers' practices and behaviours than might be the case in primary education. Instead as described above, secondary school leadership has its most significant impact on teachers through the overall managerial process that aligns appraisal with achievement outcomes and both of these with professional development.

ADDITIONAL MATERIAL

The following additional material relevant to this chapter is available on line at:

StatLink ⫘⫘ http://dx.doi.org/10.1787/608025205225

Table 6.4a   Results of multilevel linear regressions, examining the net effect of instructional and administrative leadership on teacher beliefs (2007-08)

Table 6.5a   Results of multilevel linear regressions, examining the net effect of instructional and administrative leadership on teaching practices (2007-08)

Table 6.6a   Results of multilevel linear regressions, examining the net effect of instructional and administrative leadership on co-ordination and professional collaboration among teachers (2007-08)

Table 6.7a   Results of multilevel linear regressions, examining the net effect of instructional and administrative leadership on classroom climate, time spent on learning and teacher-student relationship (2007-08)

Table 6.8a   Results of multilevel linear regressions, examining the net effect of instructional and administrative leadership on teacher's job satisfaction and self-efficacy (2007-08)

Table 6.9a   Results of multivariate linear regressions, examining the net effect of instructional and administrative leadership on aspects of teacher appraisals (2007-08)

Table 6.10a   Results of multivariate linear regressions, examining the net effect of instructional and administrative leadership on principal's use of three scenarios to improve an instructionally-weak teacher (2007-08)

Table 6.11a   Results of multilevel linear regressions, examining the net effect of instructional and administrative leadership on teachers' professional development (2007-08)

Notes

1. Based on a regression analysis of leadership style and teachers' responses to whether they received feedback or not.

Table 6.1

School principal leadership behavioral items (2007-08)

Items in behavioral indices for principals in lower secondary education

Indices	Item name	Description of the item
Management-school goals index	bcg15a	I make sure that the professional development activities of teachers are in accordance with the teaching goals of the school.
	bcg15b	I ensure that teachers work according to the school's educational goals.
	bcg15d	I use student performance results to develop the school's educational goals.
	bcg15j	I take exam results into account in decisions regarding curriculum development.
	bcg15k	I ensure that there is clarity concerning the responsibility for co-ordinating the curriculum.
	bcg16m	In this school, we work on goals and/or a school development plan.
Instructional management index	bcg15g	When a teacher has problems in his/her classroom, I take the initiative to discuss matters.
	bcg15h	I inform teachers about possibilities for updating their knowledge and skills.
	bcg15l	When a teacher brings up a classroom problem, we solve the problem together.
	bcg15m	I pay attention to disruptive behaviour in classrooms.
Direct supervision of instruction in the school index	bcg15c	I observe instruction in classrooms.
	bcg15e	I give teachers suggestions as to how they can improve their teaching.
	bcg15f	I monitor students' work.
	bcg15i	I check to see whether classroom activities are in keeping with our educational goals.
Accountable management index	bcg16a	An important part of my job is to ensure ministry approved instructional approaches are explained to new teachers, and that more experienced teachers are using these approaches.
	bcg16d	A main part of my job is to ensure that the teaching skills of the staff are always improving.
	bcg16e	An important part of my job is to ensure that teachers are held accountable for the attainment of the school's goals.
	bcg16f	An important part of my job is to present new ideas to the parents in a convincing way.
Bureaucratic management index	bcg16h	It is important for the school that I see to it that everyone sticks to the rules.
	bcg16i	It is important for the school that I check for mistakes and errors in administrative procedures and reports.
	bcg16j	An important part of my job is to resolve problems with the timetable and/or lesson planning.
	bcg16k	An important part of my job is to create an orderly atmosphere in the school.
	bcg16o	I stimulate a task-oriented atmosphere in this school.

Source: OECD, *TALIS Database*.
StatLink http://dx.doi.org/10.1787/608025205225

Table 6.2

School principal leadership behavioral indices (2007-08)

Indices for styles of leadership of principals in lower secondary education[1]

	Indices for instructional leadership						Indices for administrative leadership			
	Management-school goals index		Instructional management index		Direct supervision of instruction in the school index		Accountable management index		Bureaucratic management index	
	Mean	(S.E.)	Mean	(S.E.)	Mean	(S.E.)	Mean	(S.E.)	Mean	(S.E.)
Australia	0.47	(0.10)	-0.80	(0.08)	-0.15	(0.08)	-0.29	(0.08)	-1.00	(0.09)
Austria	-0.99	(0.05)	0.14	(0.06)	-0.47	(0.04)	-0.11	(0.06)	0.00	(0.07)
Belgium (Fl.)	-0.34	(0.08)	-0.15	(0.07)	-0.40	(0.05)	-0.54	(0.06)	-0.34	(0.05)
Brazil	0.42	(0.08)	1.10	(0.05)	1.08	(0.05)	0.63	(0.06)	0.28	(0.06)
Bulgaria	0.47	(0.11)	-0.12	(0.07)	0.62	(0.07)	1.32	(0.10)	0.87	(0.09)
Denmark	-0.77	(0.13)	0.88	(0.09)	-0.88	(0.03)	-1.65	(0.07)	-1.37	(0.05)
Estonia	0.03	(0.07)	-0.93	(0.07)	-0.79	(0.04)	-1.04	(0.06)	-0.56	(0.04)
Hungary	0.67	(0.06)	0.46	(0.07)	0.20	(0.07)	-0.09	(0.07)	0.50	(0.09)
Iceland	-0.29	(0.10)	-0.44	(0.08)	-0.41	(0.04)	-0.72	(0.07)	-0.75	(0.07)
Ireland	0.30	(0.08)	-0.24	(0.07)	-1.31	(0.07)	0.30	(0.08)	0.10	(0.07)
Italy	-0.74	(0.06)	0.68	(0.06)	0.63	(0.08)	0.13	(0.06)	0.60	(0.04)
Korea	-0.28	(0.06)	-0.27	(0.06)	0.46	(0.05)	-0.14	(0.06)	-0.70	(0.10)
Lithuania	0.06	(0.07)	0.03	(0.07)	-0.20	(0.04)	m	m	-0.18	(0.07)
Malaysia	-0.30	(0.09)	-0.87	(0.08)	0.35	(0.06)	1.03	(0.05)	0.91	(0.06)
Malta	0.27	(0.10)	0.76	(0.11)	-0.21	(0.07)	-0.24	(0.09)	-0.13	(0.10)
Mexico	0.10	(0.08)	-0.38	(0.06)	0.87	(0.06)	0.53	(0.07)	0.47	(0.09)
Norway	-0.31	(0.06)	0.12	(0.07)	-0.68	(0.04)	0.79	(0.06)	0.31	(0.06)
Poland	0.83	(0.08)	0.25	(0.08)	0.94	(0.03)	-0.27	(0.06)	-0.14	(0.06)
Portugal	0.41	(0.06)	0.25	(0.04)	-1.73	(0.07)	-0.15	(0.07)	0.15	(0.08)
Slovak Republic	0.22	(0.07)	-0.98	(0.11)	0.87	(0.06)	0.25	(0.05)	-0.21	(0.05)
Slovenia	0.63	(0.05)	0.37	(0.05)	1.16	(0.04)	0.08	(0.04)	-0.06	(0.05)
Spain	-0.67	(0.08)	-0.40	(0.07)	-0.82	(0.08)	-0.88	(0.07)	-0.24	(0.09)
Turkey	-0.40	(0.14)	0.49	(0.13)	0.36	(0.09)	0.61	(0.09)	1.04	(0.12)
TALIS average	0.00	(0.02)	0.00	(0.02)	0.00	(0.01)	0.00	(0.02)	0.00	(0.01)

1. Country values that are shaded are not statistically different from the TALIS average.
Source: OECD, *TALIS Database*.
StatLink http://dx.doi.org/10.1787/608025205225

Table 6.3

Management leadership styles (2007-08)

Indices of leadership styles adopted by principals in lower secondary education

	Instructional leadership[1]		Administrative leadership[2]	
	Mean	(S.E.)	Mean	(S.E.)
Australia	-0.22	(0.09)	-0.72	(0.08)
Austria	-0.59	(0.05)	-0.06	(0.06)
Belgium (Fl.)	-0.40	(0.08)	-0.49	(0.05)
Brazil	1.17	(0.07)	0.51	(0.06)
Bulgaria	0.43	(0.07)	1.23	(0.10)
Denmark	-0.34	(0.09)	-1.68	(0.06)
Estonia	-0.76	(0.06)	-0.89	(0.05)
Hungary	0.59	(0.07)	0.24	(0.09)
Iceland	-0.51	(0.07)	-0.81	(0.07)
Ireland	-0.56	(0.08)	0.22	(0.06)
Italy	0.26	(0.08)	0.41	(0.05)
Korea	-0.04	(0.07)	-0.46	(0.08)
Lithuania[3]	-0.05	(0.06)	-0.20	(0.08)
Malaysia	-0.37	(0.09)	1.09	(0.06)
Malta	0.37	(0.09)	-0.20	(0.09)
Mexico	0.26	(0.08)	0.56	(0.08)
Norway	-0.39	(0.05)	0.62	(0.05)
Poland	0.91	(0.07)	-0.22	(0.05)
Portugal	-0.48	(0.06)	0.01	(0.07)
Slovak Republic	0.05	(0.09)	0.03	(0.05)
Slovenia	0.97	(0.05)	0.01	(0.04)
Spain	-0.85	(0.09)	-0.62	(0.08)
Turkey	0.20	(0.15)	0.92	(0.11)
TALIS average	**0.00**	(0.02)	**0.00**	(0.01)

1. Average of the indices for Management-school goals, Instructional management and Direct supervision in the school.

2. Average of the indices for Accountable management and Bureaucratic management.

3. The score for Lithuania in the Administrative leadership index is based only on the Bureaucratic management index because of missing data in the index for Accountable management.

Source: OECD, *TALIS Database*.

StatLink http://dx.doi.org/10.1787/608025205225

Table 6.4

Relationship between school leadership style and teachers' beliefs about instruction (2007-08)

Significant variables in the multilevel linear regression of the indices for school leadership styles and the indices for beliefs about instruction in lower secondary education[1,2]

Example: In Belgium (Fl.), teachers who work with a principal with a more pronounced instructional style of leadership have a stronger belief in a direct tranmission approach to teaching.

	Teacher beliefs: Direct transmission		Teacher beliefs: Constructivist	
	Dependent on:		Dependent on:	
	Instructional leadership	Administrative leadership	Instructional leadership	Administrative leadership
Australia				
Austria				
Belgium (Fl.)	+			
Brazil				
Bulgaria		–		–
Denmark				
Estonia		+		
Hungary	+			
Iceland		+	–	+
Ireland				
Italy				
Korea				
Lithuania				
Malaysia				
Malta	–	–	+	+
Mexico				
Norway				
Poland				
Portugal	+			
Slovak Republic				
Slovenia				
Spain				
Turkey				

1. Variables where a significant positive relationship was found are indicated by a "+" while those where a significant negative relationship was found are shown with a "–". Cells are blank where no significant relationship was found. Significance was tested at the 5% level.

2. Controlling for the teacher's gender, level of education, years of experience, employment status, whether they work in another school and the size of the community in which the school is located.

Source: OECD, *TALIS Database*.

StatLink http://dx.doi.org/10.1787/608025205225

Table 6.5

Relationship between school leadership style and teaching practices (2007-08)

Significant variables in the multilevel linear regression of the indices for school leadership styles on the indices for the following teaching practices in lower secondary education[1,2]

Example: In Iceland, teachers use structuring teaching practices more frequently if they work with a principal adopting a more pronounced administrative style of leadership.

	Teacher practices: Structuring		Teacher practices: Student oriented		Teacher practices: Enhanced activities	
	Dependent on:		Dependent on:		Dependent on:	
	Instructional leadership	Administrative leadership	Instructional leadership	Administrative leadership	Instructional leadership	Administrative leadership
Australia						
Austria						
Belgium (Fl.)						
Brazil						
Bulgaria						
Denmark						
Estonia						
Hungary			+			
Iceland		+	−	+	−	+
Ireland					+	
Italy			+		+	
Korea	−					
Lithuania	+					
Malaysia						
Malta	−	+	−	+	−	+
Mexico						
Norway						−
Poland		+				
Portugal						
Slovak Republic						
Slovenia						
Spain						
Turkey						

1. Variables where a significant positive relationship was found are indicated by a "+" while those where a significant negative relationship was found are shown with a "−". Cells are blank where no significant relationship was found. Significance was tested at the 5% level.

2. Controlling for the teachers' gender, level of education, years of experience, employment status, whether they work in another school and the size of the community in which the school is located.

Source: OECD, *TALIS Database*.

StatLink ⟶ http://dx.doi.org/10.1787/608025205225

Table 6.6

Relationship between school leadership style and co-ordination and professional collaboration among teachers (2007-08)

Significant variables in the multilevel linear regression of the indices for school leadership styles on the indices for co-ordination and professional collaboration in lower secondary education[1, 2]

Example: In Hungary, teachers are more likely to exchange and co-ordinate in their teaching activities if they work with a principal who adopts a more pronounced instructional style of leadership.

| | Exchange and co-ordination for teaching | | Professional collaboration | |
| | Dependent on: | | Dependent on: | |
	Instructional leadership	Administrative leadership	Instructional leadership	Administrative leadership
Australia				
Austria				
Belgium (Fl.)				
Brazil				
Bulgaria				
Denmark				
Estonia				
Hungary	+		+	
Iceland	+	−	+	
Ireland				
Italy				
Korea				
Lithuania	+		+	
Malaysia	+	−	+	−
Malta	−	+	−	+
Mexico	+			
Norway			+	
Poland	+		+	
Portugal				
Slovak Republic				
Slovenia				
Spain				
Turkey				

1. Variables where a significant positive relationship was found are indicated by a "+" while those where a significant negative relationship was found are shown with a "−". Cells are blank where no significant relationship was found. Significance was tested at the 5% level.

2. Controlling for the teacher's gender, level of education, years of experience, employment status, whether they work in another school and the size of the community in which the school is located.

Source: OECD, *TALIS Database.*

StatLink ⇒ http://dx.doi.org/10.1787/608025205225

Table 6.7

Relationship between school leadership style and classroom disciplinary climate, time on task and teacher-student relation indices (2007-08)

Significant variables in the multilevel linear regression of the indices for school leadership styles and the indices for classroom disciplinary climate, time on task and teacher-student relations in lower secondary education[1, 2]

Example: In Denmark, teachers are more likely to report better relations with students if they work with a principal who adopts a more pronounced instructional style of leadership.

| | Classroom disciplinary climate | | Percentage of time dedicated to actual teaching and learning in class | | Teacher-Student relation | |
| | Dependent on: | | Dependent on: | | Dependent on: | |
	Instructional leadership	Administrative leadership	Instructional leadership	Administrative leadership	Instructional leadership	Administrative leadership
Australia			+			
Austria						
Belgium (Fl.)						
Brazil						
Bulgaria						
Denmark					+	
Estonia						
Hungary					+	
Iceland	−	+		−	+	+
Ireland						
Italy						
Korea						
Lithuania						
Malaysia						
Malta	+	−	+	−	+	−
Mexico					+	
Norway						
Poland						
Portugal					+	
Slovak Republic						
Slovenia						
Spain						
Turkey						

1. Variables where a significant positive relationship was found are indicated by a "+" while those where a significant negative relationship was found are shown with a "−". Cells are blank where no significant relationship was found. Significance was tested at the 5% level.

2. Controlling for the teacher's gender, level of education, years of experience, employment status, whether they work in another school and the size of the community in which the school is located.

Source: OECD, *TALIS Database.*

StatLink ⧉ http://dx.doi.org/10.1787/608025205225

Table 6.8

Relationship between school leadership style and teacher's job satisfaction and self-efficacy (2007-08)

*Significant variables in the multilevel linear regression of the indices for school leadership styles and the indices
for teacher's job satisfaction and self-efficacy in lower secondary education[1, 2]*

Example: In Estonia, teachers tend to be more satisfied with their jobs if they work with a principal who adopts a more pronounced instructional
style of leadership.

	Teachers' job satisfaction		Teachers' self-efficacy	
	Dependent on:		Dependent on:	
	Instructional leadership	Administrative leadership	Instructional leadership	Administrative leadership
Australia				
Austria				
Belgium (Fl.)				
Brazil				
Bulgaria				
Denmark				
Estonia	+			
Hungary	+		+	
Iceland	–	+		+
Ireland				
Italy				
Korea				
Lithuania				
Malaysia				
Malta	+	–	+	–
Mexico				
Norway				
Poland				
Portugal			┤	
Slovak Republic				
Slovenia				
Spain			+	
Turkey	+			

1. Variables where a significant positive relationship was found are indicated by a "+" while those where a significant negative relationship was found are shown
with a "–". Cells are blank where no significant relationship was found. Significance was tested at the 5% level.
2. Controlling for the teacher's gender, level of education, years of experience, employment status, whether they work in another school and the size of the
community in which the school is located.
Source: OECD, *TALIS Database.*
StatLink ⬛🇪🇸🇵 http://dx.doi.org/10.1787/608025205225

Table 6.9

Relationship between school leadership style and objectives of teacher appraisals (2007-08)

Significant variables in the multilevel linear regression of the indices for school leadership styles and aspects of teacher appraisals in lower secondary education[1,2]

Example: In Australia, a greater importance is given to innovative teaching practices in teacher appraisals if the school principal adopts a more pronounced instructional style of leadership.

	Factors considered in teacher appraisals								Objective of teacher appraisal is to inform an administrative level above the school[3]	
	Student test scores		Retention and pass rates of the students		Professional development undertaken by the teacher		Innovative teaching practices			
	Dependent on:		Dependent on:		Dependent on:		Dependent on:		Dependent on:	
	Instructional leadership	Administrative leadership	Instructional leadership	Administrative leadership	Instructional leadership	Administrative leadership	Instructional leadership	Administrative leadership	Instructional leadership	Administrative leadership
Australia							+			
Austria	+	+	+			+		+		
Belgium (Fl.)	+									
Brazil					+	+				
Bulgaria	+				+				+	
Denmark		+		+				+		
Estonia		+			+	+	+			+
Hungary			+		+		+		+	
Iceland		+			+		+			
Ireland			+		+					
Italy									+	
Korea							+			
Lithuania					+		+			
Malaysia										
Malta					+					
Mexico	+		+		+		+		+	
Norway	+			+						
Poland							+			
Portugal	+	−	+	−		+				
Slovak Republic					+					
Slovenia		−	+		+		+		+	
Spain	+		+		+					
Turkey					+		+			

1. Variables where a significant positive relationship was found are indicated by a "+" while those where a significant negative relationship was found are shown with a "−". Cells are blank where no significant relationship was found. Significance was tested at the 5% level.

2. Controlling for the principal's gender, level of education, years of experience, employment status, whether they work in another school and the size of the community in which the school is located, the public/private status of the school, the student-teacher ratio and average class size in the school.

3. School board, municipality, school district and school inspectorate.

Source: OECD, *TALIS Database.*

StatLink ⧉ http://dx.doi.org/10.1787/608025205225

Table 6.10

Relationship between school leadership style and outcomes of teacher appraisals (2007-08)

Significant variables in the multilevel linear regression of the indices for school leadership styles and the actions taken if a teacher appraisal reveals weaknesses in the teachers' work, in lower secondary education[1, 2]

Example: In Austria, a training or development plan is more likely to be provided for a teacher if the principal adopts a more pronounced instructional style of leadership.

| | A development or training plan is established for the teacher to address the weaknesses in their teaching | | Material sanctions are imposed on the teacher | | The underperformance is reported to another body to take action | |
| | Dependent on: | | Dependent on: | | Dependent on: | |
	Instructional leadership	Administrative leadership	Instructional leadership	Administrative leadership	Instructional leadership	Administrative leadership
Australia						
Austria	+					
Belgium (Fl.)	+					
Brazil	+					
Bulgaria	+			+	+	
Denmark						
Estonia	+					
Hungary	+					
Iceland	+					
Ireland						-
Italy						
Korea	+					
Lithuania	+					
Malaysia	+					
Malta	+				+	
Mexico	+					
Norway	+				+	
Poland						
Portugal	+					
Slovak Republic	+		+		+	
Slovenia	+					
Spain	+					
Turkey					+	

1. Variables where a significant positive relationship was found are indicated by a "+" while those where a significant negative relationship was found are shown with a "–". Cells are blank where no significant relationship was found. Significance was tested at the 5% level.

2. Controlling for the principal's gender, level of education, years of experience, employment status, whether they work in another school and the size of the community in which the school is located.

Source: OECD, *TALIS Database*.

StatLink ⟨⟩ http://dx.doi.org/10.1787/608025205225

Table 6.11

Relationship between school leadership style and the professional development of teachers (2007-08)

Significant variables in the multilevel linear regression of the indices for school leadership styles on aspects of teachers' professional development in lower secondary education[1, 2]

Example: In Bulgaria, teachers are more likely to want more professional development than they undertook if the school principal adopts a more pronounced administrative style of leadership.

	Number of days of professional development taken during the last 18 months		Teachers wanting more professional development than they received in the last 18 months	
	Dependent on:		Dependent on:	
	Instructional leadership	Administrative leadership	Instructional leadership	Administrative leadership
Australia				
Austria				
Belgium (Fl.)				
Brazil				
Bulgaria				+
Denmark				
Estonia				
Hungary			+	
Iceland	+	+	+	+
Ireland				
Italy				
Korea				
Lithuania				
Malaysia				
Malta	−	+	+	+
Mexico				
Norway				
Poland				
Portugal				
Slovak Republic				
Slovenia				+
Spain		+		
Turkey			+	

1. Variables where a significant positive relationship was found are indicated by a "+" while those where a significant negative relationship was found are shown with a "−". Cells are blank where no significant relationship was found. Significance was tested at the 5% level.

2. Controlling for the teacher's gender, level of education, years of experience, employment status, whether they work in another school and the size of the community in which the school is located.

Source: OECD, *TALIS Database*.

StatLink ⟐⟐⟐ http://dx.doi.org/10.1787/608025205225

Table 6.12

Relationship between the background characteristics of the principals and their school and the use of instructional leadership style (2007-08)

Significant values for principals in lower secondary education

	School principals' characteristics						School characteristics					Frequency of school self-evaluation		Criteria in school evaluation			Influence of school evaluations	
	Gender (Female)	Level of education (Master or higher)	Years of experience (< 5 years)	Years of experience (6-15 years)	Work in other school	Constructivist beliefs about instruction	Public school	Locality of the school: Village	Locality of the school: Town	Student-teacher ratio	Average of class size	Once in 5 years	Two or more during 5 years	Student test scores	Innovative teaching practices	Teacher's professional development	Appraisal of the school management (high influence)	Appraisal of the individual teachers (high influence)
Australia													+					
Austria											+		+	+				
Belgium (Fl.)	+	−				+							+		+			
Brazil						+						+	+					
Bulgaria		+				+	−	+							+			
Denmark		+		+					+		−	−	−					+
Estonia	+					+								+	+			
Hungary	+																	
Iceland		+	+	−	+			−	−			−		−			+	+
Ireland		+						−	−									
Italy		−					a									+	+	
Korea						+		+					+		+		−	+
Lithuania			−			+	−						−					
Malaysia	+						+	−	−			−	−			+		
Malta		+											+					
Mexico				+	+										+			
Norway	+				+							+	+	+	+			
Poland	+		−	−														
Portugal		+					+									+		
Slovak Republic		a					+											
Slovenia							a							+			+	
Spain	+			+	−	+	−				+			−	+			+
Turkey	+		+	+		+			−						+	+	−	

Note:
– Variables where a significant positive relationship was found are indicated by a "+" while those where a significant negative relationship was found are shown with a "–". Cells are blank where no significant relationship was found. Significance was tested at the 5% level.
– "a" denotes that the variable is not available.
Source: OECD, *TALIS Database*.
StatLink ᵐˢᵖ http://dx.doi.org/10.1787/608025205225

Table 6.13

Relationship between the background characteristics of the principals and their school and the use of administrative leadership style (2007-08)

Significant values for principals in lower secondary education

	School principals' characteristics						School characteristics					Frequency of school self-evaluation		Criteria in school evaluation			Influence of school evaluations	
	Gender (Female)	Level of education (Master or higher)	Years of experience (< 5 years)	Years of experience (6-15 years)	Work in other school	Constructivist beliefs about instruction	Public school	Locality of the school: Village	Locality of the school: Town	Student-teacher ratio	Average of class size	Once in 5 years	Two or more during 5 years	Student test scores	Innovative teaching practices	Teacher's professional development	Appraisal of the school management (high influence)	Appraisal of the individual teachers (high influence)
Australia						+				+		−	−					+
Austria				−										+	+			
Belgium (Fl.)							+						+					
Brazil		+				+												
Bulgaria		+				+		+	+					+				
Denmark				+		+					−							+
Estonia						+								+				
Hungary	+					+			+					+	−			
Iceland															+			
Ireland						+								+				−
Italy				−			a	+										
Korea			−	−		+		+							+			
Lithuania						+							−					
Malaysia							+					−	−					
Malta													+				+	
Mexico						+					−	−	−					
Norway	+											+	+					
Poland		+	−			+					+							
Portugal				−								+	−					
Slovak Republic		a				+												
Slovenia							a											
Spain						+												+
Turkey				+	+	+									+			

Note:

– Variables where a significant positive relationship was found are indicated by a "+" while those where a significant negative relationship was found are shown with a "−". Cells are blank where no significant relationship was found. Significance was tested at the 5% level.

– "a" denotes that the variable is not available.

Source: OECD, *TALIS Database*.

StatLink ⬛🈁 http://dx.doi.org/10.1787/608025205225

Table 6.14

Correlation between leadership styles and types of evaluation[1] (2007-08)

Correlations for school principals in lower secondary education

	Instructional leadership		Administrative leadership	
	School self-evaluation	External evaluation	School self-evaluation	External evaluation
Australia	0.24	0.10	0.14	-0.01
Austria	0.20	0.21	-0.03	-0.01
Belgium (Fl.)	0.34	0.14	0.21	0.10
Brazil	0.31	0.26	-0.05	-0.01
Bulgaria	0.10	0.19	0.02	-0.06
Denmark	0.23	0.25	0.30	0.25
Estonia	0.09	0.06	0.16	0.07
Hungary	0.11	0.16	0.00	-0.02
Iceland	0.22	0.18	-0.09	0.26
Ireland	0.22	0.17	0.19	0.08
Italy	0.09	0.09	0.03	0.17
Korea	0.21	0.16	0.18	0.14
Lithuania	0.14	-0.03	0.10	0.01
Malaysia	0.28	0.10	0.22	0.18
Malta	0.30	0.01	0.15	-0.11
Mexico	0.11	0.06	0.06	0.05
Norway	0.12	0.14	0.11	0.07
Poland	0.08	0.12	-0.02	0.01
Portugal	0.14	0.12	0.16	0.15
Slovak Republic	0.19	0.06	0.03	0.09
Slovenia	0.12	0.16	-0.02	0.10
Spain	0.23	0.13	0.33	0.12
Turkey	0.15	0.40	0.06	0.15

1. Whether or not an evaluation was conducted in the previous five years.
Note: Correlations that are significant at the 5% level are shaded in light gray.
Source: OECD, *TALIS Database*.
StatLink http://dx.doi.org/10.1787/608025205225

CHAPTER 7

Key Factors in Developing Effective Learning Environments: Classroom Disciplinary Climate and Teachers' Self-Efficacy

Highlights

- Research has shown that classroom disciplinary climate is associated with student performance and that self-efficacy is an important measure of productivity and effectiveness.

- Teachers with "constructivist" beliefs about teaching are more likely to report good classroom disciplinary climate in many countries, but those who emphasise the "direct transmission" of knowledge in instruction are more likely to teach classes with poorer disciplinary climate. Teachers who hold either of these types of beliefs strongly are more likely to report high self-efficacy.

- Structured teaching practices and student-oriented teaching practices are both associated with good classroom climate and teachers' self-efficacy in many countries. This is less true of other practices identified in the survey.

- Teacher appraisal is linked in some cases with self-efficacy, particularly when it involves public recognition of teachers' progress and is linked to innovative practices.

- More professional development is often associated with greater teacher self-efficacy, but not generally with more orderly classrooms.

- Teachers with relatively less experience and stability in their contractual status are significantly less likely to be teaching classes with a positive classroom disciplinary climate or to report high levels of self-efficacy. Teachers who are significantly more likely to report higher levels of self-efficacy are employed on permanent contracts (significant in 7 TALIS countries in the final net models estimated for each country), employed on a full-time basis (6 TALIS countries), and have more experience as a teacher (5 TALIS countries).

INTRODUCTION AND CONCEPTUAL FRAMEWORK

A number of important issues discussed in this report play an important role in school education. Chapter 3 discusses the professional development of teachers and issues such as its impact and teachers' professional development needs. Chapter 4 identifies a number of teaching practices, beliefs and attitudes across TALIS countries and analysed, among other issues, their interaction and the factors associated with them. Teachers' appraisal and feedback is the subject of Chapter 5 along with an analysis of school evaluation. Chapter 6 examines school leadership styles across and within TALIS countries as well as associations between such styles and various aspects of schools' operations and the working lives of teachers. All analyses are supplemented by Chapter 2's description of the characteristics of teachers and the schools in which they work.

This chapter focuses on two variables which are considered important pre-conditions for teachers' professional success: classroom disciplinary climate and teachers' self-efficacy (see *TALIS Technical Report* [forthcoming] for discussion of the reliability of these indices). It presents an analysis of extensive modelling (described in Annex A1.4) which incorporates variables from the previous chapters and examines their association with classroom disciplinary climate and teachers' reported self-efficacy (which are modelled separately). It builds on the analysis in other chapters, which concentrate on the specific issues that are their analytical focus. Separate modelling was conducted for each bloc of independent variables drawn from the earlier chapters estimating classroom disciplinary climate and self-efficacy. Results are contrasted with the effect of including a broad set of teacher background and various socio-economic background characteristics of classrooms and schools which better control for external factors. The final models are then presented, which include not only these background characteristics but also the significant variables from the estimations for each analytical bloc. This makes it possible to better isolate the variables that affect classroom disciplinary climate and self-efficacy and allows for a better understanding of the interaction of key variables identified in previous chapters.

The analytical model and the choice of dependent and independent variables are discussed to illustrate the development of the modelling presented here. This is complemented by a discussion of the descriptive statistics of teachers' reports of self-efficacy and of classroom disciplinary climate. The following section introduces the first results of the modelling and estimates classroom disciplinary climate and teachers' self-efficacy against various teacher background characteristics and measures of the socio-economic status of teachers' classes and the schools in which they work. Discussion is then presented of estimates of the association of classroom disciplinary climate and self-efficacy with measures of teachers' professional development from Chapter 3. Following this is discussion of the next bloc of variables included in the modelling, which encompasses measures of teachers' practices and beliefs (discussed in Chapter 4) and their association with classroom disciplinary climate and self-efficacy. Estimates of the association between measures of school evaluation and teacher appraisal and feedback (discussed in Chapter 5) and classroom disciplinary climate and self-efficacy are then discussed followed by the associations with school leadership styles from Chapter 6. Indicators of school climate and school autonomy and their relationship to the dependent variables are then discussed and finally concluding comments are presented.

Analytical model

The analytical model presented in this chapter builds upon the previous chapters of this report. Chapter 4 presents an analytical framework for the modelling presented in that chapter (see Figure 4.1). It illustrates how the various aspects of schooling that are the focus of TALIS are expected to be associated with effective schooling, with a particular emphasis on teaching practices and beliefs (the focus of that chapter). Modelling presented in Chapter 6 illustrates the associations between particular school characteristics and those of school principals and the leadership styles they adopt.

The modelling presented here is based on an analytical framework which extends that of previous chapters by including more background and socio-economic characteristics and by drawing on important elements of the analyses presented in all of the earlier chapters. The variables in the modelling include:

- teacher characteristics which describe their demographic profile and aspects of their employment and careers as teachers;
- socio-economic background characteristics measured at both the classroom and the school level;
- professional development characteristics which measure the extent and type of professional development undertaken, drawing on the analysis in Chapter 3;
- teaching practices and beliefs found across TALIS countries, drawing on the analysis in Chapter 4;
- school evaluation characteristics, with a focus upon specific aspects of the frequency and impact of school evaluation, discussed in Chapter 5;
- teacher appraisal and feedback characteristics that detail the frequency, criteria and impact of the appraisal and feedback provided to teachers, as discussed in Chapter 5; and
- school leadership styles that are prevalent across TALIS countries, as discussed in Chapter 6.

These variables are included in the modelling presented in this chapter, which estimate their association with teachers' reports of their self-efficacy and with classroom disciplinary climate. Both classroom disciplinary climate and teachers' self-efficacy are included in the analytical framework of Chapter 4, and it is important to note the differences with the considerably broader analytical framework for the modelling in this chapter. For example, a greater number of teachers' job characteristics and aspects of teachers' career structures are included in the modelling presented in this chapter which can be affected by policy. In addition, this chapter includes an analysis of school evaluation processes, of important aspects of teachers' appraisal and feedback, and of specific school leadership styles. This enables a broader analysis of the key features of the earlier chapters of the report. This broader approach requires slight changes to the modelling which are discussed below.

A focus on self-efficacy and classroom disciplinary climate

Classroom disciplinary climate and teachers' reports of their self-efficacy are the dependent variables in the modelling presented in this chapter. These variables could also be used as independent variables in other models with a different focus yet, both are considered important in school education and, as discussed below, have been shown to be important in numerous contexts. Classroom disciplinary climate not only affects student outcomes and attainment but is a prominent policy issue in a number of countries and regions (OECD, 2007). Students' actions in classrooms and a safe and productive learning environment are important for many schools and can be a challenging dimension of teachers' work. Teachers' self-efficacy is an important dimension given teachers' impact on students. The discussion below indicates that reports of self-efficacy have been linked to productivity and influence people's actions in workplaces in different industries and those of students. Given this, it is assumed here that teachers who report positive self-efficacy are more likely to undertake actions in classrooms that can enhance student learning and create a positive learning environment.

As discussed in Chapter 4, self-efficacy is an important factor for policy makers and stakeholders in school education to consider. Bandura (1994) defines self-efficacy as "the beliefs that determine how people feel, think, motivate themselves and behave", and is also related to "beliefs about their capabilities to produce designated levels of performance that exercise influence over events that affect their lives". Reports of self-efficacy can be indicative not only of knowledge about oneself, but also of idiosyncratic beliefs about social situations (Cervone, 2000). When individuals envisage ability as a skill that can be acquired, a strong feeling of self-efficacy can help them better analyse and solve problems, while a weak feeling of self-efficacy can mean self-doubt and preoccupation with concerns about evaluation if they feel their efforts to be unsuccessful (Bandura, 1989). This has been shown to affect work in a number of environments including the education sector (Ross, 1998).

In addition to the research discussed in Chapter 4 showing the linkages between self-efficacy and teachers' actions, Ross (1998) analysed its association with teachers' actions in the classroom; its influence on how they interact with students, their performance expectations, and their classroom management practices. In the health sector, a number of survey instruments have been used to measure links between health and self-efficacy. In a number of instances, they have been used to measure reductions in productivity associated with specific diseases or to assess the impact of an illness on the workplace and the effect of the treatment for that illness upon productivity (Prasad *et al.*, 2004). Such measures are used in health research to complement indicators of the direct costs of ill health upon productivity which are more easily quantifiable such as the number of days of work missed. Prasad *et al.* (2004) reviewed the validity and reliability of the survey instruments used in a number of these studies across different industries and workplaces and concluded that they can be used to show effects upon productivity. A number of studies have shown that self-efficacy is related to productivity and can contribute to efforts to better measure productivity in organisations (*e.g.* Frayne and Latham, 1987). Lema and Agrusa (2006) found in a case study in the hospitality industry that self-efficacy accounted for 13% of the variance in self-directed learning. Self-efficacy has also been found to be related to the use of technology in the workplace (Hill *et al.*, 1987).

Organisational psychology research provides evidence that supports the importance of studying self-efficacy as a factor in the ability of workers to adapt to diverse and pluralistic workplaces. Those with high levels of self-efficacy tend to do their own performance monitoring and assessment in order to improve, rather than relying only on external supervisory practices. Moreover, high levels of self-efficacy were found to influence abilities to regulate and assess responses and handle volatile situations, and to adjust to a new organisational environment (Combs, 2002; Weiss, 1978; Jones, 1986). Chen *et al.* (1998) found a relationship between self-efficacy and an intended career in entrepreneurship. Beliefs of self-efficacy for innovation and risk taking were found to differentiate entrepreneurs from managers, as well as founders from non-founders.

Student self-efficacy has also been found to be linked to performance. Results from a meta-analytic study of student performance, which analysed 36 comparable studies, show evidence of a relationship between self-efficacy and academic behaviour (Multon *et al.*, 1991). The PISA 2006 index of students' self-efficacy in science measured their belief in their ability to handle tasks effectively and overcome difficulties with a one-unit increase in the index found to correspond to a performance difference of at least 20 points (OECD, 2007). PISA 2003 also showed a positive relationship between students' concept of self-efficacy in mathematics and their performance, where a one-unit increase in the index corresponded to a performance increase of 47 points (OECD, 2004). Hocevar (2009) analysed factors relating to achievement of mathematically gifted high school students and showed a positive relationship between self-efficacy and self-regulated learning and achievement in maths and a strong negative relationship between self-efficacy and the level of worry felt by students.

Given these findings it is assumed that teachers' self-efficacy can have numerous implications for school education as it is an indicator not only of aspects of productivity but also of how teachers act in the classroom. Given the many findings on the positive impact of self-efficacy on various organisational factors, teachers' self-efficacy should also affect school culture and the operations of effective schools. Teachers with a high level of self-efficacy in diversified environments may be more likely to adapt to and moderate dynamics in schools whose students come from different environments or present particular challenges. Chapter 4 demonstrates the positive correlation between classroom disciplinary climate and reported self-efficacy.

Estimations of classroom disciplinary climate and teachers' reported self-efficacy

This chapter focuses on two variables in models estimated for each country: teachers' self-efficacy and the quality of the classroom disciplinary climate. Various estimates are made to examine how different features of teachers' working environment are associated with these variables, both of which are taken to be important pre-conditions for professional success. Estimations were conducted for each country to examine the factors associated with both classroom disciplinary climate and teachers' self-efficacy within each country. For each of these outcome variables, regression analysis was conducted separately. Missing cases in the dependent and independent variables were imputed using a multiple imputation method. The detailed procedure of the multiple imputation and the sample sizes for the estimations for each country are presented in Annex A1.4. On average across TALIS countries, the sample size for the multiple regression analysis in this chapter is 3 200 teachers.

As discussed in Chapter 4, most of the variation in the index of classroom disciplinary climate is between teachers. Among the 23 countries, the minimum *rho* (intraclass correlation coefficient) is 4%, the maximum is 19% and the median is 8%. Similarly, most of the variation in the index of teachers' self-efficacy is between teachers. Among the 23 countries, the minimum *rho* (intraclass correlation coefficient) is 0%, the maximum is 11% and the median is 4%. Since the between-school variance is very small in both the index of classroom disciplinary climate and the index of self-efficacy, it was decided to apply an ordinary least squares regression instead of multilevel regression analysis.

Explanatory variables were selected from each of the previous chapters. These variables were then grouped into six thematic blocs. Table 7.1 presents the list of independent variables in each bloc as well as the teacher and school socio-economic background variables included in the modelling.

Modelling strategy: country-by-country analysis

For each of the six thematic blocs, two sets of estimates were calculated for each dependent variable (classroom disciplinary climate and teacher self-efficacy) for each country.

- **Bloc modelling:** Separate estimates were calculated with variables in each of the six blocs detailed in Table 7.1 for each country. Two sets of estimates were analysed in each bloc for each country:
  - *Gross* models which include only the variables in each thematic bloc.
  - *Net* models which include the variables in each thematic bloc *and* the teacher and school background variables identified in Table 7.1. These models allow for better comparisons of teachers with different characteristics and of those teaching in schools with different student populations.

- **Final modelling:** For each country, estimates were calculated which include variables from each of the thematic blocs. The variables included from each bloc are those that are statistically significant in the estimates from the bloc modelling. The final models allow for analysis of the relationships between the variables across thematic blocs and classroom disciplinary climate and self-efficacy. As above, two sets of estimations are analysed:
  - *Final gross* models which include significant variables from each of the *gross* models estimated in each of the thematic blocs. These are available on the TALIS website (*www.oecd.org/edu/TALIS*).
  - *Final net* models which include significant variables from each of the *net* models estimated in each of the thematic blocs and the socio-economic background and Bloc 1 variables. The *final net* models are the main focus of the discussion below.

The blocs of variables draw on the analyses in the previous chapters of the report and are detailed in Table 7.1. Bloc 1 focuses on teachers' background characteristics. These are then used as control variables for the *net* models estimated for each country. Bloc 2 focuses on professional development characteristics and Bloc 3 on measures of teachers' beliefs and practices. Bloc 4 includes variables specifying certain aspects of teachers' appraisal and feedback and of school evaluations. Bloc 5 encompasses the school leadership styles analysed in Chapter 6 and Bloc 6 includes a number of school-level variables which measure aspects of school autonomy, school climate and school resources.

Separating each thematic group of variables into modelling blocs facilitates the analysis of the relationships between the variables in each bloc and classroom disciplinary climate and self-efficacy. However, variables in different analytical blocs may be related. For example, teachers who undertook more professional development may be more likely to employ specific teaching practices. This may have an impact on classroom disciplinary climate or self-efficacy which is not captured in the bloc modelling. Therefore, to gain a better understanding of the interaction of the variables in each bloc and the classroom disciplinary climate and self-efficacy, *final* models are estimated which include variables from each thematic bloc. *Final* models are estimated to bring together the variables that are statistically significant in the estimates for the modelling conducted in each of the six blocs. Therefore, for the *gross* and *net* models estimated for each bloc, only the significant variables in those estimations are included in the *final gross* and *final net* models. For example, in the *net* Bloc 1 modelling for Austria, years of teaching was significant in the estimate of teachers' self-efficacy. The *final net* model which estimates teachers' self-efficacy in Austria therefore includes the variable indicating years of teaching. Throughout the analysis, an effect is considered statistically significant if the p-value is below 0.05. Tables 7.10 and 7.11 (available on line) present the results of the *final net* models estimated for each TALIS country (only the significant variables and their coefficients are presented).

This is further discussed in Annex A1.4 which describes the modelling procedure in greater detail.

DESCRIPTIVE STATISTICS FOR TEACHERS' REPORTED SELF-EFFICACY

This chapter focuses on measures of teachers' self-efficacy and classroom disciplinary climate. Both of these measures are analysed as indices compiled from teachers' responses to several questionnaire items regarding these issues. The self-efficacy index and the data used to compile this index are described here to point to country differences in these areas and to provide an initial illustration of teachers' self-efficacy before turning to a discussion of the regression analyses.

Teachers' self-efficacy is measured here with an index that is a composite of four items which measures teachers' reported success in educating the students in their class. This well-established index in education research is discussed in Chapter 4. Teachers reported whether they strongly agreed, agreed, disagreed, or strongly disagreed with the following statements:

• I feel I am making a significant educational difference in the lives of my students.

• If I try really hard, I can make progress with even the most difficult and unmotivated students.

• I am successful with the students in my class.

• I usually know how to get through to students.

Reponses to these questions were compiled and an index of self-efficacy was developed from the corresponding data. In developing the index configural and metric invariance was established and the fit of the models for testing scalar invariance was acceptable. As Table 7.2 shows, the index of teachers' self-efficacy was developed with a mean of zero and a standard deviation of +/- 1 across TALIS countries. Most countries' teacher self-efficacy scores are therefore likely to be close to zero. Teachers in Norway reported considerably higher self-efficacy in their teaching than teachers in other countries, with an average self-efficacy index score of 0.51. This is considerably above the next highest group of countries which includes Italy, Iceland, Australia and Ireland, with scores at or above 0.30. At the other end of the range, teachers in Korea reported substantially lower levels of self-efficacy in their teaching. The average self-efficacy reported by Korean teachers was -0.77 and was well below the next lowest scoring group of countries – Estonia, Hungary and Spain – where teachers' reported average self-efficacy was equal to or below -0.4.

The underlying data in this index are also presented to better illustrate both the concept of self-efficacy discussed here and differences among countries. The average responses of teachers in each TALIS country to each of the four questions that comprise the index are presented in Tables 7.2a-7.2d (available on line). Over 90% of teachers across TALIS countries reported making a significant educational difference in the lives of their students. This is particularly apparent in Belgium (Fl.), Bulgaria, Italy, Malaysia, Mexico and Norway where at least 97% responded positively. While such a positive average response was less common among teachers in Estonia, Hungary, Iceland, Korea and Slovenia, over eight in ten teachers in these countries still gave a positive response to this statement. Clearly teachers in TALIS countries generally believe that they make a difference.

Making progress with students whose learning requirements are more complex or whose motivation is very low is an important aspect of education policy and a critical aspect of teaching in many schools. Some 83% of teachers reported that if they persevere they can make progress with even the most difficult and unmotivated students. While fewer teachers reported success in this area, it is important that over eight in ten reported themselves to be successful with even the most difficult and unmotivated students. This was particularly the case in Italy, Malaysia, Mexico, Norway and Slovenia where more than nine teachers in ten reported that they can make progress with these students. However, in Hungary, Portugal and Spain fewer than three-quarters of teachers reported success in this area.

On average across TALIS countries virtually all teachers considered themselves successful with the students in their class. On average, three-quarters agreed with the statement, "I am successful with the students in my class" and a further 19% strongly agreed (Table 7.2c available on line). Only in Spain and Korea did less than 90% of teachers respond positively. Very similar results are found for teachers' response to the statement, "I usually know how to get through to my students".

These figures show that the majority of teachers consider themselves to be successful in teaching students in their school. The teacher self-efficacy index presented in Table 7.2 brings these four questions together in a single index which allows for a broader analysis of teachers' self-efficacy. Regression analysis was used to disentangle the associations of different teacher and school level variables with this teacher self-efficacy index, especially those relating to the main policy themes of this report: teachers' professional development, teaching practices and beliefs, teacher appraisal and feedback, and school leadership.

DESCRIPTIVE STATISTICS FOR CLASSROOM ENVIRONMENT

As in the case of teachers' reported self-efficacy, the discussion of classroom disciplinary climate focuses on an index constructed from various questionnaire items which record teachers' reports of the climate in a randomly selected class. Classroom disciplinary climate is a multifaceted concept which is better analysed through an index that captures these separate elements. It also facilitates the regression analysis presented later in this chapter. This section examines the items underlying the index to better illustrate the meaning of the classroom disciplinary climate index, its interpretation and implications.

The classroom disciplinary climate index draws on four items in the TALIS teacher questionnaire which reflect the climate in a class taught by the teacher in the school:

- When the lesson begins, I have to wait quite a long time for students to quieten down.
- Students in this class take care to create a pleasant learning atmosphere.
- I lose quite a lot of time because of students interrupting the lesson.
- There is much noise in this classroom.

Teachers reported whether they strongly agreed, agreed, disagreed or strongly disagreed with each of these statements. An index of classroom disciplinary climate was constructed from responses to these questions. It was constructed with a mean of zero and a standard deviation of +/- 1 across TALIS countries. In developing the index configural and metric invariance was established and the fit of the models for testing scalar invariance was acceptable. Table 7.3 presents the average classroom disciplinary climate reported by teachers in each TALIS country. Given that the index was constructed with an average of zero, most countries have scores around this average. Teachers in Estonia reported a substantially more positive classroom environment than other TALIS countries with an index score of 0.45. This is considerably higher than the next highest scoring group of countries, comprising Austria, Ireland, Mexico and Slovenia where, on average, teachers reported a classroom disciplinary climate of between 0.21 and 0.25. At the other end of the range, teachers in Spain reported, on average, a more negative classroom disciplinary climate with a index score of -0.47, considerably below the next lowest scoring countries of Iceland (index score of -0.36) and Portugal (-0.39).

Descriptive statistics of the four items underlying this index are presented in Table 7.3a-7.3d (available on line). On average across TALIS countries, the majority of teachers reported that they did not have to "wait quite a long time for students to quieten down" in their class. However, this was not true of teachers in Iceland and Norway, where the majority of teachers agreed with the statement (77% in Iceland and 51% in Norway). On average, teachers have to wait considerably less for students to quieten down in classes before they can begin teaching in Bulgaria, Estonia, Ireland, Lithuania, Mexico and Poland, where less than one teacher in five reported having to wait quite a long time.

On average across TALIS countries, just fewer than three-quarters of teachers reported that "students in their class take care to create a pleasant learning environment". At least eight in ten teachers reported this to be true in Bulgaria, Italy, Korea, Lithuania and Mexico. However, it was the case for less than two-thirds of teachers in Estonia, Hungary, Iceland, Malta, Spain and Turkey (Table 7.3b available on line).

On average across TALIS countries almost one-third of teachers reported that student interruptions caused the loss of quite a lot of potential teaching time in the classes they teach (Table 7.3c available on line). In Iceland, Norway, Portugal and Spain lost time due to student interruptions was reported by at least four teachers in ten. In contrast, fewer than 20% of teachers in Estonia and Mexico reported this as a problem. Similar results are found in teachers' reports of whether "there is much noise in this classroom", a situation that can be disruptive for teaching and effective learning. On average across TALIS countries, just under one-quarter of teachers agreed with this statement (Table 7.3d available on line). The proportion rises to just fewer than 40% of teachers in Australia, Brazil and Spain but is less than 20% in Austria, Bulgaria, Estonia, Italy, Malaysia, Mexico, Poland and Slovenia.

Classroom disciplinary climate has been shown in previous research to be related to student attainment (OECD, 2007). These items have been used to construct a classroom disciplinary climate index which is used in the regression analyses described below. In the following sections, factors associated with a positive and negative classroom disciplinary climate are presented to better understand how to promote a classroom disciplinary climate that is conducive to student learning.

TEACHERS' CHARACTERISTICS AND CLASSROOM DISCIPLINARY CLIMATE AND TEACHERS' SELF-EFFICACY

As detailed in Table 7.1, the variables included in Bloc 1 are background variables describing teachers' characteristics and the schools in which they teach. They include teachers' demographic characteristics and specific characteristics of teachers' careers such as their employment status. In addition, a number of variables measuring the socio-economic background of the students in teachers' classes and schools are included in the net models estimated for each TALIS country.

Table 7.4 presents the variables in this bloc and illustrate whether they are statistically significant in the *gross*, *net* and *final net* models estimated for each country. The table also illustrates the direction of the coefficients for the variables found to be statistically significant for each country. A "+" represents a positive relationship with the dependent variable and a "–" a negative relationship. A number of variables are included in the estimates of classroom disciplinary climate and self-efficacy which describe pertinent aspects of teachers' jobs and their careers. Measures of full-time employment, employment on a permanent contract, and number of years of teaching are significantly associated with both classroom disciplinary climate and teachers' reported self-efficacy in some TALIS countries. Across TALIS countries, the strongest relationships are between classroom disciplinary climate and number of years of teaching and employment on a permanent contract. As these two variables are correlated, caution is warranted in interpreting their relationships with both classroom disciplinary climate and self-efficacy. However, it would appear that characteristics indicating greater job stability are significantly associated with both classroom disciplinary climate and teachers' reported self-efficacy (Table 7.4).

In the *final net* models estimated for each country, the number of years working as a teacher is significantly associated with a positive classroom disciplinary climate in all TALIS countries except Ireland, Korea, Mexico, Portugal and Turkey. A positive relationship with teachers' reported self-efficacy is found for Korea, Malaysia, Malta, the Slovak Republic and Turkey. Teachers employed on a permanent contract are more likely to teach classes with a more positive classroom disciplinary climate in 11 TALIS countries in the *final net* models. A positive relationship was also evident for teachers' reported self-efficacy, which is positively associated with employment on a permanent basis in the *final net* models estimated for Belgium (Fl.), Denmark, Estonia, Korea, Norway, Slovenia and Turkey. Teachers employed on a full-time basis are also significantly more likely to teach classes with a more positive classroom disciplinary climate in the *final net* models estimated for Austria, Estonia, Ireland, Lithuania and Portugal. A positive relationship with teachers' self-efficacy is also evident in the *final net* models estimated for Australia, Austria, Denmark, Italy, Korea and the Slovak Republic (Table 7.4).

This adds to the results presented in Chapter 4 which demonstrate a positive relationship between teachers' years of experience and classroom climate, teachers' reported self-efficacy and a number of teaching practices. There may be a number of explanations for these relationships. First, more experienced teachers may have honed their teaching practices and become more effective in their teaching and in creating a positive classroom climate. Second, experience may be inversely related to expectations of self-efficacy and classroom climate. Younger teachers may have high and perhaps unrealistic expectations about effective teaching and classroom disciplinary climate, which may lead to reports of less self-efficacy and a less positive classroom climate.

The gender distribution of the teacher workforce detailed in Chapter 2 shows a large majority of female teachers in a number of TALIS countries (Table 2.1). There are some significant gender differences in regard to classroom disciplinary climate and teachers' reported self-efficacy, although they are not significant in the *final net* models estimated for many TALIS countries. Female teachers are significantly more likely than male teachers to report teaching in a positive classroom disciplinary climate in Austria, Denmark, the Slovak Republic and Slovenia and significantly less likely to do so in Brazil and Malaysia.

The impact of teachers' initial level of education was estimated with a variable categorising teachers with an education qualification above the Bachelor's degree level. Teachers in Brazil, Malta and Norway with initial education of this level or above were significantly more likely to teach classes with a poorer classroom disciplinary climate in the *final net* models estimated for each country. However, the proportion of teachers with this level of education was small in some countries, particularly Brazil (see Table 2.2). In addition, these teachers reported greater levels of self-efficacy in the *final net* models for Korea, Malaysia, Mexico, Norway and Portugal (Table 7.4a). In some countries there have been concerns that less qualified teachers are working in the more challenging schools that serve either more socio-economically disadvantaged students or those with specific learning needs (OECD, 2005). If these concerns were evident in teachers' reports of classroom disciplinary climate and self-efficacy, then there would be significant differences between the results of the *gross* and *net* (which controls for socio-economic background characteristics) models estimated for each country. However, the results presented in Table 7.4 show little evidence of this. In most countries, the significance of teachers' education did not change between the estimated *gross* and *net* models.

Teachers' reports of student ability is the most significant socio-economic background variable associated with both classroom disciplinary climate teachers' and reported self-efficacy. It is significant across all TALIS countries, with lower/higher levels of reported student ability associated in the *final net* models estimated for each country with poorer/better classroom disciplinary climate. Student ability is significantly positively related to teachers' reported self-efficacy in all countries but Ireland, Malaysia, the Slovak Republic, Slovenia and Turkey. Teachers' reports of parental education levels are also significant for classroom disciplinary climate but in fewer countries. Classrooms with students with more highly qualified parents are significantly associated with a positive classroom disciplinary climate in 12 TALIS countries, even when controlling for student ability and the other factors included in the *final net* models estimated for each country (Tables 7.10 and 7.11 available on line).

Box 7.1 Classroom disciplinary climate, teachers' reported self-efficacy and the stability of employment

The length and stability of employment appear to be significantly and positively related to teachers' reported self-efficacy and to classroom disciplinary climate. Teachers with relatively less experience and with less stability in their contractual status were less likely to be teaching classes with a positive classroom disciplinary climate and to report high levels of self-efficacy in their success with students.

- Teachers teaching classes with more positive classroom disciplinary climate are those with more experience (significant in 18 TALIS countries), employed on a permanent contract (11 TALIS countries) and on a full-time basis (5 TALIS countries).

- Teachers who are significantly more likely to report higher levels of reported self-efficacy are employed on a permanent contract (significant in 7 TALIS countries), employed on a full-time basis (6 TALIS countries), and have had more experience working as a teacher (5 countries).

....

Note: All of the results are from the *final net* models estimated for each country unless otherwise specified.

TEACHERS' PROFESSIONAL DEVELOPMENT AND CLASSROOM DISCIPLINARY CLIMATE AND TEACHERS' SELF-EFFICACY

This section presents the first extensions of the regression analyses into the main analytical themes of the previous chapters through the inclusion of the thematic blocs in the modelling. It begins with the inclusion of variables representing teachers' professional development, thus building on Chapter 3. As detailed in Table 7.1, the bloc of variables measuring aspects of teachers' professional development in the estimation include:

- Number of days of professional development in the 18 months prior to the survey.
- School providing formal induction process for teachers.
- School providing mentor for new teachers.

Table 7.5 presents the variables in this bloc that are statistically significant in the *gross, net* and *final net* models estimated for each country. The table also illustrates the direction of the coefficients for the variables that are statistically significant for each country.

The amount of professional development undertaken by teachers is significantly associated with classroom disciplinary climate in the *net* models estimated for five countries. In Australia, Korea, Portugal, the Slovak Republic and Slovenia, an increase in the number of days of teachers' professional development is associated with an improved classroom disciplinary climate net of the background characteristics discussed previously (*i.e.* in the *net* models for each country). However, only in Australia is the relationship significant in the *final net* models. The amount of professional development was significantly associated with teachers' self-efficacy in 11 TALIS countries (Table 7.5a). Teachers who undertook more days of professional development were more likely to report increased self-efficacy in Denmark, Estonia, Iceland, Italy, Korea, Lithuania, Malaysia, Malta, Mexico, Portugal and Slovenia in the *final net* models (Table 7.5a). Chapter 4 shows that teachers who engage in professional development tend to use specific teaching practices more often. This may also translate into greater teacher self-efficacy, although the TALIS data do not allow for identifying causal links.

In Hungary, the number of days of teachers' professional development is significant in the *gross* but not the *net* model (Table 7.5). In other words, the greater the amount of professional development undertaken by teachers in Hungary, the greater the likelihood of teaching with a positive classroom disciplinary climate. However, this relationship is not statistically significant once background characteristics are included (the *net* model). This indicates that the amount of professional development undertaken by Hungarian teachers is related to either their personal background characteristics or to the socio-economic background characteristics of the schools in which they teach.

Two further aspects of teachers' professional development are also included in the modelling. Induction and mentoring policies and practices have grown in importance in a number of countries in recent years, with the introduction of methods to assist new teachers and to improve learning and support to teachers within schools (OECD, 2005). Chapter 3 reveals that over two-thirds of teachers work in schools with a formal induction process for teachers new to the school. Moreover, three-quarters of teachers work in schools with a mentoring programme or policy for new teachers (Table 3.6).

Box 7.2 Professional development and classroom disciplinary climate and teachers' reported self-efficacy

- The amount of professional development undertaken by teachers is significantly related to teachers' reported self-efficacy in just under half of TALIS countries. It is significantly related to classroom disciplinary climate in only one TALIS country.

  – The more days of professional development undertaken by teachers the greater the likelihood of higher reported levels of self-efficacy in 11 TALIS countries.

- Teachers working in schools with either mentoring or induction programmes are, in general, not significantly more or less likely to report higher levels of self-efficacy or classroom disciplinary climate.

Note: All of the results are from the *final net* models estimated for each country unless otherwise specified.

In terms of the association with classroom disciplinary climate, these programmes are not as significant as the number of days of professional development undertaken by teachers. The effects of these policies are only significant in a few TALIS countries and the associations are often negative, indicating that these programmes exist in schools with a relatively poorer classroom disciplinary climate. The practice of induction and mentoring programmes in schools also does not have a significant association with teachers' reported self-efficacy with significant relationships found only in Bulgaria and Estonia (Table 7.5a).

TEACHING PRACTICES, BELIEFS AND ATTITUDES AND CLASSROOM DISCIPLINARY CLIMATE AND TEACHERS' SELF-EFFICACY

The next thematic bloc of variables to be included in the estimates of classroom disciplinary climate and teachers' self-efficacy concerns the characteristics of teachers' teaching practices, beliefs and attitudes which are discussed in Chapter 4. This bloc of independent variables includes:

- Index of direct transmission beliefs about instruction.
- Index of constructivist beliefs about instruction.
- Index of classroom teaching practice: structuring.
- Index of classroom teaching practice: student-oriented.
- Index of classroom teaching practice: enhanced activities.
- Index of professional collaboration.
- Index of exchange and co-ordination for teaching.
- Index of teacher-student relations.

The modelling presented here builds upon that of Chapter 4, which, while narrower in focus than the modelling in this chapter, also analyses aspects of classroom disciplinary climate and self-efficacy. However, there are slight differences due to the scope of the variables included and the methods of estimating the models (see Annex A1.4 for further details). Given the greater scope of the objectives of the modelling in this chapter, more variables are included and missing values are imputed to ensure adequate sample size. These changes are made to reflect differences in the scope and purpose of the modelling while ensuring that accurate measures are maintained.

Table 7.6 presents the variables in this bloc that were statistically significant in the *gross*, *net* and *final net* models estimated for each country. The table also illustrates the direction of the coefficients for the variables that are statistically significant for each country.

Teaching practices, beliefs and attitudes and classroom disciplinary climate

As discussed in Chapter 4, two indices are constructed to measure teachers' beliefs: direct transmission and constructivist beliefs about instruction. Both are significantly associated with classroom disciplinary climate in a number of countries but often with opposing effects. In Hungary, Italy, Korea, Poland and Slovenia, teachers with stronger constructivist beliefs about instruction are more likely to teach classes with a positive classroom disciplinary climate in the *final net* models estimated for each of these countries. Given the positive association between classroom disciplinary climate and constructivist beliefs about instruction, it is particularly interesting that direct transmission beliefs about instruction are found to have a negative association with classroom disciplinary climate in nine countries in the *net* models. Teachers with stronger beliefs about the importance of the direct transmission style of instruction are more likely to be teaching in classrooms with a poorer classroom disciplinary climate. In the *final net* models estimated for each country, direct transmission beliefs are significantly associated with a negative classroom disciplinary climate in Belgium (Fl.), Korea, Norway, Poland, Portugal,

Slovenia and Spain. This is particularly important for policy makers, school principals, teachers and other stakeholders in Korea, Poland and Slovenia, where the positive association between constructivist beliefs and classroom disciplinary climate and the negative association with direct transmission beliefs are both significant. Teachers' reports of teacher-student relations are significantly positively associated with classroom disciplinary climate in every TALIS country except Malta in the *final net* models estimated for each country.

Four indices are developed to measure the practices teachers reported using in the classroom. As discussed in Chapter 4, these indices measure different aspects of teaching practices and complement the analysis of teachers' beliefs presented above. Teaching practices emphasising structured classes and learning programmes for students are positively associated with classroom disciplinary climate in the *final net* models estimated for 11 TALIS countries (Australia, Austria, Belgium (Fl.), Bulgaria, Hungary, Ireland, Italy, Korea, Mexico, Portugal, and Spain). In contrast, in Malaysia, teachers who reported greater use of these teaching practices are more likely to teach classes with a poorer classroom disciplinary climate. Again, care must be taken when interpreting this relationship especially in terms of causality. Teachers in Malaysia may utilise more structured techniques in their classrooms that already had a poor classroom disciplinary climate; or, alternatively, structured techniques may have created a poorer classroom disciplinary climate. TALIS does not provide evidence in support of either interpretation.

Student-oriented teaching practices are significantly associated with classroom disciplinary climate in Austria, Brazil, Estonia, Lithuania, Malaysia, Poland, Slovenia and Turkey in the *final net* models estimated for each country (Table 7.6). Teachers in these countries who reported a greater emphasis on student-oriented teaching practices are significantly more likely to have classes with a more positive classroom disciplinary climate. In Denmark and Ireland a significant relationship is also found in the *gross* models (but not the *net* models) but in these countries the association is negative. In other words, teachers are more likely to teach classes with a poor classroom disciplinary climate if they favour student-oriented teaching practices. This indicates that these teaching practices in these countries are significantly associated with various background characteristics but to differing degrees. Extending this analysis, teaching practices engaging students in enhanced activities are also significantly associated with classroom disciplinary climate in four countries. The relationship was negative in Austria, Belgium (Fl.), Lithuania and Malaysia in the *final net* models estimated for these countries.

These findings build on the results in Chapter 4 which present regressions estimating classroom climate with a narrower set of independent variables (Table 4.10). As mentioned, an additional three sets of independent variables are included in the regression results presented in this chapter. These comprise: a broader set of teacher and school background variables; variables from other analytical blocs that measure characteristics discussed in Chapters 3, 5 and 6; and the inclusion of multiple variables measuring teachers' beliefs and practices. This chapter's results confirm that the strength of these relationships with classroom disciplinary climate are not particularly affected by the inclusion of additional independent variables. Characteristics such as school leadership styles, the level and type of appraisal and feedback, and other teaching beliefs and practices do not appear to significantly affect the relationships between these teaching practices and classroom disciplinary climate. Again, this draws attention to the individual nature of teaching practices and the fact that variations in such practices are largely due to individual rather than school-level factors. In addition, the greater significance of the association between structured teaching practices and classroom disciplinary climate as compared to student-oriented and enhanced activities teaching practices still holds in estimates that include a broader set of independent variables and, perhaps of most interest, even when controlling for differences in teachers' beliefs about instruction.

Two measures of teachers' co-operation are developed in the TALIS analysis and discussed in Chapter 4: teachers' professional collaboration and the level of exchange and co-ordination for teaching. Neither of these measures is significantly associated with classroom disciplinary climate to the same extent as teachers' beliefs and practices. Teachers' professional collaboration is significantly positively associated with classroom disciplinary climate in Bulgaria, Italy and Spain and negatively associated with classroom disciplinary climate in Austria and Malaysia in the *final net* models. The level of exchange and co-ordination for teaching is significantly related to classroom disciplinary climate in Austria, Malaysia and Mexico in the *final net* models (Table 7.6).

Teaching practices, beliefs and attitudes and teachers' self-efficacy

Both direct transmission beliefs and constructivist beliefs about instruction are significantly associated with classroom disciplinary climate in some TALIS countries. Teachers with stronger constructivist beliefs about instruction are also significantly more likely to have higher levels of self-efficacy in all countries except Brazil, Bulgaria, Malaysia and Mexico in the *final net* models. Direct transmission beliefs about instruction are also significantly positively associated with self-efficacy in all countries except Australia, Estonia, Hungary, Iceland, Malaysia and Malta in the *final net* models (Table 7.6a). This reflects results presented in Chapter 4 indicating that the strength of teachers' beliefs about effective instruction are related to their self-efficacy. Previous research adds further support to this finding. Workers who have been successful with particular working methods have been found to show a stronger relationship between such methods and their perceived self-efficacy (Bandura, 1989).

A number of classroom practices that are significantly related to classroom disciplinary climate also have a significant relationship with teachers' reported self-efficacy. Structured teaching practices are positively significantly related to teachers' reported self-efficacy in 11 TALIS countries in the *final net* models. Teachers in Australia, Austria, Belgium (Fl.), Iceland, Ireland, Korea, Malaysia, Mexico, Norway, Portugal and Spain who reported emphasising structured teaching practices in their classroom have higher levels of reported self-efficacy (Table 7.6a). In Poland this relationship is significant but negative so that teachers were less likely to report higher levels of self-efficacy if they reported using structured practices in their classrooms. Student-oriented teaching practices have a significant positive relationship with teachers' reported self-efficacy in Austria, Estonia, Hungary, Korea, Lithuania, Portugal, the Slovak Republic, Slovenia and Turkey in the *final net* models. It should also be noted that, as shown in Chapter 4, there is a significant relationship in most TALIS countries between student-oriented teaching practices and constructivist beliefs about instruction (Table 4.9). This relationship may reduce the significance of that between student-oriented practices and self-efficacy found here given the finding about the significance of constructivist beliefs about instruction in estimations of teachers' reported self-efficacy.

Extending the analysis to teachers' reports of classroom practices that involve engaging students in enhanced activities, as in the case of the findings on the relationship with classroom disciplinary climate, there is a significant relationship with self-efficacy in fewer TALIS countries than for other teaching practices. In Ireland, Italy and Poland teachers who reported engaging their students in enhanced activities in the classroom were more likely to report greater levels of self-efficacy. However, in Austria a greater reported use of enhanced activities in the classroom is associated with a decrease in teachers' reported levels of self-efficacy in the *final net* model (Table 7.6a).

The two measures of teachers' co-operation used in this analysis are an index of teachers' professional collaboration and an index of exchange and co-ordination for teaching. The former is significantly associated with teachers' reported self-efficacy in ten TALIS countries in the *final net* models. The more teachers in Austria, Belgium (Fl.), Bulgaria, Estonia, Hungary, Iceland, Korea, Poland, Portugal and Spain engaged in professional collaboration, the greater their reported levels of self-efficacy. This is also true for Malaysia and Norway for teachers' levels of exchange and co-ordination for teaching in the *final net* models (Table 7.6a).

Teachers' reports about teacher-student relations in their schools is the only measure of teacher practices and beliefs that is found to have a statistically significant relationship with teachers' reported self-efficacy in all TALIS countries in the *final net* models (Table 7.6a). This is also found when modelling the relationship with classroom disciplinary climate (except for Malta), a further sign of the importance of teacher-student relations in school education.

Box 7.3 Disciplinary climate and teachers' reported self-efficacy and teaching practices and beliefs

- Stronger beliefs about instruction are related to stronger self-efficacy regardless of the type of beliefs. Teachers with stronger constructivist beliefs about instruction are significantly more likely to report higher levels of self-efficacy in all TALIS countries except Brazil, Bulgaria, Malaysia and Mexico. Moreover, direct transmission beliefs about instruction are significantly positively associated with self-efficacy in all TALIS countries except Australia, Estonia, Hungary, Iceland, Malaysia and Malta.

- Beliefs about instruction have opposing relationships with classroom disciplinary climate in some countries. Teachers with stronger constructivist beliefs are more likely to teach classes with a positive classroom disciplinary climate in 5 TALIS countries. However, direct transmission beliefs about instruction are found to have a negative association with classroom disciplinary climate in 7 TALIS countries.

  - This is particularly important for policy makers, school principals, teachers and other stakeholders in Korea, Poland and Slovenia where the positive association between constructivist beliefs and classroom disciplinary climate and the negative association with direct transmission beliefs are both significant.

- Teachers' reports of teacher-student relations is the only variable measuring teachers' beliefs and classroom practices that is significantly positively associated with classroom disciplinary climate (except in Malta) and with teachers' reported self-efficacy in every TALIS country.

- A number of teaching practices are significantly related to classroom disciplinary climate and teachers' self-efficacy:

  - Teaching practices emphasising structured classes and learning programmes for students are positively associated with classroom disciplinary climate in 11 TALIS countries and with teachers' reported self-efficacy in 11 TALIS countries.

  - Student-oriented teaching practices are significantly positively associated with classroom disciplinary climate in eight countries and with teachers' reported self-efficacy in 9 TALIS countries.

  - Teachers' professional collaboration is significantly positively associated with teachers' reported self-efficacy in ten countries but with classroom disciplinary climate in only 3 TALIS countries.

....

Note: All of the results are from the *final net* models estimated for each country unless otherwise specified.

TEACHER APPRAISAL AND FEEDBACK AND CLASSROOM DISCIPLINARY CLIMATE AND TEACHERS' SELF-EFFICACY

The next bloc of variables considered in the analysis includes aspects of school evaluations and teacher appraisal and feedback which are the focus of Chapter 5. A number of issues discussed in Chapter 5 can be considered important in school education and in the careers and working lives of teachers. They include the frequency and criteria of school evaluations, the potential impact of such evaluations, the frequency and criteria of teacher appraisal and feedback, the outcomes and impact of such appraisal and feedback, and various issues relating to the structure of school evaluation that affect teachers and their careers.

Given the breadth of the analysis in Chapter 5 and the restrictions of the modelling, only a subset of variables are included in the bloc of variables depicting school evaluations and teacher appraisal and feedback. The independent variables included in the modelling are:

- Did not have a school evaluation within the previous 5 years.
- Importance of aspect for school evaluations: student test scores.
- School evaluation published.
- Did not receive teacher appraisal or feedback from any source at this school.
- Importance in teacher appraisal and feedback: student test scores.
- Importance in teacher appraisal and feedback: innovative teaching practices.
- Importance in teacher appraisal and feedback: professional development the teacher has undertaken.
- Impact of teacher appraisal and feedback: a change in salary.
- Impact of teacher appraisal and feedback: opportunities for professional development activities.
- Impact of teacher appraisal and feedback: public recognition from the principal and/or your colleagues.
- Impact of teacher appraisal and feedback: changes in the teacher's work responsibilities that make the job more attractive.
- Whether teachers believe that the most effective teachers in their school receive the greatest monetary or non-monetary rewards.

In the same manner as for previous blocs, the bloc of variables concerned with school evaluation and teacher appraisal and feedback are included in *gross*, *net* and *final net* models estimating both classroom disciplinary climate and teachers' reported self-efficacy. Table 7.7 presents the variables in this bloc that are statistically significant in the *gross*, *net* and *final net* models estimated for each country. The table also illustrates the direction of the coefficients for the variables that are statistically significant for each country.

Two sets of estimations were carried out for the analysis of variables of teacher appraisal and feedback. The first estimates the impact of having a school evaluation and teacher appraisal and feedback, and the second estimates the impact of various important aspects and outcomes of school evaluation and teachers' appraisal and feedback. The variables measuring the important aspects and outcomes of school evaluation and teacher appraisal and feedback are only reported by teachers in schools where such activities took place. For this reason, these variables are modelled separately. The results of both sets of estimations are discussed below.

Three variables measuring important aspects of school evaluations of interest for policy makers and stakeholders are included in the modelling. The first identifies whether a school had undergone either an external or a self-evaluation within the last five years. The second measures the importance of student test scores in the school evaluation and thus indicates the role of student outcomes in the evaluations of schools. The third concerns whether or not the results of such an evaluation were published.

School evaluations are found to have little significant impact on classroom disciplinary climate. No significant relationship is found in any TALIS country between classroom disciplinary climate or teacher self-efficacy and whether or not a school had either an external or self-evaluation within the last five years in the *final net* models estimated for each country (Table 7.7a). This is also the case for the emphasis on student test scores in school evaluations and the publication of information on school evaluations. This is a contentious issue in a number of countries but does not show a significant positive or negative relationship with classroom disciplinary climate in any TALIS country.

The lack of significant findings in these relationships does not necessarily mean that the findings themselves are of little importance. These variables are included in the modelling as they are important policy malleable aspects of the evaluative framework of school education. In some countries, the publication of school evaluation results and a strong emphasis on student outcomes in evaluating schools have been contentious practices or policy issues. The finding that these factors are not significantly associated with classroom disciplinary climate may be important for policy makers or administrators considering such policy issues, particularly if, for example, the impact on classroom disciplinary climate is considered a reason for either supporting or opposing such moves.

In Brazil, Denmark, Portugal and the Slovak Republic the practice of teacher appraisal and feedback is significantly associated with classroom disciplinary climate. Teachers in these countries who had received some appraisal and feedback on their work as teachers in their school were significantly more likely to teach classes with a positive classroom disciplinary climate (Table 7.7). However, this was not significant in the *final net* models estimated for these countries. It therefore appears that in these countries, the emphasis on various criteria in appraisal and feedback discussed below (which is, by definition, correlated with whether or not teachers receive appraisal or feedback) had a stronger impact upon classroom disciplinary climate than simply whether that appraisal and feedback existed in the first place. In 11 countries a significant relationship is found between teachers who received appraisal and feedback and their reported self-efficacy. Teachers in Australia, Belgium (Fl.), Brazil, Bulgaria, Hungary, Ireland, Italy, Mexico, Portugal and Spain reported higher levels of self-efficacy if they had received appraisal and feedback on their work as teachers in their school in the *net* models (Table 7.7a). However, these relationships are not significant in the *final net* models estimated for each country. This may be because of the association between the receipt or not of appraisals and feedback and distinct aspects and impacts or outcomes of that appraisal and feedback that are also included as independent variables in the estimations

Three criteria used in teacher appraisal and feedback are included in the analysis to assess whether these are associated with classroom disciplinary climate and teacher self-efficacy. An emphasis on student test scores, innovative teaching practices and teacher professional development are considered in the analysis. Of these, teacher appraisal and feedback emphasising innovative teaching practices is found to have a significant impact in the more TALIS countries (Table 7.7 and Table 7.7a). An emphasis on innovative teaching practices in the appraisal and feedback that teachers received about their work is significantly associated with classroom disciplinary climate in seven TALIS countries in the *net* models estimated for each country (Table 7.7). Teachers in Brazil, Hungary, Lithuania, Mexico, Portugal, the Slovak Republic and Slovenia who received appraisal and feedback emphasising innovative teaching practices were more likely to report teaching classes with a more positive classroom disciplinary climate. However, once variables from other analytical blocs are included in the *final net* models, they are significantly associated with classroom disciplinary climate only in Lithuania, Portugal, the Slovak Republic and Slovenia. Teacher appraisal and feedback that emphasised innovative teaching practices is significantly associated with increased teacher self-efficacy in 11 TALIS countries in the *net* models (Table 7.7a). It is clear however, that this is also correlated with other analytical variables as it is only significant in the *final net* models estimated for Brazil, Iceland and Portugal. The link between an emphasis on innovative teaching practices and self-efficacy is an important finding in its own right. But it is also important considering the discussion in Chapter 5 shows that teachers report receiving little or no recognition for being innovative in their work. This may need to be addressed to better encourage innovative teaching practices and possibly thereby encourage greater teacher self-efficacy.

An important element of Chapter 5 concerns the linkages between teachers' professional development and teacher appraisal and feedback. The discussion emphasised the extent to which teacher appraisal and feedback is used to identify and then plan teachers' professional development activities. Once teachers have completed professional development, the impact and value of that professional development, and the changes resulting from it, can be incorporated into teachers' appraisal and feedback. The emphasis on teachers' professional development is positively associated with classroom disciplinary climate in the *net* models for Italy and Korea (Table 7.7). In addition, in the *net* models for Austria, Ireland, Korea, Lithuania, Mexico and Slovenia, teachers who received appraisal and feedback which emphasised the professional development they had undertaken reported greater levels of self-efficacy (Table 7.7a). However, this was not significant in the *final net* models for these countries. Teacher appraisal and feedback which emphasised student test scores was positively associated with classroom disciplinary climate only in Denmark and was negatively associated with teachers' self-efficacy in Estonia.

The impact and outcomes of teacher appraisal and feedback provide an indication of the role it plays in teachers' careers and their working lives. Four specific outcomes were identified and included in the estimations of classroom disciplinary climate and self-efficacy: whether a teacher had received a change in salary following appraisal and feedback; opportunities for professional development; public recognition from the school principal or school colleagues; and changes in work responsibilities that make a teacher's job more attractive. Of these, public recognition is significantly associated with classroom disciplinary climate and teachers' reported self-efficacy in the greatest number of TALIS countries (Table 7.7a).

A positive classroom disciplinary climate is more likely to exist for teachers who receive public recognition from their school principal or other colleagues in their school. In the *net* models estimated for each country, this relationship is significant in Australia, Belgium (Fl.), Brazil, Bulgaria, Estonia, Korea and Slovenia (Table 7.7). However, in the *final net* models these relationships are not significant in Australia and Slovenia; this points to correlation with variables from other analytical blocs. Associations between teachers' reported self-efficacy and public recognition from the school principal or school colleagues are significant in 11 countries in the *final net* models. Teachers in Austria, Belgium (Fl.), Estonia, Hungary, Ireland, Italy, Korea, Lithuania, Malta, Norway and Spain are significantly more likely to report greater levels of self-efficacy if they received public recognition from the school principal or school colleagues as a consequence of the appraisal and feedback they received about their work (Table 7.7a). Public recognition was the most frequent outcome following teacher appraisal and feedback (Table 5.5) so it is important that it is found to have an impact. It indicates that if the outcomes of appraisal and feedback are strengthened then it may have a greater impact upon teachers and their self-efficacy. Public recognition, while being the most frequent outcome, was only an outcome of appraisal and feedback to a moderate or large degree for 36% of teachers so there is scope to strengthen these links. Moreover, only 9% or teachers reported a moderate or large change in salary and only 16% reported a moderate or large change in career opportunities following appraisal and feedback (Table 5.5). Given that stronger outcomes of appraisal and feedback can have an impact on teacher self-efficacy, this may be an additional argument for strengthening the outcomes of teacher appraisal and feedback.

Changes in work responsibilities that make teachers' jobs more attractive have a significant relationship with teachers' reported self-efficacy in Brazil, Bulgaria, Estonia, Portugal and Slovenia in the *final net* models (Table 7.7a). Significant relationships between these variables may indicate that teacher appraisal and feedback plays a proactive and important role in school development and the organisation of teaching in schools. It may be that effective schools appraise teachers' work and fashion their teaching responsibilities to best utilise the aspects of teachers' skills and abilities that are identified in the appraisal of their work. A change in work responsibilities as a result of teacher appraisal and feedback is not significantly associated with classroom disciplinary climate in the *final net* models for any TALIS country (Table 7.7).

Chapter 5 reports that the majority of teachers do not work in schools where they believe the most effective teachers receive the greatest recognition. Similarly, approximately three-quarters of teachers reported that they would receive no recognition for increasing either the effectiveness or level of innovation in their teaching.

A similar proportion of teachers disagreed with the statement that the most effective teachers in their school receive the greatest monetary or non-monetary rewards. It is important therefore that, even given a relatively small number of teachers in a number of countries agreeing with this statement, it has a significant and positive impact upon teachers' self-efficacy in the *net* models in Brazil, Iceland, Italy, Korea, Malaysia, Portugal, Spain, and Turkey. However, this was only significant in the *final net* models in Brazil (Table 7.7a).

Box 7.4 Classroom disciplinary climate and teachers' reported self-efficacy and teachers' appraisal and feedback

- Teachers who received no appraisal and feedback were less likely to have higher levels of reported self-efficacy. Yet, this relationship was not significant in the final models indicating that it is related with other factors. There are no significant findings linking classroom disciplinary climate or teachers' self-efficacy with whether or not teachers worked in schools that had conducted school evaluations.

- Teacher appraisal and feedback that focuses on innovative teaching practices was more likely to be related to higher levels of self-efficacy in 3 TALIS countries and of classroom disciplinary climate in 4 TALIS countries. This is potentially important given that the majority of teachers reported that they received little or no recognition for being innovative in their work and that it was significant in a greater number of countries in the bloc models estimated for each country.

- Teachers who received public recognition from the school principal or their colleagues as a consequence of their appraisal and feedback were more likely to have higher levels of classroom disciplinary climate in 5 TALIS countries and reported self-efficacy in 11 TALIS countries.

- Changes in work responsibilities that make teachers' jobs more attractive are found to have a significant positive relationship with teachers' reported self-efficacy in 5 TALIS countries. This may indicate that teacher appraisal and feedback plays a proactive and important role in school development and the organisation of teaching in schools. It may be that effective schools appraise teachers' work and fashion their teaching responsibilities to make the best use of the skills and abilities identified in the appraisal of teachers' work.

....

Note: All of the results are from the *final net* models estimated for each country unless otherwise specified.

SCHOOL LEADERSHIP AND CLASSROOM DISCIPLINARY CLIMATE AND TEACHERS' SELF-EFFICACY

A final analytical bloc of variables is added to analyse the association between classroom disciplinary climate and teachers' reported self-efficacy and the specific school leadership styles discussed in Chapter 6. This bloc of school leadership variables includes:

- School leadership index: Management-school goals.

- School leadership index: Instructional management.

- School leadership index: Direct supervision of instruction in the school.

- School leadership index: Accountable management.

- School leadership index: Bureaucratic management.

Table 7.8 presents the variables in this analytical bloc that are statistically significant in the *gross*, *net* and *final net* models estimated for each country. The table also illustrates the direction of the coefficients for the variables that are statistically significant for each country.

Overall, school leadership styles are not significantly associated with teachers' reported self-efficacy or classroom disciplinary climate. For each school leadership style, significant relationships were only found in a few TALIS countries. Two important factors should be considered when interpreting these findings. First, as shown in Chapter 6, various aspects of school leadership are significantly associated with specific teaching beliefs and practices that are significantly associated with classroom disciplinary climate and teachers' reported self-efficacy. The linkages between school leadership styles and classroom disciplinary climate and teacher self-efficacy may therefore be indirect. Second, given that this is a cross-sectional study, caution must be used in inferring causality (or a lack of it). For example, if an indirect effect exists for school leadership it may be better analysed with longitudinal data which can better track impacts on classroom disciplinary climate and teachers' reported self-efficacy.

Table 7.8 shows some significant findings for school leadership styles in the *final net* models estimating classroom disciplinary climate and teacher self-efficacy. The school leadership style of framing and communicating school goals is significantly and positively related to classroom disciplinary climate in Malta and significantly and positively related to both classroom disciplinary climate and teachers' reported self-efficacy in Portugal. Promoting instructional improvements and professional development is significantly related to classroom climate only in Slovenia and the relationship is negative. But it should be emphasised that irrespective of this, teacher professional development is significantly related to both classroom disciplinary climate and teacher self-efficacy in a number of TALIS countries. School leadership emphasising the supervision of instruction in schools is also negatively related to classroom disciplinary climate in Malta. Teachers' reported self-efficacy and the accountability role of a school leader are significantly related in Ireland. The index measuring the bureaucratic role of a school leader is significantly related to classroom disciplinary climate in Estonia, Italy and Norway.

Box 7.5 Classroom disciplinary climate and teachers' reported self-efficacy and school leadership

In general school leadership styles are not found to have a significant effect on teachers' reported self-efficacy or classroom disciplinary climate. For each school leadership style, significant relationships are only found in a few TALIS countries. However, as shown in Chapter 6, various aspects of school leadership are significantly associated with specific teaching beliefs and practices that are significantly associated with classroom disciplinary climate and teachers' reported self-efficacy. The linkages between school leadership styles and classroom disciplinary climate and teacher self-efficacy may therefore be indirect.

SCHOOL AUTONOMY AND SCHOOL CLIMATE AND CLASSROOM DISCIPLINARY CLIMATE AND TEACHERS' SELF-EFFICACY

A final bloc of variables is included in the modelling to capture the relationships between certain school characteristics and teachers' self-efficacy and classroom disciplinary climate. It draws on the data first described in Chapter 2 and focuses on aspects such as the level of autonomy enjoyed by schools and specific measures of school resources. It provides a more complete estimate of classroom disciplinary climate and teachers' self-efficacy and therefore permits a more thorough analysis of the magnitude of the association with the independent variables. The following bloc of independent variables is added to the modelling:

- Index of school climate: student delinquency.
- Index of school climate: teachers' morale.
- Index of lack of personnel (teachers, technicians, instructional support personnel, other support personnel).
- Index of shortage of materials (instructional materials, computers, equipment, library materials).
- Index of school autonomy in hiring teachers, determining salaries.
- Index of school autonomy in budgeting (formulating and allocating the school budget).
- Index of school autonomy in student policy and textbooks.
- Index of school autonomy in curriculum (courses offered, course content).
- School average class size.
- Public school.

Table 7.9 presents the variables in this analytical bloc that are statistically significant in the *gross*, *net* and *final net* models estimated for each country. The table also illustrates the direction of the coefficients for the variables that are statistically significant for each country. Few significant relationships are found between these variables and classroom disciplinary climate or teachers' self-efficacy. There is a significant negative relationship between class size and classroom disciplinary climate in 19 countries in the *final net* models. However, this is not the case for teachers' reported self-efficacy. Few significant findings are evident for measures of school autonomy or school principals' reports of the extent to which a lack of school resources hinders instruction in their school.

Indices of school resources are significantly associated with teachers' reported self-efficacy only in the *final net* model estimated for Austria (Table 7.9a). However, a lack of school personnel has a positively significant relationship to classroom disciplinary climate in Iceland and Lithuania and a shortage of materials for instruction is significantly associated with classroom disciplinary climate in Poland in the *final net* models. School sector is significantly associated with classroom disciplinary climate and teachers' reported self-efficacy in four countries. A more negative classroom disciplinary climate is more likely in public schools in Denmark and Malta. In Ireland, lower levels of teachers' reported self-efficacy are also more likely to be found in public schools. However, in Norway, public school teachers are more likely to have reported higher levels of self-efficacy in the *final net* model.

School autonomy is significantly related to classroom disciplinary climate and teacher self-efficacy in a few TALIS countries (Table 7.9 and Table 7.9a). The index of school autonomy for hiring teachers and determining salaries is significantly associated with classroom disciplinary climate in Australia, Austria (where the relationship is negative) and Poland, and significantly associated with teacher self-efficacy in Belgium (Fl.) (where the relationship is negative) in the *final net* models. The index of school autonomy for school budgeting is significantly negatively related to teachers' reported self-efficacy in Poland and Portugal.

Box 7.6 Classroom disciplinary climate and teachers' reported self-efficacy and various school-level factors

In general, school-level factors measured here are not significantly associated with classroom disciplinary climate or teachers' self-efficacy. A significant negative relationship is found between class size and classroom disciplinary climate for most TALIS countries but not for teachers' reported self-efficacy.

....

Note: All of the results are from the *final net* models estimated for each country unless otherwise specified.

CONCLUSIONS AND IMPLICATIONS FOR POLICY AND PRACTICE

A number of variables are significantly associated with classroom disciplinary climate and teachers' self-efficacy. There is also substantial variation in the variables that are significant across TALIS countries, indicating that structural and school-level factors operate differently in different countries. For example, the relationships between teachers' reported self-efficacy and teachers' professional collaboration and structured teaching practices are significant in the *final net* models estimated for just over half of TALIS countries but, in the main, countries with a significant relationship between self-efficacy and professional collaboration do not exhibit a significant relationship between self-efficacy and structured teaching practices.

There are some commonalities in the findings across countries. Characteristics that are more closely related to the dependent variables of classroom disciplinary climate and teacher self-efficacy are more likely to be significant. Teachers' beliefs are significantly associated with classroom disciplinary climate across virtually all TALIS countries and other classroom factors such as student ability and class size also have significant associations in most TALIS countries. Given the connection between teaching practices and beliefs and classroom disciplinary climate and self-efficacy, it is perhaps not surprising that these variables are of greater significance. The greater proximity of these independent variables to the dependent variables is evident in their statistical significance and quantitative importance in a greater number of TALIS countries.

With regard to associations with classroom disciplinary climate, the variables that are significant in the *final net* models for over two-thirds of TALIS countries are the number of years working as a teacher, teaching practices emphasising teacher-student relations, school average class size, and lower and higher average student ability. In the *final net* models estimated for teachers' reported self-efficacy, the variables that are significant in at least two-thirds of countries are: constructivist beliefs about instruction, direct transmission beliefs about instruction and higher average student ability.

The significance of the above variables does not mean that issues such as the type of professional development, school evaluation, school leadership and other school-level variables are not important. Their effect may be indirect and more easily measured in longitudinal studies which can more readily track longer-term and indirect associations. A number of these factors are associated in the *gross* and *net* models estimated for each country but are not significant in the *final net* models which find mainly teaching beliefs and practices variables to be significant. In addition, Chapter 6 discusses significant associations between specific leadership styles and some of the teaching beliefs and practices that are significant in the *final net* models estimated for each country. This may be seen as stronger evidence of an indirect link with classroom disciplinary climate and teacher self-efficacy. It is also worth noting that the dependent variables of teachers' self-efficacy and classroom disciplinary climate can be used as independent variables in other modelling to emphasise, for example, the role of school leadership and school evaluation and teacher appraisal and feedback. Further analysis of the TALIS data may yield more findings of these relationships.

ADDITIONAL MATERIAL

The following additional material relevant to this chapter is available on line at:
StatLink 📊 http://dx.doi.org/10.1787/608030545172

List of independent variables

Blocs of independent variables	Variable name
School socio-economic background	Teacher level: ability of students in class lower than the average at the same grade level
	Teacher level: ability of students in class higher than the average at the same grade level
	Teacher level: percentage of students in class speaking instruction language
	Teacher level: percentage of students in class with at least one parent with completed ISCED 5 or higher
	School level: percentage of students in school speaking instruction language
	School level: percentage of students in school with at least one parent with completed ISCED 5 or higher
	School level: ability of students in class lower than the average
	School level: ability of students in class higher than the average
Bloc 1: Teacher characteristics	Female teacher
	Teacher employed full-time
	Teacher employed on a permanent contract
	Teacher's education: above bachelor degree
	Number of years for teaching
Bloc 2: Teacher professional development	Number of days for professional development
	School providing induction process for teachers
	School providing mentor for new teachers
Bloc 3: Teacher beliefs and practices	Index of teacher-student relations
	Index of classroom teaching practice: structuring
	Index of classroom teaching practice: student-oriented
	Index of classroom teaching practice: enhanced activities
	Index of direct transmission beliefs about instruction
	Index of constructivist beliefs about instruction
	Index of exchange and co-ordination for teaching
	Index of professional collaboration
Bloc 4: Teacher appraisal and feedback	Never received appraisal or feedback from any source
	Never received a school evaluation within the last 5 years
	Teacher perceives that effective teachers receive more monetary or non-monetary rewards in the school
	Important aspect for teacher appraisal: student test scores
	Important aspect for teacher appraisal: innovative teaching practices
	Important aspect for teacher appraisal: professional development the teacher has undertaken
	Teacher appraisal and feedback impact: a change in salary
	Teacher appraisal and feedback impact: opportunities for professional development activities
	Teacher appraisal and feedback impact: public-private recognition from the principal and/or your colleagues
	Teacher appraisal and feedback impact: changes in the teacher's work responsibilities that make the job more attractive (1=moderate or large change; 0=others)
	School evaluation published
	Important aspect for school evaluations: student test scores
Bloc 5: School leadership	Index of management-school goals
	Index of instructional management
	Index of direct supervision of instruction in the school
	Index of accountable management
	Index of bureaucratic management
Bloc 6: School autonomy and resources	Index of school climate: student delinquency
	Index of school climate: teachers' working morale
	Index of a lack of personnel
	Index of school resources: shortage of materials
	Index of school autonomy in hiring teachers, determining salaries
	Index of school autonomy in budgeting (formulating and allocating the school budget)
	Index of school autonomy: student policy and textbooks
	Index of school autonomy in curriculum (courses offered, course content)
	School average class size
	Public school

Source: OECD, *TALIS Database*.
StatLink http://dx.doi.org/10.1787/608030545172

Table 7.2
Index of self-efficacy (2007-08)
In lower secondary schools

	Self Efficacy index	
	Mean	(S.E.)
Australia	0.30	(0.03)
Austria	0.24	(0.02)
Belgium (Fl.)	0.05	(0.02)
Brazil	-0.10	(0.03)
Bulgaria	0.22	(0.03)
Denmark	0.28	(0.03)
Estonia	-0.40	(0.01)
Hungary	-0.42	(0.02)
Iceland	0.34	(0.03)
Ireland	0.30	(0.03)
Italy	0.36	(0.02)
Korea	-0.77	(0.02)
Lithuania	0.06	(0.02)
Malaysia	0.01	(0.03)
Malta	-0.05	(0.03)
Mexico	0.08	(0.03)
Norway	0.51	(0.03)
Poland	-0.14	(0.02)
Portugal	-0.08	(0.02)
Slovak Republic	-0.30	(0.02)
Slovenia	0.01	(0.01)
Spain	-0.45	(0.02)
Turkey	0.00	(0.04)
TALIS average	0.00	(0.01)

Source: OECD, *TALIS Database*.
StatLink http://dx.doi.org/10.1787/608030545172

Table 7.3
Classroom disciplinary climate index (2007-08)
In lower secondary schools

	Classroom disciplinary climate index	
	Mean	(S.E.)
Australia	0.05	(0.03)
Austria	0.25	(0.02)
Belgium (Fl.)	0.08	(0.03)
Brazil	-0.25	(0.02)
Bulgaria	0.15	(0.04)
Denmark	-0.08	(0.04)
Estonia	0.45	(0.02)
Hungary	0.13	(0.04)
Iceland	-0.36	(0.03)
Ireland	0.21	(0.03)
Italy	0.09	(0.02)
Korea	-0.12	(0.02)
Lithuania	0.15	(0.02)
Malaysia	-0.06	(0.03)
Malta	-0.19	(0.03)
Mexico	0.25	(0.02)
Norway	-0.13	(0.04)
Poland	0.14	(0.02)
Portugal	-0.39	(0.03)
Slovak Republic	-0.11	(0.03)
Slovenia	0.24	(0.03)
Spain	-0.47	(0.03)
Turkey	-0.07	(0.05)
TALIS average	0.00	(0.01)

Source: OECD, *TALIS Database*.
StatLink http://dx.doi.org/10.1787/608030545172

Table 7.4
Significant variables and the direction of coefficients of Bloc 1 variables in the *gross, net* and *final net* models estimating classroom disciplinary climate (2007-08)[1]
Significant variables in the multiple regression of the index of classroom disciplinary climate that include the following lower secondary education teachers' characteristics[2]

Example: In Austria, teachers employed on a full-time basis are more likely to teach classes with a better classroom disciplinary climate.

	>ISCED5 (Bachelor degree)			Female			Full-time employment			Permanent Contract			Years of teaching		
	Gross	Net	Final net	Gross	Net	Final net	Gross	Net	Final net	Gross	Net	Final net	Gross	Net	Final net
Australia							+	+		+	+		+	+	+
Austria		−		+	+	+	+	+	+				+	+	+
Belgium (Fl.)										+	+	+	+	+	+
Brazil	−	−	−	−	−	−							+	+	+
Bulgaria													+	+	+
Denmark	+			+	+	+							+	+	+
Estonia					+				+	+	+	+	+	+	+
Hungary										+	+	+	+	+	+
Iceland													+	+	+
Ireland				+	+			+	+	+	+	+			
Italy	+	+	+										+	+	+
Korea															
Lithuania	+			+	+		+	+	+	+	+	+	+	+	+
Malaysia						−				−			+	+	+
Malta			−							+	+	+	+	+	+
Mexico													+		
Norway	−	−	−							+	+	+	+	+	+
Poland										+	+	+	+	+	+
Portugal							+	+	+						
Slovak Republic				+	+	+							+	+	+
Slovenia				+	+	+				+	+	+	+	+	+
Spain										+		+	+	+	+
Turkey							+	+							

1. Gross model includes only the variables in this analytic bloc. Net model includes the variables in this analytic bloc and socio-economic background variables (see Table 7.1) and final net model includes the variables found to be statistically significant in the net model in each analytic bloc and socio-economic background and Bloc 1 variables.

2. Variables where a significant positive relationship was found are indicated by a "+" while those where a significant negative relationship was found are shown with a "−". Cells are blank where no significant relationship was found. Significance was tested at the 5% level.

Source: OECD, *TALIS Database*.
StatLink http://dx.doi.org/10.1787/608030545172

Table 7.4a

Significant variables and the direction of coefficients of Bloc 1 variables in the *gross, net* and *final net* models estimating teachers' reported self-efficacy (2007-08)[1]

Significant variables in the multiple regression of the index of teachers' self-efficacy that include the following lower secondary education teachers' characteristics[2]

Example: In Australia, teachers employed on a full-time basis are more likely to have higher levels of reported self-efficacy.

	>ISCED5 (Bachelor degree)			Female			Full-time employment			Permanent Contract			Years of teaching		
	Gross	Net	Final net	Gross	Net	Final net	Gross	Net	Final net	Gross	Net	Final net	Gross	Net	Final net
Australia							+	+	+	+	+				
Austria		−		+	+		+	+	+				−	−	−
Belgium (Fl.)	−	−	−				+	+		+	+	+			
Brazil	−	−		−						−	−	−			
Bulgaria						−							+	+	
Denmark							+	+	+	+	+	+			
Estonia										+	+	+			
Hungary															
Iceland															
Ireland															
Italy							+	+	+						
Korea	+	+	+	−	−	−		+	+	+	+	+	+	+	+
Lithuania				+	+										
Malaysia		+	+	−	−	−							+	+	+
Malta													+	+	+
Mexico		+					+	+							
Norway	+	+	+					+		+	+	+			
Poland						−							+	+	
Portugal	+	+	+										−	−	
Slovak Republic							+	+	+				+	+	+
Slovenia												+			−
Spain															
Turkey							+	+				+	+	+	+

1. Gross model includes only the variables in this analytic bloc. Net model includes the variables in this analytic bloc and socio-economic background variables (see Table 7.1) and final net model includes the variables found to be statistically significant in the net model in each analytic bloc and socio-economic background and Bloc 1 variables.

2. Variables where a significant positive relationship was found are indicated by a "+" while those where a significant negative relationship was found are shown with a "−". Cells are blank where no significant relationship was found. Significance was tested at the 5% level.

Source: OECD, *TALIS Database*.

StatLink http://dx.doi.org/10.1787/608030545172

Table 7.5

Significant variables and the direction of coefficients of Bloc 2 variables in the *gross*, *net* and *final net* models estimating classroom disciplinary climate[1]

Significant variables in the multiple regression of the index of classroom disciplinary climate that include the following professional development variables for lower secondary education teachers[2]

Example: In Malta, teachers who work in schools with a mentoring programme are more likely to teach classes with a more positive disciplinary climate.

	Number of days of professional development			School providing induction process for teachers			School providing mentor for new teachers		
	Gross	Net	Final net	Gross	Net	Final net	Gross	Net	Final net
Australia	+	+	+				+		
Austria									
Belgium (Fl.)									
Brazil								−	−
Bulgaria									
Denmark							+		
Estonia									
Hungary	+								
Iceland									
Ireland									
Italy									
Korea	+	+							
Lithuania									
Malaysia							+		
Malta				−	−	−	+	+	+
Mexico									
Norway									
Poland				−	−				
Portugal	+	+							
Slovak Republic	+	+							
Slovenia		+		−	−	−			
Spain									
Turkey									

1. Gross model includes only the variables in this analytic bloc. Net model includes the variables in this analytic bloc and socio-economic background variables (see Table 7.1) and final net model includes the variables found to be statistically significant in the net model in each analytic bloc and socio-economic background and Bloc 1 variables.

2. Variables where a significant positive relationship was found are indicated by a "+" while those where a significant negative relationship was found are shown with a "−". Cells are blank where no significant relationship was found. Significance was tested at the 5% level.

Source: OECD, *TALIS Database.*

StatLink ⧉ http://dx.doi.org/10.1787/608030545172

Table 7.5a

Significant variables and the direction of coefficients of Bloc 2 variables in the *gross, net* and *final net* models estimating teachers' reported self-efficacy[1]

Significant variables in the multiple regression of the index of teachers' self-efficacy that include the following professional development variables for lower secondary education teachers[2]

Example: In Denmark, teachers are more likely to have higher levels of self-efficacy if they have undertaken more days of professional development.

	Number of days of professional development			School providing induction process for teachers			School providing mentor for new teachers		
	Gross	Net	Final net	Gross	Net	Final net	Gross	Net	Final net
Australia									
Austria	+	+							
Belgium (Fl.)									
Brazil									
Bulgaria	+	+					+	+	+
Denmark	+	+	+						
Estonia	+	+	+				+	+	+
Hungary	+	+		−					
Iceland	+	+	+						
Ireland									
Italy	+	+	+						
Korea	+	+	+						
Lithuania	+	+	+						
Malaysia	+	+	+				+	+	
Malta	+	+	+				+	+	
Mexico		+	+						
Norway	+	+							
Poland									
Portugal	+	+	+						
Slovak Republic				+					
Slovenia	+	+	+						
Spain									
Turkey				−					

1. Gross model includes only the variables in this analytic bloc. Net model includes the variables in this analytic bloc and socio-economic background variables (see Table 7.1) and final net model includes the variables found to be statistically significant in the net model in each analytic bloc and socio-economic background and Bloc 1 variables.

2. Variables where a significant positive relationship was found are indicated by a "+" while those where a significant negative relationship was found are shown with a "−". Cells are blank where no significant relationship was found. Significance was tested at the 5% level.

Source: OECD, *TALIS Database.*

StatLink http://dx.doi.org/10.1787/608030545172

Table 7.6

Significant variables and the direction of coefficients of Bloc 3 variables in the *gross, net* and *final net* models estimating classroom disciplinary climate[1]

Significant variables in the multiple regression of the index of classroom disciplinary climate that include the following indices of teachers' beliefs and practices in lower secondary education[2]

Example: In Italy, teachers reporting more frequent use of structured teaching practices are more likely to teach classes with a more positive disciplinary climate.

	Index of teacher-student relations			Index of classroom teaching practice: structuring			Index of classroom teaching practice: student-oriented			Index of classroom teaching practice: enhanced activities		
	Gross	Net	Final net	Gross	Net	Final net	Gross	Net	Final net	Gross	Net	Final net
Australia	+	+	+	+	+	+						
Austria	+	+	+	+	+	+	+	+	+	−	−	−
Belgium (Fl.)	+	+	+	+	+	+				−	−	−
Brazil	+	+	+				+	+	+			
Bulgaria	+	+	+	+	+	+						
Denmark	+	+	+	+			−			+		
Estonia	+	+	+				+	+	+			
Hungary	+	+	+		+	+						
Iceland	+	+	+									
Ireland	+	+	+	+	+	+	−					
Italy	+	+	+	+	+	+						
Korea	+	+	+	+	+	+						
Lithuania	+	+	+	+				+	+	−	−	−
Malaysia	+	+	+	−	−	−	+	+	+	−	−	−
Malta	+			+								
Mexico	+	+	+	+	+	+						
Norway	+	+	+									
Poland	+	+	+	−			+	+	+			
Portugal	+	+	+	+	+	+		+				
Slovak Republic	+	+	+				+					
Slovenia	+	+	+				+	+	+		−	
Spain	+	+	+	+	+	+						
Turkey	+	+	+				+	+	+			

	Index of direct transmission beliefs about instruction			Index of constructivist beliefs about instruction			Index of exchange and co-ordination for teaching			Index of professional collaboration		
	Gross	Net	Final net	Gross	Net	Final net	Gross	Net	Final net	Gross	Net	Final net
Australia												
Austria							+	+	+	−	−	−
Belgium (Fl.)		−	−									
Brazil												
Bulgaria	−	−								+	+	
Denmark												
Estonia	−	−										
Hungary				+	+	+						
Iceland												
Ireland												
Italy				+	+	+				+	+	+
Korea	−	−	−	+	+	+						
Lithuania										+		
Malaysia							+	+	+		−	−
Malta												
Mexico								+	+			
Norway	−	−	−									
Poland	−	−	−	+	+	+						
Portugal	−											
Slovak Republic	−									+		
Slovenia	−	−	−	+	+	+						
Spain	−	−	−							+	+	+
Turkey												

1. Gross model includes only the variables in this analytic bloc. Net model includes the variables in this analytic bloc and socio-economic background variables (see Table 7.1) and final net model includes the variables found to be statistically significant in the net model in each analytic bloc and socio-economic background and Bloc 1 variables.

2. Variables where a significant positive relationship was found are indicated by a "+" while those where a significant negative relationship was found are shown with a "−". Cells are blank where no significant relationship was found. Significance was tested at the 5% level.

Source: OECD, *TALIS* Database.

StatLink ᴍᴤᴘ http://dx.doi.org/10.1787/608030545172

Table 7.6a

Significant variables and the direction of coefficients of Bloc 3 variables in the *gross*, *net* and *final net* models estimating teachers' reported self-efficacy[1]

Significant variables in the multiple regression of the index of teachers' self-efficacy that include the following indices of teachers' beliefs and practices in lower secondary education[2]

Example: In Hungary, teachers reporting more frequent use of student-oriented teaching practices are more likely to report a higher level of self-efficacy.

	Index of teacher-student relations			Index of classroom teaching practice: structuring			Index of classroom teaching practice: student-oriented			Index of classroom teaching practice: enhanced activities		
	Gross	Net	Final net	Gross	Net	Final net	Gross	Net	Final net	Gross	Net	Final net
Australia	+	+	+	+	+	+						
Austria	+	+	+	+	+	+	+	+	+	−	−	−
Belgium (Fl.)	+	+	+	+	+	+	+					
Brazil	+	+	+				+					
Bulgaria	+	+	+							+		
Denmark	+	+	+	+								
Estonia	+	+	+				+	+	+			
Hungary	+	+	+				+	+				
Iceland	+	+	+	+	+	+						
Ireland	+	+	+	+	+	+				+	+	+
Italy	+	+	+				−			+	+	+
Korea	+	+	+	+	+	+	+	+	+			
Lithuania	+	+	+				+	+	+			
Malaysia	+	+	+	+								
Malta	+	+	+	+								
Mexico	+	+	+	+	+	+						
Norway	+	+	+	+	+	+						
Poland	+	+	+	−	−	−	+			+	+	+
Portugal	+	+	+		+	+	+	+	+			
Slovak Republic	+	+	+				+	+	+			
Slovenia	+	+	+				+	+	+			
Spain	+	+	+	+	+	+						
Turkey	+	+	+				+	+	+			

	Index of direct transmission beliefs about instruction			Index of constructivist beliefs about instruction			Index of exchange and co-ordination for teaching			Index of professional collaboration		
	Gross	Net	Final net	Gross	Net	Final net	Gross	Net	Final net	Gross	Net	Final net
Australia				+	+	+	+					
Austria	+	+	+	+	+	+				+	+	+
Belgium (Fl.)	+	+	+	+	+	+				+	+	+
Brazil	+	+	+									
Bulgaria	+	+	+	+						+	+	+
Denmark		+	+	+	+	+						
Estonia				+	+	+	−			+	+	+
Hungary				+	+	+				+	+	+
Iceland				+	+	+					+	+
Ireland	+	+	+	+	+	+						
Italy	+	+	+	+	+	+						
Korea	+	+	+	+	+	+				+	+	+
Lithuania	+	+	+	+	+	+						
Malaysia								+	+			
Malta				+	+	+						
Mexico	+	+	+									
Norway	+	+	+	+	+	+	+	+	+			
Poland	+	+	+	+	+	+				+	+	+
Portugal	+	+	+	+	+	+				+	+	
Slovak Republic	+	+	+	+	+	+				+		
Slovenia	+	+	+	+	+	+						
Spain	+	+	+	+	+	+				+	+	+
Turkey		+	+	+	+	+						

1. Gross model includes only the variables in this analytic bloc. Net model includes the variables in this analytic bloc and socio-economic background variables (see Table 7.1) and final net model includes the variables found to be statistically significant in the net model in each analytic bloc and socio-economic background and Bloc 1 variables.

2. Variables where a significant positive relationship was found are indicated by a "+" while those where a significant negative relationship was found are shown with a "−". Cells are blank where no significant relationship was found. Significance was tested at the 5% level.

Source: OECD, *TALIS* Database.

StatLink ⬛ http://dx.doi.org/10.1787/608030545172

Table 7.7 (1/2)

Significant variables and the direction of coefficients of Bloc 4 variables in the *gross*, *net* and *final net* models estimating classroom disciplinary climate[1]

Significant variables in the multiple regression of the index of classroom disciplinary climate that include the following appraisal and feedback variables for teachers in lower secondary education[2]

Example: In Italy, teachers who work in schools where effective teachers are better rewarded are more likely to teach classes with a better disciplinary climate.

	Never received appraisal or feedback from any source			Work in schools that did not have an evaluation within the last 5 years			Effective teachers receive more monetary or non-monetary rewards in the school.			Important aspect for teacher appraisal: student test scores[3]		
	Gross	Net	Final net	Gross	Net	Final net	Gross	Net	Final net	Gross	Net	Final net
Australia												
Austria					+							
Belgium (Fl.)												
Brazil	−	−		+	+							
Bulgaria	−						+					
Denmark		−								+	+	+
Estonia												
Hungary							+					
Iceland												
Ireland												
Italy							+	+	+			
Korea												
Lithuania												
Malaysia	−											
Malta				+						+		
Mexico												
Norway							−	−	−	+		
Poland	−											
Portugal	−	−										
Slovak Republic	−	−					+	+				
Slovenia	−											
Spain												
Turkey												

	Important aspect for teacher appraisal: innovative teaching practices[3]			Important aspect for teacher appraisal: professional development undertaken[3]			Appraisal impact: a change in salary[3]			Appraisal impact: opportunities for professional development activities[3]		
	Gross	Net	Final net	Gross	Net	Final net	Gross	Net	Final net	Gross	Net	Final net
Australia												
Austria												
Belgium (Fl.)												
Brazil	+	+										
Bulgaria												
Denmark												
Estonia												
Hungary	+	+								+	+	+
Iceland												
Ireland												
Italy				+	+		−					
Korea				+	+		−	−	−	+		
Lithuania	+	+	+									
Malaysia				+								
Malta							−	−	−			
Mexico	+	+										
Norway												
Poland	+											
Portugal	+	+	+							+	+	+
Slovak Republic	+	+	+	+			+	+	+			
Slovenia	+	+	+									
Spain												
Turkey												

1. Gross model includes only the variables in this analytic bloc. Net model includes the variables in this analytic bloc and socio-economic background variables (see Table 7.1) and final net model includes the variables found to be statistically significant in the net model in each analytic bloc and socio-economic background and Bloc 1 variables.

2. Variables where a significant positive relationship was found are indicated by a "+" while those where a significant negative relationship was found are shown with a "−". Cells are blank where no significant relationship was found. Significance was tested at the 5% level.

3. Due to high rates of missing values for some variables in this analytic bloc, a substantial degree of bias may exist in the results for particular variables included in the estimations for each country. Caution should therefore be taken in any interpretation of the results.

Source: OECD, *TALIS Database.*

StatLink ⟶ http://dx.doi.org/10.1787/608030545172

Table 7.7 (2/2)

Significant variables and the direction of coefficients of Bloc 4 variables in the *gross*, *net* and *final net* models estimating classroom disciplinary climate[1]

Significant variables in the multiple regression of the index of classroom disciplinary climate that include the following appraisal and feedback variables for teachers in lower secondary education[2]

Example: In Korea, teachers who received public recognition following an appraisal.

	Appraisal impact: public recognition from the principal and/or your colleagues[3]			Appraisal impact: changes in teachers' work responsibilities that make the job more attractive[3]			School evaluation published[3]			Important aspect for school evaluations: student test scores[3]		
	Gross	Net	Final net	Gross	Net	Final net	Gross	Net	Final net	Gross	Net	Final net
Australia	+	+										
Austria												
Belgium (Fl.)	+	+	+									
Brazil	+	+	+								−	
Bulgaria	+	+	+									
Denmark										−	−	
Estonia	+	+	+									
Hungary												
Iceland												
Ireland												
Italy										+	+	
Korea	+	+	+									
Lithuania	+											
Malaysia	+									+		
Malta							−					
Mexico				+	+							
Norway												
Poland	+											
Portugal												
Slovak Republic												
Slovenia	+	+										
Spain												
Turkey	+											

1. Gross model includes only the variables in this analytic bloc. Net model includes the variables in this analytic bloc and socio-economic background variables (see Table 7.1) and final net model includes the variables found to be statistically significant in the net model in each analytic bloc and socio-economic background and Bloc 1 variables.

2. Variables where a significant positive relationship was found are indicated by a "+" while those where a significant negative relationship was found are shown with a "−". Cells are blank where no significant relationship was found. Significance was tested at the 5% level.

3. Due to high rates of missing values for some variables in this analytic bloc, a substantial degree of bias may exist in the results for particular variables included in the estimations for each country. Caution should therefore be taken in any interpretation of the results.

Source: OECD, *TALIS Database.*

StatLink ᵍᵖ http://dx.doi.org/10.1787/608030545172

Table 7.7a (1/2)

Significant variables and the direction of coefficients of Bloc 4 variables in the *gross*, *net* and *final net* models estimating teachers' reported self-efficacy[1]

Significant variables in the multiple regression of the index of teachers' self-efficacy that include the following appraisal and feedback variables for teachers in lower secondary education[2]

Example: In Mexico, teachers who have never received appraisal or feedback in their school are more likely to have lower levels of reported self-efficacy. However, this was not found to be true when including the significant variables from each analytic bloc in the final net estimation.

	Never received appraisal or feedback from any source			Work in schools that did not have an evaluation within the last 5 years			Effective teachers receive more monetary or non-monetary rewards in the school.			Important aspect for teacher appraisal: student test scores[3]		
	Gross	Net	Final net	Gross	Net	Final net	Gross	Net	Final net	Gross	Net	Final net
Australia		–										
Austria	–	–										
Belgium (Fl.)	–	–										
Brazil	–	–	+	+			+	+	+			
Bulgaria	–											
Denmark												
Estonia				–	–					–	–	–
Hungary	–	–					+					
Iceland	–	–					+	+				
Ireland												
Italy	–	–					+	+				
Korea	–						+	+				
Lithuania	–											
Malaysia							+	+				
Malta												
Mexico	–						+					
Norway												
Poland												
Portugal	–	–					+	+				
Slovak Republic										+	+	
Slovenia												
Spain	–	–					+	+				
Turkey							+	+				

	Important aspect for teacher appraisal: innovative teaching practices[3]			Important aspect for teacher appraisal: professional development undertaken[3]			Appraisal impact: a change in salary[3]			Appraisal impact: opportunities for professional development activities[3]		
	Gross	Net	Final net	Gross	Net	Final net	Gross	Net	Final net	Gross	Net	Final net
Australia	+	+										
Austria	+	+		+	+							
Belgium (Fl.)												
Brazil	+	+	+									
Bulgaria	+	+										
Denmark												
Estonia	+	+										
Hungary											+	
Iceland	+	+	+									
Ireland				+	+							
Italy	+	+										
Korea				+	+					+		
Lithuania	+	+			+							
Malaysia										+	+	
Malta				+								
Mexico	+			+	+					+		
Norway												
Poland	+	+										
Portugal	+	+	+									
Slovak Republic	+											
Slovenia	+	+		+	+							
Spain				+						+		
Turkey							+					

1. Gross model includes only the variables in this analytic bloc. Net model includes the variables in this analytic bloc and socio-economic background variables (see Table 7.1) and final net model includes the variables found to be statistically significant in the net model in each analytic bloc and socio-economic background and Bloc 1 variables.

2. Variables where a significant positive relationship was found are indicated by a "+" while those where a significant negative relationship was found are shown with a "–". Cells are blank where no significant relationship was found. Significance was tested at the 5% level.

3. Due to high rates of missing values for some variables in this analytic bloc, a substantial degree of bias may exist in the results for particular variables included in the estimations for each country. Caution should therefore be taken in any interpretation of the results.

Source: OECD, *TALIS Database.*

StatLink ᴍᴤᴾ http://dx.doi.org/10.1787/608030545172

253

Table 7.7a (2/2)

Significant variables and the direction of coefficients of Bloc 4 variables in the *gross, net* and *final net* models estimating teachers' reported self-efficacy[1]

Significant variables in the multiple regression of the index of teachers' self-efficacy that include the following appraisal and feedback variables for teachers in lower secondary education[2]

Example: In Portugal, teachers who have changes in their work responsibilities following an appraisal are more likely to have higher levels of reported self-efficacy.

	Appraisal impact: public recognition from the principal and/or your colleagues[3]			Appraisal impact: changes in teachers' work responsibilities that make the job more attractive[3]			School evaluation published[3]			Important aspect for school evaluations: student test scores[3]		
	Gross	Net	Final net	Gross	Net	Final net	Gross	Net	Final net	Gross	Net	Final net
Australia	+	+										
Austria	+	+	+									
Belgium (Fl.)	+	+	+	+	+		+					
Brazil	+	+		+	+	+					-	
Bulgaria	+	+		+	+	+						
Denmark												
Estonia	+	+	+	+	+	+		+				
Hungary	+	+	+									
Iceland												
Ireland	+	+	+							-		
Italy	+	+	+	+	+							
Korea	+	+	+									
Lithuania	+	+	+									
Malaysia				+	+							
Malta	+	+	+							+	+	
Mexico	+	+		+								
Norway	+	+	+									
Poland	+	+		+	+							
Portugal	+			+	+	+						
Slovak Republic	+	+										
Slovenia				+	+	+						
Spain	+	+	+									
Turkey												

1. Gross model includes only the variables in this analytic bloc. Net model includes the variables in this analytic bloc and socio-economic background variables (see Table 7.1) and final net model includes the variables found to be statistically significant in the net model in each analytic bloc and socio-economic background and Bloc 1 variables.

2. Variables where a significant positive relationship was found are indicated by a "+" while those where a significant negative relationship was found are shown with a "–". Cells are blank where no significant relationship was found. Significance was tested at the 5% level.

3. Due to high rates of missing values for some variables in this analytic bloc, a substantial degree of bias may exist in the results for particular variables included in the estimations for each country. Caution should therefore be taken in any interpretation of the results.

Source: OECD, *TALIS Database.*

StatLink ⬛➡ http://dx.doi.org/10.1787/608030545172

Table 7.8

Significant variables and the direction of coefficients of Bloc 5 variables in the *gross*, *net* and *final net* models estimating classroom disciplinary climate[1]

Significant variables in the multiple regression of the index of classroom disciplinary climate that include the following indices for school leadership in lower secondary education[2]

Example: In Portugal, teachers whose school principal reported more frequent framing and communicating school goals and curricular development were more likely to teach classes with a better disciplinary climate.

	Index of framing and communicating the school goals and curricular development			Index of promoting instructional improvements and professional development			Index of supervision of instruction in the school			Index of accountability role of the principal			Index of bureaucratic rule-following		
	Gross	Net	Final net	Gross	Net	Final net	Gross	Net	Final net	Gross	Net	Final net	Gross	Net	Final net
Australia	+														
Austria															
Belgium (Fl.)				+											
Brazil															
Bulgaria													+		
Denmark[3]										−					
Estonia														+	+
Hungary															
Iceland[3]															
Ireland[3]															
Italy							−						+	+	+
Korea[3]															
Lithuania										−	−				
Malaysia															
Malta		+	+	+			−	−	−	−	−				
Mexico															
Norway										−			+	+	+
Poland															
Portugal	+	+	+												
Slovak Republic															
Slovenia				−	−	−									
Spain														−	
Turkey										+	+	+	−	−	

1. Gross model includes only the variables in this analytic bloc. Net model includes the variables in this analytic bloc and socio-economic background variables (see Table 7.1) and final net model includes the variables found to be statistically significant in the net model in each analytic bloc and socio-economic background and Bloc 1 variables.

2. Variables where a significant positive relationship was found are indicated by a "+" while those where a significant negative relationship was found are shown with a "−". Cells are blank where no significant relationship was found. Significance was tested at the 5% level.

3. Due to higher rates of missing values for these variables in these countries, the results should be treated with considerable caution.

Source: OECD, *TALIS Database*.

StatLink ⬛🔜 http://dx.doi.org/10.1787/608030545172

Table 7.8a

Significant variables and the direction of coefficients of Bloc 5 variables in the *gross, net* and *final net* models estimating teachers' reported self-efficacy[1]

Significant variables in the multiple regression of the index of teachers' self-efficacy that include the following indices for school leadership in lower secondary education[2]

Example: In Lithuania, teachers whose school principal reported more frequent supervision of instruction were more likely to report higher levels of self-efficacy.

	Index of framing and communicating the school goals and curricular development			Index of promoting instructional improvements and professional development			Index of supervision of instruction in the school			Index of accountability role of the principal			Index of bureaucratic rule-following		
	Gross	Net	Final net	Gross	Net	Final net	Gross	Net	Final net	Gross	Net	Final net	Gross	Net	Final net
Australia															
Austria	+	+													
Belgium (Fl.)															
Brazil							+								
Bulgaria															
Denmark[3]															
Estonia															
Hungary							+	+							
Iceland[3]															
Ireland[3]										+	+	+			
Italy										–	–		+	+	
Korea[3]															
Lithuania							+	+	+	–	–				
Malaysia															
Malta															
Mexico															
Norway															
Poland															
Portugal	+	I	+												
Slovak Republic															
Slovenia															
Spain															
Turkey															

1. Gross model includes only the variables in this analytic bloc. Net model includes the variables in this analytic bloc and socio-economic background variables (see Table 7.1) and final net model includes the variables found to be statistically significant in the net model in each analytic bloc and socio-economic background and Bloc 1 variables.

2. Variables where a significant positive relationship was found are indicated by a "+" while those where a significant negative relationship was found are shown with a "–". Cells are blank where no significant relationship was found. Significance was tested at the 5% level.

3. Due to higher rates of missing values for these variables in these countries, the results should be treated with considerable caution.

Source: OECD, *TALIS Database.*

StatLink http://dx.doi.org/10.1787/608030545172

Table 7.9

Significant variables and the direction of coefficients of Bloc 6 variables in the *gross*, *net* and *final net* models estimating classroom disciplinary climate[1]

Significant variables in the multiple regression of the index of classroom disciplinary climate that include the following indices of school autonomy and resources in lower secondary education[2]

Example: In Australia, teachers whose school principals reported higher levels of student delinquency are more likely to teach classes with a worse disciplinary climate.

	Index of school climate: student delinquency			Index of school climate: teachers' working morale			Index of a lack of personnel			Index of school resources: shortage of materials			Index of school autonomy in hiring teachers and determining salaries		
	Gross	Net	Final net	Gross	Net	Final net	Gross	Net	Final net	Gross	Net	Final net	Gross	Net	Final net
Australia	−	−	−	+			−			+			+	+	+
Austria							−	−	−					−	−
Belgium (Fl.)															
Brazil	−									+	+				
Bulgaria	−	−	−												
Denmark[3]													−		
Estonia															
Hungary	−	−	−												
Iceland[3]	−						+	+	+						
Ireland[3]	−	−	−												
Italy	−														
Korea[3]															
Lithuania								+	+						
Malaysia															
Malta							−	−					+		
Mexico															
Norway															
Poland	−										+	+		+	+
Portugal															
Slovak Republic															
Slovenia															
Spain															
Turkey															

	Index of school autonomy in budgeting (formulating and allocating the school budget)			Index of school autonomy: student policy and textbooks			Index of school autonomy in curriculum (courses offered, course content)			School average class size			Public school		
	Gross	Net	Final net	Gross	Net	Final net	Gross	Net	Final net	Gross	Net	Final net	Gross	Net	Final net
Australia										−					
Austria				+						−	−	−			
Belgium (Fl.)										−	−				
Brazil	−	−	−	+	+	+				−	−	−			
Bulgaria				+	+					−	−	−			
Denmark[3]										−	−	−	−	−	−
Estonia										−	−				
Hungary										−	−				
Iceland[3]										−	−				
Ireland[3]										+	−	−	−		
Italy										−	−				
Korea[3]										−	−				
Lithuania										−	−				
Malaysia										−	−				
Malta							−	−	−	−	−		−	−	−
Mexico															
Norway	−	−								−	−				
Poland	−														
Portugal										−	−				
Slovak Republic	+	+	+							−					
Slovenia										−	−	−	−	−	
Spain										−	−	−			
Turkey										−	−	−			

1. Gross model includes only the variables in this analytic bloc. Net model includes the variables in this analytic bloc and socio-economic background variables (see Table 7.1) and final net model includes the variables found to be statistically significant in the net model in each analytic bloc and socio-economic background and Bloc 1 variables.

2. Variables where a significant positive relationship was found are indicated by a "+" while those where a significant negative relationship was found are shown with a "−". Cells are blank where no significant relationship was found. Significance was tested at the 5% level.

3. Due to higher rates of missing values for these variables in these countries, the results should be treated with considerable caution.

Source: OECD, *TALIS* Database.

StatLink ⬛📈 http://dx.doi.org/10.1787/608030545172

Table 7.9a

Significant variables and the direction of coefficients of Bloc 6 variables in the *gross*, *net* and *final net* models estimating teachers' reported self-efficacy[1]

Significant variables in the multiple regression of the index of teachers' self-efficacy that include the following indices of school autonomy and resources in lower secondary education[2]

Example: In Norway, teachers who work in public schools are more likely to report higher levels of self-efficacy.

	Index of school climate: student delinquency			Index of school climate: teachers' working morale			Index of a lack of personnel			Index of school resources: shortage of materials			Index of school autonomy in hiring teachers and determining salaries		
	Gross	Net	Final net	Gross	Net	Final net	Gross	Net	Final net	Gross	Net	Final net	Gross	Net	Final net
Australia													+	+	
Austria				−	−	−				+	+	+			
Belgium (Fl.)													−	−	−
Brazil															
Bulgaria					−										
Denmark[3]															
Estonia															
Hungary	−	−													
Iceland[3]															
Ireland[3]														−	
Italy															
Korea[3]										+	+				
Lithuania															
Malaysia															
Malta															
Mexico															
Norway										−					
Poland															
Portugal	−														
Slovak Republic				−	−	−					+				
Slovenia															
Spain													+	+	
Turkey															

	Index of school autonomy in budgeting (formulating and allocating the school budget)			Index of school autonomy: student policy and textbooks			Index of school autonomy in curriculum (courses offered, course content)			School average class size			Public school		
	Gross	Net	Final net	Gross	Net	Final net	Gross	Net	Final net	Gross	Net	Final net	Gross	Net	Final net
Australia										+					
Austria															
Belgium (Fl.)															
Brazil				+	+										
Bulgaria										+					
Denmark[3]															
Estonia													−		
Hungary				−	−	−		+					−		
Iceland[3]		+											−		
Ireland[3]													−		−
Italy															
Korea[3]															
Lithuania										+			−		
Malaysia															
Malta															
Mexico															
Norway	−	−								+					+
Poland	−	−	−							+					
Portugal	−	−	−												
Slovak Republic								+		+					
Slovenia													−		
Spain							−								
Turkey							+						−		

1. Gross model includes only the variables in this analytic bloc. Net model includes the variables in this analytic bloc and socio-economic background variables (see Table 7.1) and final net model includes the variables found to be statistically significant in the net model in each analytic bloc and socio-economic background and Bloc 1 variables.

2. Variables where a significant positive relationship was found are indicated by a "+" while those where a significant negative relationship was found are shown with a "−". Cells are blank where no significant relationship was found. Significance was tested at the 5% level.

3. Due to higher rates of missing values for these variables in these countries, the results should be treated with considerable caution.

Source: OECD, *TALIS Database*.

StatLink ⟐ http://dx.doi.org/10.1787/608030545172

References

CHAPTER 1

Council (Education) of the European Union (2002), "Detailed work programme on the follow-up of the objectives of Education and training systems in Europe", OJ C 142, 14 June 2002.

Council (Education) of the European Union (2005), "Council Conclusions 2005", OJ C141, 10 June 2005.

Council (Education) of the European Union (2007), "Council Conclusions 2007", OJ C 300, 12 December 2007.

OECD (2005), *Teachers Matter: Attracting, Developing and Retaining Effective Teachers*, OECD, Paris.

OECD (2008a), *Education at a Glance - OECD Indicators 2008*, OECD, Paris.

CHAPTER 2

Atkinson, T. (2005), *Atkinson Review: Final Report, Measurement of Government Output and Productivity for the National Accounts*, Palgrave Macmillan, London.

Ballou, D. and **M. Podgursky** (1997), *Teacher Pay and Teacher Quality*, W.E. Upjohn Institute for Employment Research, Kalamazoo, Michigan.

Boyd, D., P. Grossman, H. Lankford, S. Loeb, and **J. Wyckoff,** (2008), "Who Leaves? Teacher Attrition and Student Achievement", NBER Working Paper No. 14022, May 2008.

Dixit, A. (2002), "Incentives and Organisations in the Public Sector: An Interpretive Review", *Journal of Human Resources*, No. 37 (4), pp. 696-727.

Hoxby, C. (2003), *The Economics of School Choice, National Bureau of Economic Research Conference Report,* University of Chicago Press.

Lazear, E.P. (2000), The Future of Personnel Economics, *The Economic Journal,* No. 110, 467, pp. 611-639.

Mante, B. and **G. O'Brien** (2002), "Efficiency Measurement of Australian Public Sector Organisations: The Case of State Secondary Schools in Victoria", *Journal of Educational Administration*, No. 30 (7), pp. 274-91.

McKewen, N. (1995), "Accountability in Education in Canada", *Canadian Journal of Education,* No. 20 (1).

OECD (2004), *Completing the Foundation for Lifelong Learning: An OECD Survey of Upper Secondary Schools*, OECD, Paris.

OECD (2006a), *Demand Sensitive Schooling? Evidence and Issues,* OECD, Paris.

OECD (2007), *PISA 2006: Science Competencies For Tomorrow's World*, OECD, Paris.

OECD (2008b), *No More Failures: Ten Steps to Equity in Education*, OECD, Paris.

Podgursky, M., Monroe, R. and **D. Watson** (2004), "The academic quality of public school teachers: An analysis of entry and exit behaviour", *Economics of Education Review,* No. 23 (5) (October), pp. 507-518.

Rockoff, J. (2004), "The Impact of Individual Teachers on Student Achievement: Evidence from Panel Data", *American Economic Review Proceedings,* No. 92 (2), pp. 247-252.

Rockoff, J.E. (2008), "Does Mentoring Reduce Turnover and Improve Skills of New Employees? Evidence from teachers in New York City", *NBER Working Paper,* No. 13868, March 2008.

CHAPTER 3

OECD (1998), *Staying Ahead: In-Service Training and Teacher Professional Development*, OECD, Paris.

OECD (2008c), *Students with Disabilities, Learning Difficulties and Disadvantages*, OECD, Paris.

International Association for the Evaluation of Educational Achievement (2008), "Pedagogy and ICT use in schools around the world: Findings from the IEA SITES 2006 study", Law, N., Pelgrum, W.J. and T. Plomp (eds.), CERC-Springer, Hong Kong.

CHAPTER 4

Ashton, P. and **N. Webb** (1986), *Making a Difference: Teacher Efficacy and Student Achievement*, Monogram, Longman, White Plains, New York.

Bandura, A. (1986), *Social Foundations of Thought and Action: A Social Cognitive Theory*, Prentice Hall, Englewood Cliffs, New Jersey.

Bandura, A. (1997), *Self-Efficacy: The Exercise of Control*, Freeman, New York.

Baumert, J. and **M. Kunter** (2006), "Stichwort: Professionelle Kompetenz von Lehrkräften", *Zeitschrift für Erziehungswissenschaft*, No.9 (4), pp. 469-520.

Blum, R.W., C.A. McNeely and **P.M. Rinehart** (2002), *Improving the Odds: The Untapped Power of Schools to Improve the Health of Teens*, University of Minnesota, Center for Adolescent Health and Development, Minneapolis.

Brophy, J.E. and **T.L. Good** (1986), "Teacher Behaviour and Pupil Achievement", *in* M.C. Wittrock (ed.), *Handbook of Research on Teaching*, MacMillan, New York, pp. 328-375.

Campbell, A., O. McNamara and **P. Gilroy** (2004), *Practitioner Research and Professional Development in Education*, Chapman, London.

Caprara, G.V., C. Barbranelli, P. Steca and **S. Malone** (2006), "Teachers' Self-Efficacy Beliefs as Determinants of Job Satisfaction and Students' Academic Achievement: A Study at the School Level", *Journal of School Psychology*, No. 44 (6), pp. 473-490.

Chacón, C. (2005), "Teachers' Perceived Efficacy among English as a Foreign Language Teachers in Middle Schools in Venezuela", *Teaching and Teacher Education*, No. 21, pp. 257-272.

Clausen, M. (2002), *Unterrichtsqualität: Eine Frage der Perspektive? Pädagogische Psychologie und Entwicklungspsychologie*, D.H. Rost (ed.), Waxmann, Munster.

Clement, M. and **R. Vandenberghe,** (2000), "Teachers' Professional Development: A Solitary or Collegial (Ad)venture", *Teaching and Teacher Education*, Vol. 16, pp. 81–101.

Cohen, J. (2006), "Social, Emotional, Ethical and Academic Education: Creating a Climate for Learning, Participation in Democracy and Well-being", *Harvard Educational Review*, Vol. 76, No. 2, Summer, pp. 201-237.

Cronbach, L. (1957), "The Two Disciplines of Scientific Psychology", *American Psychologist*, pp. 671-684.

Creemers, B.P.M. and **G.J. Reezigt** (1999), "The Role of School and Classroom Climate in Elementary School Learning Environments", *in* H.J. Freiberg (wd.), *School Climate: Measuring, Improving and Sustaining Healthy Learning Environments*, Falmer Press, London.

Darling-Hammond, L., D.J. Holtzman, S.J. Gatlin and **J.V. Heilig** (2005), "Does Teacher Preparation Matter? Evidence about Teacher Certification, Teach for America, and Teacher Effectiveness", *Education Policy Analysis Archives*, No. 13 (42).

Dormann, C. and **D. Zapf** (2001), "Job Satisfaction – A Meta-Analysis of Stabilities", *Journal of Organizational Behavior*, No. 22, pp. 483-504.

Harris, A. and **J.H. Chrispeels** (eds.) (2006), *Improving Schools and Educational Systems: International Perspectives*, Routledge, London.

Hiebert, J., R. Gallimore, H. Garnier, K.B. Givven, H. Hollingsworth, J. Jacobs, A.M.-Y. Chui, D. Wearne, M. Smith, A. Manaster, E. Tseng, W. Etterbeek, C. Manaster, P. Gonzales and J.W. Stigler (2003), *Teaching Mathematics in Seven Countries: Results from the TIMSS 1999 Video Study*, US Department of Education, National Center for Education Statistics, Washington, D.C.

Hopkins, D. (ed.) (2005), *The Practice and Theory of School Improvement: International Handbook of Educational Change,* Springer, Dordrecht.

Kim, J.S. (2005), "The Effects of a Constructivist Teaching Approach on Student Academic Achievement, Self-concept, and Learning Strategies", *Asia Pacific Education Review*, No. 6 (1), pp. 7-19.

Klieme, E. and K. Rakoczy (2003), "Unterrichtsqualität aus Schülerperspektive: Kulturspezifische Profile, regionale Unterschiede und Zusammenhänge mit Effekten von Unterricht"; *in* J. Baumert, C. Artelt, E. Klieme, M. Neubrand, M. Prenzel, U. Schiefele, W. Schneider and K.-J. Tillmann, (eds.), *PISA 2000: Ein differenzierter Blick auf die Länder der Bundesrepublik Deutschland* (pp. 334-359), Leske & Budrich, Opladen.

Klieme, E., F. Lipowsky, K. Rakoczy and N. Ratzka (2006), "Qualitätsdimensionen und Wirksamkeit von Mathematikunterricht: Theoretische Grundlagen und ausgewählte Ergebnisse des Projekts 'Pythagoras'", *in*: M. Prenzel and L. Allolio-Näcke (eds.), *Untersuchungen zur Bildungsqualität von Schule, Abschlussbericht des DFG-Schwerpunktprogramms,* pp. 128-146, Waxmann, Munster.

Lee, J.C.K. and M. Williams, (eds.) (2006), *School Improvement: International Perspectives*, Nova Science Publishers Inc., New York.

Levitt, K.E. (2001), "An Analysis of Elementary Teachers' Beliefs Regarding the Teaching and Learning of Science", *Science Education*, No. 85, pp. 1-22.

Lipowsky, F., K. Rakoczy, C. Pauli, B. Drollinger-Vetter, E. Klieme and K. Reusser (2008), "Quality of Geometry Instruction and its Short-term Impact on Students' Understanding of the Pythagorean Theorem", *Learning and Instruction*, Science Direct Website, Doi:10.1016/j.learninstruc.2008.11.001.

Mortimore, P., P. Sammons, L. Stoll, D. Lewis and E. Russell (1988*), School Matters: The Junior Years*, Open Books, Wells.

Muijs, R.D. and D. Reynolds (1999), "School Effectiveness and Teacher Effectiveness: Some Preliminary Findings from the Evaluation of the Mathematics Enhancement Programme", Paper presented at the American Educational Research Association Conference, Montreal, Quebec, 19 April.

Nettle, E.B. (1998), "Stability and Change in the Belief of Student Teachers During Practice Teaching", *Teaching and Teacher Education*, No. 14 (2), pp. 193-204.

OECD (forthcoming), *TALIS Technical Report*, OECD, Paris.

Peterson, P.L., E. Fennema, T.P. Carpenter and M. Loef (1989), "Teachers' Pedagogical Content Beliefs in Mathematics", *Cognition and Instruction,* No. 6 (1), pp. 1–40.

Podell, D. and L. Soodak (1993), "Teacher Efficacy and Bias in Special Education Referrals", *Journal of Educational Research,* No. 86, pp. 247-253.

Rakoczy, K., E. Klieme, B. Drollinger-Vetter, F. Lipowsky, C. Pauli and K. Reusser (2007), "Structure as a Quality Feature in Mathematics Instruction of the Learning Environment versus a Structured Presentation of Learning Content", *in* M. Prenzel (ed.), *Studies on the Educational Quality of Schools: The Final Report of the DFG Priority Programme,* pp. 101-120, Waxmann, Munster.

Rosenholtz, S. (1989), *Teachers' Workplace: The Social Organization of Schools*, Longman, New York.

Ross, J.A. (1998), "The Antecedents and Consequences of Teacher Efficacy", *in* J. Brophy (ed.) *Advances in Research on Teaching*, Vol. 7, pp. 49-74, JAI Press, Greenwich, Connecticut.

Rutter, M., B. Maughan, P. Mortimore and J. Ouston (1979), "Fifteen Thousand Hours: Secondary Schools and their Effects on Children", Harvard University Press, Cambridge, Massachusetts.

Schagen, I. and **K. Elliot** (eds.) (2004), *But What Does It Mean? The Use of Effect Sizes in Educational Research*, NFER, Slough.

Scheerens, J. and **R.J. Bosker** (1997), *The Foundations of Educational Effectiveness*, Pergamon, Oxford.

Shulman, L. (1987), "Knowledge and Teaching: Foundations of the New Reform", *Harvard Educational Review*, No. 57 (1), pp. 1-22.

Singer, E. (1996), "Espoused Teaching Paradigms of College Faculty", *Research in Higher Education,* No. 37 (6), pp. 659-679.

Snow, E.R., and **D.F. Lohman** (1984), "Toward a Theory of Cognitive Aptitude for Learning from Instruction", *Journal of Educational Psychology*, No. 76, pp.347–376.

Staub, F. and **E. Stern** (2002), "The Nature of teachers' Pedagogical Content Beliefs Matters for Students' Achievement Gains: Quasi-experimental Evidence from Elementary Mathematics", *Journal of Educational Psychology*, No. 93, pp. 144-155.

Steinert, B., E. Klieme, K. Maag Merki, P. Döbrich, U. Halbheer and **A. Kunz** (2006), "Lehrerkooperation in der Schule: Konzeption, Erfassung, Ergebnisse", *Zeitschrift für Pädagogik*, No. 52 (2), pp.185-203.

Topping, K.J. (2005), "Trends in Peer Learning", *Educational Psychology*, No. 25 (6), pp. 631-645.

Wang, M.C., G.D. Haertel and **H.J. Walberg** (1993), "Toward a Knowledge Base for School Learning", *Review of Educational Research*, No. 63 (3), pp. 249 -294.

Wang, M.C., G.D. Haertel and **H.J. Walberg** (1997), "Learning Influences", *in* H.J. Walberg and G.D. Haertel (eds.), *Psychology and Educational Practice*, McCuthan, Berkeley, California.

Wheatley, K.F. (2005), "The Case for Reconceptualizing Teacher Efficacy Research", *Teaching and Teacher Education*, No. 21, pp. 747-766.

Wilcox-Herzog, A. (2002), "Is There a Link Between Teachers' Beliefs and Behaviors?", *Early Education and Development*, No. 13 (1), pp. 81-106.

CHAPTER 5

Bethell, G. (2005), *Value-Added Indicators of School Performance: The English Experience Anglia Assessment,* Battisford, Suffolk, England (unpublished report).

Bolen, K. (1989), *Structural Equations with Latent Variables*, John Wiley & Sons, New York.

Bourque, M. L. (2005), The History of No Child Left Behind, *in* Richard P. Phelps (ed.), *Defending Standardized Testing* (pp. 227-254). Hillsdale, NJ: Lawrence Erlbaum Associates.

Caldwell, B. (2002), Autonomy and Self-managment: Concepts and Evidence. *In* T. Bush and L. Bell, *The Principles and Practice of Educational Management*, Paul Chapman, London, pp. 34-48.

Caldwell, B. and **J. Spinks.** (1998), *Beyond the Self-Managing School,* Falmer Press, London.

Glenn, C. and **de J. Groof.** (2005), *Balancing Freedom, Autonomy and Accountability in Education,* Wolf Legal Publishers, Nijmegan, Netherlands.

Hanushek, E. A. and **M. E. Raymond.** (2004), The Effect of School Accountability Systems on the Level and Distribution of Student Achievement, *European Economic Review,* forthcoming.

Gorard, S., J. Fitz, and **C. Taylor** (2001), School Choice Impacts: What Do We Know?, *Educational Researcher,* No. 30 (7), pp. 18-23.

Ingersoll, R. and **Smith, T.** (2004), "What are the Effects of Mentoring and Induction on beginning Teacher Turnover?" *American Educational Research Journal,* No. 41 (3), pp. 681-714.

Ladd, H.F. (2007), *Holding Schools Accountable Revisited*, 2007 Spencer Foundation Lecture in Education Policy and Management, Association for Public Policy Analysis and Management.

Malone, L.J. (2002), *Peer Critical Learning*, CASTL Final Report, June 2002.

Ladd, H. and **Figlio, D.** (2008), "School Accountability and Student Achievement", in Helen F. Ladd and Edward B. Fiske, (eds.) *Handbook of Research on Education Finance and Policy*, Routledge.

O'Day, J. (2002), Complexity, Accountability, and School Improvement. *Harvard Educational Review*, No. 72, (3), pp. 293-329.

Odden, A. and **Busch, C.** (1998), *Financing Schools for High Performance*, San Francisco, Jossey-Bass.

OECD (2008d), *Measuring Improvements in Learning Outcomes: Best practices to Assess the Value-Added of Schools*, OECD, Paris.

OECD (2006b), *Where Immigrant Students Succeed: A Comparative Review of Performance and Engagement in PISA 2003*, OECD, Paris.

Pont B., D. Nusche and **H. Moorman** (2008), *Improving School Leadership, Volume 1: Policy and Practice*, OECD, Paris.

Plank, D.N. and **B.A. Smith** (2008), "Autonomous Schools: Theory, Evidence and Policy", *in* H.F. Ladd and E. B. Fiske, *Handbook of Research in Education Finance and Policy*, Lawrence Erlbaum/ Routledge Press.

Sammons, P., S. Thomas, P. Mortimore, C. Owen and **H. Pennell** (1994), *Assessing School Effectiveness: Developing Measures to put School Performance in Context*, Office for Standards in Education, London.

Saunders, L. (2000), "Understanding Schools Use of 'Value-Added' Data: The Psychology and Sociology of Numbers", *Research Papers in Education*, No.15 (3), pp. 241-58.

Schumacker, R., and **R. Lomax,** (2004), *A Beginner's Guide to Structural Equation Modeling* (2nd edition), Lawrence Erlbaum, Mahwah, New Jersey.

Senge, P. (2000), *Schools that Learn: A Fifth Discipline Fieldbook for Educators, Parents, and Everyone Who Cares About Education*, Doubleday, New York.

Serpell, Z. (2000), *Beginning Teacher Induction: A Review of the Literature*, American Association of Colleges for Teacher Education, Washington, DC.

Smith, M.S. and **J. O'Day** (1991), "Systemic School Reform", *in* S.H. Fuhrman and B. Malen (eds.), *The Politics of Curriculum and Testing: The 1990 Politics of Education Association Yearbook*, Falmer Prero, New York, pp. 233-267.

Van de Grift, W. and **A.A.M. Houtveen,** (2006*), Underperformance in Primary Schools: School Effectiveness and School Improvement*, No. 17 (3) pp. 255-273.

Webster, W. J. (2005), "The Dallas School-Level Accountability Model: The Marriage of Status and Value-Added Approaches", *in* R. L. (ed.), *Value-added models in education: Theory and Applications*, Maple Grove, JAM Press, Minnesota.

CHAPTER 6

Baker, D. and **G.K. LeTendre** (2005), *National Differences, Global Similarities: World Culture and the future of Schooling*, Stanford University Press, Stanford, California.

Barzelay, M. (2001), *The New Public Management: Improving Research and Policy Dialogue*, University of California Press, Berkeley, California.

Blase, J. and **J. Blase** (1998), *Handbook of Instructional Leadership: How Really Good Principals Promote Teaching and Learning*, Corwin Press, Thousand Oaks, California.

Blumberg, A. and **W. Greenfield** (1980), *The Effective Principal: Perspectives on School Leadership*, Allyn and Bacon, Boston, Massachusetts.

Bossert, S., D.C. Dwyer, B. Rowan and **G.V. Lee** (1981), *The Instructional Management Role of the Principal: A Preliminary Review and Conceptualization*, Far West Laboratory for Education Research, San Francisco, California.

Boyd, B. (1996), "The Principal as Teacher: A Model for Instructional Leadership", *NASSP Bulletin*, No. 80 (580), pp. 65-73.

Duke, D. and M. Grogan (1987), *Ethics in Educational Leadership Programs: Emerging Models*, University Council for Educational Administration, Columbia, Missouri.

Fullan, M. (2000), *The Jossey-Bass Reader on Educational Leadership*, JB Publishers, San Francisco, California.

Hallinger, P. and **J. Murphy** (1986), "The Social Context of Effective Schools", *American Journal of Education*, No. 94 (3), pp. 328-355.

Heck, R.H., T.J. Larsen and **G.A. Marcoulides** (1990), "Instructional Leadership and School Achievement: Validation of a Causal Model", *Educational Administration Quarterly*, No. 26 (2), pp. 94-125.

Jones, L., K. Schedler and **S. Wade** (1997), *International Perspectives on the New Public Management*, Jai Press, Greenwhich, Connecticut.

Kleine-Kracht, P. (1993), "Indirect Instructional Leadership: An Administrator's Choice", *Educational Administration Quarterly*, No. 29 (2), pp. 187-212.

Lemahieu, P.G., P.A. Roy and **H.K. Foss** (1997), "Through a Lens Clearly: A Model to Guide the Instructional Leadership of Principals", *Urban Education*, No. 31 (5), pp. 582-608.

National Commission on Excellence for Education (1983), *A Nation at Risk: The Imperative for Educational Reform*, Washington, DC.

OECD (2001), *What works in Innovation in Education,* Centre for Educational Research and Innovation, OECD, Paris.

Reitzug, U. (1997), "Images of Principal Instructional Leadership: From Super-Vision to Collaborative Inquiry", *Journal of Curriculum and Supervision*, No. 12 (4), pp. 324-43.

Sahlin-Andersson, K. (2001), "National, International and Transnational Constructions of New Public Management", *in* T. Christensen and P. Lægreid (eds.), *New Public Management: The Transformation of Ideas and Practice,* Ashgate, Aldershot.

Schedler, K. and **A.D. Proeller** (2000), *New Public Management,* Paul Haupt, Bern.

Wiseman, A.W. (2002), "Principals' Instructional Management Activity and Student Achievement: A Meta-Analysis", Paper presented at the Annual Meeting of the Southwestern Educational Research, Austin, Texas.

Wiseman, A.W. (2004a), "Management of Semi-Public Organizations in Complex Environments", *Public Administration and Management*, No. 9 (2), pp.166-181.

Wiseman, A.W. (2004b), *Principals under Pressure: The Growing Crisis*, Scarecrow Press Lanham, Maryland.

CHAPTER 7

Bandura, A. (1989), "Perceived Self-Efficacy in the Exercise of Personal Agency", *The Psychologist: Bulletin of the British Psychological Society*, Vol. 2, pp. 411-424.

Bandura, A. (1994), "Self-Efficacy", *in* V. S. Ramachaudran (Ed.), *Encyclopedia of Human Behavior* , Vol. 4, pp. 71-81, Academic Press, New York.

Cervone, D. (2000), "Thinking About Self-efficacy", *Behavior Modification*, Sage Publications, Vol. 24, No. 30, pp. 30-56.

Chen, C., Greene, P. and **A. Crick** (1998), "Does Entrepreneurial Self-Efficacy Distinguish Entrepreneurs from Managers?", *Journal of Business Venturing*, Vol.13, pp. 295-316.

Combs G. (2002), "Meeting the Leadership Challenge of a Diverse and Pluralistic Workplace: Implications of Self-Efficacy for Diversity Training" *Journal of Leadership and Organizational Studies*, pp. 1–11.

Hill, T., Smith, N. and **M. Mann** (1987), *Role of Efficacy Expectations in Predicting the Decision to Use Advanced Technologies: The Case of Computers,* Journal of Applied Psychology, Vol. 72, No. 2, pp. 307-313.

Hocevar, D. (2009), "Self-Regulation, Goal Orientation, Self-Efficacy, Worry, and High-Stakes Math Achievement for Mathematically Gifted High School Students" *The Free Library* 01 May 1999, 24 March 2009. <http://www.thefreelibrary. com/Self-Regulation, Goal Orientation, Self-Efficacy, Worry, and...-a055127608>.

Frayne, C. A. and **G. P. Latham** (1987), "Application of Social Learning Theory to Employee Self-Management of Attendance", *Journal of Applied Psychology*, Vol. 72, No. 3, pp. 387-392.

Jones, G.R. (1986), "Socialization Tactics, Self-Efficacy, and Newcomers' Adjustments to Organizations", *The Academy of Management Journal*, Vol. 29, No. 2, pp. 262-279.

Multon, D., Brown, S. and **R. Lent** (1991), "Relation of Self-Efficacy Beliefs to Academic Outcomes: A Meta-Analytic Investigation", *Journal of Counseling Psychology*, Vol. 38, No. 1, pp. 30-38.

Lema, J. and **J. Agrusa** (2006), "Self-Efficacy, Industry Experience and the Self-Directed Learning Readiness of Hospitality Industry College Students", *Journal of Teaching in Travel and Tourism*, Vol. 6, No. 4, pp. 37-50.

Lerner, A. Lee, B., Rooney, J., Rogers, T., Chang, W. and **E. Berndt** (2003), "Relationship of Employee-Reported Work Limitations to Work Productivity", *Med Care*, Vol. 41, No. 5, pp. 649-659.

OECD (2007), *PISA 2006: Science Competencies For Tomorrow's World*, OECD, Paris.

OECD (2004), *Learning for Tomorrow's World: First Results from PISA 2003*, OECD, Paris.

Prasad, M., Wahlqvist, P., Shikiar, R., and **T. Ya-Chen** (2004), "A Review of Self-Report Instruments Measuring Health-Related Work Productivity: A Patient-Reported Outcomes Perspective" *PharmacoEconomics*, Vol. 22, No. 4, pp. 225-244.

Weiss, H. (1978), "Social Learning of Work Values in Organizations", *Journal of Applied Psychology*, No. 63, pp. 711-718.

ANNEXES

Baumgartner, H. and **J.-B. E.M. Steenkamp** (2001), "Response Styles in Marketing Research: A Cross-national Investigation", *Journal of Marketing Research*, No. 18, pp. 143-156.

Cohen, J. (1969), "Statistical Power Analysis for the Behavioural Sciences", *Academic Press*, London.

Little, R.J.A. and **Rubin, D.B.** (2002), *Statistical analysis with missing data: second edition*, John Wiley & Sons, Inc., New Jersey.

Raudenbush, S.W. and **A.S. Bryk** (2002), *Hierarchical Linear Models: Applications and Data Analysis Methods,* Sage, London.

Royston, P. (2004), "Multiple imputation of missing values", *The Stata Journal*, Vol. 4, No. 3, pp. 227-241.

Schafer, J. L. and **J. W. Graham** (2002), "Missing Data: Our view of the State of the Art", *Psychological Methods*, No. 7 (2), pp. 147-177.

Snijders, T. and **R. Bosker** (1999), *Multilevel Analysis: An Introduction to Basic and Advanced Multilevel Modelling,* Sage, London.

Van de Vijver, F. J. R. and **Leung, K.** (1997), "Methods and Data-Analysis for Cross-Cultural Research", *in* W.J. Lonner and J.W. Berry (eds.): *Cross-Cultural Psychology Series*, Sage Publications, Thousand Oaks.

Annex A1

Technical Notes on
Survey Procedures and Analysis

Annex A1.1

CONSTRUCTION OF INDICES AND OTHER DERIVED MEASURES

This annex explains the indices (or scales) and other measures derived from the TALIS teacher and principal questionnaires. Terms enclosed in brackets < > in the descriptions were replaced in the national versions of the questionnaires by the appropriate national equivalent term.

For a detailed description of the methods used to construct and test the reliability of these indices, see the *TALIS Technical Report* (forthcoming).

Cross-cultural validity of the indices

TALIS measures teachers' and school principals' self-reported beliefs, attitudes and practices across a range of topics in 23 countries. The development of these beliefs, attitudes and practices is influenced by individual characteristics, but also by the cultural background and the school system. Furthermore, cultural factors affect the interpretation of questions and the ways in which responses are given (Van de Vijver and Leung, 1997). These influences may produce differences in levels of endorsement or frequency in survey responses, but they may also affect the index structure used to compile responses and thus limit the comparability of the resulting scores. As a consequence, cross-cultural studies entail special methodological challenges. TALIS uses items from indices which are well-established in national and, where possible, cross-national research. When developing the questionnaire care was taken to ensure that items were compatible with the culture and school system of each TALIS country and that the indices had high-quality translation and verification. Furthermore, the cross-cultural comparability – or "invariance" – of the indices measuring beliefs, attitudes and practices in Chapters 4 and 6 was tested by means of confirmatory factor analysis.

Cross-cultural survey methods often differentiate among three levels of invariance: configural, metric and scalar.

- **Configural invariance** is established when the same items are associated with the same underlying factors in all participating countries. This implies an acceptable fit of confirmatory factor analysis models using the same factor structure for all countries.

- **Metric invariance** is achieved when the strength of the associations between each of the items and the underlying factor is also equivalent across countries

- **Scalar invariance** is the most rigorous form. It implies that cross-country differences in the means of the observed items are a result of differences in the means of their corresponding factors. At least partial scalar invariance is needed to make meaningful comparisons of mean scores across countries (*e.g.* Baumgartner and Steenkamp, 2001).

The *TALIS Technical Report* (forthcoming) discusses the construction of the indices reported in Chapter 4 and Chapter 6 and the results from the invariance analysis in greater detail.

Indices derived from TALIS data

Teachers' beliefs about teaching

To assess beliefs about teaching and learning, TALIS asked teachers (and principals) to indicate how strongly they agreed with various statements on a 4-point likert scale, ranging from 1 = "strongly disagree" to 4 = "strongly agree". A statistical factor analysis of the results revealed that responses to groups of these statements were correlated in each country so that it was possible to summarise teachers' beliefs about teaching across two indices: Direct transmission beliefs and Constructivist beliefs.

In short, constructivist beliefs are characterised by a view of the teacher as the facilitator of learning with more autonomy given to students whereas a direct transmission view sees the teacher as the instructor, providing information and demonstrating solutions.

In the analysis to test the cross-cultural validity of these indices, configural and metric invariance was achieved but scalar invariance was not. Country means on the index are therefore not directly comparable. The analysis therefore focuses more on the pattern of cross-cultural differences than on specific country-by-country comparisons of the index scores.

The questionnaire items comprising these indices are as follows:

Index of direct transmission beliefs about teaching

- Effective/good teachers demonstrate the correct way to solve a problem.
- Instruction should be built around problems with clear, correct answers, and around ideas that most students can grasp quickly.
- How much students learn depends on how much background knowledge they have – that is why teaching facts is so necessary.
- A quiet classroom is generally needed for effective learning.

Index of constructivist beliefs about teaching

- My role as a teacher is to facilitate students' own inquiry.
- Students learn best by finding solutions to problems on their own.
- Students should be allowed to think of solutions to practical problems themselves before the teacher shows them how they are solved.
- Thinking and reasoning processes are more important than specific curriculum content.

Each index was calculated with an international mean of zero and a standard deviation of one.

Teachers' teaching practices

To assess teachers' classroom teaching practices, TALIS asked teachers to indicate the frequency – on a 5-point scale ranging from "never or hardly ever" to "in almost every lesson" – with which specified activities happened in a certain "target class" that they taught. In order to randomise the choice of the class, the "target class" was defined as the first ISCED level 2 class that the teacher (typically) taught in the school after 11 am on Tuesdays.

A statistical factor analysis of the results revealed that responses to groups of these activities were correlated in each country so that it was possible to summarise teachers' classroom practices across three indices: Structuring practices; Student-oriented practices and Enhanced activities.

In the analysis to test the cross-cultural validity of these indices, configural and metric invariance was achieved but scalar invariance was not. Country means on the index are therefore not directly comparable. The analysis therefore focuses more on the pattern of cross-cultural differences than on specific country-by-country comparisons of the index scores.

The questionnaire items comprising these indices are as follows:

Index of structuring practices

- I explicitly state learning goals.
- I review with the students the homework they have prepared.

- At the beginning of the lesson I present a short summary of the previous lesson.
- I check my students' exercise books.
- I check, by asking questions, whether or not the subject matter has been understood.

Index of student oriented practices
- Students work in small groups to come up with a joint solution to a problem or task.
- I give different work to the students that have difficulties learning and/or to those who can advance faster.
- I ask my students to suggest or to help plan classroom activities or topics.
- Students work in groups based upon their abilities.

Index of enhanced activities
- Students work on projects that require at least one week to complete.
- Students make a product that will be used by someone else.
- I ask my students to write an essay in which they are expected to explain their thinking or reasoning at some length.
- Students hold a debate and argue for a particular point of view which may not be their own.

Each index was calculated with an international mean of zero and a standard deviation of one.

Co-operation among teaching staff

To assess the co-operation among teaching staff, TALIS asked teachers to indicate the frequency – on a 6-point scale ranging from "never" to "weekly" – with which they undertook specified activities.

A statistical factor analysis of the results revealed that responses to groups of these activities were correlated in each country so that it was possible to summarise teachers' co-operative practices across two indices: Exchange and co-ordination for teaching and Professional collaboration.

In the analysis to test the cross-cultural validity of these indices, configural and metric invariance was achieved but scalar invariance was not. Country means on the index are therefore not directly comparable. The analysis therefore focuses more on the pattern of cross-cultural differences than on specific country-by-country comparisons of the index scores.

The questionnaire items comprising these indices are as follows:

Index of exchange and co-ordination for teaching
- Discuss and decide on the selection of instructional media (*e.g.* textbooks, exercise books).
- Exchange teaching materials with colleagues.
- Attend team conferences for the age group I teach.
- Ensure common standards in evaluations for assessing student progress.
- Engage in discussion about the learning development of specific students.

Index of professional collaboration
- Teach jointly as a team in the same class.
- Take part in professional learning activities (*e.g.* team supervision).

- Observe other teachers' classes and provide feedback.
- Engage in joint activities across different classes and age groups (*e.g.* projects).
- Discuss and co-ordinate homework practice across subjects.

Each index was calculated with an international mean of zero and a standard deviation of one.

Classroom disciplinary climate

To assess the classroom disciplinary climate, TALIS asked teachers to indicate how strongly they agreed – on a 4-point scale ranging from "strongly disagree" to "strongly agree" – with a number of statements about a "target class" that they taught. This "target class" was defined as the first ISCED level 2 class that the teacher (typically) taught in the school s/he works in after 11 am on Tuesdays.

A statistical factor analysis of the results revealed that responses to these statements were correlated in each country so that it was possible to summarise the classroom disciplinary climate in a single index.

In the analysis to test the cross-cultural validity of this index, configural and metric invariance was achieved. Although full scalar invariance was not established, the fit of the models for testing this was sufficiently close to justify an examination of the global picture of mean score differences, though direct comparisons of country means should be avoided.

The questionnaire items comprising this index are as follows:

Index of classroom disciplinary climate

- When the lesson begins, I have to wait quite a long time for students to <quieten down>.
- Students in this class take care to create a pleasant learning atmosphere.
- I lose quite a lot of time because of students interrupting the lesson.
- There is much noise in this classroom.

The index was calculated with an international mean of zero and a standard deviation of one.

Teacher-student relations

To assess teacher-student relations, TALIS asked teachers to indicate how strongly they agreed – on a 4-point scale ranging from "strongly disagree" to "strongly agree" – with a number of statements about how they relate to students in the school.

A statistical factor analysis of the results revealed that responses to these statements were correlated in each country so that it was possible to summarise teacher-student relations in a single index.

In the analysis to test the cross-cultural validity of this index, configural and metric invariance was achieved. Although full scalar invariance was not established, the fit of the models for testing this was sufficiently close to justify an examination of the global picture of mean score differences, though direct comparisons of country means should be avoided.

The questionnaire items comprising this index are as follows:

Index of teacher-student relations

- In this school, teachers and students usually get on well with each other.
- Most teachers in this school believe that students' well-being is important.

- Most teachers in this school are interested in what students have to say.
- If a student from this school needs extra assistance, the school provides it.

The index was calculated with an international mean of zero and a standard deviation of one.

Teachers' self-efficacy

To assess teachers' self-efficacy, TALIS asked teachers to indicate how strongly they agreed – on a 4-point scale ranging from "strongly disagree" to "strongly agree" – with a number of statements about their work in the school.

In the analysis to test the cross-cultural validity of this index, configural and metric invariance was achieved. Although full scalar invariance was not established, the fit of the models for testing this was sufficiently close to justify an examination of the global picture of mean score differences, though direct comparisons of country means should be avoided.

A statistical factor analysis of the results revealed that responses to these statements were correlated in each country so that it was possible to summarise teachers' self-efficacy in a single index.

The questionnaire items comprising this index are as follows:

Index of teachers' self-efficacy

- I feel that I am making a significant educational difference in the lives of my students.
- If I try really hard, I can make progress with even the most difficult and unmotivated students.
- I am successful with the students in my class.
- I usually know how to get through to students.

The index was calculated with an international mean of zero and a standard deviation of one.

School leadership

To assess school leadership behaviours, TALIS asked school principals to indicate the frequency – on a 4-point scale ranging from "never" to "very often" – with which they undertook specified activities in the school. A statistical factor analysis of the results revealed that responses to groups of these activities were correlated in each country so that it was possible to summarise school leadership behaviours across five indices: Management-school goals; Instructional management; Direct supervision of instruction; Accountable management; Bureaucratic management.

In the analysis to test the cross-cultural validity of these indices, configural and metric invariance was achieved but scalar invariance was not. Country means on the index are therefore not directly comparable. The analysis therefore focuses more on the pattern of cross-cultural differences than on specific country-by-country comparisons of the index scores.

The questionnaire items comprising these indices are as follows:

Index of management of school goals

- I make sure that the professional development activities of teachers are in accordance with the teaching goals of the school.
- I ensure that teachers work according to the school's educational goals.
- I use student performance results to develop the school's educational goals.
- I take exam results into account in decisions regarding curriculum development.

- I ensure that there is clarity concerning the responsibility for co-ordinating the curriculum.
- In this school, we work on goals and/or a school development plan.

Index of instructional management

- When a teacher has problems in his/her classroom, I take the initiative to discuss matters.
- I inform teachers about possibilities for updating their knowledge and skills.
- When a teacher brings up a classroom problem, we solve the problem together.
- I pay attention to disruptive behaviour in classrooms.

Index of direct supervision of instruction

- I observe instruction in classrooms.
- I give teachers suggestions as to how they can improve their teaching.
- I monitor students' work.
- I check to see whether classroom activities are in keeping with our educational goals.

Index of accountable management

- An important part of my job is to ensure ministry-approved instructional approaches are explained to new teachers, and that more experienced teachers are using these approaches.
- A main part of my job is to ensure that the teaching skills of the staff are always improving.
- An important part of my job is to ensure that teachers are held accountable for the attainment of the school's goals.
- An important part of my job is to present new ideas to the parents in a convincing way.

Index of bureaucratic management

- It is important for the school that I see to it that everyone sticks to the rules.
- It is important for the school that I check for mistakes and errors in administrative procedures and reports.
- An important part of my job is to resolve problems with the timetable and/or lesson planning.
- An important part of my job is to create an orderly atmosphere in the school.
- I stimulate a task-oriented atmosphere in this school.

To summarise these five leadership behaviour indices further, two indices of leadership styles were derived by averaging the individual leadership behaviour indices as follows:

Index of instructional leadership

- Index of management of school goals.
- Index of instructional management.
- Index of direct supervision of instruction.

Index of administrative leadership

- Index of bureaucratic management.
- Index of accountable management.

Each index was calculated with an international mean of zero and a standard deviation of one.

School resources

TALIS asked school principals to indicate on a 4-point scale ranging from "not at all" to "a lot", the extent to which the school's capacity to provide instruction was hindered by various resource issues. A statistical factor analysis of the results revealed that responses to groups of these issues were correlated in each country so that it was possible to summarise them into two indices measuring the extent to which instruction was hindered by a lack of resources: Index of lack of personnel and Index of shortage of materials.

The questionnaire items comprising these indices are as follows:

Index of lack of personnel

The school's capacity to provide instruction is hindered by:

- A lack of qualified teachers.
- A lack of laboratory technicians.
- A lack of instructional support personnel.

Index of shortage of materials

The school's capacity to provide instruction is hindered by:

- Shortage or inadequacy of instructional materials (e.g. textbooks).
- Shortage or inadequacy of computers for instruction.
- Shortage or inadequacy of other equipment.
- Shortage or inadequacy of library materials.

Each index was calculated with an international mean of zero and a standard deviation of one.

School autonomy

TALIS asked school principals who, among the principal, teachers, the <school governing board>, <regional or local authority> and <national education authority>, had a considerable responsibility for a range of specified tasks. School autonomy was defined as those decisions for which a considerable responsibility lay with the principal, the teachers or the <school governing board>. A "considerable responsibility" was defined as one where an active role is played in decision making. A statistical factor analysis of the results revealed that responses to groups of these tasks were correlated in each country so that it was possible to summarise them into separate indices measuring school autonomy in four broad areas: Hiring teachers and determining salaries, Formulating and allocating the school budget, Student policy and textbook choice and Curriculum.

The questionnaire items comprising these indices are as follows:

Index of autonomy: Hiring teachers and determining salaries

- Selecting teachers for hire.
- Firing teachers.
- Establishing teachers' starting salaries.
- Determining teachers' salary increases.

Index of autonomy: Formulating and allocating the school budget

- Formulating the school budget.
- Deciding on budget allocations within the school.

Index of autonomy: Student policy and textbook choice

- Establishing student disciplinary policies.
- Establishing student assessment policies.
- Approving students for admission to the school.
- Choosing which textbooks are used.

Index of autonomy: Curriculum

- Determining course content.
- Deciding which courses are offered.

Each index was calculated with an international mean of zero and a standard deviation of one.

Ratios derived from TALIS data

Student-teacher ratio

This was derived from school principals' responses to a question about the number of staff (headcounts) currently working in the school and the total number of students (headcounts) of all grades in the school. The measure is not therefore restricted to those teaching or supporting ISCED level 2 education in the school but covers education of all levels provided in the school. The ratio is derived by dividing the number of students by the number of teachers (those whose main activity is the provision of instruction to students).

Ratio of teachers to number of personnel for pedagogical support

This was derived from school principals' responses to a question about the number of staff (headcounts) currently working in the whole school and so is not restricted to only those teaching or supporting ISCED level 2 education in the school. The ratio is derived by dividing the number of teachers (those whose main activity is the provision of instruction to students) by the number of personnel for pedagogical support. Pedagogical support personnel include all teacher aides or other non-professional personnel who provide instruction or support teachers in providing instruction, professional curricular/instructional specialists and educational media specialists.

Ratio of teachers to number of school administrative or management personnel

This was derived from school principals' responses to a question about the number of staff (headcounts) currently working in the whole school and so is not restricted to only those teaching or supporting ISCED level 2 education in the school. The ratio is derived by dividing the number of teachers (those whose main activity is the provision of instruction to students) by the number of school administrative or management personnel. School administrative or management personnel include principals, assistant principals, other management staff, receptionists, secretaries and administration assistants whose main activity is administration or management.

Percentage of professional development that is compulsory

This was derived from teachers' responses to the questions "In all, how many days of professional development did you attend during the last 18 months" (rounded to whole days) and "Of these, how many were compulsory for you to attend as part of your job as a teacher". For each teacher, the percentage was calculated by dividing the number of compulsory days by the total number of days and multiplying by 100. Where this percentage is reported at the country level (Table 3.1), this is the average of the percentages calculated for the individual teachers in that country.

Average class size

In the section of the teacher questionnaire which asked teachers were asked about their classroom teaching practices, they were asked to report on a "target class" that they taught. This "target class" was defined as the first ISCED level 2 class that the teacher (typically) taught in the school after 11am on Tuesdays. Among the characteristics of the "target class", teachers were asked to report the number of students in this class on average throughout the year. In some analyses, the class size was considered at the school level by averaging the reported numbers across the teachers in the school. Similarly, when average class size is reported at the country level (Table 2.4) this is the average of the class sizes reported by the individual teachers in that country.

Annex A1.2

TALIS SAMPLING PROCEDURES AND RESPONSE RATES

The objective of TALIS was to obtain a representative sample of ISCED level 2 teachers in each participating country. TALIS identified policy issues that encompass the classroom, the teacher, the school, and the school management so the coverage of TALIS extends to all teachers of ISCED level 2 and to the principals of the schools where they teach. The international sampling plan prepared for TALIS used a stratified two-stage probability sampling design. This means that teachers (second stage units or secondary sampling units) were to be randomly selected from the list of in-scope teachers in each of the randomly selected schools (first stage units, or primary sampling units). A more detailed description of the survey design and its implementation can be found in the *TALIS Technical Report* (forthcoming).

A teacher of ISCED level 2 is one who, as part of his or her regular duties in their school, provides instruction in programmes at the ISCED level 2. Teachers who teach a mixture of programmes at different levels including ISCED level 2 programmes in the target school are included in the TALIS universe. There is no minimum cut-off for how much ISCED level 2 teaching these teachers need to be engaged in.

The *international target population* of TALIS restricts the survey to those teachers who teach regular classes in ordinary schools and to the principals of those schools. Teachers teaching to adults and teachers working with children with special needs are not part of the international target population and are deemed "out of scope". When schools are comprised exclusively of these teachers, the school itself is said to be "out of scope". Teacher aides, pedagogical support staff (*e.g.* guidance counsellors, librarians) and health and social support staff (*e.g.* doctors, nurses, psychiatrists, psychologists, occupational therapists, and social workers) were not considered as teachers and thus not part of the TALIS international target population.

For national reasons, participating countries could choose to restrict the coverage of their national implementation of TALIS to parts of the country. For example, a province or state experiencing civil unrest or an area struck by a natural disaster could be removed from the international target population to create a *national target population*. Participating countries were invited to keep these exclusions to a minimum.

TALIS recognised that attempting to survey teachers in very small schools, those in schools with no more than three teachers of ISCED level 2, and those teaching in schools located in geographically remote areas could be a costly, time-consuming and statistically inefficient exercise. Therefore, participating countries were allowed to exclude those teachers for TALIS data collection, thus creating a *national survey population* different from the national target population. The National Project Manager for each country was required to document the reasons for exclusion, the size, the location, the clientele, etc. of each excluded school.

Within a selected in-scope school, some teachers were excluded from the sample:

- Teachers teaching only to special needs students.
- Teachers who also act as school principals: no teacher data collected, but school principal data collected.
- Substitute, emergency or occasional teachers.
- Teachers on long-term leave.
- Teachers teaching exclusively to adults.
- In Malta and Iceland, teachers who had taken part in the TALIS 2007 field trial.

Sample size requirements

To allow for reliable estimation and modelling, while allowing for some amount of non-response, the minimum sample size was set at 20 teachers within each participating school. A minimum sample of 200 schools was to be drawn from the population of in-scope schools. Thus, the nominal international sample size was a minimum of 4 000 teachers.

Participating countries could choose to augment their national sample by selecting more schools, or by selecting more teachers within each selected school, or by increasing both. Some countries were asked to increase the within-school sample to counterbalance the effect of selecting too many schools with fewer than 20 teachers.

The sample size requirement was reduced for some participating countries because of the smaller number of schools available for sampling. In a few cases, because the average number of teachers in the schools was less than expected in the international plan, the number of schools sampled was increased to maintain a minimum total number of participating teachers.

Participation rates

The quality requirements for TALIS translate into participation rates (response rates) for schools and for teachers. Reaching these levels of participation does not preclude that some amount of bias may be present in the results but should minimise the negative impact of non-response biases. As TALIS is one of the first large-scale international surveys of active teachers, little is known of "reasonable" response rates for this population. Hence, when compared to large-scale student-level international surveys on education (*e.g.* PISA, PIRLS, TIMSS), TALIS' requirements may appear somewhat lower.

The minimum school participation rate was set at 75% after replacement. Though replacement schools could be called upon as substitutes for non-responding schools, National Project Managers were encouraged to do all they could to obtain the participation of the schools in the original sample. Responding schools that yielded at least 50% of responding teachers were considered as "participating" schools; schools that failed to meet that threshold were considered as "non-participating" even though the number of responding teachers may have been enough to contribute to some of the analyses.

The minimum teacher participation rate was 75% of the selected teachers in participating schools (original sample or replacement schools). Teacher participation was calculated over all participating schools, whether the schools were in the original sample or used as a replacement, and thus the participation rate for the teachers is a requirement at the national level but not at the school level. The overall unweighted and weighted participation rates are the product of the respective school and teacher participation rates.

Table A1.2.1 presents the unweighted school participation rates, before and after replacement of non-participating schools, the unweighted teacher participation rate, the unweighted overall participation rates by country, and a weighted estimated size of the teacher population. Nearly 74 000 teachers participated, which corresponded to 78% of all teachers sampled.

Definition of teachers

TALIS followed the INES (International Indicator of Educational System) data collection definition of a teacher for sampling and analysis:

> "*the formal definition of a classroom teacher is a person whose professional activity involves the planning, organising and conducting of group activities whereby students' knowledge, skills and attitudes develop as stipulated by educational programmes. In short, it is one whose main activity is teaching*" (OECD, 2004).

| Table A1.2.1 | Unweighted participation rates and weighted estimated size of the teacher population by country |

	Number of participating schools	Responding teachers in participating schools	School participation before replacement	School participation after replacement	Teacher participation in participating schools	Overall participation	Weighted estimated size of teacher population
Australia	149	2 275	45.0	74.5	78.6	58.6	92 691
Austria	248	4 265	78.7	89.5	84.8	75.9	42 372
Belgium (Fl.)	197	3 473	61.8	76.1	83.8	63.7	19 580
Brazil	380	5 834	90.6	96.2	90.6	87.1	569 553
Bulgaria	199	3 796	97.5	99.0	95.4	94.5	29 166
Denmark	137	1 722	47.0	68.5	79.4	54.4	25 735
Estonia	195	3 154	94.9	98.5	96.3	94.8	7 567
Hungary	183	2 934	89.4	96.8	91.7	88.8	47 492
Ireland	142	2 227	63.5	71.0	76.4	54.2	22 039
Iceland	133	1 394	92.4	92.4	79.7	73.6	1 916
Italy	298	5 263	87.0	99.3	92.9	92.2	177 539
Korea	171	2 970	66.5	85.5	92.5	79.1	78 052
Lithuania	206	3 535	96.6	99.5	96.1	95.6	28 961
Mexico	192	3 368	95.5	96.0	87.5	84.0	248 197
Malta	58	1 142	100.0	100.0	97.2	97.2	2 618
Malaysia	217	4 248	98.6	99.1	98.1	97.2	81 958
Netherlands	39	484	11.4	26.2	63.7	16.7	28 316
Norway	156	2 458	49.2	78.4	75.7	59.4	18 990
Poland	172	3 184	85.0	86.0	96.3	82.8	120 604
Portugal	173	3 046	81.3	87.4	86.6	75.7	48 381
Slovak Republic	186	3 157	86.8	94.4	93.1	87.9	25 738
Slovenia	184	3 069	88.5	92.0	88.6	81.5	7 244
Spain	193	3 362	93.0	97.0	88.7	86.1	200 101
Turkey	193	3 224	93.5	96.5	90.9	87.7	148 304
TALIS average	4 401	73 584	79.3	88.2	88.4	78.0	2 073 114

Source: OECD.
StatLink ▒▒▒ http://dx.doi.org/10.1787/608033612455

Annex A1.3

QUALITY ASSURANCE

This annex provides an overview of the quality assurance procedures followed in conducting TALIS. Full details are provided in the *TALIS Technical Report* (forthcoming).

Quality control of translation and cultural adaptation of survey questionnaires

The TALIS survey instruments were developed by the Instrument Development Expert Group (IDEG) in English and translated into French, the other working language of the OECD. Although countries were free to choose which language should be their source, all participating countries solely used the international English version as source for translation and adaptations, adhering to the procedures described in the *TALIS Manual for National Project Managers* (MS-01-03). The detailed procedures helped ensure that the 31 national versions of the instruments were as close as possible to the international original, whilst allowing for appropriate adaptations to the national context.

Each version of the TALIS questionnaires was subject to a stringent independent translation and layout verification process prior to both the field trial (FT) and main survey (MS). Independent language experts compared the translated instruments side by side with the international version. The verified instruments with verifiers' comments and suggestions were then returned to the National Project Managers (NPM) for review and improvement of translation/adaptation. Questionnaires were then sent to the International Study Centre (ISC) for verification of the layout, before they were finalised for data collection.

Quality control in TALIS survey administration

For the TALIS main survey (MS) a standardised quality control programme of school visits was prepared by the Secretariat of the International Association for the Evaluation of Educational Achievement (IEA) in its role as the international contractor for TALIS. The programme consisted of an international and a national component; its major aim was to document the quality of the survey administration in each country and flag any issues that may influence the quality of comparability of the data. A secondary aim was to learn about the experiences with TALIS directly from the people administering it, so as to better understand how to improve procedures for subsequent cycles.

The materials and procedures developed for the TALIS survey administration were standardised across all participating countries and languages to ensure, as far as possible, that participants in each country received comparable survey materials under comparable survey conditions. The purpose of the TALIS quality control programme was to document the extent to which the standard operating procedures were followed in each country.

Quality control of data collection in TALIS was composed of three different parts:

- An international programme of school visits and visits at the national centres by International Quality Control Monitors (IQCM), organised and overseen by the IEA Secretariat.
- The national quality control programme of school visits, which was the responsibility of the National Project Manager (NPM) in each country. However, the IEA Secretariat supplied a manual template that could be adapted according to the individual country needs, which was used by 19 out of 21 countries that ran a national quality control programme.
- The online Survey Activities Questionnaire (SAQ) to be completed by NPMs after survey administration, which was administered by the ISC. NPMs were asked about their experiences with the TALIS survey administration. Outcomes of the national quality control programme were reported in the final section of the SAQ.

Field trial operations checklist

The full quality control programme was administered only for the MS. Quality control for the field trial at international level consisted of the Field Trial Operations Checklist, which outlined major steps in survey administration activities: sampling, preparing survey materials and data collection, data entry and data submission. This checklist asked NPMs to fill in the date each task was completed, and to list any comments or any problems they experienced. The completed checklists were used by the ISC to identify weak points in the survey administration and improve survey operation procedures for the MS.

International quality control monitoring programme

For the international programme, the IEA Secretariat, in co-operation with each national centre, identified and appointed one IQCM in each of the 24 participating countries, to visit 10% of the sampled TALIS schools and to interview the school co-ordinators (SC) about aspects of TALIS administration. Schools to be visited were randomly selected from a subset of schools that met specific criteria.

The results from these school visits are discussed in the *TALIS Technical Report* (forthcoming).

Survey Activities Questionnaire

The SAQ covered all aspects of survey administration. It was delivered on line to NPMs by the ISC after all data had arrived at the ISC. The intention of the questionnaire was to obtain information about activities, the extent to which procedures and guidelines were followed and to provide NPMs with an opportunity to give feedback about all aspects of survey administration, including procedures and manuals.

Survey anonymity

A major concern among teachers sampled for participating in TALIS was whether the completed questionnaires and results of the survey would be anonymous and confidential. Whilst confidentiality was guaranteed in the written introduction to the survey, many respondents sought further assurances. School Co-ordinators (SCs) and NPMs in around half of the participating countries reported teacher questions or concerns regarding the confidentiality of responses. Teachers' names were recorded on questionnaires and tracking forms for only one-third of these countries. The others relied on ID numbers, codes, or aliases to disguise teacher identities.

The importance of maintaining the confidentiality of respondents and the completed questionnaires was impressed upon both SCs and QCMs. Many SCs mentioned that the completed questionnaires were in sealed envelopes and/or did not have teachers' names on them. In the majority of countries, teachers' names were not used as identifiers on tracking/listing forms and questionnaire/cover letter labels so as to comply with the legal requirements in their country or to meet teachers' concerns.

Summary

Quality control for TALIS was performed at different levels throughout the survey. All important steps were monitored and documented by independent people or agencies. Analyses of the *School Visit Records* and the SAQ have revealed that the high quality of TALIS data reflects the fact that the standardised procedures for survey preparation as well as administration and data entry were followed by all participating countries.

Annex A1.4

TECHNICAL NOTES ON MULTIPLE REGRESSION ANALYSES

The statistics in this report represent estimates of national characteristics, beliefs and general reports of teachers based on samples of teachers rather than values that could be calculated if every teacher in every country had answered every question. Consequently, it is important to have measures of the degree of uncertainty of the estimates. In TALIS, each estimate has an associated degree of uncertainty, which is expressed through a standard error. The use of confidence intervals provides a way to make inferences about the population means and proportions in a manner that reflects the uncertainty associated with the sample estimates. From an observed sample statistic it can, under the assumption of a normal distribution, be inferred that the corresponding population result would lie within the confidence interval in 95 out of 100 replications of the measurement on different samples drawn from the same population.

Regression analysis enables the estimation of the effects of one or multiple dichotomous and continuous predictor variables on dichotomous or continuous predicted variables. This annex describes the regression methods used in the analysis presented in Chapters 4, 6 and 7.

Regression analysis was carried out for each country separately, as prior analysis showed noticeable differences in regression coefficients between countries.

The regressions were computed with population weights and Balanced Repeated Replicates (BRR) methodology with Fay's adjustment for variance estimation, given the complex sample design of TALIS. Standardised beta weights are available on line for Chapters 4 and 6 at www.oecd.org/edu/talis. Beta weights illustrate the relation between the respective predictor variable and the predicted variable for each country. The standardisation of the weights enables comparisons across measures that differ in their metric. For continuous variables both the variance of the predictor and of the predicted variable were used for standardisation; for dichotomous predictor variables only the variance of the predicted variable was used. Beta weights based on multiple regressions with continuous variables are interpreted as the change in the predicted variable relative to its variance per one standard deviation change in the predictor variable, controlling for the effects of the other variables included in the model. Beta weights for dichotomous variables are interpreted as the difference between, say males and females, in the predicted variable relative to its variance.

An effect has been considered statistically significant if the p-value is below 0.05 for all regression analyses presented in the TALIS report.

Multilevel regression analysis

In addition to the regression analysis on the individual level, described above, multilevel multiple regressions were also used in Chapters 4 and 6. In multilevel regressions the variance for each predicted variable is broken down into a teacher- and a school-level variance. Therefore, both teacher- and school-level variables can be used as predictor variables.

Random intercept models were used. These allow the intercepts to vary between schools, but not the slopes. Thus, the predicted value of the predicted variable is allowed to vary between schools, but not the strength of the association between predictor variables and predicted variable. All variables, including both background and predictor variables, were centred on the grand mean of each country, as models were computed for each country separately. Grand mean centering is a linear transformation of variables by subtracting the overall country mean from each individual score. Data files were weighted at the teacher level with the "final teacher weight". To deal with missing data listwise deletion was used.

In multilevel models effect sizes were additionally computed for school-level variables that use residual variances instead of simple variances. These take both the within-level and the between-level variance into account and therefore enable more realistic estimations of effect sizes at the school level (*e.g.* Schagen and Elliott, 2004). For their computation the following formulas are used

For continuous variables: $\Delta = 2 \times B \times SD_{predictor} / \sigma_e$

For dichotomous variables: $\Delta = B / \sigma_e$

The unstandardised beta weight is multiplied by the standard deviation of the predictor and divided by the residual variance at the individual level for continuous variables, while for dichotomous variables the unstandardised beta coefficient is only divided by the residual variance at the individual level. Based on standards from experimental research, and analogous to Cohen's *d*, $\Delta > .20$ can be interpreted as a small but significant effect size (Cohen, 1969).

To fully understand the meaning of these results, it is important to be aware of the methodology and the assumptions on which it is grounded. In the section above, some technical information is given. Even more important is the following aspect: regression analysis describes the effect of a set of conditions (independent, explanatory or predictor variables) on one or several predicted or dependent variables. Whereas the predicted variables have been treated separately, one by one, all the independent variables (conditions) included in a table have been entered jointly into the statistical procedure. Thus, the conditions are mutually controlled for. For example, the impact of gender on direct transmission beliefs that is estimated in Table 4.3 is the "net" effect after controlling for all the other teacher background variables that are mentioned, namely subject taught, experience and level of education. The effect can be interpreted as the "pure" gender effect that remains if only male and female teachers with similar background in terms of subject, experience, level of education are compared. "Net" effects tend to be smaller than "gross" effects which are calculated without controlling for other variables, but the net estimators come closer to the very meaning of "effect": the association of a factor with a predicted variable, when everything else that might have an influence is taken out of the equation.

Technical notes on the regression analysis presented in Chapter 4

The regression analysis in Chapter 4 largely followed the above. In this chapter on teachers' beliefs and teaching practices, regression analysis was carried out for each country separately. After analysing this background model, the predictor variables considered to be relevant based on theoretical considerations were added. Thus, in each of the models net effects are reported instead of gross effects.

The teacher background variables included in the regression analyses in Chapter 4 are presented in Table A1.4.1.

Multiple regression analysis for the TALIS chapter on teachers' beliefs and teaching practices were mainly computed with the programme SPSS and a special macro using population weights and BRR methodology with Fay's adjustment for variance estimation, given the complex sample design of TALIS. In addition to the regression analysis at the individual level, described above, some multilevel multiple regressions were computed with the programme Mplus, version 5.1.

Technical notes on regression analysis presented in Chapter 6

In the TALIS chapter on school leadership styles, regression analysis was carried out for each country separately. The same background variables were included as control variables in each of the models. These differ slightly from Chapter 4 given the difference in focus, particularly on the school principal. After analysing the background model, the predictor variables considered to be relevant were added based on theoretical considerations. Thus, in each of the models net effects are reported instead of gross effects.

The teacher background variables included in the regression analyses in Chapter 6 are presented in Table A1.4.2.

Multiple regression analyses were mainly computed with the programme STATA® and the standard errors were adjusted using population weights and BRR methodology with Fay's adjustment for variance estimation, given the complex sample design of TALIS. To deal with missing data, listwise deletion was used for the regression analyses.

In addition to the regression analyses on individual level, described above, some multilevel multiple regressions were computed. Prerequisites for the use of multilevel models were: variables were included in the model that are conceptually school-level variables for which multilevel confirmatory factor analysis confirmed an adequate fit on the school level; and the proportion of variance at the school level for the predicted variable equals at least 5%.

Technical notes on regression analysis presented in Chapter 7

Analyses conducted in Chapter 7 differ from those in previous chapters in that they incorporate variables from each of the analytical chapters of the TALIS report. Given the greater scope of the modelling presented in this chapter, a greater number of variables were included in the estimations and missing values were imputed to ensure adequate sample size. These changes were made to reflect differences in the scope and purpose of the modelling while still ensuring that accurate measures were maintained.

For each of the two dependent variables – the index of classroom disciplinary climate and the index of teachers' reported self efficacy – a separate regression analysis was conducted. Cases missing a value in the dependent variables and the independent variables were imputed with a multiple imputation method. Estimations were run for each country and for each dependent variable. The sample sizes for the estimations of each model for each country are presented in Table A1.4.3.

The regression analysis described in Chapter 7 was performed using STATA® and SAS®. Most of the variation in the index of classroom climate is between teachers. Table A1.4.4 presents the between-school variance in classroom disciplinary climate and teachers' reported self-efficacy for each country. This is often reported as the intra-class correlation coefficient. Among 23 countries, the minimum *rho* (intraclass correlation coefficient) is 4%, the maximum is 19% and the median is 8%. Similarly, most of the variation in the index of teachers' self-efficacy is between teachers. Among 23 countries, the minimum *rho* (intraclass correlation coefficient) is 0%, the maximum is 11% and the median is 4%. Since the between-schools variance is very small in the index of classroom climate and the index of self-efficacy, it was decided to apply an ordinary least squares regression instead of multilevel regression analysis. This also facilitated the multiple imputation approach. Within each country, an ordinary least squares regression analysis was carried out with a set of independent variables. The index of teachers' self-efficacy (SELEF) and the index of classroom disciplinary climate (CCLIMATE) served as the dependent variables separately.

Selecting and recoding variables

Based on both theoretical considerations and previous empirical findings, several teacher- and school-level explanatory variables were selected from Chapters 2-6 in order to examine their association with teachers' self-efficacy as well as classroom disciplinary climate. The variables were grouped into six thematic blocs:

• Bloc 1: Teachers' characteristics (mainly from Chapter 2).
• Bloc 2: Teachers' professional development (mainly from Chapter 3).
• Bloc 3: Teachers' beliefs and practices (mainly from Chapter 4).
• Bloc 4: Teachers' appraisal and feedback (mainly from Chapter 5).
• Bloc 5: School leadership (mainly from Chapter 6).
• Bloc 6: School autonomy and resources (Chapter 2).

In the selection of independent variables, indices were preferred over single-item statements whenever they were available since more information could be combined in one index and the problem of measurement error is less severe for indices than for single items (see the *TALIS Technical Report* [forthcoming] for details of indices).

Demographic and socio-economic background variables, which are less likely to be policy amenable for schools and educational systems, were selected on the basis of previous empirical findings. These background variables were included in the net models (that is, models accounting for background factors) in order to examine the net effects of the teacher- and school-level variables. The background variables used in the net model are detailed in Table A1.4.5 in the categories socio-economic background characteristics and teacher characteristics.

The selected independent variables were re-coded where necessary. The description of the independent variables is presented in Table A1.4.5. A detailed SAS® syntax for recoding variables is available on line at *www.oecd.org/edu/talis.*

Missing data

TALIS data include responses from both teachers and school principals. While the focus of the analysis is on teachers, missing data can be a problem if either teachers or school principals have not responded to particular items or questions included in the models presented in Chapter 7. Missing data for a variable can have an adverse effect on the results of the estimations if non-respondents have particular characteristics or circumstances that are different from those for whom there are responses in the data set and if these differences are important for the variable in the analysis. In that case, this can affect both the variance and bias in the estimations.

The assumption made regarding these data is that the missing data are "missing at random". This is not as strong an assumption as "missing completely at random" but it still makes assumptions about the pattern of the missing and actual data that is difficult to analyse. The key assumption for cases of "missing completely at random" is that the pattern of missing data is not systematically different from the non-missing data (Little and Rubin, 1987). This may not hold, for example, if teachers who do not respond to questions about their teaching practices have particular teaching practices or if school principals who do not respond to questions about school evaluations are those who received a particularly negative evaluation.

"Missing at random" also assumes that the missing values can be predicted from other variables in the data set and therefore justifies imputing the missing data. In the Chapter 7 modelling, missing data need to be imputed in order to include the maximum number of cases in the analysis. As more than 50 variables were included in the models, a listwise deletion of all observations that have a missing value for at least one variable would have significantly reduced the sample. The proportion of missing cases for each variable by country is presented in Table A1.4.6. A multiple imputation method was therefore used based on the assumption of "missing at random" to circumvent the problem of missing data (Schafer and Graham, 2002).

Multiple imputation refers to the procedure of replacing each missing value by a vector of $D \geq 2$ imputed values. The D values are ordered in the sense that D completed data sets can be created from the vectors of imputations; replacing each missing value by the first component in its vector of imputations creates the first completed data set, replacing each missing value by the second component in its vector creates the second completed data set, and so on. Standard complete-data methods are used to analyse each data set. When the D sets of imputations are repeated random draws from the predictive distribution of the missing values under a particular model for nonresponse, the D complete-data inferences can be combined to form one inference that properly reflects uncertainty due to nonresponse under that model. (Little and Rubin, 2002, p, 85)

The advantage of multiple imputation over single imputation methods (*e.g.* replacing missing values with the mean or mode of the non-missing values for that variable) is that multiple imputation can take randomness into account in the imputations and incorporate uncertainty when estimating regression coefficients and standard errors.

There are three steps in conducting an analysis with multiple imputation: *i)* create multiply imputed data sets; *ii)* analyse complete data using standard procedures; and *iii)* combine complete data results to obtain the final estimates. The analysis in Chapter 7 followed the procedures below:

i)   Five imputed data sets were prepared using STATA®-ice-procedure.[1] This procedure imputes missing values in the set of variables by using switching regression, an iterative multivariable regression technique (Royston, 2004). The variables used in the multiple imputation model included two dependent variables and all the independent variables listed in Table A1.4.5.[2]

ii) A linear regression analysis was conducted with 100 replicates for each of these 5 data sets in SAS®.

iii) The regression results from 5 independent data sets were combined in SAS® to compute the final estimates based on the following formulae:

Final estimate for regression coefficients (*e.g.* $\bar{\beta}$)

$$\bar{\beta} = (\beta_1 + \beta_2 + \beta_3 + \beta_4 + \beta_5)/5$$

Where β_1 is the regression coefficient from the first data set;

β_2 is the regression coefficient from the second data set;

β_3 is the regression coefficient from the third data set;

β_4 is the regression coefficient from the fourth data set; and

β_5 is the regression coefficient from the fifth data set.

Final estimate for standard error (*e.g.* $\sigma_{(error)}$)

$$\sigma^2_{(w)} = (\sigma^2_{(\beta_1)} + \sigma^2_{(\beta_2)} + \sigma^2_{(\beta_3)} + \sigma^2_{(\beta_4)} + \sigma^2_{(\beta_5)})/5$$

$$\sigma^2_{(b)} = \frac{1}{4}\sum_{i=1}^{5}(\beta_i - \bar{\beta})^2$$

$$\sigma_{(error)} = \sqrt{\sigma^2_{(w)} + (1 + \frac{1}{5}\sigma^2_{(b)})}$$

The STATA® syntax for the first step and the SAS® syntax for the second and third steps can be found at *www.oecd.org/edu/TALIS*.

Teacher weights

The teacher final weights (TCHWGT) as well as the 100 replicates (TRWGT1 to TRWGT100) were used to conduct the regression analysis.

Modelling strategy

This section outlines the modelling strategy used in the regression analysis of teacher- and school-level variables related to two dependent variables—the index of teachers' self-efficacy and the index of classroom disciplinary climate. Modelling for the index of teachers' self-efficacy and modelling for the index of classroom disciplinary climate were conducted independently, but followed exactly the same procedure.

A two-step procedure was applied following the model specification suggested by Raudenbush and Bryk (2002), as well as by Snijders and Bosker (1999):

- Step 1: the effects of the variables of each of the six blocs were examined in turn, estimating separate models for each bloc.
- Step 2: for each of the separate models run in the first step, only the significant variables were selected for the final model. Throughout the regression analysis, an effect is considered statistically significant if the p-value is below 0.05.

The impact of selected teacher and school-level variables on the dependent variables was analysed before and after accounting for the demographic and socio-economic background variables. A gross model is defined as the model without accounting for the background variables, while a net model is defined as the model accounting for the background variables. In the net Bloc 1 model, socio-economic background variables listed at the top of Table A1.4.5 were introduced in addition to the independent variables listed as Bloc 1. In the net Bloc 2 to Bloc 6 models, socio-economic background variables and Bloc 1 variables listed in Table A1.4.5 were introduced in addition to the variables in each bloc.

In the end, each country has four different final models: two models for teachers' self-efficacy (gross and net) and two for classroom disciplinary climate (gross and net). The summary of these four models is presented in Box A1.4.1. The set of independent variables in the final models differ among the countries.

Box A1.4.1 **Summary of four final models per country**

Dependent variables	With/without accounting for the background variables	Step 1		Step 2		Final model
Index of teachers' self-efficacy	Without background variables	Bloc-by-bloc analysis (six separate models: Bloc 1 to 6 models)	→	Select only significant variables	→	**Final gross self-efficacy model**
	With background variables	Bloc-by-bloc analysis (six separate models: Bloc 1 to 6 models) with background variables	→	Select only significant variables with background variables	→	**Final net self-efficacy model**
Index of classroom disciplinary climate	Without background variables	Bloc-by-bloc analysis (six separate models: Bloc 1 to 6 models)	→	Select only significant variables	→	**Final gross classroom disciplinary climate model**
	With background variables	Bloc-by-bloc analysis (six separate models: Bloc 1 to 6 models) with background variables	→	Select only significant variables with background variables	→	**Final net classroom disciplinary climate model**

NOTES

1. Stata®-ice-procedure was used instead of SAS® for creating multiple imputed data sets as the SAS® PROC multiple imputation procedure does not allow the use of fractional weights.

2. Four school-level variables (*e.g.* BTG39A, BTG40A, BTG40C) were created by aggregating the teacher-level variables at the school level before imputing the data.

Table A14.1 List of independent variables in the Chapter 4 regression analyses

Variable	Level	Based on variable in data set
Teacher background		
Teacher's gender (1=female; 0=male)	Teacher	BTG01
Subject taught: Mathematics/science (0=other, 1=mathematics or science)	Teacher	BTG34
Subject taught: Humanities (0=other, 1=reading, social studies, foreign languages or religion)	Teacher	BTG34
Number of years of teaching[1]	Teacher	BTG09
Teacher's education: high (1=ISCED5A masters or higher; 0=ISCED5A bachelor or below)	Teacher	BTG07
Classroom background		
Class size	Teacher	BTG38
Average ability (compared to other students in the same year/level)	Teacher	BTG39B
Percentage of students with a mother tongue different from the language of instruction	Teacher	BTG40A
School backgroun		
Public school	School	PUBLIC
School location: (1= city, 0= other)	School	BCG10
School size (number of students)	School	BCG12
Percentage of students in school with at least one parent having completed an ISCED3 qualification or higher	School	BTG40B
Ability of students in class compared to the average at the same grade level	School	BTG39B
Professional development		
Number of days of professional development	Teacher	BTG12
Type of professional development: workshops/courses (0=no, 1=yes)	Teacher	BTG11A1
Type of professional development: Networks (0=no, 1=yes)	Teacher	BTG11E1
School providing mentor for new teachers (1=yes; 0=no)	School	BCG35
Teachers' beliefs, attitudes and practices		
Index of classroom climate	Teacher	CCLIMATE
Index of teacher-student relations	Teacher	TSRELAT
Index of self-efficacy	Teacher	SELFEF
Index of classroom teaching practice: structuring	Teacher	TPSTRUC
Index of classroom teaching practice: student-oriented	Teacher	TPSTUD
Index of classroom teaching practice: enhanced activities	Teacher	TPACTIV
Index of direct transmission beliefs about instruction	Teacher	TBTRAD
Index of constructivist beliefs about instruction	Teacher	TBCONS
Index of exchange and co-ordination for teaching	Teacher	TCEXCHAN
Index of professional collaboration	Teacher	TCCOLLAB

1. Continuous variables were z-standardised.
Source: OECD, *TALIS Database*.
StatLink http://dx.doi.org/10.1787/608033612455

Table A1.4.2 List of independent variables in the Chapter 6 regression analyses

Variable	Level	Based on variable in data set
Average class size	Teacher	BTG38
Important aspect of teacher appraisal: innovative teaching practices (1 = considered of moderate or high importance; 0 = others)	Teacher	BTG22H
Important aspect of teacher appraisal: professional development the teacher has undertaken (1 = considered of moderate or high	Teacher	BTG22J
Important aspect of teacher appraisal: retention and pass rates of students (1 = considered of moderate or high importance; 0 = others)	Teacher	BTG22B
Important aspect of teacher appraisal: student test scores (1 = considered of moderate or high importance; 0 = others)	Teacher	BTG22A
Index of classroom climate	Teacher	CCLIMATE
Index of constructivist beliefs about instruction	Teacher	TBCONS
Index of exchange and co-ordination for teaching	Teacher	TCEXCHAN
Index of professional collaboration	Teacher	TCCOLLAB
Index of self-efficacy	Teacher	SELFEF
Index of teacher-student relations	Teacher	TSRELAT
Number of days of professional development	Teacher	BTG12
Number of years of teaching (categorised into 0-5 years and 6-15 years)	Teacher	BTG09
Teacher job satisfaction	Teacher	BCG31A
Teacher wanted more professional development	Teacher	BTG19
Teacher's contract status (1 = permanent; 0 = fixed-term contract)	Teacher	BTG06
Teacher's education: high (1 = ISCED 5A masters or higher; 0 = ISCED 5A bachelor or below)	Teacher	BTG07
Teacher's employment status (1 = full-time; 0 = part-time)	Teacher	BTG03
Teacher's gender (1 = female; 0 = male)	Teacher	BTG01
Time in class spent on actual teaching and learning	Teacher	BTG41C
Works in another school (1 = yes, 0 = no)	Teacher	BTG04
Action taken following identification of a weakness in teacher appraisal: Establish a development plan	School	BCG28C
Action taken following identification of a weakness in teacher appraisal: Impose material sanctions	School	BCG28D
Action taken following identification of a weakness in teacher appraisal: Report to another body to take action	School	BCG28E
Important aspect of school evaluation: innovative teaching practices (1 = considered of high importance; 0 = other)	School	BCG19H
Important aspect of school evaluation: student test scores (1 = considered of high importance; 0 = other)	School	BCG19A
Important aspect of school evaluation: teacher professional development (1 = considered of high importance; 0 = other)	School	BCG19J
Index of a lack of personnel (teachers, technicians, instructional support personnel, other support personnel)	School	LACKPERS
Index of school autonomy in hiring teachers, determining salaries	School	AUTHIRE
Index of school leadership: Administrative leadership	School	ADMINL
Index of school leadership: Instructional leadership	School	INSTRL
Influence of school evaluation: Appraisal of individual teachers (1 = high influence; 0 = other)	School	BCG20D
Influence of school evaluation: Appraisal of the school management (1 = high influence; 0 = other)	School	BCG20C
Number of years as school principal (categorised into 0-5 years and 6-15 years)	School	BCG05
Objective of teachers' appraisal: Inform administrative body	School	BCG26B
School autonomy (1 = school principal has responsibility for all areas, 0 = other)	School	BCG31
School being public (1 = public; 0 = private)	School	PUBLIC
School location (two variables: one = village, one = small town)	School	BCG10
School principal in another school (1 = yes, 0 = no)	School	BCG03
School principal's education: high (1 = ISCED 5A masters or higher; 0=ISCED 5A bachelor or below)	School	BCG04
School principal's gender (1 = female, 0 = male)	School	BCG01
Self-evaluation report (two variables: one = if it had been conducted, one = more than twice in 5 years)	School	BCG18A

Source: OECD, *TALIS Database*.
StatLink ᴍᴸᴸ http://dx.doi.org/10.1787/608033612455

Table A1.4.3	Sample sizes for the Chapter 7 regression analyses

	Number of teachers
Australia	2 275
Austria	4 285
Belgium (Fl.)	3 511
Brazil	5 867
Bulgaria	3 817
Denmark	1 740
Estonia	3 155
Hungary	2 938
Iceland	1 409
Ireland	2 227
Italy	5 382
Korea	2 975
Lithuania	3 609
Malaysia	4 315
Malta	1 145
Mexico	3 409
Norway	2 458
Poland	3 209
Portugal	3 046
Slovak Republic	3 164
Slovenia	3 071
Spain	3 362
Turkey	3 224

Source: OECD, *TALIS Database*.
StatLink ᵀᵐˢ⁺ http://dx.doi.org/10.1787/608033612455

Table A1.4.4	Between-school variance in classroom disciplinary climate and teachers' reported self-efficacy for each country

	Total variance between schools expressed as a percentage of the total variance within country[1]	
	Classroom disciplinary climate (%)	Teacher self-efficacy (%)
Australia	9.31	2.59
Austria	6.52	2.25
Belgium (Fl.)	5.89	2.59
Brazil	18.83	11.48
Bulgaria	11.35	4.36
Denmark	11.13	3.83
Estonia	4.48	1.84
Hungary	10.42	4.59
Iceland	6.88	0.16
Ireland	11.93	3.64
Italy	6.60	3.93
Korea	7.18	4.42
Lithuania	5.70	4.89
Malaysia	12.74	10.10
Malta	11.71	5.28
Mexico	6.01	4.64
Norway	10.33	4.48
Poland	6.32	3.69
Portugal	8.63	2.51
Slovak Republic	5.97	2.99
Slovenia	6.64	2.45
Spain	7.53	3.21
Turkey	11.41	6.08
TALIS Average	**8.85**	**4.17**

1. This index is often referred to as the intra-class correlation (rho).
Source: OECD, *TALIS Database*.
StatLink ᵀᵐˢ⁺ http://dx.doi.org/10.1787/608033612455

Table A1.4.5	List of independent variables in the Chapter 7 regression analyses		

Blocs of Independent variables	Variable name	Level	Based on variable in data set
Socio-economic background characteristics	Ability of students in class lower than the average at the same grade level (1 = lower; 0 = average or higher)	Teacher	BTG39B
	Ability of students in class higher than the average at the same grade level (1 = higher; 0 = average or lower)	Teacher	BTG39B
	Percentage of students in class speaking a different language than the language of instruction	Teacher	BTG40A
	Percentage of students in class with at least one parents completed ISCED5 qualification or higher	Teacher	BTG40C
	Percentage of students in school speaking a different language than the language of instruction	School	BTG40A
	Percentage of students in school with at least one parent having completed ISCED5 qualification or higher	School	BTG40C
	Ability of students in class lower than the average at the same grade level (1 = lower; 0 = average or higher)	School	BTG39B
	Ability of students in class higher than the average at the same grade level (1 = higher; 0 = average or lower)	School	BTG39B
Bloc 1: Teacher characteristics	Teacher's gender (1 = female; 0 = male)	Teacher	BTG01
	Teacher's employment status (1 = full-time; 0 = part-time)	Teacher	BTG03
	Teacher's contract status (1 = permanent; 0 = fixed-term contract)	Teacher	BTG06
	Teacher's education: high (1 = ISCED5A masters or higher; 0 = ISCED5A bachelor or below)	Teacher	BTG07
	Number of years of teaching	Teacher	BTG09
Bloc 2: Teacher professional development	Number of days of professional development	Teacher	BTG12
	School providing induction process for teachers (1 = yes; 0 = no)	School	BCG33
	School providing mentor for new teachers (1 = yes; 0 = no)	School	BCG35
Bloc 3: Teacher beliefs and practices	Index of teacher-student relations	Teacher	TSRELAT
	Index of classroom teaching practice: structuring	Teacher	TPSTRUC
	Index of classroom teaching practice: student-oriented	Teacher	TPSTUD
	Index of classroom teaching practice: enhanced activities	Teacher	TPACTIV
	Index of direct transmission beliefs about instruction	Teacher	TBTRAD
	Index of constructivist beliefs about instruction	Teacher	TBCONS
	Index of exchange and co-ordination for teaching	Teacher	TCEXCHAN
	Index of professional collaboration	Teacher	TCCOLLAB
Bloc 4: Teacher appraisal and feedback	Never received appraisal or feedback from any source (1 = true; 0 = false)	Teacher	NEVERAF
	School evaluation within 5 years (1 = never; 0 = at least once)	School	NEVEREVAL
	Effective teachers receive more monetary or non-monetary rewards in the school. It is a dichotomous variable (1 = strongly agree or agree, 0 = strongly disagree or disagree).	Teacher	BTG28F
	Important aspect of teacher appraisal: student test scores (1 = considered of moderate or high importance; 0 = others)	Teacher	BTG22A
	Important aspect of teacher appraisal: innovative teaching practices (1 = considered of moderate or high importance; 0 = others)	Teacher	BTG22H
	Important aspect of teacher appraisal: professional development the teacher has undertaken (1 = considered of moderate or high importance; 0 = others)	Teacher	BTG22J
	Appraisal impact: a change in salary (1 = moderate or large change; 0 = others)	Teacher	BTG23A
	Appraisal impact: opportunities for professional development activities (1 = moderate or large change; 0 = others)	Teacher	BTG23C
	Appraisal impact: public recognition from the principal and/or colleagues (1 = moderate or large change; 0 = others)	Teacher	BTG23E
	Appraisal impact: changes in the teacher's work responsibilities that make the job more attractive (1 = moderate or large change; 0 = others)	Teacher	BTG23F
	School evaluation published (1 = yes; 0 = no)	School	BCG21
	Important aspect for school evaluations: student test scores (1 = considered of moderate or high importance; 0 = others)	School	BCG19A
Bloc 5: School leadership	Index of management-school goals	School	FCSGCD
	Index of instructional management	School	PROIIPD
	Index of direct supervision of instruction in the school	School	SUPINSTR
	Index of accountable management	School	ACCROLE
	Index of bureaucratic management	School	BURRULEF
Bloc 6: School autonomy and resources	Index of school climate: student delinquency	School	SCDELINQ
	Index of school climate: teachers' working morale	School	SCTMORAL
	Index of a lack of personnel (teachers, technicians, instructional support personnel, other support personnel)	School	LACKPERS
	Index of shortage of materials (instructional materials, computers, equipment, library materials)	School	LACKMAT
	Index of school autonomy in hiring teachers, determining salaries	School	AUTHIRE
	Index of school autonomy in budgeting (formulating and allocating the school budget)	School	AUTBUDGT
	Index of school autonomy in student policy and textbooks	School	AUTSTUDP
	Index of school autonomy in curriculum (courses offered, course content)	School	AUTCURR
	Average class size	School	BTG38
	School being public (1 = public; 0 = private)	School	PUBLIC

Source: OECD, *TALIS Database*.
StatLink ⧉ http://dx.doi.org/10.1787/608033612455

Table A14.6 (1/5) The percentage of missing cases for each country for each variable included in the Chapter 7 regression analyses

	N	Cclimate	Self-efficacy	BTG39B	BTG39B	BTG40A
		Index of classroom climate	Index of Teacher (%)s' reported self-efficacy	Ability of students in class lower than the average at the same grade level (1=lower; 0=average or higher)	Ability of students in class higher than the average at the same grade level (1=higher; 0=average or lower)	Percentage of students in class speaking a different language than the language of instruction
		Teacher (%)	Teacher (%)	Teacher (%)	Teacher (%)	Teacher (%)
Australia	2275	6.94	3.65	8.81	8.81	6.95
Austria	4285	6.14	3.48	8.96	8.96	6.39
Belgium (Fl.)	3511	3.87	2.45	7.27	7.27	4.25
Brazil	5867	4.61	2.02	5.90	5.90	8.13
Bulgaria	3817	5.00	1.64	8.08	8.08	10.17
Denmark	1740	4.65	3.64	7.43	7.43	5.11
Estonia	3155	1.96	0.84	4.88	4.88	6.18
Hungary	2938	4.17	1.64	3.28	3.28	4.73
Iceland	1409	14.93	9.83	19.01	19.01	14.83
Ireland	2227	2.39	0.76	5.07	5.07	3.11
Italy	5382	7.66	4.22	10.20	10.20	11.65
Korea	2975	2.02	1.85	3.75	3.75	3.93
Lithuania	3609	6.42	3.40	13.28	13.28	16.45
Malaysia	4315	2.62	2.24	2.53	2.53	2.82
Malta	1145	2.21	2.10	4.10	4.10	6.03
Mexico	3409	3.48	1.76	4.32	4.32	5.18
Norway	2458	6.73	4.94	13.65	13.65	7.12
Poland	3209	3.33	2.06	7.24	7.24	18.18
Portugal	3046	3.23	1.44	4.29	4.29	4.31
Slovak Republic	3164	3.18	1.32	8.39	8.39	6.87
Slovenia	3071	4.00	1.56	5.85	5.85	9.60
Spain	3362	2.81	1.08	5.01	5.01	5.50
Turkey	3224	3.49	3.37	4.73	4.73	100.00

	BTG40C	BTG40A	BTG40C	BTG39B	BTG39B	BTG01
	Percentage of students in class with at least one parents having completed ISCED5 or higher	Percentage of students in school speaking a different language than the language of instruction	Percentage of students in school with at least one parent having completed ISCED5 or higher	Ability of students in class lower than the average at the same grade level (1=lower; 0=average or higher)	Ability of students in class higher than the average at the same grade level (1=higher; 0=average or lower)	Teacher (%)'s gender (1=female; 0=male)
	Teacher (%)	School (%)	School (%)	School (%)	School (%)	Teacher (%)
Australia	11.26	0.00	0.00	0.00	0.00	0.00
Austria	11.57	0.00	0.00	0.00	0.00	0.42
Belgium (Fl.)	10.90	0.00	0.00	0.00	0.00	0.79
Brazil	8.49	0.00	0.00	0.00	0.00	0.53
Bulgaria	14.01	0.00	0.00	0.00	0.00	0.38
Denmark	8.25	0.00	0.00	0.00	0.00	0.76
Estonia	14.89	0.00	0.00	0.00	0.00	0.07
Hungary	8.06	0.00	0.00	0.00	0.00	0.47
Iceland	30.17	0.00	0.00	0.00	0.00	0.83
Ireland	12.37	0.00	0.00	0.00	0.00	0.00
Italy	17.28	0.00	0.00	0.00	0.00	2.11
Korea	3.69	0.00	0.00	0.00	0.00	0.15
Lithuania	13.45	0.00	0.00	0.00	0.00	2.08
Malaysia	3.18	0.00	0.00	0.00	0.00	1.65
Malta	13.68	0.00	0.00	0.00	0.00	0.36
Mexico	5.67	0.00	0.00	0.00	0.00	0.89
Norway	20.00	0.00	0.00	0.00	0.00	0.00
Poland	16.21	0.00	0.00	0.00	0.00	0.80
Portugal	6.64	0.00	0.00	0.00	0.00	0.00
Slovak Republic	7.90	0.00	0.00	0.00	0.00	0.15
Slovenia	22.53	0.00	0.00	0.00	0.00	0.08
Spain	18.43	0.00	0.00	0.00	0.00	0.00
Turkey	5.25	100.00	0.00	0.00	0.00	0.00

Source: OECD, *TALIS Database*.
StatLink ᘛᗑᗑ http://dx.doi.org/10.1787/608033612455

Table A1.4.6
(2/5)

The percentage of missing cases for each country for each variable included in the Chapter 7 regression analyses

	BTG03	BTG06	BTG07	BTG09	BTG12	BCG33
	Teacher's employment status (1=full-time; 0=part-time)	Teacher's contract status (1=permanent; 0=fixed-term contract)	Teacher's education: high [1=ISCED5A masters or higher; 0=(No suggestion) bachelor or below]	Number of years of teaching	Number of days of professional development	School providing induction process for teachers (1=yes; 0=no)
	Teacher (%)	Teacher (%)	Teacher (%)	Teacher (%)	Teacher (%)	School (%)
Australia	0.43	1.67	0.53	1.22	2.01	5.30
Austria	0.81	3.84	1.99	1.82	3.91	4.71
Belgium (Fl.)	1.33	3.18	1.53	1.41	3.40	9.74
Brazil	4.84	3.91	3.79	1.35	7.69	4.18
Bulgaria	1.07	1.24	1.62	0.60	9.40	0.66
Denmark	0.97	1.82	1.11	1.32	4.73	15.36
Estonia	0.53	3.21	1.03	1.19	2.58	0.84
Hungary	0.93	1.43	1.29	0.79	7.55	0.84
Iceland	1.35	3.27	1.47	3.16	8.70	34.66
Ireland	0.39	3.60	0.27	0.54	3.15	18.27
Italy	3.55	3.52	4.21	3.08	9.76	4.31
Korea	1.56	1.57	0.47	0.59	1.57	12.19
Lithuania	3.47	3.64	3.79	3.29	4.66	2.42
Malaysia	2.04	2.13	2.01	2.19	2.66	1.18
Malta	1.23	2.15	1.49	0.36	5.23	5.77
Mexico	2.45	3.27	2.68	2.55	6.46	3.60
Norway	0.41	1.68	0.54	1.91	3.55	4.03
Poland	1.15	2.41	1.43	1.38	3.84	1.93
Portugal	0.45	1.01	0.22	0.21	5.24	9.20
Slovak Republic	0.92	1.82	0.87	0.96	3.17	2.24
Slovenia	0.70	2.62	0.77	0.74	6.41	4.38
Spain	0.56	2.89	0.76	0.64	17.63	5.81
Turkey	2.59	3.50	0.58	1.01	5.50	3.97

	BCG35	TSRELAT	TPSTRUC	TPSTUD	TPACTIV	TBTRAD
	School providing mentor for new teachers (1=yes; 0=no)	Index of teacher-student relations	Index of classroom teaching practice: structuring	Index of classroom teaching practice: student-oriented	Index of classroom teaching practice: enhanced activities	Index of direct transmission beliefs about instruction
	School (%)	Teacher (%)	Teacher (%)	Teacher (%)	Teacher (%)	Teacher (%)
Australia	6.12	3.70	7.41	7.41	7.41	2.93
Austria	3.64	3.60	6.28	6.28	6.28	3.20
Belgium (Fl.)	9.36	2.46	4.06	4.06	4.06	2.96
Brazil	4.01	1.97	4.73	4.73	4.73	1.93
Bulgaria	1.46	1.56	5.17	5.17	5.17	1.28
Denmark	17.86	3.64	4.84	4.84	4.84	3.65
Estonia	1.50	0.99	2.29	2.29	2.29	1.11
Hungary	0.84	1.52	2.48	2.48	2.48	1.24
Iceland	34.66	9.66	16.70	16.70	16.70	10.21
Ireland	16.23	0.80	2.28	2.28	2.28	0.73
Italy	3.25	4.45	7.06	7.06	7.06	4.68
Korea	14.56	1.85	2.14	2.14	2.14	1.52
Lithuania	3.59	3.30	6.60	6.60	6.60	3.48
Malaysia	0.75	2.20	2.44	2.44	2.44	2.06
Malta	0.00	2.14	2.57	2.57	2.57	2.35
Mexico	4.71	1.68	3.39	3.39	3.39	1.45
Norway	5.36	4.84	7.60	7.60	7.60	5.06
Poland	1.47	2.10	3.20	3.20	3.20	1.88
Portugal	11.08	1.40	3.12	3.12	3.12	1.24
Slovak Republic	2.05	1.35	3.34	3.34	3.34	1.32
Slovenia	4.40	1.53	3.60	3.60	3.60	1.68
Spain	5.81	1.08	3.01	3.01	3.01	1.01
Turkey	6.25	3.36	3.85	3.85	3.85	2.98

Source: OECD, *TALIS Database*.
StatLink ⬛▥▤ http://dx.doi.org/10.1787/608033612455

Table A14.6
(3/5)

The percentage of missing cases for each country for each variable included in the Chapter 7 regression analyses

	TBCONS	TCEXCHAN	TCCOLLAB	NEVERAF	NEVEREVAL	BTG28F
	Index of constructivist beliefs about instruction	Index of exchange and co-ordination for teaching	Index of professional collaboration	Never received appraisal or feedback from any source (1=true; 0=false)	School evaluation within 5 years (1=never; 0=at least once)	Effective teachers receive more monetary or non-monetary rewards in the school. It is a dichotomous variable (1=strongly agree or agree; 0=strongly disagree or disagree).
	Teacher (%)	Teacher (%)	Teacher (%)	Teacher (%)	School (%)	Teacher (%)
Australia	2.93	3.33	3.33	2.83	5.51	4.76
Austria	3.20	3.66	3.66	3.56	5.90	7.20
Belgium (Fl.)	2.96	2.56	2.56	2.76	8.91	4.71
Brazil	1.93	2.05	2.05	5.63	4.52	4.75
Bulgaria	1.28	1.37	1.37	2.68	2.40	5.76
Denmark	3.65	3.95	3.95	3.67	18.65	4.91
Estonia	1.11	1.24	1.24	2.04	1.49	3.58
Hungary	1.24	1.54	1.54	2.21	1.28	7.03
Iceland	10.21	10.55	10.55	7.65	32.88	14.40
Ireland	0.73	0.69	0.69	2.84	19.44	4.37
Italy	4.68	4.77	4.77	10.22	6.36	14.67
Korea	1.52	1.67	1.67	1.69	13.97	1.56
Lithuania	3.48	3.27	3.27	3.90	3.53	4.72
Malaysia	2.06	2.15	2.15	2.04	1.06	2.66
Malta	2.35	2.40	2.40	2.35	1.84	6.19
Mexico	1.45	1.61	1.61	2.89	3.01	2.86
Norway	5.06	5.04	5.04	5.23	4.89	7.49
Poland	1.88	1.99	1.99	3.44	0.51	5.21
Portugal	1.24	1.21	1.21	2.17	8.95	4.95
Slovak Republic	1.32	1.41	1.41	1.48	1.85	3.93
Slovenia	1.68	1.54	1.54	2.35	6.02	6.58
Spain	1.01	0.93	0.93	3.43	7.45	6.06
Turkey	2.98	3.04	3.04	3.08	3.54	3.88

	BTG22A	BTG22H	BTG22J	BTG23A	BTG23C	BTG23E
	Important aspect of teacher appraisal: student test scores (1=considered of moderate or high importance; 0=others)	Important aspect of teacher appraisal: innovative teaching practices (1=considered of moderate or high importance; 0=others)	Important aspect of teacher appraisal: professional development the teacher has undertaken (1=considered of moderate or high importance; 0=others)	Appraisal impact: a change in salary (1=moderate or large change; 0=others)	Appraisal impact: opportunities for professional development activities (1=moderate or large change; 0=others)	Appraisal impact: public recognition from the principal and/or colleagues (1=moderate or large change; 0=others)
	Teacher (%)	Teacher (%)	Teacher (%)	Teacher (%)	Teacher (%)	Teacher (%)
Australia	25.29	19.54	21.58	3.47	4.17	3.73
Austria	33.27	20.34	25.57	5.75	6.39	6.15
Belgium (Fl.)	31.44	23.61	22.95	3.78	4.12	4.47
Brazil	15.87	11.49	12.81	4.39	5.21	4.72
Bulgaria	13.37	18.14	12.63	5.70	6.62	6.34
Denmark	23.95	29.29	20.96	5.16	5.52	5.59
Estonia	27.40	24.45	21.19	3.79	4.97	4.18
Hungary	40.46	26.67	29.27	4.59	6.38	5.58
Iceland	36.73	34.64	37.14	9.06	10.56	10.41
Ireland	24.66	23.93	26.86	3.21	3.98	3.80
Italy	21.25	16.09	16.03	8.61	10.00	8.98
Korea	11.89	8.42	9.41	2.46	2.70	2.70
Lithuania	33.57	21.11	20.57	5.23	6.76	5.87
Malaysia	3.74	2.76	4.01	2.42	2.61	2.46
Malta	24.45	15.90	25.61	3.84	3.98	4.41
Mexico	23.64	14.16	16.12	3.06	3.75	3.32
Norway	35.84	39.22	33.36	7.50	7.90	8.39
Poland	28.96	16.68	13.39	5.58	6.53	5.12
Portugal	23.44	20.52	19.57	3.29	3.37	3.36
Slovak Republic	18.84	15.26	20.50	2.25	3.33	3.53
Slovenia	27.38	20.75	25.82	4.85	6.03	5.43
Spain	16.43	21.89	20.42	3.87	4.20	4.21
Turkey	16.60	13.51	16.50	5.04	5.51	5.82

Source: OECD, *TALIS* Database.
StatLink ᵐ🔗 http://dx.doi.org/10.1787/608033612455

ANNEX A1.4 TECHNICAL NOTES ON MULTIPLE REGRESSION ANALYSES

Table A1.4.6 (4/5) The percentage of missing cases for each country for each variable included in the Chapter 7 regression analyses

	BTG23F	BCG21	BCG19A	FCSGCD	PROIIPD	SUPINSTR
	Appraisal impact: changes in the teacher's work responsibilities that make the job more attractive (1=moderate or large change; 0=others)	School evaluation published (1=yes; 0=no)	Important aspect for school evaluations: student test scores (1=considered of moderate or high importance; 0=others)	Index of framing and communicating the school goals and curricular development	Index of promoting instructional improvements and professional development	Index of supervision of instruction in the school
	Teacher (%)	School (%)	School (%)	School (%)	School (%)	School (%)
Australia	3.85	6.03	7.66	3.88	3.88	3.88
Austria	6.20	6.77	15.25	2.79	2.79	2.79
Belgium (Fl.)	4.17	8.91	12.39	8.08	8.40	8.08
Brazil	4.82	5.15	8.56	1.71	1.75	1.75
Bulgaria	6.57	3.07	5.00	0.43	0.43	0.43
Denmark	5.59	20.64	19.15	14.83	15.26	15.26
Estonia	4.91	2.80	5.58	0.55	0.55	0.55
Hungary	6.04	2.73	5.90	0.00	0.37	0.37
Iceland	9.97	34.43	44.72	28.94	28.94	28.94
Ireland	3.58	17.42	19.95	15.56	18.16	18.16
Italy	9.31	10.65	12.00	2.88	2.88	2.88
Korea	2.87	15.56	17.67	11.49	11.49	11.49
Lithuania	6.32	6.29	11.24	1.04	1.04	1.04
Malaysia	2.48	1.06	1.06	0.43	0.43	0.43
Malta	4.10	3.92	5.22	0.00	0.00	0.00
Mexico	2.91	3.93	5.58	1.92	3.24	3.24
Norway	8.18	7.92	11.70	2.78	2.78	2.78
Poland	5.45	1.16	7.25	0.72	0.95	0.95
Portugal	3.25	7.56	13.73	7.56	7.56	7.56
Slovak Republic	2.93	2.09	3.52	1.85	1.85	1.85
Slovenia	5.84	6.71	8.60	3.13	3.13	3.13
Spain	4.00	8.56	15.67	5.29	5.29	5.29
Turkey	5.13	4.15	8.53	3.42	3.82	3.82

	ACCROLE	BURRULEF	SCDELINQ	SCTMORAL	LACKPERS	LACKMAT
	Index of accountability role of the principal	Index of bureaucratic rule-following	Index of school climate: student delinquency	Index of school climate: teachers' working morale	Index of a lack of personnel (teachers, technicians, instructional support personnel, other support personnel)	Index of shortage of materials (instructional materials, computers, equipment, library materials)
	School (%)	School (%)	School (%)	School (%)	School (%)	School (%)
Australia	4.59	4.59	5.30	5.30	8.68	8.08
Austria	2.79	2.79	3.23	3.23	9.42	8.15
Belgium (Fl.)	8.64	8.64	9.84	9.84	13.32	10.50
Brazil	2.09	2.76	2.35	2.35	6.74	3.38
Bulgaria	0.43	0.43	1.06	1.06	7.30	2.18
Denmark	14.83	14.83	15.36	15.36	17.05	16.01
Estonia	0.55	0.55	0.55	0.55	2.30	1.54
Hungary	0.37	0.37	0.00	0.00	2.08	1.54
Iceland	29.44	30.23	34.66	34.66	34.66	35.11
Ireland	15.56	15.56	15.56	15.56	18.61	16.23
Italy	2.88	2.88	2.88	2.88	8.43	4.52
Korea	12.20	12.20	12.07	12.07	14.51	15.05
Lithuania	100.00	1.04	1.04	1.04	7.40	2.06
Malaysia	0.86	0.86	0.43	0.43	1.63	2.52
Malta	0.00	0.00	0.00	0.00	1.36	1.36
Mexico	1.92	1.92	1.92	1.92	3.85	4.30
Norway	2.78	2.78	4.03	4.03	8.31	5.54
Poland	0.72	0.72	0.23	0.23	3.32	1.27
Portugal	7.56	7.56	8.32	8.32	9.03	8.00
Slovak Republic	2.37	2.37	1.85	1.85	5.66	4.97
Slovenia	3.68	3.68	3.72	3.72	4.81	5.05
Spain	7.10	7.10	5.29	5.29	10.32	7.87
Turkey	3.63	3.96	4.99	4.99	6.01	5.85

Source: OECD, *TALIS Database*.
StatLink ᴹᔕᴾᴸ http://dx.doi.org/10.1787/608033612455

Table A14.6
(5/5)
The percentage of missing cases for each country for each variable included in the Chapter 7 regression analyses

	AUTHIRE	AUTBUDGT	AUTSTUDP	AUTCURR	BTG38	Public
	Index of school autonomy in hiring teachers, determining salaries	Index of school autonomy in budgeting (formulating and allocating the school budget)	Index of school autonomy in student policy and textbooks	Index of school autonomy in curriculum (courses offered, course content)	Average class size	Public school (1=public; 0=private)
	School (%)	School (%)	School (%)	School (%)	School (%)	School (%)
Australia	9.66	8.75	8.05	10.36	6.72	0.50
Austria	11.95	4.29	4.59	4.40	6.43	4.58
Belgium (Fl.)	11.68	10.29	11.90	10.94	3.52	8.08
Brazil	5.10	5.34	17.55	3.42	5.87	2.76
Bulgaria	3.56	1.02	4.67	0.89	6.49	0.43
Denmark	21.01	16.88	17.89	16.64	4.47	14.83
Estonia	2.75	1.41	2.39	1.74	2.67	0.55
Hungary	10.51	1.50	1.91	0.38	4.33	0.00
Iceland	43.62	35.56	37.73	36.07	13.81	24.38
Ireland	21.22	15.56	16.45	15.56	2.52	15.56
Italy	11.19	6.97	8.66	4.57	8.40	4.51
Korea	15.82	14.49	13.38	13.27	2.18	22.51
Lithuania	8.59	2.72	4.12	4.24	6.91	1.28
Malaysia	5.81	3.93	4.47	5.67	2.64	1.34
Malta	4.24	4.81	3.93	0.00	4.45	0.00
Mexico	10.48	5.17	5.22	3.41	8.93	5.06
Norway	10.08	4.33	14.94	6.73	6.32	2.50
Poland	0.94	3.18	3.63	0.87	5.58	0.23
Portugal	17.18	10.06	11.07	9.51	2.95	7.56
Slovak Republic	4.73	3.44	2.76	2.63	3.29	1.98
Slovenia	9.28	3.72	4.82	4.20	4.54	3.78
Spain	8.55	6.88	6.29	7.54	3.09	5.31
Turkey	10.19	5.68	6.36	7.76	3.41	3.57

Source: OECD, *TALIS Database*.
StatLink ⟨≋⟩ http://dx.doi.org/10.1787/608033612455

Annex A2

Selected Characteristics of Data Collected from the Netherlands

The Netherlands participated in TALIS but unfortunately was unable to meet the sampling requirements agreed by the TALIS Board of Participating Countries (see *TALIS Technical Report* [forthcoming]). Therefore, data from teachers and school principals collected in the Netherlands could not be included in the main contents of this report. Instead, some selected characteristics are described here to provide some information about teachers and school principals who completed the TALIS questionnaires in the Netherlands.

The sample obtained from the Netherlands was not representative of the teacher population. Therefore, extreme caution must be taken in interpreting the data. The data are not population estimates but summaries of the responses received. The raw data relate to all of the responses received. Thus, unlike the other participating countries, all respondents in the Netherlands are covered regardless of whether the minimum participation rate of teachers within each school was reached.

In the tables provided in this annex, only selected indicators from the survey are presented, alongside the TALIS country average. The selected indicators were chosen in conjunction with the member of the TALIS Board of Participating Countries from the Netherlands. The four tables presented coincide with the main analytical chapters of the report: Table A1.1 presents data on teachers' professional development; Table A2.2 focuses on teaching practices, beliefs and attitudes; Table A2.3 presents data on school evaluation and teacher appraisal and feedback in schools; and Table A2.4 presents characteristics of school leadership.

Table A2.1 **The professional development of teachers: selected data for the Netherlands**

	Netherlands[1]	TALIS average
Participation in development activities		
Percentage of teachers who undertook some professional development in the previous 18 months	91.4%	88.5%
	N=613	(0.20)
Average days of professional development across all teachers	13.5	15.3
	N=613	(0.14)
Unsatisfied demand for development		
Teachers who wanted to participate in more development that they did in the previous 18 months	47.8%	54.8%
	N=646	(0.27)
Percentage of teachers who reported "lack of employer support" as a reason for not participating in more development	29.7%	15.0%
	N=300	(0.27)
Induction and mentoring		
Percentage of teachers in schools that do not operate formal induction programmes	8.2%	29.0%
	N=549	(0.62)
Percentage of teachers in schools that do not operate formal mentoring programmes	0%	25.1%
	N=549	(0.60)

1. Because the sampling standards were not achieved in the Netherlands, the results for the Netherlands cannot be directly compared with those of other participating countries.
Note: Standard errors are presented in parentheses. Standard errors are not presented for the data from the Netherlands as the data are not population estimates.
Source: OECD, *TALIS Database.*
StatLink ⏱️ http://dx.doi.org/10.1787/608033612455

Table A2.2 **Teaching practices beliefs and attitudes: selected data for the Netherlands**

	Netherlands[1]	TALIS average
Teaching activities		
Percentage of teachers who report that in almost every lesson students work in groups based upon their abilities	4.9%	9.5%
	N=627	(0.17)
Percentage of teachers who report that in almost every lesson they review with students the homework they have prepared	34.1%	34%
	N=624	(0.25)
Perceptions of the job and the school environment		
Percentage of teachers who agree or strongly agree that they are satisfied with their job	89%	89.6%
	N=637	(0.17)
Collaborative activities		
Percentage of teachers who observe other teachers' classes and provide feedback at least on a monthly basis	7.3%	6.6%
	N=642	(0.15)

1. Because the sampling standards were not achieved in the Netherlands, the results for the Netherlands cannot be directly compared with those of other participating countries.
Note: Standard errors are presented in parentheses. Standard errors are not presented for the data from the Netherlands as the data are not population estimates.
Source: OECD, *TALIS Database.*
StatLink ⏱️ http://dx.doi.org/10.1787/608033612455

Table A2.3	School evaluation, teacher appraisal and feedback, and the impact on schools and teachers: selected data for the Netherlands

	Netherlands[1]	TALIS average
School evaluations		
Percentage of teachers in schools that have had no school evaluation in the previous five years	2.8%	13.8%
	N=545	(0.56)
Percentage of teachers in schools where the principal reports that retention and pass rates of students are of moderate or high importance in school evaluations	100%	70.8%
	N=534	(0.77)
Percentage of teachers in schools where school evaluation results are published	90.7%	55.3%
	N=505	(0.88)
Teacher appraisal and feedback		
Percentage of teachers who have never received an appraisal or feedback in their school	8.9%	13.4%
	N=637	(0.18)
Percentage of teachers who report that retention and pass rates of students are of moderate or high importance in appraisal and feedback	42.4%	56.2%
	N=429	(0.34)
Percentage of teachers who report that teaching in a multicultural setting is of moderate or high importance in appraisal and feedback	27%	45%
	N=433	(0.36)
Outcome of appraisal and feedback		
Percentage of teachers reporting a moderate or large change in their salary	5.6%	9.1%
	N=572	(0.16)
Percentage of teachers reporting a moderate or large change in the likelihood of their career advancement	7.2%	16.2%
	N=568	(0.19)
Perceptions of system of appraisal and feedback		
Percentage of teachers who agreed or strongly agreed that sustained poor performance of a teacher would be tolerated by the rest of the staff	55.2%	33.8%
	N=623	(0.26)
Percentage of teachers who agreed or strongly agreed that the most effective teachers receive the greatest monetary or non-monetary rewards in their school	7.9%	26.2%
	N=622	(0.28)

1. Because the sampling standards were not achieved in the Netherlands, the results for the Netherlands cannot be directly compared with those of other participating countries.
Note: Standard errors are presented in parentheses. Standard errors are not presented for the data from the Netherlands as the data are not population estimates.
Source: OECD, *TALIS Database*.
StatLink ⟊ http://dx.doi.org/10.1787/608033612455

Table A2.4	School leadership: selected data for the Netherlands

	Netherlands[1]	TALIS average
School leadership behaviour (percentages of teachers in schools where the principal agreeed or strongly agreeed) about the following statements		
A main part of my job is to ensure that the teaching skills of the staff are always improving	90.7%	90.5%
	N=538	(0.44)

1. Because the sampling standards were not achieved in the Netherlands, the results for the Netherlands cannot be directly compared with those of other participating countries.
Note: Standard errors are presented in parentheses. Standard errors are not presented for the data from the Netherlands as the data are not population estimates.
Source: OECD, *TALIS Database*.
StatLink ⟊ http://dx.doi.org/10.1787/608033612455

Annex A3
List of Contributors

TALIS is a collaborative effort, bringing together expertise from participating countries that share an interest in developing a survey programme to inform their policies about teachers, teaching and learning. This report is the product of collaboration and co-operation between the member countries of the OECD and the partner countries participating in the first round of TALIS. Engagement with bodies representing teachers and regular briefings and exchanges with the Trades Union Advisory Council at the OECD have been very important in the development and implementation of TALIS. In particular, the co-operation of the teachers and principals in the participating schools has been crucial in ensuring the success of TALIS.

The TALIS Board of Participating Countries has, in the context of OECD objectives, driven the development of TALIS and has determined its policy objectives. This includes the objectives of the analysis and reports produced, the conceptual framework, and the development of the TALIS questionnaires. The Board has also overseen the implementation of the survey.

Participating countries implemented TALIS at the national level through National Project Managers (NPMs) and National Data Managers (NDMs), who were subject to rigorous technical and operational procedures. The NPMs played a crucial role in helping to secure the co-operation of schools, to validate the questionnaires, to manage the national data collection and processing and to verify the results from TALIS. The NDMs co-ordinated data processing at the national level and liaised in the cleaning of the data.

An Instrument Development Expert Group (IDEG) was established to translate the policy priorities into questionnaires to address the policy and analytical questions that had been agreed by the participating countries. Technical experts were also critical in the analytical phase of the development of the initial report.

The co-ordination and management of implementation at the international level was the responsibility of the appointed contractor, the Data Processing Centre of the International Association for the Evaluation of Educational Achievement (IEA). The IEA Secretariat was responsible for overseeing the verification of the translation and for quality control in general. Statistics Canada, as a sub-contractor of the IEA, developed the sampling plan, advised countries on its application, calculated the sampling weights and advised on the calculation of sampling errors.

The OECD Secretariat had overall responsibility for managing the programme, monitoring its implementation on a day-to-day basis and serving as the Secretariat of the Board of Participating Countries.

Members of the TALIS Board of Participating Countries

Chair: Anne-Berit Kavli

Australia: Oon Ying Chin and Nicole Panting

Austria: Josef Neumueller

Belgium (Flemish Community): Isabelle Erauw

Brazil: Maria das Graças Moreira Costa and Carmilva Souza Flôres

Bulgaria: Marina Mavrodieva

Denmark: Tine Bak

Estonia: Priit Laanoja

Hungary: Judit Kádár Fülöp

Iceland: Julius K. Björnsson

Ireland: Gerry Shiel

Italy: Fiorella Farinelli

Korea: Yeonkee Gu

Lithuania: Marytė Speičienė

Malaysia: Khalijah Mohammad and Muhammad Zaini Mohd Zain

Malta: Raymond Camilleri

Mexico: Jorge Santibanez Romellon

Netherlands: Hans Ruesink

Norway: Anne-Berit Kavli

Poland: Magdalena Krawczyk

Portugal: João Trocado da Mata and Nuno Neto Rodrigues

Slovak Republic: Paulina Korsnakova

Slovenia: Mitja Sardoc

Spain: Carmen Tovar Sánchez

Turkey: Zuhal Gökçesu

TALIS National Project Managers

Australia: Christopher Freeman

Austria: Claudia Schreiner and Juliane Schmich

Belgium (Flemish Community): Peter Van Petegem

Brazil: Carmilva Souza Flôres and Ana Carolina da Silva Cirotto

Bulgaria: Marina Mavrodieva

Denmark: Charlotte Rotbøll and Tue Halgreen

Estonia: Krista Loogma

Hungary: Matild Sági

Iceland: Arnheidor Arnadottir and Ragnar F. Ólafsson

Ireland: Laura McAvinue and Rachel Perkins

Italy: Maria Gemma de Sanctis

Korea: Kapsung Kim

Lithuania: Mindaugas Stundža

Malaysia: Khalijah Mohammad and Muhammad Zaini Mohd Zain

Malta: Raymond Camilleri

Mexico: Ana Maria Aceves Estrada

Netherlands: Sjerp Willem van der Ploeg and Kees van Bergen

Norway: Per Olaf Aamodt, Nils Vibe and Tone Cecilie Carlsten

Poland: Rafał Piwowarski

Portugal: João Trocado da Mata

Slovak Republic: Paulina Korsnakova

Slovenia: Mitja Sardoc

Spain: Carmen Tovar Sánchez

Turkey: Ozlem Kalkan and Zühal Gkokcesu

TALIS National Database Managers

Australia: Christopher Freeman

Austria: Martin Pointinger

Belgium (Flemish Community): Alexia Deneire and Annelies Sweygers

Brazil: Carlos Daniel Araújo Mathias and Carmilva Souza Flôres

Bulgaria: Marina Mavrodieva

Denmark: Jesper Lund

Estonia: Eeva Keskula

Hungary: Matild Sagi

Iceland: Ragnar F. Ólafsson and Arnheidor Arnadottir

Ireland: Rachel Perkins, Maeve Proctor

Italy: Maria Teresa Morana

Korea: Kapsung Kim

Lithuania: Mindaugas Stundža

Malaysia: Khalijah Mohammad and Muhammad Zaini Mohd Zain

Malta: Raymond Camilleri

Mexico: Jorge Rendon Albarran and Marina Santos

Netherlands: Eva van Cooten

Norway: Nils Vibe

Poland: Krzysztof Dziurzyński, Magdalena Krawczyk and Artur Pokropek

Portugal: Nuno Neto Rodrigues

Slovak Republic: Jana Kovacova

Slovenia: Mitja Sardoc, Tina Vrsnik Perse

Spain: Enrique Gallego Palomero and Julián Garcia Crisóstomo

Turkey: Nilgün Duran

OECD Secretariat

Andreas Schleicher (Head of Indicators and Analysis Division)

Michael Davidson (overall co-ordination and management of TALIS)

Ben Jensen (project management and analytical services)

Miyako Ikeda (analytical services)

Maciej Jakubowski (analytical services)

Soojin Park (analytical services)

Diana Toledo Figueroa (analytical services)

Pedro Lenin Garcia De Leon (analytical services)

Elisabeth Villoutreix (editorial support)

Isabelle Moulherat (administrative support)

Fionnuala Canning (administrative support)

Shayne Maclachlan (administrative support)

Alexandra Weiss (support for the preparation of the initial report)

TALIS Expert Groups

Instrument Development Expert Group

David Baker (Pennsylvania State University, United States)

Michael Davidson (OECD Secretariat)

Aletta Grisay (consultant, Paris, France)

Ben Jensen (OECD Secretariat)

Eckhard Klieme (German Institute for International Educational Research (DIPF), Frankfurt, Germany)

Jaap Scheerens (University of Twente, the Netherlands)

Technical experts

David Kaplan University of Wisconsin – Madison, United States) (statistical modelling)

Fons van de Vijver (University of Tilburg, the Netherlands) (cross-cultural validity)

TALIS Consortium

IEA Data Processing Centre (Hamburg, Germany)

Dirk Hastedt (International Project Director)

Steffen Knoll (International Project Director)

Ralph Carstens (International Project Manager, data and analysis)

Friederike Westphal (project co-ordinator, field operations)

Alena Becker (International Deputy Project Manager, data and analysis)

Plamen Mirazchiyski (data analysis and quality control)

Leslie Rutkowski (data analysis and quality control)

Simone Uecker (data processing and quality control)

Dirk Oehler (data processing)

Tim Daniel (data processing)

Michael Jung (data processing)

Alexander Konn (software development)

Stephan Petzchen (software development)

Harpreet Singh Choudry (software development)

Christian Harries (software development)

Statistics Canada (Ottawa, Canada)

Jean Dumais (sampling referee)

Sylvie LaRoche (sampling and weighting)

IEA Secretariat (Amsterdam, Netherlands)

Barbara Malak-Minkiewicz (translation verification and international quality control)

Suzanne Morony (translation verification and international quality control)

Juriaan Hartenberg (financial control)

OECD PUBLISHING, 2, rue André-Pascal, 75775 PARIS CEDEX 16
PRINTED IN FRANCE
(87 2009 01 1 P) ISBN 978-92-64-05605-3 – No. 56913 2009